the

psychology

of

motivation

ABRAHAM K. KORMAN

Baruch College
City University of New York

Prentice-Hall, Inc., Englewood Cliffs, New Jersey

Library of Congress Cataloging in Publication Data

Korman, Abraham K.   1933
    The psychology of motivation.

    Bibliography: p.
    1. Motivation (Psychology)   I. Title.
BF683.K67   153.8   73-21541
ISBN   0-13-733279-3

The Prentice-Hall Psychology Series
James J. Jenkins, Editor

Printed in the United States of America

10   9   8   7   6   5   4   3   2

Prentice-Hall International, Inc., London
Prentice-Hall of Australia, Pty, Ltd., Sydney
Prentice-Hall of Canada, Ltd., Toronto
Prentice-Hall of India Private Limited, New Delhi
Prentice-Hall of Japan, Inc., Tokyo

To Rhoda

contents

preface

Since an understanding of the motivational processes underlying any task effort is a matter of continuing controversy, it is particularly difficult for an author of a book on motivation to explicate the factors that led him to the undertaking. Of those influences of which I am aware, I would cite first an increasing dissatisfaction with the books that have been available for my own particular teaching purposes. I have taught courses in motivation on both a graduate and undergraduate level for a number of years and each term found myself searching for adequate reading assignments. Some books were far too difficult while others were highly simplified approaches to some very complex questions.

Somewhat orthogonal to this problem has been, I think, a preponderance of narrow approaches to the field. The area of motivation is a diverse one, as I have tried to show in this book, and should not be defined as being identical with the theoretical constructs of one particular school.

A third influence has been my belief that changes in the degree of viability of theories take place over time and it is well to recognize this. A historical perspective is, I believe, crucial, and I have used such an approach here. However, this approach should lead us to some assessments of the value of different approaches, i.e., where they are valuable and where they are not. Basically, I believe we should not reify theories (particularly our own) and I have tried to emphasize this here.

The tendency to reify our own work comes in part because of our tendency to read in highly specialized areas. Thus, part of my motivation stems from a "missionary" desire to introduce my fellow psychologists in other areas to much of the exciting work relevant to basic motivational theory that is taking place in my own specialty of industrial and organizational psychology and other "field" areas. This is a book on motivation and what I have tried to show is that we can learn much about general motivational processes outside the laboratory as well as in it.

Specifically, there are many people I would like to cite. John Atkinson's book on motivation a decade ago influenced the organization of the early chapters and I wish to emphasize it. Although our conclusions may be different, his research and writing has done much to clarify my own thinking. Professors Reuben Baron of the University of Connecticut and James Uleman of New York University made incisive penetrating comments on an earlier draft which were of inestimable value in developing a final version. Of particular value have been the working atmospheres, first at New York University and now at Baruch College. Each has contributed greatly to my being able to develop this book.

Most important of all has been my wife Rhoda and our children, Stacey and Scott. As we have observed one another's motivational processes and have learned from one another, my appreciation of the importance of understanding this crucial aspect of human behavior has continually increased.

Abraham K. Korman
New York, New York

the
psychology
of
motivation

AN INTRODUCTION

ONE

If one were to do a public-opinion survey concerning the field of psychology, why it exists, and why it is of importance in our world, there would undoubtedly be many answers. In this diversity, certain themes would probably emerge more often than others.

It helps us understand why people do the strange things that they do.
It helps us understand why people don't always do what is best for them.
It helps us understand why people make the choices that they do.
It helps us understand why our common beliefs and practices as to how to help and influence people don't always work.
It helps us understand why people are always changing and why they are so difficult to understand.

A glance at these specific statements, and more could certainly be listed, indicates a certain commonality among them. This commonality may be summarized by the following statement:

Psychology can help us to understand the factors that influence the arousal of behavior, the direction of behavior, and the persistence of behavior.

In essence, this statement leads to the purpose of this book. Basically, this book is interested in the field of psychology that has been concerned with the study of those factors that influence the arousal of behavior, the direction of behavior, and the persistence of behavior. This field is known as the psychology of motivation, and it is this area of psychology that will be the focus of our attention. Thus, we shall be dealing with such questions as:

What kinds of theoretical frameworks, methods, and approaches have been developed in order to help us understand (and eventually predict) the arousal, direction, and persistence of behavior? In what ways are these approaches adequate and in what ways are they not? In what ways have they been of value in helping us to understand the basic processes involved? In what ways has the psychology of motivation helped to shed light on some of the persisting questions and problems that dominate human society? In what ways do psychologists interested in motivation agree as to the basic processes involved? In what ways do they disagree? What needs to be done in order to increase future theoretical understanding in the psychology of motivation? What needs to be done in order to help resolve some persisting societal dilemmas?

These are some of the questions that will concern us in this book. In dealing with them, it will become clearer to the reader what the psychology of motivation is and how it differs from other such basic psychological processes as learning and perception. As a starting point, we may say that the psychology of motivation concerns itself with attempting to understand (and predict) the arousal, direction, and persistence of behavior, given the characteristics of the behaving subject at the time and the characteristics of the environment (both real and perceived) at the time. The psychology of learning concerns itself with how and why the subject develops the characteristics he has, and the psychology of perception deals with the processes of how and why stimuli (both within the self and the environment) come to be perceived the way they are. Each of these also attempts to understand behavioral direction, persistence, and arousal, but they use different vantage points, deal with more narrowly defined aspects of behavior (neither attempts to account for both personal and environmental variables as joint effects), and are concerned with different kinds of questions. Thus, while overlap exists between all of these, the three separate fields developed because all were needed if we were to develop a more complete understanding of basic psychological processes.

VARIOUS APPROACHES
TO THE STUDY OF MOTIVATION

As we will see, there are a variety of different approaches that can be, have been, and continue to be used in the study of motivational processes. It is possible to integrate and classify these various approaches according to the nature of the psychological traditions from which they stem. There are three such major traditions in the psychology of motivation. One is a biological, physicalistic tradition stemming from the work of the physiologists of the nineteenth century and the Darwinian revolution in scientific thought. Thus, we shall be discussing, in Chapters 2 through 4, the thinking and theorizing of psychologists such as Clark Hull, John Watson, and Kenneth Spence. These psychologists use such terms as *drives* and *instincts* in explaining the arousal, direction, and persistence of behavior. Secondly, there is a cultural tradition in the study of motivational processes, and it is this school of psychology that uses terms such as *wishes, feelings, desires, demands, needs,* and *motives* in its thinking and writings. Learned experiences and the nature of the psychosocial environment are important for them in developing explanatory variables for understanding the arousal, direction, and persistence of behavior. The work of many of the psychologists we shall be discussing in Chapters 5 through 10 can be ordered to this type of framework. Finally, there is a philosophical-theological tradition in motivational thinking, one that dominated the field prior to the twentieth century and that has had a recent resurgence in the form of the "humanistic" psychology we shall be discussing in Chapter 10. With the exception of the brief discussion in Chapter 10 and our historical survey later in this chapter, this tradition will not concern us greatly in this book because it has not lent itself to the kinds of empirical, systematic research we feel to be necessary in the study of motivational processes.

One note of caution is that this general classification of approaches should not be seen as a rigid system with no overlap between the different groups. As we will see, this is not so, since similar terms and conceptualizations do occur among psychologists working in different traditions and from different assumptions. Similarly, most psychologists working in the field of motivation agree on the need for utilizing both characteristics of the behaving individual and characteristics of the environment in developing an adequate framework for understanding the arousal, direction, and persistence of behavior. Despite these similarities, however, there are differences, and these differences will become apparent as our discussion proceeds.

There are some limits to our interests in this book, and it is well to make them explicit at this point. First, our interest is essentially in all of the factors that affect motivational processes as we have defined them, not only the effect of motive differences between people on behavior. As we will see, the fact that people differ in motive characteristics is only one aspect of the psychology of motivation and as such is only one influence on behavioral arousal, direction, and persistence. Other factors are also highly crucial as influences on behavior, and we shall also be dealing with factors such as environmental demands, environmental stimulation, and so forth. Secondly, our interest is more in the motivational processes underlying complex human behavior, and it is within this framework that our discussion will take place. This does not mean that we will not cite animal research. We will, from time to time. It also does not mean that we will make a fetish of "humanism," for we will not. There is much that can be learned from animal research. However, our interests are in the development of a framework for eventually understanding human motivation, and this will undoubtedly influence our discussion of animal research at the times when these are cited. The reader should, therefore, be aware of this predisposing attitude. Third, we will be interested here in a psychology of motivation, and this will also guide our discussion. This is not meant to deprecate in any way the importance of physiological research in motivation. Such research is highly crucial and important in certain limited areas of motivation. However, it is not relevant at this time to many of the interests of those who wish to build a psychological understanding of motivation applicable to humans. Hence, except for minor references from time to time, this area will not be of concern in this book. Finally, since our interest is in the various approaches to motivational processes that are based on laboratory and field research and involve the gathering of empirical data relevant to their propositions, our primary focus will be on developments since psychology became an empirical science. However, since contemporary empirical work does have historical antecedents, and since these antecedents served to define in a general way the various traditions spoken of above and that will be reflected in our later discussions, it will be of value for us to briefly review these historical antecedents. Following this review, we will conclude this introductory discussion by previewing the particular topics that will interest us in this book.

THE PSYCHOLOGY OF MOTIVATION:
A HISTORICAL BACKGROUND

It is almost a truism to observe that interest in the personal and environmental factors that influence the arousal, direction, and persistence of behavior did not begin in the twentieth century. Such interest can be traced back to the dawn of recorded history, and it is undoubtedly true that thoughts about these matters occured even before then. Thus, one can point to the consideration of these questions by the Greek philosophers, by the writers of the medieval era such as Saint Augustine and Saint Thomas Aquinas, by the English associationists, and by the Eastern philosophers, just to cite a few who have concerned themselves with the kinds of questions dealt with in a book on the psychology of motivation.

At the risk of some oversimplification, however, much of this preempirical research thinking on motivational processes does lend itself to some meaningful integration into different groups, an integration that anticipates many contemporary concerns. One of the most important of these philosophical traditions is that for a significant number of these writers, responsibility for the arousal, direction, and persistence of behavior was seen as resulting from different factors for animals as opposed to humans. These differences can be exemplified by the following quotations:

... man has sensous desire, and rational desire or will. He is not absolutely determined in his desires and actions by sense impressions as is the brute, but possesses a faculty of self-determination, whereby he is able to act or not to act. ... The will is determined by what intelligence concerns to be the good, by a rational purpose. This, however, is not compulsion; compulsion exists where a being is inevitably determined by an external cause. Man is free because he is rational, because he is not driven into action by an external cause without his consent, and because he can choose between the means of realizing good or the purpose which his reason conceives. (Thilly, 1957, pp. 232–33)

According to this view, animals, lacking rational souls, were merely automata. Their behavior was held to be due to the physical forces acting upon them. Some forces were external but others were internal, caused by agitations within the physical organism. For example, if an animal was without food its physiology would be disturbed in such a way that it would eat; it was compelled to eat by its physical structure. (Bolles, 1967, p. 25)

Basically, up until the time of Darwin, the major forces thought to cause behavior arousal, direction, and persistence were seen to be physical for the animal and both physical and spiritual for the human. Such a division stemmed from a number of philosophical and theological considerations developed over a period of more than two thousand years, with the philosophical theory of dualism the most important of these influences. While this theory had different forms at different times, its logic in most cases consisted of the assumption that there was a physical reality and a nonphysical reality. The former is controlled in a mechanistic fashion by the manipulation of environmental events, while the latter is controlled by the soul of the individual, his reason, his knowledge, and his will. Furthermore, whereas both animals and humans have bodies under the control of environmental events, only humans have a soul, reason, and a will to implement their knowledge in specific directions. Hence, the understanding of the motivational processes of animals could be done in a mechanistic fashion, but the motivational process of the human was under the control of his physiological needs and desires, his knowledge, and his will. Furthermore, in many of these philosophical writings, this conscious will of the human could serve to balance and control the gluttonous, physical, and sexual desires of the body, desires seen in many cases as being either undesirable in and of themselves, or at least worthy of only limited expression. This is not to say that the will was completely free-floating and under no influence at all from bodily and/or environmental variation. Some such influence was, in fact, postulated by Descartes. However, even here, much greater reliance was placed on the freedom and choice of the will as opposed to other influences.

This, then, was the type of thinking that prevailed among writers concerned with motivational questions until about the middle of the nineteenth century. Perhaps the full flavor of this thought can be seen even more clearly by examining the specific thoughts and ideas of a sampling of pre-Darwinian thinkers and the kinds of concepts they developed. Most prominent of these were the Greek philosophers, in whose writings we can find so many of the antecedents to later thought. For our purposes here, perhaps the most significant writing was that by Plato and Aristotle, both of whom extended the prevailing thought that what was crucial was to gain knowledge, since knowledge was the determinant of behavior arousal, direction, and persistence. It was their belief that knowledge in and of itself was not sufficient to determine behavior. A concept such as will, as developed by practice, was an even more important determinant, they argued. A slightly different, but still similar, conceptualization is found centuries later in the writings of Saint Augustine, who argued that behavior was ruled by the will and the will was different from both feeling and knowing. Thus, it was through the functioning of the will that control was obtained over the physical determinants of behavior, behaviors he saw as weaknesses (i.e., the animal passions). In addition, there is the writing of Saint Thomas Aquinas, who saw animal behavior as being motivated primarily by instincts and the senses, while human behavior was more a function of rational insight into the relation between the act and its end. Finally, almost as an epitome of this type of thinking, there is the famous theoretical work of Descartes, who also adopted a dualistic system arguing for physical determinants of animal behavior and a rational will for explaining human activity. However, he also extended his argument by hypothesizing physiological determinants of the emotions and, henceforth, of the will. In this sense, then, Descartes was the first to propose that the will, the determinant of behavior, was in turn a function of other variables that were at least theoretically understandable and controllable.

There were also a number of writers who concerned themselves with the proposition that behavior was due to the desire to achieve pleasure and avoid pain. Known as hedonism, this way of thinking, while it also had its origin in Greek thought, probably reached its greatest flowering in the writings of the English utilitarianism movement of the early nineteenth century. Led by Jeremy Bentham and the Mills, James and his son John Stuart, it argued that the desire to achieve the "greatest pleasure" was universal in mankind. As we will see, the idea that responsibility for the motivation of behavior can be attributed to both the desire for pleasure and the knowledge of what will bring pleasure finds representation in contemporary theorizing.

The third great tradition of preempirical work in motivation is the postulation of specific motives of various kinds as highly important and crucial in the understanding of human behavior. Typical of this last group are the writings of Machiavelli and Hobbes, both of whom developed proposals for the nature of political leadership based on the postulation of such motives as egotism, fear, love, hunger, thirst, and sex. Machiavelli, for example, wrote that leaders are motivated by egotism and that they can control people best by fear, and then by love. Hobbes's thought was somewhat different, his major proposals centering around the belief that man's desires (e.g., hunger, thirst, sex) are in conflict with one another and that, therefore, a strong sovereign is necessary. As we will see, the notion that motives such as these are important in understanding behavior will appear quite frequently in contemporary work on motivational processes. In addition, Hobbes is also notable for the same reason as Descartes, in that he made some attempt to hypothesize various physical and environmental determinants of the will and of motives. The importance of this theorizing cannot be overemphasized, because it is only through this type of thinking that a psychology of motivation and the factors that affect it became possible.

These, then, are some of the major philosophical thoughts on motivation prevalent prior to the time when psychology became an empirical science. These thoughts were clearly interesting and significant but, unfortunately, not based on systematic empirical observation and research of the kind we think necessary today. Before such observation based on systematic experimentation and field research could become the norm for the psychology of motivation, however, two further events had to take place. First, the British associationist philosophers had to establish the principle that the content of the mind was a function of experience and learning. Basically, the significance of this argument for us was that it established on a firm philosophical basis the position that thought and the content of the mind were understandable and predictable from previous experiences to which the individual had been exposed. Hence, the will, the determinant of behavior choice and direction, was not "free," but rather a function of experiences that could be determined and, thus, used to predict variations of the will. It is clear that this type of thinking had to develop before we could begin to understand such questions as why people commit suicide, why people choose the mates that they do, why they persist in certain tasks rather than others, and all the other questions that a psychology of motivation attempts to answer.

In addition to the British associationists, another event needed to take place before a psychology of motivation could get started, and that was the Darwinian revolution.

Darwin and the Theory of Evolution

There are, of course, a number of reasons why Charles Darwin is considered by many as the man who stands at the very top in any ranking of figures of importance in the scientific study of living creatures. However, rather than attempt to summarize these reasons in detail, our comments here (and in Chapter 2) will be limited to those aspects of his work of crucial importance in the development of a psychology of motivation. These are that (a) the survival and reproduction of each member of a species is a function of the degree to which it fits the particular environment in which it finds itself, and (b) the characteristics of a species change as some of its members survive and reproduce while others die out because of their inability to survive in the particular environment. These proposals were important for the psychology of motivation in at least two crucial ways. First, they destroyed the carefully built distinctions between human and animal motivation that had been built up and supported over centuries. Dualism was destroyed because it became clear that there could not be a duality if it could be shown that the basic human and animal processes were fundamentally the same. How could there be differences and how could dualism be defended if the function of instincts (supposedly an animal characteristic) could be shown to be highly similar to the function of intelligent, rational choice (supposedly an exclusively human property)? Were there really any differences between instincts and intelligence at all, if the functions of both were to assist in the functioning and survival of the organism?

There was also a second implication of Darwin's proposals that destroyed the arguments of the previous centuries. Theoretically, *all* motivational processes could now be studied as a function of their antecedent conditions. If we could study animal motivational processes as a function of the external and internal environmental conditions that affected them, why then could we not extend the earlier steps of Descartes and Hobbes the whole way and study human motivational processes in the same way? The answer was, of course, that we could, and it is this basic philosophical presupposition that has guided work in the psychology of motivation ever since. The basic proposition that we engaged in certain behaviors because we had a will to do so now became unacceptable unless the investigator concerned himself with the determinants of that will and the environmental variables that affected it. Framed this way, the next step was to say that we did not need will at all. It was unnecessary and superfluous. All we needed was knowledge of the antecedent environmental conditions. Hence, for many, Darwin's work eliminated such notions as will and other forms of nonphysical concepts, such as wants, motives, and the like, as unnecessary in the study of motivational phenomena. These were the psychologists who then went on to develop motivational theories without nonphysicalistic terms and who keyed their constructs to Darwin-like hypotheses concerning survival as a rationale for behavior.

For others, however, Darwin's theory did not have to be interpreted in that limited a fashion. The nature of behavioral arousal, direction, and persistence could be studied, they proposed, in terms of how the antecedent variables affected them for both animals *and* humans, but with no need to use the same concepts for both. Different kinds of concepts could be developed in order to describe different motivational processes, and one could develop constructs that signify uniquely human motivational processes, provided they were of the kind that would enable us to ascertain the factors affecting such motivational processes and, hopefully, study them in the laboratory and/or in the field. For these psychologists, then, the major significance of Darwin's work was that behavior, both simple and complex, animal and human, could be studied for the antecedent variables affecting and determining them. Both of these approaches to motivational theorizing will be discussed in this book, since it is essentially these frameworks that have served as orienting systems underlying the various kinds of theories and research we shall study, the methods followed by the theorists involved, and the procedures proposed for the future.

THE PLAN OF THIS BOOK

We have reviewed, albeit too briefly, the historical context within which the systematic empirical study of motivational processes emerged in the twentieth century. The field that developed assumed that the arousal, direction, and persistence of behavior, no matter how complex, could be studied for the antecedent variables that influenced their occurrence and that such antecedent variables were of the type that could lend themselves to laboratory research, field research, and sometimes both. Furthermore, it also assumed that theories could be developed to account for these phenomena in a meaningful way and, hopefully, in a manner that would eventually lead to interventions that could be made for the good of the individual and society. It is this field of motivation, the ideas that were developed, the research that was undertaken, the problems that were found, and other similar questions that will comprise the subject matter of this book. The procedure that we will follow is as follows:

Chapter 2 – We will begin by first showing how the thinking we have outlined here led to the development of the two major theoretical approaches to the psychology of motivation in the first half of the twentieth century, the work of Freud and Clark Hull. We will see that while the former was a psychiatrist and the other a strict experimentalist who worked with animals, their thinking was amazingly similar in some areas. In addition, we will see how they were different and why they were both important enough for us to use their work as our departure point.

Chapter 3 – This chapter will show how revisions in the Hullian framework took place as a function of the research it stimulated and why it remains important today as a significant laboratory-oriented natural-science approach to the understanding of motivational processes, animal and human. In addition, attention will be paid in both Chapters 2 and 3 to the overall general fruitfulness of viewing motivational processes as resting on an evolutionary framework and as capable of being dealt with in a physical-science approach similar to the kind we use in experimenting with physical materials such as chemicals and machines. The usefulness of viewing motivational processes in this manner will be dealt with here.

Chapter 4 – A contemporary natural-science approach to motivational processes known as activation-arousal theory is explored here in its various aspects. Among our concerns will be the research it has stimulated, the methodological and logical problems involved in the approach, and its possible significance in resolving such contemporary problems as the effects of different kinds of physical environments, urban problems, and the like.

Chapter 5 — Our attention in this chapter will focus on expectancy-value theory, an alternative to the pure physical-science view of motivation. This approach tends to stress cognitive variables, such as motives and expectations, rather than those that are physical and palpable in nature, but tries to do so within an experimentally oriented approach. It also deals with motivational questions that are human, rather than animal, oriented. Both traditional and contemporary examples of this approach will be discussed here.

Chapter 6 — The various types of tests and measurements utilized in assessing individual differences in motives are dealt with here. As an example, it is here that we will concern ourselves with such questions as, How do we know that Person A has a higher achievement motive than Person B? Is Person C higher in need of independence than Person D? The methods we might use in answering these questions will be discussed here, as well as the criteria we would use for evaluating the adequacy of these methods.

Chapter 7 — The motivation to attain consistency, as opposed to the assumption that people are necessarily motivated to achieve only "good" outcomes, as a framework for understanding human behavior has gained a great number of adherents since World War II. The characteristics of this approach, the different ways in which it has developed, and its various strengths and weaknesses will be discussed here.

Chapters 8 and 9 — Achievement and aggression motivation are two specific types of motivational processes that are highly significant in our society. An examination will be made in these chapters of the ways in which these processes have been studied and what we currently know about them. In addition, we will examine the fruitfulness of understanding these specific types of behavior by utilizing general theories of motivation, as opposed to developing limited theories designed for just these specific motivational processes in and of themselves.

Chapter 10 — A theory designed to deal with the motivation toward achievement, aggression, and change will be presented here as an example of an approach midway between developing overall motivational frameworks and developing motivational theories aimed at explaining narrow, specific behaviors. The various relationships between the theory presented here and the other material discussed in this book will also be explored.

Chapter 11 — This final chapter will concern itself with the various implications for future work in the psychology of motivation that our discussions in previous chapters have indicated and the directions this future activity might take.

SUMMARY

The goals of this book have been set forth in this chapter. Our purpose is to know the theories, research, and thoughts of those psychologists concerned with factors leading to the arousal, direction, and persistence of behavior, that is, the field that has come to be known as the psychology of motivation. Interest in these types of questions far predates psychology and can be shown to have been of major interest to writers since recorded history began. For the most part, prepsychological concern with the field of motivation postulated mechanical, objective, physiologically based determinants of motivational processes for animals, while concepts such as rational will and other subjective notions were utilized for understanding human behavior arousal, choice, and persistence. However, the Darwinian revolution ended this perspective, and the viewpoint was adopted that both human and animal motivational processes could be studied by understanding the antecedent factors leading to the behavior in each case. A continuing argument that marks the field today is whether different concepts have to be used for humans and animals.

behavioristic approaches to motivational processes

THE HULLIAN TRADITION

TWO

In this chapter we will begin our study of the psychology of motivation by discussing the work of those psychologists who have operated within what has been called a natural-science tradition (a term we will attempt to clarify a little later). Our concern here will first be to detail the historical influences on the work of this group and how such influences led to the guiding assumptions under which they have operated in the past and continue to work today. Following this, we will show how such influences led to the most significant statement of this type of approach, the theory proposed in 1943 by Clark Hull. Our analysis of this major event will then enable us to show in later chapters how more recent attempts using this type of approach to the psychology of motivation stemmed from the strengths and weaknesses of Hull's work.

THE BACKGROUND:
PHYSICALISM, INSTINCTS, AND OTHER INFLUENCES

Although psychology arose in the late nineteenth century as a merger of both philosophy and physiology, it would not be unfair to say that the first half of the twentieth century saw much more effort devoted to following the procedures and methods of the latter rather than the former. There are several reasons for this, with two in particular standing out. First, there was the

12

explosive growth in theory and methodology of the natural sciences during the previous two centuries. Second, there was the shattering influence of Darwin's theory of evolution. These two influences were crucial in affecting the course of Hull's 1943 formulation, and both continue to be important today because of their influence on the work of his students.

Physicalism and Objective Psychology

Perhaps the most famous example of this influence was John Watson's (1913) clarion call for a psychology that would be objective in nature. The subject matter of this psychology would be the hard, physical matter of behavior that one could touch, feel, and experiment with in the same way that one could experiment in physiology and physics. Rejected from the science, according to Watson, would be attempts to utilize "consciousness" as the subject matter of psychology, the then prevailing approach. According to Watson, it was only in this way that psychology could take its place with the other sciences that had been advancing so rapidly, sciences such as physics and biology, which also dealt with hard, physical matter and looked for explanatory systems in such manipulable phenomena. Furthermore, Watson declared, psychology could also operate from the same philosophical framework as these other sciences, in the sense that the general approach for psychology would be to search for the "basic elements" of behavior, physically defined and understood. The rules of combination would be sought according to which these basic elements determined the directional aspects of behavior. According to Watson, this basic behavioral unit was already known. This was the *conditioned-response* model used in showing how stimuli that were originally unable to elicit a certain type of behavior develop the capacity to elicit the behavior. Thus, after these neutral stimuli were paired contiguously with stimuli that elicited the desired type of behavior intrinsically, the organism made the same responses to both types of stimuli. This model, in basic outline form, is as follows:

Stage One		Stage Two	Stage Three	
Stimulus	*Response*	Buzzer	*Stimulus*	*Response*
		Food		
Buzzer ⟶ Ears perk		Presented as paired over period of time, with buzzer presented first	Buzzer ⟶ Salivation	
Food ⟶ Salivation			Food ⟶ Salivation	

This process, which Watson favored, is known as *classical* or *Pavlovian* (after the Russian phychologist who first illustrated and studied it) *conditioning* in the psychological literature, and this was the basis upon which we can understand changes in behavior, or so Watson suggested. As an example of his approach, he showed how he could condition a young boy to emit a fear response to a white rabbit that he had not feared originally. The way he did it was as follows:

Stage One		Loud Noise Rabbit	Stage Two	Stage Three	
Stimulus	*Response*		Presented as paired over period of time, with loud noise presented first	*Stimulus*	*Response*
Loud Noise → Fear				Loud Noise → Fear	
Rabbit → Nonfear curiosity				Rabbit → Fear	

Watson was then able to recondition the child not to fear the rabbit by presenting it in a context where there was no strong fear-inducing stimulus present. Eventually, the child's conditioned fear response was eliminated in the same way that it had originally been developed, thus further substantiating to Watson that he had, indeed, a meaningful way of understanding the antecedents to behavioral choice and direction and that he could do it without resorting to what was, for him, the mysticism of conscious experience.

Watson was oversimplified. It has not been as easy as he or his followers (cf. Kuo, 1921) thought it would be. For one thing, the conditioned response (CR) to the conditioned stimulus (CS) (i.e., salivation to the buzzer) is rarely, if ever, the same as the unconditioned response (UR) to the unconditioned stimulus (US) (i.e., salivation to the food in our example). It is usually weaker and more easily eliminated in favor of other behaviors than the response of innate origin. Hence, stimulus substitution cannot completely account for the change in the direction of behavior, one of the primary concerns of the psychology of motivation. Something else must be involved. Second, responses are not infinitely transferable (that is, while one could use the buzzer as an unconditioned stimulus to develop a salivation response to an electric light), such learning (a process known as *higher-order conditioning*) is generally not as effective, and the response to the light will be even more different from the original salivation than the response to the buzzer. Similarly, attempts to then use the electric light as an unconditioned stimulus are extremely difficult to achieve (Keller and Schoenfield, 1950). Finally, even when such higher-order conditioning occurs, the responses established are far easier to extinguish in favor of other responses than the original, innately determined response, or that from *first-order conditioning*. These results substantiate further our earlier remark that attempts to use the stimulus substitution process, in the simple physical sense proposed by Watson as a framework for understanding the direction of behavior, are not adequate. Other variables must be involved in guiding and affecting such directional change.

This same general conclusion has been made by Brown (1961) after first reviewing the relevant research evidence for what an associative (i.e., Watsonian) view of motivational processes would imply. According to Brown, this type of approach would hold that variables such as hunger and thirst, variables we often call motivational because they arouse and direct behavior, are really just sets of stimuli and act like any other stimuli that become linked to responses through classical conditioning. Such stimulus-response linkings, once they are learned, can thus affect behavior whenever these stimuli are present in the future. The behavior that results in the new situation is a function of the qualitative and quantitative similarity between the stimuli currently being utilized and the stimuli to which the response was originally learned. For example, suppose a rat has been trained to press a lever for food when he has not been fed for four hours. According to a strictly Watsonian (associative) view, it would be predicted that lever pressing would be higher in the future after the rat had been starved for four hours as opposed to being starved for two hours, a prediction supported in the literature. Similarly, it also says, and this is also supported, that lever pressing, if learned when hungry as a way of getting food, is most likely to take place in the future when the rat is hungry, not thirsty. All well and good. The problem, however, is that the rat trained under four hours of deprivation is more likely to exhibit the behavior when he is deprived for six hours than when he is deprived for four. This behavior Watson would not and could not predict. A strictly associative theory of motivation of the type proposed by Watson would have to predict just the opposite. Clearly, then, increasing hunger and thirst deprivation seem to have effects on behavior in addition to just serving as stimuli for specific responses in the way that Watson argued.

Despite all this, however, Watson's dream of an objective, behavioral, nonmentalistic, nonconsciousness-oriented psychology, one that operated without such variables as will and desire as determinants of behavior, has persisted to this day. There exist today a number of psychologists who are interested in the psychology of motivation and who approach it from this type of philosophical framework. What is particularly intriguing, however, is that motivational processes, particularly of a complex nature, are at this stage of our knowledge extremely difficult to equate with physiological processes. How, then, can an approach of this nature be successful? Can it overcome the problem we have seen in an associative viewpoint such as Watson's and deal with such questions as the choice of one goal as opposed to another? Can it explain the anticipation and expectancy of achieving goals and incentives? Can these really be translated into a physicalistic system? Do not such questions, of necessity, need such mentalistic, nonphysicalistic concepts as purpose, goals, plans? We will see presently how one group of psychologists working in this tradition attempted to deal with these questions.

Before doing so, however, it will be necessary for us to turn our attention to the other major influence. This is the group of biologists, physiologists, and psychologists who traced their intellectual heritage from Darwin. The key notion around which this group formed and the reason why they are important for us here is their common interest in innate instincts of evolutionary significance as determinants of the arousal and direction of behavior.

Instincts as Determinants of Behavioral Arousal and Direction

Charles Darwin was certainly not the only man to propose the idea that both humans and animals had instincts that led them to behave in certain ways and directions rather than others. Nor was he the only one to propose that these instinctual, innate behaviors had biological significance in that their performance determined the likelihood of both individual and species survival. Darwin's position in psychology is similar to Columbus's in history. It is really irrelevant how many Europeans visited the New World before Columbus, because nothing much happened until Columbus made the trip. In the same sense, it is irrelevant how many others observed the same phenomena as Darwin — Darwin's is the voice that was heard. Darwin's proposal of evolutionary theory burst like a thunderclap, shaking the worlds of theology, education, and science to their foundations. For us, the point of greatest significance is Darwin's proposal that certain behavioral tendencies which are innately built into organisms to respond to certain stimuli, such as hunger, thirst, and pain, cause behaviors designed to eliminate them. The reason, Darwin postulated, that such behavior takes place is that the survival of the organism depends upon their performance, and if we did not engage in such activities, we would die. It is the thesis of Darwinian evolutionary theory that those who were not programmed for such stimulus-reduction activity died out a long time ago and that we today are those who survived to reproduce. Among the stimuli involved here are thirst, hunger, pain, and perhaps, sex. (The latter, however, is a controversial issue as an innate instinct since it is clearly necessary only for species, rather than individual, survival.)

Actually, the proposition that basic instincts are determinants of behavioral arousal and direction divides, after Darwin, into two separate, only partially related directions. One group, whose most prominent representatives were William James and William McDougall, made lists of instincts that were seen as mainsprings of all kinds of behaviors, simple and complex, necessary and unnecessary, for biological survival. We shall devote some attention in a later chapter to this aspect of "instinct" psychology, its foremost exponent, McDougall, and the problems that developed from this type of approach. What concerns us here is the other direction that the utilization of instinct theory took, and this was the effort to utilize the innate mechanisms of biological survival significance as a base upon which to build frameworks and themes designed to explain human motivation of a complex, nonbiological nature. It is this latter work that interests us in this chapter.

Our discussion will take two directions. First, we will see how Darwin's theory influenced the motivational hypotheses of Sigmund Freud. Second, we will examine its influence on the work of Clark Hull and his students.

There are several reasons for examining them in this order. First, Freud came before Hull chronologically and much of his theorizing served as a challenge to Hull in the sense that Hull felt it was very important to examine many Freudian concepts experimentally. Secondly, Freud's work was the final blow to the concept of rational will as a determinant of behavior directionality, choice, and persistence. Because Freud insisted that overt behavior reflected instinctual drives as disguised and distorted by societal pressures and constraints, the principle that we could understand motivational processes by looking at the antecedent variables that led to them became firmly established. From Freud's time on, the basic argument that behavior varied because of antecedent variables, variables theoretically able to be understood and measured prior to the behavior, became the basic framework for understanding and viewing the study of motivational processes in general.

SIGMUND FREUD

Sigmund Freud was, of course, a genius of first-order magnitude. Witness the work he published, the disciples he attracted, the enemies he made, and the thousands upon thousands of pages written about him. Our interest here is not in reviewing all the work of this fertile, innovative mind and the theories, arguments, and ideas he stimulated. This would be a task for many writers and many books. Rather our purpose will be to discuss a limited segment of his writings, namely, his theory of motivational processes, in order to indicate how Freud followed rather directly from the ideas of Darwin, and how he, descriptive and clinical though he was, had many ideas that appear in the work of later, more research-oriented psychologists.

The purpose of activity, according to Freud, or the reason that behavior arousal occurs and takes the direction that it does, is that man has innate needs that must be satisfied. Each of these innate needs gives rise to tensions and stimulation represented as instincts in the mental life of the individual, and the reduction of these tensions is the ultimate cause of all activity. Thus, the reader will note that Freud's answer as to the determinants of behavioral arousal, direction, and vigor lies, at least partially, in the assumption of the existence of innate needs, which may also be called instincts in a psychological sense. (Freud also proposed other directive influences on behavior once aroused, as we will see.)

There are four distinguishing characteristics to each instinct. First, each instinct has a *source*. This is internal body stimulation and differs from external sources of stimulation in three ways. One, obviously, is that it comes from the body itself rather than from the environment (although environmental manipulation such as starvation can affect the internal stimuli). A second difference is that the internal stimulation associated with an instinct is constant and recurring, rather than episodic. Finally, one can not escape from this type of stimulation as one can escape from external stimuli. The second characteristic of an instinct is its *impetus*. This, according to Freud, is the force or energy that the instinct represents and is a function of the need intensity from which the instinctual stimulation arises. Third, each instinct has an *aim*, which is to end the stimulation that gave rise to it. This ceasing of stimulation is satisfying and, hence, what is sought, Freud proposed. Furthermore, various intermediary steps along the way to the ending of stimulation may be sought if these are perceived as leading to desired end states. Last, but far from least, every instinct has an *object*. This is postulated as anything that will abolish the stimulation, and it is assumed that there is no innate link between any instinct and any given object. Thus, it is clear from this assumption that there are an infinite variety of objects that might reduce any given instinctual drive. Which is chosen in a given context? This varies depending on the learning experiences of the given individual and what he expects to occur in the given environment at the time. Obviously, the same objects reduce different instinctual stimulation in different individuals and might also reduce different stimuli in the same person at different points in time. This is why, Freud argued, people have so many strange types of obsessions in sexual and other areas of life and why they act differently in different environments. From our point of view, Freud's conception of the instinct object as a function of an individual's learning history and contemporary expectancies introduces, in addition to instincts, second and third determinants of the direction behavior takes in a given situation. What we have learned in the past will reduce stimulation, and the extent to which we see these similar conditions existing in the present are directional influences on behavior. These general ideas, as we will see, are highly similar to the "habit" and "expectancy" concepts postulated by later, more experimentally oriented psychologists as directive influences on behavior.

Basically, then, Freud's model of the motivation of behavior is that of a tension-reduction system. Stimulation stemming from basic instinctual sources of biological significance arouses the individual and he seeks out ways to reduce such stimulation. The direction and persistence of the behavior is determined partially by the nature of the instinct itself, partially by the individual's past learning experiences concerning successful stimulation reduction, and partially by the individual's expectations of successful reduction of instinctual stimulation in the contemporary environment. These rational expectancies operate together with previous learning and instinctual drives to partially determine the arousal and direction of behavior. In addition, there are other influences to be considered in determining behavior direction stemming from the developmental history of the individual, as we will now see.

We begin with Freud's basic proposal that the individual is born with a depository of basic, biologically significant instinctual drives called the *id*. These drives are life maintaining (e.g., hunger, thirst), and reproductive (e.g., sexual),[1]

---

[1]Freud, in his later life, became more pessimistic and, perhaps as a result of W.W. I and his own illness, postulated a death instinct that usually became displaced into aggression against others by the life-maintaining instincts. Sometimes, however, such displacement does not take place and the result is self-mutilation and self-destruction. This conceptualization of Freud's never proved very popular, however, and few accepted it. Hence, we will not deal with it further except to note that we will indicate later that a major problem of many motivational theories, in general, is how to deal with and explain self-destructive behavior.

and have the characteristics detailed above. It is they that serve as mainsprings to behavior. Originally, when these drives (and the stimuli constituting them) become too great in the infant, the tension is reduced by *wish fulfillment,* rather than by seeking out appropriate objects in the real world. Such behavior is called *primary-process* functioning, and it is marked mainly by the development of mental content, realistic or not, that results in pleasurable sensations, namely, the reduction of stimulation. This is why primary-process thinking has been conceptualized as operating according to the *pleasure principle.* Eventually, however, the ability to satisfy instinctual desires by wish alone decreases, and interaction with the real world begins in order to seek out those objects that once attained will lead to the pleasure that comes from satisfaction of the basic instinct. (For example, satisfaction of the hunger drives eventually needs to come from real, digestible objects, not just wishful thinking.) Out of such interaction with the real world, two further structures of the mind develop that eventually come to operate in conjunction with the id. One of these is the *superego,* which is the internalized representation of parental and societal requirements as to which objects and behaviors are permissible as mechanisms for instinctual satisfaction, which are not, and which are "ideal" as a way of satisfying the instincts. The second development (actually, it comes first chronologically according to Freud) is the *ego,* which is, in essence, the "executive" part of the personality structure. The reason for describing the ego in this way is that it basically operates as a control mechanism, balancing the desires of the id and the constraints of the superego by directing the behavior of the individual toward those objects that will lead to both instinctual satisfaction and serve an appropriate source of gratification. At the same time, it attempts to steer him away from those objects and behaviors not permissible as sources of satisfaction. These operations of the ego, directing and controlling the means of instinctual expression by balancing id against superego demands and require-ments, are called *secondary-process* functioning, with such functioning operating according to the *reality principle.* (It should be noted, incidentally, that "pleasure" is sought both in primary- and secondary-process thinking. The difference is that in the latter case, the objects decided upon as a means for achieving pleasure are as a result of interaction with the real world, not wishful thinking.)

One further influence on the ego in seeking appropriate means of instinctual expression is found in Freud's postulation of one other source of behavior directionality, at least as far as sexual instincts are concerned. This is his famous theory of stages, whereby he stated that the areas of the body where gratification of the sexual instincts are sought follow an invariant developmental progression. Thus, the first two years of life comprise the *oral stage,* where means of sexual satisfaction are sought in the area of the mouth. This is followed by the *anal stage,* from about the ages of two to four years, which corresponds to the period of toilet training. The third stage is the *phallic stage,* whereby children find pleasure in their genital areas and become greatly attracted in a sexual sense toward their opposite sex parents. As a result of the fears that such interest elicits, Freud argued, sexual interest then becomes repressed and a *latency period* of no sexual interest develops. Finally, the individual emerges at adolescence into the *genital stage,* a period when the individual is ready for mature sexual expression with the opposite sex.

The picture that Freud presented of the motivational mechanisms of behavior is that of a conflict between the basic instincts of man and the opportunities afforded by the environment, a picture not too unlike that of Darwin. The one who survived, according to Darwin *and* according to Freud, was the one who developed mechanisms that allowed the gratification of those instincts necessary for survival.

However, we should not make this analogy too close, since Freud, while trained as a neuroanatomist, was mainly concerned with psychological processes, not biology. As an example, there is his primary interest in the sexual instinct, an instinct necessary for species survival, but not seemingly for individual survival (although Freud would have argued this latter point). Similarly, Freud developed concepts such as expectancy as guides to behavioral direction and choice, concepts that, as we will see, are necessary in a psychology of motivation but that have never been satisfactorily developed in a theoretical sense by those who are oriented to a natural-science, biological approach to motivation. Finally, Freud was also a clinician who developed such concepts as unconscious motivational processes and ego-defense mechanisms, ideas of crucial importance for Freud and anyone else interested in a psychology of human motivation, but not very relevant for anyone interested in the biological survival of animals. It is these hypotheses of unconscious motivational processes and ego-defense mechanisms that constitute the last elements in our all too brief recounting of Freud's motivational theorizing. They are important both in helping us to understand Freud and because of their influence on the work of later motivational theorists.

Basically, Freud's concepts of unconscious motivation and the ego-defense mechanisms are important for us because they serve as the final set of constructs that Freud developed for understanding why behavior takes the direction it does. Underlying this set of theoretical proposals aimed at understanding why we sometimes do things without knowing why we do them and why we sometimes do what seem to be very strange things is the notion of anxiety. Basically, Freud argued in his later, more generally accepted theorizing in this area, anxiety develops when the ego is caught between the instinctual demands of the id wanting to be gratified and the constraints of the superego not allowing these instinctual demands to be satisfied. Usually, Freud proposed, this type of conflict stems from the sexual instincts, but theoretically, of course, the proposed situation could occur with any instinctual demand. As a result of this conflict, the ego seeks out a different direction and a different means by which the instinctual demands will be satisfied. It needs to select behavior of which the superego approves. (Remember, any object may, through learning, serve as a source of instinct gratification.) The process by which this is done, it is important to realize, is unconscious in nature, that is, the individual is unaware that his ego is operating in a manner to seek out situations where the expectancy of being able to satisfy instinctual demands is high, given the constraints of the superego. All the person is aware of is that he is engaging in a given set of behaviors. It might be noted that this is the reason, Freud believed, that psychoanalytic therapy takes so long. Behavior patterns designed to satisfy instinctual needs develop unconsciously, thereby making analysis designed to overcome those behavior patterns that are dysfunctional, highly time-consuming,

Table 2.1 Some Ego-defense Mechanisms and Illustrations in Organizational Situations

Mechanism	Psychological Process	Illustration
Regression	Individual returns to an earlier and less mature level of adjustment in the face of frustration	A manager having been blocked in some administrative pursuit busies himself with clerical duties or technical details more appropriate for subordinates
Compensation	Individual devotes himself to a pursuit with increased vigor to make up for some feeling of real or imagined inadequacy	Zealous, hard-working president of the 25-year club who has never advanced very far in the company hierarchy
Conversion	Emotional conflicts are expressed in muscular, sensory, or bodily symptoms of disability, malfunctioning, or pain	A disabling headache keeping a staff member off the job the day after a cherished project has been rejected
Fantasy	Daydreaming or other forms of imaginative activity provide an escape from reality and imagined satisfactions	An employee's daydream of the day in the staff meeting when he corrects the mistakes of his boss and is publicly acknowledged as the real leader of the industry
Negativism	Active or passive resistance, operating unconsciously	The manager who, having been unsuccessful in getting out of a committee assignment, picks apart every suggestion that anyone makes in the meeting
Resignation, apathy, or boredom	Breaking psychological contact with the environment; withholding any sense of emotional or personal involvement	Employee who, receiving no reward, praise, or encouragement, no longer cares whether or not he does a good job
Flight or withdrawal	Leaving the field in which frustration is experienced, either physically or psychologically	The salesman's big order falls through and he takes the rest of the day off

Source: Timothy W. Costello and Sheldon S. Zalkind, *Psychology in administration: a research orientation,* pp. 148-49. © 1963 by Prentice-Hall, Inc. Reprinted by permission.

and arduous. What has to be done is to pierce these behavioral mechanisms that the ego has developed unconsciously in order to satisfy the needs of the id and the demands of the superego and thus protect itself from being destroyed by their conflicting requirements. It is when the conflicts are difficult to reconcile that therapy is necessary. However, we will not deal with these aspects of Freud's work here.

What kinds of behaviors resolve these types of conflicts? Freud called them the *ego-defense mechanisms* and suggested a considerable number of them, some of which are listed in Table 2.1, along with illustrations as to how they might manifest themselves in organizational situations.

In addition to these behavioral patterns, Freud also saw dreaming as a major way in which impulses unacceptable to the superego are expressed. It was here, also, that Freud looked for clues concerning the motivational characteristics of the patient he was dealing with at the time. It is worth noting that it was because of the kinds of analyses indicated in the following quotation, that is, Freud's tracing of instinctual determinants of dreams as distorted by superego pressures of the kind we have described, that Freud developed his notion of determinants of behavior stemming from desires that had been buried in the unconscious by societal constraints. It was this type of evidence and argument, as well as the repeated observation that people under hypnosis did things of which they were later unaware, behavior that seemed highly irrational to the onlooker, that buried forever the concept of rational will as the major motivational construct it had been since Grecian times, and led psychologists to the deterministic type of thinking exemplified by Freud.

The Interpretation of Dreams was considered by Freud to be his most important work and the significance of dreams as the "royal road to the unconscious" is accepted as a major aspect of psychoanalysis; the symbol is one of the means whereby forbidden wishes from the unconscious id are allowed to manifest themselves in disguised form in consciousness when they would otherwise clash with the moral demands of the superego. It is the function of the dream to preserve sleep by permitting expression to the wishes in such a form as not to shock the ego and so awaken the dreamer, and it thus happens that the manifest content of the dream (i.e. the dream as recalled upon waking) differs considerably from its latent content (i.e. its unconscious significance). However, by the process of free-association the latent content can be revealed, in spite of condensation, displacement, plastic representation, and fixed symbolism. Condensation means that some parts of the latent content are left out and elements possessing a common trait are fused together, so that a figure appearing in a dream may be a composite image of several people in real life. In displacement, elements which are invested with great emotional significance may be made to appear insignificant and vice versa in order to conceal their importance from the dreamer. Plastic representation is described by Freud as a "plastic, concrete piece of imagery, originating in the sound of a word." For example, the dreamer's impression of climbing a high mountain from which he has a wide *view* of the surrounding land is connected by free association with the recollection of a friend who is publishing a *Review* on the subject of foreign relations. The dreamer is identifying himself with the "reviewer," since he is making a survey of his own life in his analysis. In fixed symbolism, Freud drew attention to his belief that certain modes of symbolic expression in dreams have a fixed meaning which cannot be further analysed, since they are not individual but common to all humanity. Examples of such fixed symbols have been given in Chapter 3, and in the Freudian sense the meanings are usually sexual ones. As if these disguises were not enough, there is a final process which complicates dream analysis: that of secondary elaboration. On awaking, the dreamer recalls the dream's manifest content, but his mind soon sets to work to give what he only vaguely remembers as some semblance of order and coherence, a coherence which it did not originally possess, so that the dream as told is a much more orderly and rational entity than it was when originally presented during sleep. Thus the latent content is disguised to form the manifest content and this is further distorted by secondary elaboration.[2]

This completes our overview of Freud's motivational theorizing, a discussion that has been summarized in Figure 2.1 and that the reader will note has been nonevaluative and essentially descriptive in character. Since our procedure in later chapters will be far more analytic and evaluative, it may be desirable at this point to explain why we have followed the procedure we have. Basically, we view Freud as a theorist of overwhelming historical influence, one whose ideas will appear in refined, renamed fashion throughout this book. Thus, we will be discussing at various times many of Freud's notions, such as (a) basic instinctual drives as the determinants of behavior arousal; (b) the tension-reduction hypothesis; and (c) the ego-defense mechanisms. These formulations have been studied by psychologists who knew of their indebtedness to Freud, but who were more experimentally and research oriented than he was. It is on the basis of this later work that we will be able to deal with and evaluate some of these ideas.

In terms of Freud's own specific motivation theory, however, we view it as primarily of historical importance as an influence on later motivational theories. It is still, we feel, basically untested in a research sense and is, perhaps, untestable in any experimental sense with human beings. Similarly, while field tests of Freud's work might be undertaken, these have rarely been done in the past with anything approaching sufficient sampling, satisfactory measuring instruments, or controls for investigator bias.

It is for these reasons we have adopted the position we have and why we will be more concerned throughout this book with tracing the *influence* of Freud's concepts and the research evidence relating to them, rather than looking at the evidence relating to the specific theory itself.

[2] J. A. C. Brown, *Freud and the Post-Freudians* (Pelican Original, 1961), pp. 112-13. Copyright © The Estate of J. A. C. Brown, 1961, 1964.

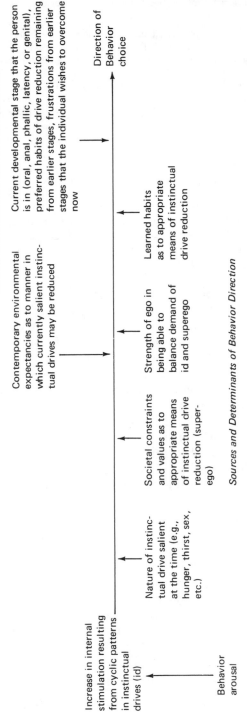

Figure 2.1 Outline of Freudian theory of motivation.

CLARK HULL: THE 1943 SYSTEM

Clark Hull is remembered today as the author of a seemingly highly sophisticated attempt at constructing a rigorous, locally tight, mathematically oriented theory of motivation. His theory, developed during the first half of the twentieth century, constituted a major effort to reject mentalistic, subjective notions, such as the will, in favor of physically defined variables in dealing with the phenomena we call motivational processes. In this section we will begin our discussion of his work.

Hull received his degree relatively late in life (he was in his thirties), and his early professional work, while conceded to be very good, was in such unrelated areas as aptitude testing and hypnosis. However, beginning in the late 1920s, when he moved to Yale University from the University of Wisconsin, he began to develop a theoretical system that, for comprehensiveness, systematization, and influence on other psychologists and their work, probably stands second only to Freud's in the history of psychology. Indeed, even today, more than forty years after Hull began his theorizing, his concepts and ideas dominate the work of many contemporary psychologists, and his approach still constitutes the standard against which later theoretical models are compared. Furthermore, the fact that the systems he proposed have had to be and continue to be revised is no discredit to him but is actually the opposite, since he explicitly designed his work in order that this be possible.

From the point of view of the longevity of hypotheses, it is extremely dangerous for them to become specific. The very definiteness of an hypothesis makes it possible to determine with relative ease whether its implications agree with known phenomena which it proposes to explain. In case of failure to conform, the unambiguous nature of the comparison is peculiarly fatal. Worse yet, an unambiguous hypothesis is likely to permit the deductive forecast of what should be observed under various experimental conditions which may as yet be untried. A single well-planned experiment may at any moment yield results quite different from the deductive forecast, and thus topple the entire hypothetical structure. This, of course, is all quite as it should be. The healthy development of a science demands that the implications of its hypotheses be deduced as promptly and unambiguously as possible. This will make it possible for them, if verified by experiment, to be incorporated into the structure or system of the science, or if found to disagree with experimental findings, the hypotheses may be recast or simply discarded as errors in the long trial-and-error process of system construction. At the least, such hypotheses may be credited with the virtue of having stimulated experimental research. But if an hypothesis be so vague and indefinite, or so lacking in relevancy to the phenomena which it seeks to explain that the results neither of previous experiments nor those of experiments subsequently to be performed may be deduced from it, it will be difficult indeed to prove it false. And if, in addition, the hypotheses should appeal in some subtle fashion to the predilections of a culture in which it gains currency, it should enjoy a long and honored existence. Unfortunately, because of its very sterility and barrenness in the above deductive sense, such an hypothesis should have no status whatever in science. It savours more of metaphysics, religion or theology.[3]

Hull's theorizing, through which he attempted to implement this philosophical stance, actually developed over a period of time. Generally, his work is described as having involved two major stages, with the first evolving into his 1943 system (Hull, 1943) and the second into his 1952 theory (Hull, 1952). The theories were similar in that they both involved the setting up of a system of postulates and theorems from which specific predictions could be made, with the results of the experiments to then be interpreted as either supporting the postulate or theorem from which they were derived or as necessitating a revision of them. However, although both postulate systems used this method of theory building and hypothesis generation (known more formally as the hypothetic-deductive method), both were physicalistic in nature, and both showed the influence of the Darwinian tradition. They were different in that the 1952 model was radically changed in order to overcome the weaknesses found in the 1943 approach. Hence, we will begin by first discussing the 1943 system and its strengths and weaknesses. Following this, we will examine the 1952 revision and the ways it differed from the earlier version. In addition, we will discuss the work of other psychologists who utilized the Hullian approach in studying motivational phenomena during this period. We will conclude our discussion by assessing the contemporary adequacy of the Hullian approach in the study of motivational processes, discussing both the reasons why it remains viable today and what its continuing weaknesses are. As we will see, it is primarily because of these weaknesses that a new way of looking at motivational phenomena in an objective, physicalistic framework has begun to gain popularity. It is this school of thought, known as the activation-arousal school, that will command our attention in Chapter 4.

The Basic Theory: An Overview

Hull's orientation, as we have already seen, was very much in a natural-science tradition. The tradition included, for him, the physically oriented behaviorism of John Watson and the notions of instinctual behavior stemming from Darwin's theory of evolution. For Hull, following Darwin, the problem of arousal of behavior, or why man originally behaved at all, stemmed clearly from evolutionary considerations. Man engaged in behavior, or behavior was aroused, because it had survival value. Whenever an organism was in the type of situation whereby his survival was threatened, behavior was aroused and engaged

[3]Clark Hull, Simple trial-and-error learning: A study in psychological theory. *Psychological Review,* 37 (1930): 251-52.

in, with this behavior directed primarily toward those activities that, either through innate endowment or through learning, had become associated with survival value in the past. Overall, this was Hull's basic answer to the question of the arousal and direction of behavior. An organism behaved when its survival was threatened, and the direction it took stemmed either from innate behavioral characteristics that had survival value (as these had been developed by evolutionary processes) or from learned behaviors that had been associated with survival value in the past. From this preliminary assumption, Hull believed most forms of behavior could and would eventually be derived.

What kinds of situations threatened survival? For Hull, these could be physically defined, and they consisted of such things as the presence of hunger, thirst, pain (or tissue injury), sexual deprivation, and the like. The presence of stimulation associated with these conditions consisted of threats to survival, according to Hull, and when they occurred the stimuli associated with them had to be reduced. This, then, was what determined the arousal of behavior; it was engaged in to reduce stimulation. Another way of saying this is that man is motivated to achieve an inert condition, that is, a condition without stimulation. This is a position that we recall was encountered in our examination of Freud's motivational position, and it is an argument that has aroused much opposition, as we will see. The behavior itself, and its direction, was either that which had been bred into the organism by evolution as a means of achieving survival or that which the organism had learned in the past had led to the reduction of the particular stimulation of the moment.

The genius of Hull, however, was not just that he attempted to provide some clear answers to the "why" of behavior or the reasons certain behaviors were engaged in more than others. Nor was it because he sought to distinguish the "why," or arousal, of behavior from the "how," or direction, of behavior. Others before him had made this distinction. In Table 2.2, for example, are listed summaries of the thinking of other psychologists, both predecessors and contemporaries who had thoughts and engaged in research that led to similar types of conceptualizations. Rather the genius of Hull was in attempting to spell out in precise detail how these mechanisms worked, how they combined, and so on. It is when we examine these aspects of his work that we can begin to get a truer appreciation of his accomplishments.

For Hull, the newborn organism possesses a set of receptors capable of being stimulated by such sources as external (to the organism) stimuli (called S_E by Hull) and internal stimuli of the type associated with biological states of a threatening nature. Examples of the latter are stomach contractions (hunger), dryness of the mouth (thirst), and tissue injury (pain). These stimuli, both internal and external, may give rise to an internal state marked by two major characteristics. The first of these is a general drive state (called D by Hull) that acts as a general stimulant to the arousal of behavior in that it stimulates activation of whatever behavior tendencies exist in the organism at the time. But

Table 2.2 Theoretical Proposals and Empirical Research that Preceded, Led to, and Accompanied the Development of Hull's System

Theoretical and Research Statements	Source
1. The research by the Würzburg School in Germany in the late nineteenth and early twentieth centuries argued that there is a dynamic factor or energizing force that activates and determines what mental content (i.e., ideas, images, etc.) will occur in consciousness. Such mental content of the mind, i.e., the associative structure learned through experience, is used by the energizing force, which determines the mental content that will appear at any given time.	Humphrey (1951)
2. a. Deprivation leads to random, nondirectional states of restlessness. b. The "appetites" are internal stimuli that keep the organism restless until it acquires through learning those modes of response that will allay the internal stimulation.	Holt (1931)

3. a. Drives are stimuli that goad people to consummatory reactions (e.g., eating, drinking, etc.).
  b. Drives are stimuli that activate stimulus-response mechanisms, which prepare the way and facilitate the attaining of the consummatory response; such stimulus-response mechanisms are called preparatory responses and are, in essence, the "how" of behavior, whereas the drive is the "why" of behavior.
  c. Any mechanism might become a drive if it is directed toward a consummatory, rather than preparatory, reaction.
	Woodworth (1918)

4. As biological deprivation becomes greater, the result is greater general diffuse activity as well as specific behaviors keyed to the specific source of deprivation.	Richter (1927)
5. Each motivational condition has associated with it a central motive state (CMS), the major properties of which are (a) persistence of motivation after original stimulation has been removed, (b) heightened level of activity, (c) responses to condition, and (d) preparation of organism to engage in consummatory behavior. There is some overlap between different CMS's.	Morgan (1943)

which tendencies exist at that time? This is a function of the second characteristic, which is that these biological states have associated characteristic sets of physical stimulation unique to each state. Thus, hunger involves stomach contractions, thirst a dry mouth, and so on, or so Hull thought, and it is these physical stimuli that determine the direction of behavior. The reason for this is that these are the stimuli most relevant at the time (due to the biological state), and these stimuli then activate behavior sequences that have in the past been associated with reduction of these physical stimuli. The behavior sequence that is activated might be of two kinds. It might be an unlearned sequence, one innate to the organism possibly bred into him by evolutionary adaptation because of its survival value. This innate response tendency Hull termed $_sU_R$, with the subscripts S and R not having any significance other than indicating that the behavior consists of an unlearned (U) stimulus-response (S-R) sequence. The second type of behavior sequence that might be activated, and far more important in Hull's thinking, is analogous to this, except that instead of being an innately bred mechanism for reducing stimulation, it is a learned behavior sequence. It is the behaviors that the organism has engaged in in the past that have led to the reduction of these specific drive stimuli. This learned stimulus-response link Hull called $_SH_R$ (H indicates habit), and it is on the basis of biological survival value that these stimulus-response links develop, or are learned, or so Hull proposed in 1943. To recapitulate for a moment, Hull's basic paradigm may be diagrammed as follows:

$$
\begin{array}{lll}
 & \textit{Internal States} & \\
 & \textit{of Organism} & \\
\end{array}
$$

	Internal States of Organism	
Environmental stimuli $\longrightarrow$	Drive (D) ─────────────→	Arousal of behavior
		↓
Internal stimuli $\longrightarrow$	Drive Stimuli (S_D)	stimulates stimulus-response connections that are most salient at the time
	high saliency of specific stimuli associated with particular internal state appropriate to specific stimulation of the moment (e.g., hunger, thirst, pain, sex, etc.)	↓ behavior sequences designed to reduce stimuli

$$ S^U_R \qquad S^H_R $$

unlearned behavior sequences that will reduce stimulation	learned behavior sequences that will reduce stimulation

These then, are Hull's major 1943 concepts or building blocks of behavior, D, $_SH_R$, and in a much more minor sense, particularly for humans, $_SU_R$. Several questions remain, however, if we are to see exactly how Hull's theory worked as an explanatory system for motivation processes and how it could actually be used in the prediction of behavioral arousal, direction, and vigor. First, we need to know the determinants of D and $_SH_R$, how they develop, what determines their strength, and, since they are both crucial, how they combine in the prediction of behavior. Secondly, we need to know how Hull attempted to account for the obviously common observation that there are many kinds of stimulation able to arouse behavior that bear little or no similarity to biological need states and have little significance for the survival of the organism. Similarly, there are many kinds of responses that become linked to given stimuli and are regularly elicited by them, despite their having seemingly little or no biological utility. How Hull and his successors accounted for these questions will be discussed below.

The Nature of D and $_SH_R$: Conceptualization and Measurement

Let us begin with some abstract statements concerning the nature of Hullian theorizing, and then we will see what Hull's approach meant in a concrete sense. Thus, for Hull, D and $_SH_R$ are conceptual, theoretical variables, rather than observable, physical stimuli. According to him, they occur and vary as a function of physically defined stimuli, and then, in turn, they "cause" differences in observable, physically defined responses as a function of their values. They are defined and conceptualized as a function of variables under the experimenter's control, thus making empirical tests based on them susceptible to empirical research, but the theoretical structure is not concerned with those specific variables that the experimenter can control. The theory itself is concerned with the significance of D and $_SH_R$ in the prediction of behavior and it is in terms of these intervening variables that the hypotheses are stated.

What was Hull's point in building his approach this way? What were the advantages he saw? What were the problems Hull had to overcome in utilizing this approach? Perhaps these questions can best be answered by some more concrete discussions.

Assume for a moment that at least four of the basic instinctual forces of behavior are the desires to reduce (1) hunger, (2) thirst, (3) pain from tissue injury, and (4) sexual stimulation. It is possible to study each of these separately in terms of the factors that influence them in their variation. Similarly, we can also determine how variations in each of them are in turn related to and determinant of other behaviors, with this being even simpler to do if we define all of these variables in a physicalistic sense. This is conceptually easy to do in measuring hunger (i.e., stomach contractions would be the physical manifestation), thirst (i.e., dryness of the throat), pain (i.e., tissue injury), and sexual stimulation (i.e., blood chemical changes). Why, then, didn't Hull do this? The answer, basically, was one of theoretical parsimony and the desire for psychological understanding. Thus, if Hull kept them separate, he would need to develop four separate theoretical systems and postulate four separate hypotheses as to how each would have psychological effects on behavior. Suppose, however, he could postulate that all four instinctual forces were determinants of the *same* psychological variable and that it was this variable that determined behavior of various kinds. If this were in fact so, then he had one theory to account for the same set of behaviors for which he previously needed four sets of propositions.

The problem, however, is that the psychological variables, the ones proposed to determine the behavior and in this case called D and $_SH_R$, are conceptual variables, which are assumed to vary as a function of such factors as hunger, thirst, pain, and sexual stimulation, but which are not the same. This is perfectly all right, and D and $_SH_R$ can be defined and utilized in this way *as long as* the empirical operations and the rationale used in determining, measuring, and identifying differences in them have been clearly specified and defended. Obviously, unless such operations were developed, we would have no way of knowing that we were actually measuring and manipulating D and $_SH_R$, and without such knowledge the theory cannot be tested. Hull, thus, was very interested in dealing with these questions and in developing clear statements indicating how certain observable stimuli were determinants of D and $_SH_R$ and how these explanatory, psychological variables in his system varied as a function of these observable antecedents. Having developed this coordinating system between his theoretical constructs and the empirical operations that would determine them, he would then develop predictions as to the effects of different levels of D and $_SH_R$ on behavior and proceed to test them.

Given, then, that D (drive) was basically conceptualized as a function of such manipulable variables as number of hours since last feeding (for hunger), number of hours since last drinking (for thirst), degree of shock (for pain), and the like, it was further postulated that these stimuli combine in a summative fashion at any particular time to determine the general level of D. Because D was viewed as a general arousal agent, it was hypothesized that it would be affected by all the sources of stimulation operative on the organism at any particular point in time, and it is this total sum of stimulation that determines the level of D. Hence, according to Hull, whatever biological need states happen to operate at a time (e.g., sexual, hunger, and thirst), all would serve as general activators or contributors to D. Furthermore, this would happen whether these drives were relevant or irrelevant to whatever primary need state might be operative at the time. Thus, a relevant drive in a hunger experiment would be as a result of the stomach contractions occurring at the time in the subject's (Ss) stomachs. However, in addition to this, there would be further contributions to D by whatever thirst, sex, or pain stimuli also happened to be operative at the time. In such an experiment, then, when food deprivation was under study as the major contributor to D, these latter sources of stimulation would then be termed irrelevant sources of drive for this particular experiment. Relevant or irrelevant, though, all would have to be measured to determine the level of D and to predict arousal. In this sense, all would operate in the same way. However, they would operate differently in determining the direction of behavior.[4] Thus, if we assume that we have experimentally manipulated the hunger deprivation of Ss running a maze originally learned under hunger deprivation, the theory clearly predicts that performance would be facilitated by adding thirst deprivation stimuli to those stemming from hunger. However, this facilitation would occur only up to a certain point of thirst deprivation. Increasing it beyond this point would lead to a decline in maze performance because now drive stimuli (S_D) relating to thirst deprivation are more salient than drive stimuli relating to hunger

---

[4]The reader should note that we are using behavior as Hull's dependent variable. Actually, as a dependent variable, he stated his predictions using $_SE_P$ (excitory potential). However, since $_SE_P$ was closely related to behavior, and since it varied as a function of other, minor factors we shall not consider here, the more convenient behavior has been utilized as Hull's dependent variable in our discussion.

deprivation as directive influences on behavior. However, these thirst S_D have not been associated with drive reduction in this particular maze, and thus, the behavior sequences these stimuli elicit are not particularly facilitative of performance in this situation, being instead more random in nature.

In terms of $_SH_R$, the 1943 Hullian system postulated a number of determinants and procedures for measuring these determinants. First and foremost, an $_SH_R$ (i.e., a habit) develops because the responses involved have biological utility in that they have led to the reduction of drive stimuli. The speed and development of $_SH_R$, however, is a function of the following variables, all of which are theoretically under the control of the experimenter:

1. The closeness in time of the stimulus-response coupling to the actual stimulus reduction; such stimulus reduction in the interest of biological utility was Hull's definition of reinforcement, that is, each stimulus-reduction occurrence constituted a reinforcement for him. It should be noted that this definition of reinforcement overcame the charges of "circularity" that had been made against other psychologists who defined reinforcement, on the one hand, by saying it was a stimulus that led to a repetition of behavior, while on the other, they said that one could see if something was a reinforcer if it led to repetition. However, this charge was never an accurate one since it could easily be shown that many reinforcers were transsituational and not circular since they had effects in different situations from where they had originally been observed acting as reinforcers [Meehl, 1950]. The inaccuracy of the charge of "circularity" against other psychologists does not, however, detract from the value of Hull's definition. Nor does the fact that the definition eventually proved inaccurate detract from the value of his attempts. Hull made a valiant attempt to define his key concepts clearly, logically, with a rationale attached to them, and in a way that they could be tested experimentally. The fact that they were eventually found wanting through research is, as we said earlier, a credit rather than a disservice to him.
2. The number of reinforced trials.
3. The magnitude of reinforcement during training.

These are the determinants of $_SH_R$, according to Hull, and its level at any particular time is measureable by the probability of response to stimulation, the latency of response, and the degree to which the response to stimulation is resistant to extinction.

These procedures then determine how D and $_SH_R$ are measured. How do they combine in the predicting of behavior? Hull, basing his statements on the results of experiments by Perrin (1942) and Williams (1938), suggested that the strength of the impetus to respond is a multiplicative function of habit and drive, assuming the general form:

$$_SE_R = D \times {_SH_R}$$

Behavior = $f(D) \times f(_SH_R)$

This model means, of course, that zero levels of either D or $_SH_R$ would result in a complete lack of behavior, a prediction easily tested for the case where $D = 0$. However, for the converse, the implications of this equation are clearly not accurate, since high levels of D will always have some S_D, thus initiating response sequences of some nature aimed at drive reduction, either $_SU_R$ or $_SH_R$. Hence, it is hard to conceive of a case where behavior could approach zero at high levels of D, since some S_D must always be involved by definition of the components making up the high stimulus state. This S_D will always stimulate some behavior, even if it is only of an innate nature stemming from evolutionary adaptation that might have little usefulness for achieving drive reduction in a specific situation. This situation, stemming from the lack of independence between D and S_D, constitutes a logical problem of the Hull model, which we shall mention later when we discuss other weaknesses of the approach.

Expanding the Basic 1943 Framework:
Conditioned Stimuli and Secondary Reinforcers

It is clearly the case that most forms of complex human behavior cannot be viewed simply as the attempt to get food, drink, or avoid shock, the forms of motivated behavior that constitute much of the data psychologists working in the Hullian tradition tend to report. Human behavior is symbolic, conceptual, and not easily controllable by what seems to be the physical type of external stimulation found in animal experiments. Yet, according to the philosophical framework under which Hull operated, his "building blocks" would eventually be able to account for these complex behaviors. Could this be done? Could the basic system we have described actually be used to understand more complex forms of behavior? As it turned out, the answer was mixed, with some forms of complex behavior adequately accounted for by the Hullian system, and some less so. It is to this research that we now turn.

First, it is important to realize that the basic mechanism Hull proposed to use for explaining complex behavior was, at least conceptually, a simple one, essentially Pavlovian in nature. As it turned out, however, the simplicity was illusory. Hull proposed that stimuli associated contiguously with primary drive states (such as hunger, thirst, and pain) come to elicit behaviors similar to those that the primary drive states elicit. That is, they become conditioned stimuli, eliciting those behaviors that had in the past led to reduction of the stimulation associated with the specific primary drive (i.e., the original unconditioned stimulus). Similarly, and in an analogous fashion, stimuli that have been closely and contiguously associated with primary reinforcement (i.e., a reduction of biological drives) come in and of themselves to assume reinforcing properties.

Hence, behavior that, in the presence of certain eliciting stimuli, leads to the attainment of these secondary reinforcers tends to recur in the same sense that behavior that leads to primary reinforcement in the presence of these eliciting stimuli tends to recur. In other words, these stimuli have now become conditioned or secondary reinforcers. Thus, it was basically by using the conditioned stimulus-conditioned reinforcers framework developed on the basis of contiguity that Hull proposed to account for complex behavior in his 1943 theory.

More recently, a former colleague of Hull's, O. H. Mowrer (1960), has proposed a theory of behavior explicitly designed to use much of the Hullian approach and terminology in accounting for complex behavior. However, Mowrer's approach differs significantly from that of the 1943 Hull in that his interests are not particularly in the conditioned stimulus aspect discussed above, but, rather, mostly in conditioned reinforcers and their implications for controlling human behavior. According to Mowrer, various stimuli become associated with various kinds of outcomes and thus assume symbolic significance to the organism, sometimes positive and sometimes negative. Because of this, he goes on to propose, these stimuli assume reinforcing properties and, hence, are influences on later behavior. What kinds of symbolic significance are involved here? Mowrer distinguishes at least four separate cases:

1. Stimuli that become associated with outcomes of behavior that are negative (e.g., drive increasing) in nature; these become stimuli that are called "fear" stimuli (note: by *drive increasing* is meant hunger increasing, pain increasing, etc.).
2. Stimuli that become associated with outcomes of behavior that are positive (e.g., drive decreasing) in nature; these become "hope" stimuli.
3. Stimuli that become associated with outcomes of behavior that involve the disappearance of signals that meant the reduction of drives; these become "disappointment" stimuli.
4. Stimuli that become associated with outcomes of behavior that involve the termination of danger stimuli; these become "relief" stimuli.

It is here in Mowrer's theorizing that we see an example of how the Hullian approach might eventually be refined enough to bring into the laboratory and there study such human, cognitive, emotional concepts as fear, hope, relief, and disappointment in a more rigorous manner. Thus, it is Mowrer's basic prediction that "hope" and "relief" stimuli become positive reinforcers of behavior and can be utilized to build habits, since organisms are motivated to achieve them. On the other hand, "fear" and "disappointment" are negative outcomes that, Mowrer argues, organisms try to avoid and that will not build up habit (i.e., S-R connections).

Conditioned stimuli and conditioned reinforcers, then, are the proposed explanatory concepts for complex behavior in the Hullian tradition. The question that concerns us, however, is how well they work in this context, and, as we have suggested previously, the answer to this is mixed. Thus, let us first look at where the approach is adequate, and then we will look at some of the problems.

Anxiety and fear as conditioned stimuli.   Assume that you are a rat and that you live in a black box and your life is generally pretty pleasant. Then one day somebody picks you up and puts you in a white box and the moment you are set down, you receive a severe electric shock. Assume that this happens a couple of times. What would you then do if you saw a white box? You'd probably be rather upset and more than a little nervous, or maybe *fearful* would be a better word. Once you felt that way, you'd probably do something to try to reduce the fear, like avoiding the white box if you could or escaping from it if you were placed in it against your will.

This experimental paradigm constitutes what is probably the best example of how Hull thought his "building-block" approach would eventually be useful in the understanding of complex human behavior. Thus, it is particularly interesting that it has been in as significant an area of human behavior as fear and anxiety that Hull's conditioned-stimulus hypotheses have been most investigated as an explanatory system. Furthermore, while much of this work was supportive of Hull's ideas, the same research became, conversely, one of the reasons Hull's system failed in the eyes of many psychologists.

Among the most significant investigators in this area has been Neal Miller, one of Hull's students, who was actually responsible for the research study discussed in the beginning of this section. In this research (Miller, 1948), it was successfully shown that a white box that had been associated with an electric shock would serve as a conditioned stimulus in the sense predicted by Hull. That is, rats when placed in it would (a) attempt to escape even before the shock was administered, and (b) learn new habits that would enable escape from the white box when earlier learned escape routes were unavailable. The implications of this research finding were that fear could be considered a secondary or acquired drive because it acted like a drive even though it was not innate, but was learned, and conditions for its acquisition could be demonstrated experimentally. Despite such differences in its origin, it had effects on behavior similar to that of pain, hunger, thirst, and the other biologically based drives. The differences are highly important, however. Even though fear and other similarly conceptualized variables such as frustration and anxiety, which use this framework for research, might have specific, physicalistic stimulation attached to them such as changes in autonomic nervous system functioning, the fact that the behavior is learned and does not need to have any biological significance attached to it is very crucial. This research was one of the reasons why the adequacy of Hull's theoretical system was eventually challenged by many psychologists. The reason is that Hull's achievement of linking behavior and its arousal to cases of biological significance was now called into question, since, clearly, anxiety and frustration develop for many other reasons than threat to biological survival, although survival may still be considered one cause of these variables.

Since the basic conclusions of this experiment have been supported in a wide variety of other studies (cf. Brown and Jacobs, 1949), the effect can be considered to be fairly well substantiated. But what is the significance of these secondary drives, or secondary sources of drive, as Brown (1961) prefers to call them? At least four different implications seem to be indicated.

First, as we have mentioned, it suggests that the definition of D as being biologically based had to be changed. It is clear that environmental variables having little biological significance would elicit anxiety and that such anxiety could assume drive properties in the same sense as pain and hunger have drive properties. The effect of this finding was, on the one hand, to support Hullian predictions. At the same time, doubt was cast on the logical underpinnings of the whole system, in that the variable that Hull wanted to work as a source of drive and that did work the way he wanted (i.e., a neutral experimental variable) was, on reflection, the type of variable that did not need Hull's theory to be justified.

A second implication of the successful establishment of anxiety as a source of drive was that it suggested an experimental procedure whereby psychologists who preferred the rigorous methods of the laboratory could investigate a phenomenon of considerable clinical significance. The significance of anxiety for understanding neurotic behavior had been pointed out by Freud (1933), among many others, and psychologists such as Mowrer (1960) have spent significant parts of their careers studying the anxiety phenomenon by using experimental techniques inspired by Hullian theory. Miller, himself, suggested this significance in his 1948 article.

> The mechanism of acquired drives allows behavior to be more adaptable in complex variable situations. It also allows behavior to appear more baffling and apparently lawless to any investigator who has not had the opportunity to observe the conditions under which the acquired drive was established. In the present experiment the white and black compartments are very obvious features of the animal's environment. If more obscure external cues or internal ones had been involved, the habit of turning the wheel and pressing the bar might seem to be completely bizarre and maladaptive. One hypothesis is that neurotic symptoms, such as compulsions, are habits which are motivated by fear (or anxiety as it is called when its source is vague or obscured by repression) and reinforced by a reduction in fear. (Pp. 100-101)

A third implication of this successful experimental development of an acquired drive was that it led to a proposed mechanism for integrating within a relatively parsimonious theoretical framework the diverse mutiplicity of human goals. Thus, instead of going through the process of postulating separate motives for such things as money, status, prestige, a new car, a big house, and the like, Brown (1952) was moved to suggest:

The important motivating component of many of the supposed acquired drives for specific goal objects is actually a learned tendency to be discontented or anxious in the absence of these goal objects. On this view, stimulus cues signifying a lack of affection, a lack of prestige, insufficient money, etc. would be said to acquire, through learning, the capacity to arouse an anxiety reaction having drive properties. This learned anxiety would then function to energize whatever behavior is directed toward goal objects by stimuli, and its reduction, following the achievement of these goals, would be powerfully reinforcing.[5]

Brown then goes on to cite an example of how this mechanism would operate.

During the first few years of a child's life there are innumerable occasions upon which the child experiences genuine pain. Its fingers get cut. . . . And on nearly all these occasions, normally solicitous parents behave in a worried, anxious manner. The frequent combination of pain with these cues provided by the sight of the worried parents could result in the acquisition by those cues of the capacity to elicit anxiety reactions in the child. . . . Now if at the time anxiety is indicated by the parents' worried looks, they were to complain of being worried by a lack of money, the words "we have no money." could become a higher-order conditioned stimulus with power to arouse the child's anxiety on subsequent occasions. . . . if this is true, then the actual presence of money is the specific condition for producing the cessation of the anxiety-arousing cues. Having money in one's possession is equivalent to escaping from the white-box cues into the black-box cues. . . . Money thus functions as a reward or reinforcement.[6]

Brown's argument is a fascinating one because of its promise of being able to integrate the concerns of personality and social psychology with that of clinical work, all within what would appear to be a relatively rigorous framework. What is needed, however, to move this from a programmatic statement to theoretical adequacy is to have it tested, for example, to find out if children whose parents are anxious in the absence of money develop a greater drive toward money. Research of a longitudinal nature in which children would be studied over time would be most desirable here, although laboratory experimental studies are also of considerable value and would be most helpful. Unfortunately, very little of the necessary work of either type has been done as yet and Brown's hypothesis remains still untested for the most part.

Finally, the successful study of fear and anxiety as acquired drives and their gradual incorporation into the Hullian model made it possible to increase the amount of testing that could be made of the theory with human subjects. The reason for this was that once anxiety was established as a drive and a determinant of D in the Hullian sense, then one could differentiate people as to

[5] J. S. Brown, Problems presented by the concept of acquired drive. *Current theory and research in motivation,* pp. 1-21 (Lincoln: University of Nebraska Press). Copyright 1952 by the University of Nebraska Press.

[6] Ibid.

the degree to which they were chronically highly anxious or chronically low in anxiety. Then, once having classified people as high or low anxiety, or high and low D in terms of the theory, it would be possible to test various predictions of the theory with human subjects. The major necessary requirement for this was, of course, that some valid and reliable measure of chronic anxiety (or D) be available.

In 1953, Janet Taylor reported the development of the Manifest Anxiety Scale (MAS), a questionnaire explicitly designed as a measure of chronic differences in drive level (D) between individuals in order that it might be used in tests of the Hullian model. Since then, Taylor (now known professionally as Janet Taylor Spence), the late Kenneth Spence, and their co-workers have reported considerable research aimed at such tests. Before turning to their research, however, it is important to note, as Spence (1958) himself has pointed out, that this research could just as easily have used any other measure of drive. The interest was in drive (D) as a theoretical variable, not in anxiety as a content variable, although the items used in the MAS are those from a larger personality questionnaire (the Minnesota Multiphasic Inventory) that had been rated by experimental clinicians as being highly significant for the diagnosis of anxiety. The reason we bring this up at this point (and a matter that also concerned Spence) is that some psychologists have, on occasion, used the MAS clinically, a purpose for which it was never intended.

Turning now to the actual research of the Taylor-Spence group, the major focus has been on the influence of anxiety (as measured by the MAS) on task performance and how this influence might be affected by task difficulty. Starting from the basic Hullian notion that performance ($_SE_R$) is a multiplicative function of drive (motivation) and habit, high drive should activate whatever habits a person has, whether good or bad. Hence, if a task is easy, high drive should facilitate performance, since the correct (or "good") response is likely to be something a person has (since the task is easy). On the other hand, for a hard task, the person's habits are likely to be incorrect for a task. Thus, if these habits are activated, they will result in poor performance. This, then, leads to the interesting prediction, diagrammed below, that high anxiety should facilitate performance on easy tasks but hinder performance on hard tasks.

In 1964 Spence reviewed a body of research on eyelid conditioning concerned with testing the predictions of Figure 2.2 and found support in twenty-one of twenty-five investigations (Spence, 1964). For those that did not show support, Spence suggested that small samples and other such methodological problems were responsible. For our purposes, an obvious conclusion (and one made also by Spence) is that the $D \times H$ model, as utilized by the Spences, can have considerable usefulness in the study of such a significant variable as anxiety and its possible effects on task performance.

Unfortunately, a similar research-based statement to this cannot be made if we turn our attention to a highly related variable, frustration. Frustration has

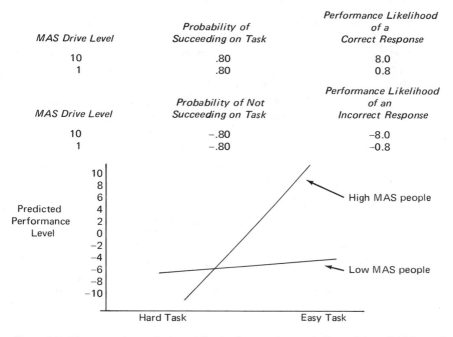

MAS Drive Level	Probability of Succeeding on Task	Performance Likelihood of a Correct Response
10	.80	8.0
1	.80	0.8

MAS Drive Level	Probability of Not Succeeding on Task	Performance Likelihood of an Incorrect Response
10	−.80	−8.0
1	−.80	−0.8

Figure 2.2 Diagrammatic prediction of Taylor-Spence theory of effect of drive (MAS score) on performance as a function of task difficulty.

been defined and conceptualized in many different ways (cf. Lawson, 1965), but what is perhaps most relevant for us here is the way that frustration has been conceptualized by Judson Brown and I. E. Farber, two psychologists working in the Hullian tradition.

Frustration, then, according to Brown and Farber, is a conflict between two opposing tendencies — one response tendency being the one originally evoked by the situation (presumably some kind of goal response), the other being some alternative response aroused by the frustrating interfering conditions themselves. This conflict between opposing tendencies leads to whatever could be said to be the unique behavioral consequences of frustration. Because frustration is defined in terms of the relationship between two hypothetical constructs – the opposing response "tendencies" – frustration is a higher-order construct; it is defined in terms of first order constructs (which can theoretically be related directly to observables). . . . One effect . . . is an increase in drive. Frustration adds to the total motivation of the organism, and thus strengthens more whatever responses are already strong in the situation. Thus, for example, if the goal directed response is far stronger than any other behavior in the situation, frustrating it may lead to its occurrence with even greater vigor. The second effect is to produce unique internal stimuli (which might be called "emotional" or "affective"). These stimuli, in turn, may be related to other responses not previously present in the situation.[7]

[7] R. Lawson, *Frustration: the study of a concept,* pp. 31-32. © 1965 by The Macmillan Company. Reprinted by permission.

First, a complex variable such as frustration has been defined in an experimentally useful fashion, that is, as a function of two experimentally manipulable drives. Secondly, a prediction is made that habitual responses to frustration stimuli may also develop if such responses reduce stimuli. However, despite the rigor of this approach, little research has taken place that would allow evaluation of the approach. Hence, the effect has been that this Brown-Farber hypothesis has had much the same undeserved fate as Brown's other hypothesis concerning the desire for social goods, status, and so forth, as functions of the desire to reduce the anxiety that occurs in the absence of these common behavioral incentives.

In addition, there is a third interesting suggestion by Brown as to how the Hullian framework can be used to account for complex human behavior that falls within the general category of anxiety and fear as conditioned drive states and that has also had a similar fate in that it has stimulated little or no research. The suggestion here concerns the possible significance of verbal stimuli as acquired sources of drive (Brown, 1961). Starting from the fact that behavior is affected by words, Brown considers the possibility that certain words, because of the responses they evoke, may actually contribute to a person's level of drive. Thus, for example, such words as *hurry up, pay attention, come on now,* and *get ready* may, because they are learned under certain conditions, actually operate as secondary sources of drive. Furthermore, such stimulation would occur whether a person spoke them to himself or somebody else was speaking to him. As an example, Brown suggests that perhaps the difference between high and low achieving individuals is that in situations that call for achievement, the high achiever is more likely to administer to himself such commands as *pay attention, hurry up,* and *try harder.* Such verbal stimuli then directly operate to increase his body tension and/or anxiety level. Whichever is the case, and they both may be so, the result is an increase in drive and, hence, task performance. One question that does arise is whether this relationship would hold for hard tasks also. Clearly, the Taylor-Spence hypothesis would say it would not. Perhaps, then, the high achiever uses these verbal stimuli less for hard tasks than for easy ones, with the reverse being true for the low achievers. On the other hand, perhaps some other type of self-administered verbal stimulation (such as *relax, take it easy*) occurs in both groups, and the difference is the ratio of different self-administered commands under the different conditions.

As a general overall conclusion, it would appear that the Hullian framework has proven useful in a number of ways in studying such phenomena as anxiety, fear, and, potentially, frustration. It has generated meaningful conceptualizations susceptible to empirical testing, and when such tests have been made, the degree of support has been considerable. Hence, in this sense, Hull's notion that complex behavior might be viewed as a function of differential conditioning processes and the attachment of different stimuli to more basic drive and drive-reduction stimuli has received support, at least insofar as this research area is concerned.

However, as we implied previously, there is some reason to think that the success of the research effort within the Hullian framework of conditioned sources of drive was a Pyrrhic victory for this type of theorizing. The reason we are referring to it in this manner is that the incorporation of anxiety as a legitimate drive variable meant that the Hullian formulation could no longer be based on biological mechanistic thinking in a Darwinian evolutionary sense. Rather, it meant that determinants of behavior arousal that were purely psychological in nature had to be allowed into the system, an opening which, of course, meant to many psychologists that a purely physicalistic orientation to the study of motivational processes must be incomplete at best. We shall expand considerably on this point in a later section.

Conditioned appetitive drive states.   In almost exact opposition to the work on anxiety, there is little or no evidence that stimuli (e.g., restaurants) associated with appetitive drives, such as hunger and thirst deprivation states, assume drive-eliciting properties of their own in that exposure to them systematically increases drive level when other factors are held constant. In a recent review of the literature, Cravens and Renner (1970), finding little support for Hull's postulation that stimuli contiguous with hunger and thirst develop drive properties, suggested that there were at least four possible reasons for the lack of confirmation. The first of these was that the dependent variable in many of the studies, eating and drinking rate, might not be a sensitive enough variable to be able to reflect the effects of conditioning previously neutral stimuli to have drive properties. (By *sensitivity* here is meant not easily aroused by either primary *or* secondary stimuli.) Secondly, eating and drinking rates might not only not be sensitive enough to reflect conditioning, but they may also be unreliable variables. That is, eating and/or drinking rate may be an inconsistent variable over time, thus decreasing the probability of finding them affected by experimental variations in any consistent manner. Third, it might be too difficult to pair an external stimulus with hunger-state stimuli, particularly since the latter involves a gradual onset over time. Such growth in hunger is, of course, much different from the sudden onset of the shock stimuli to which fear and anxiety seem so easily conditioned. Finally, they suggest that perhaps it is difficult for an organism to discriminate between those internal stimuli associated with different degrees of hunger deprivation.

Whatever the reason, and they may all be operative, there would seem to be little reason to disagree with the conclusion that appetitive drive states can not be conditioned as effectively as anxiety. In addition, we will soon suggest another possible reason for this lack of support for the hypothesis of conditioned appetitive drive states and that is the operational confusion in Hull's system between conditioned sources of drive and conditioned reinforcers.

Conditioned reinforcers.   This is the second basic mechanism by which Hull eventually hoped to account for the complexities of human behavior. It will be recalled that his proposal was that stimuli associated with primary reinforcing events (i.e., reduction of biological-need states) would come to assume reinforcing power in and of themselves and, hence, serve as the kinds of outcomes that organisms would be motivated to achieve.

Unfortunately, the concept of secondary reinforcement in the "stimulus substitution" sense that Hull used it does not rest on as strong a foundation as one would like. Thus, while Hull was able to cite studies supporting his ideas, the notion has always had difficulties. First, as an example of a positive study, there is the research reported by Bugelski (1938) in which rats learned to press a lever to obtain food, with each press of the lever accompanied by a click. After withdrawing the food, the rats eventually ceased to press the lever (this is known as the extinction process). However, in the group where the press of the lever still resulted in clicks, the extinction process took considerably longer than the group where the clicking mechanism had been detached along with the withdrawal of food.

Although there are other studies to support Hull's predictions (cf. Wolfe, 1936; Cowles, 1937), the hypothesis has always had problems. For example, there is evidence that secondary reinforcers may quickly lose their effect over time if they are not associated often enough with the primary reinforcer (Isaacson, Hutt, and Blum, 1965; Wike, 1969). On the other hand, this is not always the case and there are experiments that do show secondary reinforcing effects over long periods of time. For example, Zimmerman (1957) has shown that a secondary reinforcer can have long-lasting effects if it has been periodically associated with the primary reinforcer to begin with, rather than constant association with it. This is as a result of the partial-reinforcement effect, a phenomenon we will discuss later. Suffice it to say here that one of the reasons conditioned reinforcers in these situations may continue to have long-lasting effects may be that an organism comes not to expect primary reinforcement since the conditioned reinforcers have not been continuously associated with primary reinforcers during the time of acquisition. However, we may ask why we keep working for these stimuli since it means working for no primary reinforcement. Or does it? And isn't "expect" a cognitive nonphysicalistic concept? We shall deal with these questions a little later. Turning back for a moment, it may be noted that Siegal and Milty (1969) have recently found little experimental support for the proposal that stimuli that signal the termination of electric shock take on secondary reinforcing properties in the manner that Hull and Mowrer predict.

What, then, can we say overall about these mechanisms by which Hull hoped to account for the complexities of human behavior? It seems clear that the answer is a mixed one in that sometimes his predictions received support, but sometimes the ideas were definitely not adequate. A legitimate question, then, is why? Why haven't hypotheses of conditioned stimuli and conditioned reinforcers worked out better than they have?

In addition to the problems we have suggested previously, there is a major difficulty with the logic of the Hullian approach to the study of complex behavior, which may be a major contributor to these inconsistent findings. This logical problem can be seen in the example of a hungry person who walks into a restaurant of distinguishable characteristics, orders a meal after he sits down at a table, and then proceeds to eat the meal when he is served, thus reducing his hunger, and perhaps some other drives. A logical examination of this simple example would have to come to the conclusion that the restaurant is, at one and the same time:

1. A conditioned stimulus (the person entered and sat down while he was hungry)
2. A conditioned reinforcer (the person was there as he ate and reduced his hunger)
3. A source of frustration (since he probably started making eating responses of an anticipatory nature, like smacking his lips, as soon as he walked in, and these responses were frustrated until the meal was served)

In other words, in the Hullian system, it is apparent that the same stimulus can serve as a conditioned stimulus, a conditioned reinforcer, and a source of frustration, all at the same time! The experimental clarity and rigor of the Hullian system turns out, at least in this instance, to be somewhat illusory in nature, and it is perhaps no wonder that the results are as confusing as they are. Variables that are defined as ambiguously as these turn out to be are not very likely to lead to systematic findings in any given direction, positive or negative.

Why, then, are the results for anxiety relatively favorable, given this logical problem? We really don't know. One answer may be that anxiety is really the key arousal agent, not just any conditioned stimuli, as postulated by Hull, and that if the conditioned stimuli (e.g., the restaurant cues) do not arouse anxiety, there is no increment in behavior arousal. The problem, therefore, may be that external cues associated with hunger states are not anxiety arousing to the same degree as those associated with shock and pain. While, in a sense, this explanation could be fit into a Hullian system, such assignment of crucial importance to anxiety would lead to considerable logical and theoretical difficulties for followers of this approach for the reasons discussed earlier.

This logical problem with the Hullian approach to motivational processes was not all that was wrong with the 1943 system, and there were other reasons why a revision became necessary. It is these other difficulties, and the changes that resulted, that will concern us in Chapter 3.

SUMMARY

In this chapter we have begun our discussion of psychological research and theory in the area of motivation as it has developed since psychology became an empirical science. The discussion here has focused primarily on the work of two of the giants in the history of motivational theory, Sigmund Freud and Clark Hull.

Freud, who came first chronologically, saw himself as stemming from the Darwinian tradition of the need for survival as dictating behavioral arousal and direction, and as operating within the scientific framework of viewing motivational phenomena as resulting from specifiable antecedent events. It was Freud's basic hypothesis that the major antecedent events leading to the arousal and direction of behavior were instinctual sources of stimulation (e.g., hunger, thirst, tissue injury, sexual deprivation stimuli) in the organism. It was the reduction of such stimuli that would be satisfying, with some of this stimulation having direct biological evolutionary significance, and some having developed as a result of being linked by learning to basic needs. The determinants of how this stimulation is reduced, or behavior direction, are innate physiological developmental factors and societal learning experiences concerning the likelihood of success in choosing different approaches to stimulus reduction.

In his emphasis on Darwinian evolutionary theory as a logic for behavior and in his emphasis on a stimulus-reduction model as a basic explanatory system, Hull was quite similar to Freud. In most other respects, however, he was different. Hull was a physicalistically oriented behaviorist who attempted to deal with motivational processes by postulating physiologically based stimuli of evolutionary significance as leading to the arousal of behavior. Once behavior was aroused and drive (D) was operative, Hull suggested that direction was due to the linkage of physiologically based stimuli and responses. Despite his objective goals, however, logical and empirical problems began to appear when Hull applied his thoughts to complex human processes.

behavioristic
approaches
to
motivational
processes
CONTEMPORARY HULLIAN FRAMEWORKS

THREE

From the time Hull's work was first published, it became what he hoped it would be. It stimulated research by both opponents and proponents, research that had significance for differing theoretical positions and, more importantly, for the understanding of motivational processes in general. It would probably be fair to say, even now, thirty years later, that Hull's 1943 theory can still be cited as the acme of what a theory should be, in that its fertility as a research-generating system has been an immeasurable aid in the understanding of behavior. The fact that there were serious errors in the approach and that revisions became necessary does not detract from the value of the attempt, since such problems indicated the theory was stated clearly enough that empirical tests could be made. This was Hull's desire and in this way the theory was a success. Furthermore, even after the revisions we will be discussing in this chapter, a considerable segment of the theory has remained viable for many as a useful explanatory system in the understanding of behavior. However, before discussing these revisions, let us turn to some of the other major criticisms of the 1943 model besides those we have already mentioned.

HULL'S 1943 SYSTEM: AN EVALUATION

Biological Needs as Determinants of D (drive):
A Basic Assumption

There are a number of problems that have been associated with this basic assumption of the 1943 Hull model. As we have already indicated, while stimuli associated with shock do assume fear- or anxiety-arousing properties and do function as drives in the Hullian sense, stimuli associated with hunger and thirst deprivation states do *not* become conditioned stimuli and do *not* assume drive characteristics (Cravens and Renner, 1970). In addition to the fact that this provides evidence that shock and hunger states are not similar in their effects on learning and conditioning, something Hull did not postulate, it provides negative evidence of a second nature by indicating that stimuli that may, but do not necessarily, have biological significance (such as anxiety) can still act as drives. Thus, Hull's desire to refer all behavior back to a biological base with evolutionary significance was dealt a severe blow by this research. In another similar direction are the findings that some kinds of increased biological-need states do not lead to increased behavior. For example, people may suffer from vitamin B_{12} deficiency (anemia) and not do anything to correct it. Similarly, the breathing of carbon monoxide in a closed car does not lead to lifesaving behavior. Rather, people can and do die from it.

Another set of findings that did not jibe with Hull's work is the evidence that obese individuals do not use biological deprivation as cues for how and when they should eat. Their eating behavior seems to be a function of variables having little or nothing to do with the degree of their physiological deprivation at the time (Nisbett, 1968; Schacter, Goldman, and Gordon, 1968).

Third, as a continuing demonstration of the difficulty of coordinating *D*, as conceptualized by Hull, to biological-need states and the various stimuli conditioned to them, there is Zajonc's recent program supporting the theoretical assumption that the presence of other people may act as a drive state in the Hullian sense (Zajonc, 1965). This also only adds to the confusion as to what *D* is.

Finally, there is considerable additional evidence that such biologically linked need states as hunger, thirst, pain, and sex are a function of many other vairables besides physiological determinants. Vernon (1969) has pointed out that (a) food preferences are very much culturally determined and some individuals will and do starve rather than eat forbidden foods; (b) sexual behavior is under hormonal influence for organisms low in the evolutionary hierarchy, but such behaviors are very much a function of learning experience for humans and higher animals; (c) there is some basis for biologically linked instinctual maternal behaviors in lower animals, but such behavior is culturally determined in humans; and (d) fear and anxiety are very much culturally learned, with great differences between individuals and groups in the degree to which they will admit such reactions and base their behavior on them.

Need Reduction as a Determinant of Habit Formation

Does the learning of stimulus-response connections (i.e., habit) depend on primary- and/or conditioned-stimulus (i.e., need) reduction?

In a very real sense the logic of Hull's entire approach rested on the answer to this question, since he based his system on the principle of the biological utility of behavior and its derivatives. Today, it is clear that while habits can be learned on the basis of primary- (or conditioned-) need reduction, it is not necessary that such reduction occur for learning to take place. The evidence for this statement comes from a variety of sources, some of which are as follows:

1. Nonnutritive saccharin (a substance that passes through the body without providing any food value) can reinforce the learning of an instrumental response (Sheffield and Roby, 1950).
2. Infant monkeys can obtain satisfaction from ersatz mothers who have not provided milk (Harlow and Zimmerman, 1959).
3. Rats can be reinforced by copulating responses without being given the opportunity to ejaculate (Sheffield, Wulf, and Backe, 1951).
4. Habits can be learned when the outcome of the behavior involved is not the reduction of some primary or conditioned need, but rather the opportunity to explore some "new" stimulus field (Harlow, 1953; Montgomery, 1953; Glanzer, 1953). (By a "new" stimulus field is meant one that is different from the one in which the organism is currently behaving and one not previously associated with primary-need reduction.)

One of the first, and still one of the most convincing, of the studies that have provided negative evidence for this aspect of Hull's theory was a series of experiments performed more than a decade before Hull's 1943 monograph. Yet, for some reason not clearly understandable, no account of them was taken in the first set of formulations. These studies, the famous *latent-learning* experiments (Blodgett, 1929), showed quite conclusively that drive reduction (reinforcement) was not necessary for learning of habits, but that it was important for the performing of habits already learned. In other words, drive reduction, which defines reinforcement in the Hullian sense, seems to influence engaging in behavior patterns already known, but may not be necessary for learning them. The major experiment of Blodgett's that showed this was one involving three groups of rats learning a maze. For one of the groups, food was provided at the end of the maze, whereas for the other two it was not. Using error score as a performance measure, the data clearly indicated that for the first group of trials, the food-reinforced group performed better than the other two. At first glance, this seems to provide support for the Hullian notion. However, looking at the curves for Groups II and III in Figure 3.1, representing the basic data of the experiment, it is evident that a different conclusion must present itself. What has happened to the performance of each group after the trial where they are provided food for the first time? It seems appropriate to infer that both

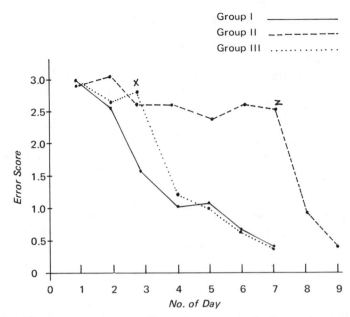

Figure 3.1. The latent phenomenon. Group I was given a food reward on every trial. In Group II, the food was not introduced until the seventh day (at point z). In Group III, the food reward was not introduced until the third day (at point x). Both Group II and Group III show a substantial decrease in errors after the first rewarded trial.

Source: J. W. Atkinson, *An Introduction to Motivation,* p. 139. © 1964 by Litton Educational Publishing, Inc. Reprinted by permission of Van Nostrand Reinhold Company.

Groups II and III almost immediately attain the level of proficiency of Group I, thus suggesting that they knew how to run the maze all the time but that there was no reason to do so. Once they learned that there was food available, then there was some reason to show the learned behavior patterns.

The latent-learning experiments were crucial for at least two reasons. First, by showing that need reduction is not necessary for learning, but that the opportunity for need gratification could generate quick, significant changes in behavior, considerable doubt was cast on the 1943 Hull theory. The best Hull could predict was that there would be a steady increase in performance, such as in the first few trials for Group I in Figure 3.1. It is clear that this did not happen. Second, these results also suggest that a complete theory of motivation would have to include some consideration of how changes in the environment affect behavior, and among these effects might be the availability of the types of incentives used by Blodgett. As an example, it was clear that the rats behaved differently when the food was in the goal box at the end of the maze than when it was not, a phenomenon that had to be accounted for theoretically by the Hullian approach. Thus, it was this research that led Hull and his co-workers to develop K, a type of environmental incentive, as part of the later 1952 postulates and Spence's 1956 theory. As we will see, this is an approach that views environmental incentives as having both an energizing and directive influence on behavior in the same way that D does. On the other hand, it is also possible, as other theorists have argued, to view environmental incentives as perceptions primarily providing knowledge on where to satisfy desires. There are, as we shall see, certain advantages to the latter.

Drive Reduction as a Determinant of Behavior

Is behavior just a desire to reduce stimulation? Is this where behavior arousal comes from (e.g., the desire to reduce stimulation)? The question is a theoretically crucial one, not only for Hull and for Freud, but for other theorists as well. For example, there is a well-known formulation by Miller and Dollard (1941), who suggested:

> A drive is a strong stimulus which impels action. Any stimulus can become a drive if it is made strong enough. The stronger the stimulus, the more drive function it possesses.

While the general logic of this proposal is similar to that of Hull's D, Miller and Dollard's approach turned out to have certain advantages that eventually led Hull, himself, to adopt their argument in 1952. These are that it does not force one to hold to a biological-utility hypothesis as the basis for all behavior, and it enables the interpretation of innate and learned sources of stimulation within one framework.

Whichever approach one uses, however, the early or late Hull, Miller and Dollard, or Freud, there is considerable negative evidence for all of them. Thus, it seems clear that (a) behavior sometimes is more than just the reduction of stimulation, and (b) high stimulation may lead to less behavior, rather than to more. Consider, for example, the following studies:

1. Direct electrical stimulation of certain parts of the brain can seem to reinforce behavior in the same manner as food, thirst, and pain reduction (Olds and Milner, 1954); here is a case where reinforcement can come from more stimulation, rather than less.
2. Harlow (1953), Montgomery (1953), and Glanzer (1953) have all shown, along with others, that the opportunity to explore and see "newness" and "difference" can be a great incentive to behavior; "newness" and "difference" can be assumed to be increases in stimulation.
3. Common sense suggests that there are times when decreases in stimulation may cause increases in motivated behavior (e.g., a person hurrying home on a dark night), whereas an increase in stimulation may cause a decrease in motivated behavior (e.g., the person slows down at the first sign of light since this means he is almost home). It is interesting to note that Miller and Dollard agree as to the saliency of

this example, but argue that perhaps such behavior may occur because the increase in external stimulation (the light) is still less than the internal stimulation associated with the anxiety (due to the dark night). This argument at first glance has some degree of reasonableness attached to it and should certainly be investigated. There is, however, an interesting, possibly negative, implication for theorists of the Hullian persuasion, even if it should be supported. The implication is that such support would mean that, here again, one of the supposed real advantages of this type of approach to motivational processes, that is, the clear manner in which its key concepts can be experimentally controlled by the investigator, turns out to be somewhat illusory in nature. Thus, the testing of this type of explanation would demand adequate physiological indices of emotional arousal in order to distinguish between the anxiety-arousing darkness and the anxiety-reducing light. Theoretically, while such tests are possible, they have not as yet been done. Even if they were and Miller and Dollard were correct, all this would mean is that there is no simple relation between physical stimulation and psychological arousal. In fact, the two may, in certain situations, be negatively related. This would not be the clear, physicalistic system Hull envisioned.

4. Brown and Jacobs (1949) have found that increased amounts of drive do not always result in increased physical activity and might actually result in less. As an example, they cite their own research finding that some anxious rats "freeze," rather than increase their motor behavior. This, again, is one of those situations where it is possible to argue that "freezing" is the form of behavior that reduces the drive for these rats. All well and good, except that if this is so, then we must move even further away from the physicalistic system Hull wanted.

5. Research with different forms of drug addition and drug-taking behavior indicate both support and difficulties for the Hullian drive concept. On one hand, the taking of opiates (opium, morphine, heroin, codeine) and barbituates provides support, since in these cases the result is some kind of stimulation-reducing process. On the other hand, the taking of hallucinogenic drugs (e.g., hashish, marijuana, and LSD) and those termed analeptic (e.g., cocaine and amphetamines) would be considered negative evidence, since the outcome is generally increased excitement and stimulation (Cohen, 1969). The sum total of these findings seems to be that behavior can, at times, clearly be shown to be, at least in its appearance, something more than just the reduction of stimulation. Furthermore, it is also true that, under some conditions, organisms may act in order to increase stimulation.

Can one handle these findings within a Hullian framework, or does this research constitute a fatal blow to the logic of the whole system? There is really no clear answer to this question. For some psychologists, it has constituted a fatal blow, and as a result they have turned to different ways of theorizing about motivational processes, while at the same time retaining much of the rigorous laboratory flavor of Hull and his students. In the next chapter we shall talk about this group of psychologists and their work, a group that has come to be known as the activation theorists.

However, there are others, also of a physicalistic, natural-science bent, who are not quite ready to give up on the logic of Hullian theory in trying to account for this stimulation-seeking behavior, difficult though it may be at first glance. Thus, there are at least two suggested theories to account for this behavior consistent with a Hullian approach.

One of these is a theoretical hypothesis suggested by Berlyne (1960), the essence of which is to propose that the stimulation that organisms try to reduce is not environmental, but rather in the reticular activating system (RAS) of the brain. Such RAS stimulation, Berlyne argues, is a curvilinear function of physical environmental stimulus complexity, so that RAS arousal is greatest when environmental stimulation is either very great or very small. According to this system, the following behavioral predictions are made as a function of the given physical environmental stimulus conditions. The crucial question here is the

Table 3.1 Outline of Berlyne (1960) Theory for Handling Stimulus-seeking Behavior Within a Hullian Framework

Degree of Stimulation in the Physical Environment	Degree of RAS Stimulation Assumed to Occur as a Function of Given Physical Environment	Levels of Environmental Stimulation Sought for Predicted Behaviors	Reasoning Underlying Behavioral Predictions
1. Low	High	Higher than previous	Since RAS arousal is less at moderate levels of stimulation than at low levels of external stimulation and it is the reduction of the RAS system that is reinforcing.
2. Moderate	Moderate	Same as previous	
3. High	High	Lower than previous	Since RAS arousal is less at moderate levels of stimulation than at high levels of external stimulation

degree of support for the major innovation of the theory, namely, that low levels of environmental stimulation lead to high RAS arousal. It is this assumption that would enable this approach to handle stimulus-seeking behavior within a basically Hullian framework. Unfortunately, however, the degree of support for this assumption is not very impressive at this time. While there is some indication that boredom does lead to high RAS arousal, the evidence to support this is still generally scanty (deCharms, 1968, p. 101). In fact, about the best that can be said at this time is that relevant research really still remains to be done. (The reader might note here the similarity between this argument and the Miller and Dollard "darkness-light" example discussed earlier.)

The second suggested framework for handling stimulation seeking within a stimulus-reduction framework has been suggested by a number of different psychologists, including Berlyne and Freud. Here again, it is still just an idea with little research data either for or against. The framework is known as *arousal-jag* theory, and its basic idea is that increased stimulation is tolerated and even sought out because of the anticipated reduction that will follow. Somewhat oversimplified, but not too far from the general idea here, is that "a person may keep banging his head because it feels so good when he stops." Freud, for example, used this type of hypothesis in attempting to explain why people engage in the increased stimulation known as sexual foreplay and the like. According to him, it is because of the increased pleasure that will come when stimulus reduction (i.e., sexual climax) takes place. This kind of evidence for the hypothesis is not very satisfactory, and we need more systematic research data in order to fully evaluate the idea. Unfortunately, little of the necessary research has been undertaken.

Effects of Reinforcement Levels and Patterns on Later Behavior

A major part of the 1943 Hull system that has turned out to be very difficult to support can perhaps best be illustrated by the following propositions.

1. 1943 Hull proposition:

Drive		Behavior
(hunger, anxiety	⟶	designed to reduce drive
pain, etc.)		stimulation

2. Related proposition stemming from 1943 Hullian framework (also found in Mowrer, 1960):

The physical stimulation (kinesthetic and otherwise) accompanying that behavior which has led to "bad" outcomes in the past (e.g., no rewards or incentives, punishments, etc.)	⟶	Stimuli become associated with anxiety and stress (because the behavior has become conditioned to "bad" outcomes by classical-conditioning procedures)	⟶	Behavior designed to reduce this stimulation, e.g., refusal to engage in that behavior which has caused the anxiety because it has led to poor outcomes in the past and the choosing of different behaviors which will lead to the reduction of the anxiety-laden stimuli

The problem is that, despite the apparent simplicity of these propositions and their almost common-sense nature, there is an increasing body of evidence from a variety of different empirical areas of research that does not jibe with them.

3.

The longer organisms engage in behavior that leads to "bad" outcomes (e.g., punishment, lack of reward, etc.), the more behavior occurs which does lead to "bad" outcomes	→	The less the anxiety at one's behavior	→	The less behavior designed to reduce anxiety	→	The greater the occurrence of behavior that leads to "bad" outcomes

The implication of this paradigm is that the previous history of the organism (i.e., the degree to which it has been rewarded and/or punished in the past) determines its degree of responsiveness to later positive and negative outcomes and how significant these possible or expected outcomes may be in affecting its behavior. Thus, the "poorer" the previous history, the less likely it is that "good" outcomes will be necessary in order to solidify or reinforce approach behavior. Similarly, the "poorer" the history of the organism, the less likely it is that expected "bad" outcomes will lead to avoidance behavior. In general, then, the effectiveness of possible outcomes, whether the achievement of the positive or the reduction of the negative, in controlling and reinforcing behavior is lessened, the more negative the history of the organism. This conclusion seems to be warranted whether we refer to outcomes as reinforcers of behavior, operating in a somewhat mechanistic fashion to stamp in certain behaviors rather than others, or to outcomes operating as incentives to (or expected outcomes of) behavior, a matter we will deal with more completely later. In both cases, the point is that it is possible to specify those individuals for whom positive outcomes are not necessary as directive influences on behavior. In Table 3.2 we present a brief summary of a large number of research studies that support these conclusions. The studies outlined range from laboratory research on the effects that experiencing negative outcomes have on later responsiveness to rewards and punishments to field studies of people making complex, life-long decisions such as making a career choice. It is an analysis of these studies that leads us to conclude that the more an organism (animal or human) is punished for its behavior, the less likely it is that it will engage in behavior to achieve rewards and avoid punishments in the future. Conversely, the less it is punished, the more it will be oriented to achieving "good" outcomes, such as engaging in behavior to achieve positive outcomes and avoid those that are negative.

As further support for the data of Table 3.2, there is a vast body of research that points to the fact that organisms that have not been continuously positively reinforced for engaging in certain behaviors are more likely to engage in that behavior when no reinforcement is available (i.e., during the extinction process) than those who have a history of continuous positive reinforcement. Known as the *partial-reinforcement* effect, this should not occur, according to

Table 3.2 Summary of Research Supporting the Conclusion that Individuals Will Perform in a Manner Consistent with Previous Reinforcement Patterns

General Finding	Investigators
1. Individuals who have high social reinforcement standards (i.e., degree to which they have been rewarded previously) are more likely to perform in a manner designed to achieve high rewards than those who have low social reinforcement standards.	Baron (1966)
2. Self-perceived ability on a task based on previous task performance is positively related to later task performance.	Kaufman (1963); Feather (1965)
3. Individuals of high self-esteem* are more likely to choose occupations where they perceive themselves to have a great degree of ability than those of low self-esteem.	Korman (1967a); Korman (1967b)
4. Individuals who are told they are incompetent to achieve specific goals on a task, even though they have had no previous experience with the task, will perform worse than those who are told they are competent to achieve the task goals.	Korman (1968)
5. Individuals and groups of low self-esteem are less likely to achieve difficult goals they have set for themselves than individuals of high self-esteem.	Korman (1968)
6. Groups that have failed previously set their goals in ways that increase the probability of their failing again.	Zander, Forward, and Albert (1969)
7. Academic underachievers have a more negative self-concept than achievers.	Shaw (1968)
8. There is a significant positive relationship between self-concept of ability and grade-point average.	Brookover and Thomas (1963-64)
9. The individual who has had a long series of frustrations engages in behavior that is (a) persistent beyond degree of reward, (b) not alterable by punishment, (c) nongoal oriented, and (d) not affected by consequences or by the anticipation of same.	Maier (1949)
10. Overlearning a response so that one becomes very competent at it increases the effectiveness of punishment as an eventual response suppressor.	Karsh (1962); Miller (1960)
11. Adaptation to punishment can occur, and this decreases its effectiveness.	Miller (1960)
12. If a subject is habituated to receiving shock together with positive reinforcement during reward training, punishment during extinction can actually increase resistance to extinction.	Holz and Azrin (1961)
13. Research has indicated that punishment can lead to self-defeating behavior oriented toward no goal.	Masserman (1943)
14. Rewarding others has greater influence on their behavior than punishing them.	Miller, Butler, and McMartin (1969)

*We have an assumption in this table that we will defend elsewhere and that, we believe, has considerable empirical support. This is that individuals of high self-esteem can be theoretically defined as those who have prior histories of high positive reinforcement and whose interaction history with others has primarily been supportive and ego-enhancing. Such interactions, we assume, also consist of high positive reinforcement. Low self-esteem people we assume, of course, to have had opposite reinforcement and interaction histories.

Hullian theory, since habits are a function of the amount of reinforcement attained by the organism for the stimulus-response connection. Yet, it has been shown that organisms only partially reinforced for learning a given habit (e.g., for every fifth response) will engage in that behavior far longer without any reinforcement at all than organisms reinforced for all responses while learning the habit. In essence, it seems that patterns of reinforcements, both positive and negative, result in changes in the organism, which in turn affect later responsiveness to positive and negative outcomes as influences on behavior. In a later part of this book, we will attempt to account for these findings by proposing an intermediary concept, self-evaluation, which is a function of these antecedent outcomes and which in turn affects the level of outcomes sought. However, self-evaluation is a cognitive concept and does not constitute the type of theorizing one can easily put into a Hullian-type system. Can we account for these phenomena using Hullian variables and the logic of a physicalistic system?

There has been one major attempt to handle these phenomena within the confines of a physicalistic system and that is Spence's (1960) application of some ideas by Amsel (1958). The hypothesis he proposes is directed primarily at explaining the partial-reinforcement effect, but, given the nature of our discussion, his argument can probably be generalized to the whole problem as we have defined it here; that is, the general question of why organisms that are continually exposed over time to "poor" outcomes gradually come to behave in such a way as to reflect lack of responsivity to the differences between "good" and "poor" outcomes. According to Spence and Amsel, organisms put on a partial-reinforcement schedule learn to link two types of stimuli with approach responses in a given goal-box situation. That is, they learn two habits, not one, under partial reinforcement. First, they learn to associate the goal box and its characteristics with reward (e.g., food). Because of this generalization process, anticipatory consummatory responses (i.e., anticipatory eating behavior) start to take place as soon as the organism enters the goal box with its distinctive characteristics. Since these anticipatory behaviors are physical in nature (salivation, jaw movements, etc.), they are also stimuli to the organism, as are the characteristics of the goal box. Hence, these physical stimuli become part of the stimulus-response link that is developed, such association taking place by classical-conditioning procedures (i.e., contiguity). Similarly, since by definition partial reinforcement consists of rewarded trials interspersed with nonrewarded trials, there are the stimulus cues resulting from the physical behaviors that we can call anticipatory frustration (since some trials are frustrated). Hence, two sets of cues are conditioned to approach responses; one set consists of anticipatory rewarded behavior (e.g., eating), and, after initial aversive responsing, the other consists of anticipatory frustrated behavior (e.g., teeth gnashing). This contrasts with the full-reinforcement situation, where the only anticipatory stimulus cues conditioned to approach behavior are those signifying consummatory behavior (e.g., eating). Once frustration appears for this group, as in extinction where all rewards have been withdrawn, the anticipatory behavior for this outcome has not been conditioned to approach behavior during previous learning. As there are no S-R connections (or habits) supporting continuing approach habits when there is no reward at the end, their level of responding drops more quickly; this leads to the partial-reinforcement effect we spoke of previously. Similarly, it would also seem to predict the general finding that organisms used to "poor" outcomes in the past are more likely to behave in ways likely to achieve "poor" outcomes in the future.

The Spence-Amsel attempt to account for what might be termed, in a lay sense, self-defeating behavior within a physicalistic system has received considerable research attention, with some results being supportive (cf. Haggard, 1959; Goodrich, 1959) and others not so (Hill, 1968). For our purposes here, there are several major points worth noting. First, the theory seems to predict quicker running speed later in the goal box rather than earlier, a prediction not supported by data (Hill, 1968). Second, the attempt to use anticipatory behavior resulting from stimulus generalization from the goal box to earlier environmental cues and the stimulus cues resulting from them as influences on behavior is highly intriguing, since it represents a possible physical representation of the cognitive notion of expectancy. It is an approach typical of the recent theorizing of the Hullian school, and one we shall soon meet more fully. However, there is a dilemma attached to the approach which we noted in our earlier discussion on secondary reinforcement and which is relevant here also. This is that the same environment being proposed as an incentive to behavior (i.e., the stimulus cues resulting from the physical movements in anticipatory eating and anticipatory frustration) can just as easily be seen as a source of secondary reinforcement. In this capacity, then, these stimuli should operate to decrease the behavior designed to achieve it, that is, the "approach" behavior. This is particularly true in the full-reinforcement case, but it also operates in the partial-reinforcement situation. The dilemma comes from attempting to use the same variables (i.e., environmental cues) in mutually contradictory ways. Sometimes they are suggested, as we have already seen, as a directive influence on behavior. Sometimes, as we will see, they are postulated as a source of general behavior arousal. Finally, they can be a behavior reducer (secondary reinforcer) under other conditions. The effect of such theorizing, of course, is to minimize one of the hoped-for greater values of physicalistic approaches to the study of motivational processes, namely, the ease with which it lends itself to operationally clear and experimentally manipulable concepts.[1]

[1] Wike (1969) has recently argued that while there are some conditions under which this problem does occur, there are others where it does not. For example, he argues that the possible effect of a secondary reinforcer can be seen by utilizing it in new learning situations as a reinforcer of behavior, a point with which we would agree. Nevertheless, we would argue, there is something questionable about a concept from the viewpoint of theoretical clarity that is postulated to operate in a mutually contradictory manner in different situations. At the very least, it throws doubt on the supposed advantage of physicalistic thinking, which is that it tends to encourage rigorous thinking.

HULL AND SPENCE: THE LATER MODELS

It seems clear from our discussion that Hull's 1943 theory had an imposing list of problems, problems that had to be overcome if the approach was to remain a viable one in the study of motivational processes. As a result, the decade of the 1950s did indeed see such attempted revisions of the general framework, with the most prominent being those by Hull himself and the revisions suggested by one of his students, Kenneth Spence. In the rest of this chapter we will discuss these newer theoretical frameworks suggested by the Hullian school, frameworks still being used by many psychologists today, and also attempt an evaluation of the general Hullian approach to the psychology of motivation in light of contemporary psychological knowledge, theory, and methodology.

A Physicalistic Approach to Expectancy

One of the most important revisions in the later statements of the Hullian school stemmed from the necessity to account for the findings of the latent-learning experiments and others similar to it within a physicalistic system. As we have seen, the dilemma for Hull, Spence, and their students was that there was clear experimental evidence that organisms could and did change their behavior almost immediately when the levels of reward and/or incentive available in the environment changed.

To recall for a moment, a condition of nonreward at the end of a maze will stimulate wandering aimlessly through that maze. However, on the first or second trial after reward is provided, the newly rewarded rat will run as quickly to the goal box as one that had been rewarded all along (Blodgett, 1929). This suggests that perhaps both groups of subjects, rewarded and nonrewarded, had been learning all along, but the latter had no reason to show the effects of the learning since they didn't "expect" to receive any food at the end of the maze. However, once *expectancy* changed, behavior changed, and they ran as quickly through the maze as the first group. It *is* possible that habits (i.e., $_SH_R$) developed far more quickly once reinforcement occurred than when positive reinforcement had been taking place all over. The reason for this would be unknown, but it is the only explanation the 1943 Hull system could provide. Similarly, there were extensive data on the low resistance to extinction among organisms continuously reinforced as in the research by Zeaman (1949) that showed there was an almost immediate drop in performance when reward was withdrawn from these organisms used to obtaining it on all responses. In these cases, also, the data indicated that as soon as the expectancy of reinforcement changed, behavior changed. The only explanation possible by the 1943 Hull system was that $_SH_R$ decreased suddenly, an explanation no more satisfactory here than it is in explaining why a rat that shows no learning during nonrewarded trial after nonrewarded trial shows highly skilled behavior almost immediately after the introduction of reward.

The dilemma, then, for Hull and his followers was how to account for the fact that behavior is not only determined by previous learning (habit) and current condition (drive), but also by the contemporary characterisitcs of the environment (i.e., the amount of reward that is available and expected). But how can expectancy, an inherently subjective concept, be translated into a physicalistic concept? The actual answer to this question had been anticipated by Hull in an early paper (Hull, 1930), but it was not until 1952 that Hull resurrected his original notion as to how expectancy could be defined physically, an idea we have already introduced in a general sense in our discussion of Spence and Amsel's work. It was this notion that was used as a base by Spence (1956) in developing his answers to the above question, and it is Spence's work that we shall lean on primarily as the most influential answer to this problem from the Hullian school.

Consider a rat running a maze to get to a goal box that has food in it. Once he gets to the food, he begins eating, and the more food, the longer and more vigorously he eats, generally up to the saturation point. Since this eating behavior becomes conditioned by stimulus-generalization processes to the various stimulus characteristics of the goal box, the rat, when later reintroduced into the goal box, immediately starts eating behavior again, even before the food is present. This anticipatory behavior (i.e., eating before food) is thus engaged in prior to actual eating behavior and might, in fact, be engaged in other parts of the maze prior to actually entering the goal box. Hence, when a rat runs a maze, the physical stimuli affecting him are the stimuli of the maze and his anticipatory goal (or eating) responses at each part of the maze prior to the goal (or food) box.

> Stimulus cues in the goal box and from the alley just preceding the goal box become conditioned to the goal response, R_g. Through generalization the stimulus cues at earlier points in the runway are also assumed to acquire the capacity to elicit R_g, or at least noncompetitional components of R_g that can occur without the actual presence of the food (e.g. salivating and chewing movements). As a result this fractional conditioned response, which we shall designate as rg, moves forward to the beginning of the instrumental sequence. Furthermore, the intereoceptive stimulus cue (sg) produced by this response also becomes part of the stimulus complex in the alley and thus should become conditioned to the instrumental location response. But more important, in addition to this associative function, we have assumed this rg-sg mechanism also has motivational properties that vary with the magnitude or vigor with which it occurs. (Spence, 1956, pp. 134-35)

In other words, what Spence has argued is that these anticipatory reponses (*rg*'s), which are also stimuli (*sg*'s) since they are physical-motor behavior, serve two major functions. First, they become conditioned to the maze-running responses just as the stimulus aspects of the maze become conditioned. Secondly, Spence suggests, the *rg-sg* mechanism also operates as a motivational mechanism in that they are a set of stimuli which the organism wishes to reduce just as he wishes to reduce other drive stimuli. Why does Spence consider these rg-sg mechanisms to be drive stimuli? Possibly, he goes on, these anticipatory responses have a certain degree of tension, frustration, and anxiety attached to them, since they involve the making of goal-achieving (consummatory) responses without any goal achievement at that point of the maze. The reader will notice the resemblance of this argument to our previous discussion of anxiety as a learned drive that an organism wishes to reduce. Hence, like any other tension stimuli (e.g., anxiety, fear, frustration), behavior designed to reduce them will take place. They will thus serve to arouse behaviors in a general sense and also stimulate into behavior the directional determinants of behavior; in this case, these would be the maze-running habits of the organism previously learned as ways of reducing drivelike stimulation.

Spence called this motivational property of the conditioned rg-sg mechanism K and defined it as an incentive variable representing the influence of contemporaneous events in the environment on behavior. This influence can be summarized briefly by saying that the introduction of food into the goal box would lead, according to Spence, to greater anticipatory responding on the immediately following trials. Such responding leads to higher levels of frustrationlike stimuli and, hence, greater behavior designed to reduce the stimulation. Similarly, a decrease in food at the goal box would lead, in later trials, to less anticipatory responding earlier in the goal box, a lower $K,$ and hence a lower level of behavior. Consider the following examples (all numbers are purely illustrative in nature):

	Amount of food in goal box	Vigor and intensity of food-eating responses (as determined by arbitrary measurement)	Vigor and intensity of anticipatory responses earlier in goal box (as determined by arbitrary measurement	Hypothesized resulting level of K
Case 1	3 oz.	100	30	30
Case 2	2 oz.	75	25	25
Case 3	1 oz.	45	15	15

What else determines K besides the vigor and intensity of the consummatory response (food eating)? The question is a crucial one, since K is like D and $_SH_R$ in that it is a theoretical intervening variable that must be susceptible to and derivable from empirical, experimental operations. Thus, in addition to the vigor and intensity of the unconditioned consummatory response (eating), Spence suggested that K might be a function of the following:

1. The number of conditioned trials in the goal box;

2. The similarity of the specific environmental cues to those originally conditioned to the goal (food-eating) response in the goal box;
3. The distance from the goal box (since internal, proprioceptive cues are important and these are more similar to the goal-box responses the closer one is to it).

K as an incentive variable, and as a physicalistically oriented construct representing expectancy, became highly crucial to the later Hull system and to the theoretical notions developed by Spence in the 1950s with much attention being devoted to it, particularly by the latter. However, there was a difference between them in how they postulated it would work as an influence on behavior. For Hull, K was incorporated as one of the variables to insert into his multiplicative equation as follows:

$$_S E_R = D \times K \times _S H_R$$

Behavior = Drive $\times$ Incentive $\times$ Habit

On the other hand, Spence felt that K, as a general arousal agent acting in the same manner as D, should be placed in the same conceptual category, as follows:

$$\text{Behavior} = (D + K) \times _S H_R$$

$$= (\text{Drive} + \text{Incentive}) \times \text{Habit}$$

In other words, Hull proposed that D and K combine multiplicatively, whereas Spence proposed that they combine additively, a difference illustrated in Figure 3.2. In addition to the different types of curves the two approaches predict, a big difference is that in the Hull case a zero value for D or K would mean no behavior, whereas in the Spence case behavior would take place. Which one is correct? We don't really know at this point. What is perhaps a more important question, however, is whether the logic of the entire approach is a fruitful one, a matter we will be discussing shortly.

A New Definition of Drive (D)

In addition to the introduction of K, the later Hull and Spence theories also involved other changes from the 1943 model, with almost all stemming from some of the criticisms we have mentioned previously. One of these changes was that Hull gave up the assumption that behavior (or drive) is basically aroused by biological-need deprivation or by some stimulus conditioned to it. Instead, he went over to the Miller and Dollard (1941) assumption that any strong stimulus can become a drive, the reduction of which is reinforcing. This was a change that had several advantages. The fact that we generally try to reduce high levels of noise, strong light, and the like, now became easily accounted for by the Hullian approach. A second advantage is that it freed Hull from having to tie all

If $D = 2$ and $_SH_R = 2$ and K is as indicated.

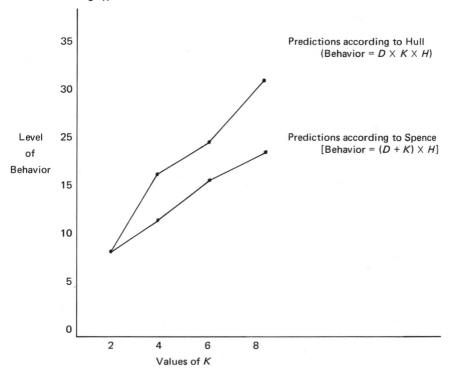

Figure 3.2 Illustrative differences between Hull (1952) and Spence (1956) conceptualizations of the incentive variable K.

secondary drives (e.g., anxiety) back to a biological base and thus enabled him to handle those experiments that showed that learning and performance could take place without biological-need reduction (cf. the Sheffield experiments we cited earlier). However, even though the concept of drive was now being refined so that the framework could handle experiments showing that copulatory activity without ejaculation could reinforce behavior, it was not at all clear what the nature of the drive was that was being reduced by the increased stimulation of copulatory activity. In other words, this redefinition of drive did not provide a coherent position as to where drives and arousal come from. This position needed to handle the fact that stimulation-increasing activities (e.g., copulatory activities) could serve to reinforce behavior as well as stimulation-reducing activities, and it needed to do it within a framework that started from the position that the raison d'être of behavior was to reduce a theoretically defined set of drive stimuli. The 1943 model had provided such a coherent model, based on its hypothesis of biologically based drives of evolutionary significance. As it turned out, this was manifestly unsatisfactory, but now nothing was being offered in its place.

A New Definition of Habit ($_SH_R$)

Finally, both the Hull (1952) and Spence (1956) models changed the 1943 conception as to the determinants of $_SH_R$ and its strength. Whereas it had originally been assumed that $_SH_R$ was a function of the amount of reinforcement that a particular S-R connection had been subjected to, Spence, in particular, moved to the position that the level of $_SH_R$ is determined solely by the number of times a particular stimulus-response connection has occurred. The frequency with which such connections occur is in turn a function of other variables such as drive (D) and incentive (K), and it is in this indirect sense that the amount of reinforcement affects the amount of learning (or the development of $_SH_R$) in a given situation. In other words, reinforcement influences the propensity to behavior, and once a person is behaving, he will learn to associate whatever stimuli and responses happen to be occurring contiguously at that time, with such contiguity being the reason for the association. Finally, the more frequently these S-R connections occur together, the more likely that particular stimulus will elicit that particular response in the future, all other things being equal.

Hull's 1952 definition of $_SH_R$ is, at first glance, a little different from Spence's in that he postulates that there is some reinforcement necessary for the learning of an S-R connection. However, the distinction is really a meaningless one since he makes no predictions about any particular level of reinforcement being necessary for the development of a habit. Since, theoretically, even an infinitesimal degree of reinforcement would be sufficient for the development of $_SH_R$ in the 1952 Hull system, the position is, in effect, a contiguity one like Spence's. Habits would be developed on the basis of the frequency with which the stimulus and response have occurred together, with such frequency a function of the person's reasons for such behavioral frequency (i.e., D, K, and H).

THE HULLIAN TRADITION: A SUMMARY

These, then, are the major ways in which the Hullians changed as a result of the criticisms directed at the 1943 model. What can be said of the Hullian approach to a theory of motivation today, three decades after the publication of the original theoretical papers? There are a number of conclusions that seem justified, and as with almost anything else, some are positive and some are negative.

Clearly, the tradition is a strong one and remains highly viable as a fruitful source of research ideas for many psychologists. One source of its great appeal is the relatively explicit manner in which D and K are defined as the causes of behavior arousal, in which habits are defined as the source of behavior directedness, and the general ease with which its variables lend themselves to rigorous laboratory experimentation.

As an example of the pervasiveness of the Hullian scheme, Weiss (1968) has adopted this type of approach in trying to delimit the conditions under which attitude change as a function of persuasive communication will occur. Basically, Weiss suggests that the likelihood of change as a result of persuasive communication is greater the more we have changed our attitudes in the past, the more anxiety we feel about our current attitudes (and hence the greater the impetus toward change), and the more reason we see for the change. Conceptually, as Table 3.3 indicates, these three conditions correspond to

Table 3.3 Conceptual Similarities Between Attitude-change Variables and Hullian Concepts

(1)	(2)	(3)	(4)
(a) The frequency with which he has engaged in attitude change opinions in the past	(a) Degree of manifest anxiety felt in the given situation	(a) Strength of argument being made for change of attitude	(a) Speed of agreement with attitude-change argument
+	+	+	(b) Degree of agreement with new opinion
(b) The extent to which he has actively participated in stating such opinions	(b) Time stress felt in given situation	(b) Number of exposures to attitude-change argument	
	+	+	
	(c) Presence of anxiety-inducing others	(c) Delay of argument being made for change	
		+	
		(d) Credibility of source making the change argument	
Can be considered to be analogous to	Can be considered to be analogous to	Can be considered to be analogous to	Can be considered to be analogous to
$_sH_R$ X	$(D$ X	$K)$ =	E

Source: Adapted from Weiss, 1968.

$_sH_R$, D, and K, and they can, in fact, be coordinated to these theoretical constructs.

In another direction, Zajonc (1965) has recently shown the fruitfulness of the approach in developing a hypothesis as to why the presence of others will sometimes facilitate performance and sometimes debilitate it. Basically, he postulates that the presence of others is a source of drive (D). In other words, while other people can be directional influences on behavior in the sense of producing specific cues and reinforcement, Zajonc argues they are also a source of general arousal, energizing all responses likely to be emitted in the given situation. The effects, then, are similar to those predicted by the Spence-Taylor theory discussed earlier. That is, if the subject's dominant responses are appropriate from the point of view of the experimental situation (i.e., if the task is easy), then the presence of others will enhance performance. If the dominant responses are largely inappropriate (i.e., if the task is hard), performance will be impaired. Zajonc has reported a number of studies that have shown support for these predictions (Zajonc, 1965; Zajonc and Sales, 1966; Wheeler and Davis, 1967; Cottrell, Rittle, and Wack, 1967; Zajonc, Heingartner, and Herman, 1969). There is little doubt that in this situation, as well as in the Spence-Taylor research and other studies we have not mentioned here, the approach has been a fruitful one. In addition, this particular application has been further solidified and related to the general Hullian tradition by the theorizing of Cottrell et al. (1968), Weiss and Miller (1971), and Paulus and Murdock (1971). In this more recent work, the basis for Zajonc's argument has been shown to rest in the data that indicate anxiety as the basic mediating variable that determines whether the presence of others has a drivelike effect. Thus, when others are acting in an evaluative, testlike manner, the effect of their presence will be to increase D. However, if they are acting in a relaxed, nonjudgmental manner, their presence or absence will have no effect.

Despite such value, however, it is clear that a number of significant problems remain. Thus, as we have said, D has lost its simplicity and the rigor with which it was once defined. As Hull expanded his definition to make it any strong stimulus, regardless of its biological evolutionary significance, and thus brought his thinking into line with that of Miller and Dollard and that of Woodworth many years previously, he lost what was uniquely his. The elegance and the rigor and the biological underpinning were clearly inadequate for the job, and the theory had to change. And yet, the expanded definition led to other questions as: How and under what conditions does external stimulation lead to increased drive since, clearly, sometimes it does not (cf. our discussion of the effects of previous punishment on current responsiveness above)? How do different antecedent conditions leading to drive summate? Is it just a matter of adding the amount of hunger to the amount of thirst to the amount of pain, and so on? Or does the presence of one incentive result in the loss of effectiveness of other incentives? Recent research by Deci (1971, 1972) suggests that this may, in fact, be the case. When and under what conditions do these antecedent variables leading to drive differ in the relative strengths of their contributions to the levels of arousal? The complexity of these questions is very great, and Hull never came close to answering them. In addition, recent evidence suggests that these different sources of drive are not interchangeable in contributing to general arousal, a finding contrary to Hull's predictions (Bolles, 1967).

A second problem concerns the by now accepted findings that organisms will sometimes act in a manner designed to increase stimulation as well as reduce it. There have been at least three types of theories that have attempted to account for these findings within a framework consistent with the Hullian approach, two of which we mentioned earlier. One of these was Berlyne's hypothesis that both low and high external stimulation lead to high reticular activating system (RAS) arousal and that behavior arousal is determined by the desire to reduce RAS stimulation. Secondly, there is the arousal-jag theory, which postulates that the desire to increase stimulation results from the expectancy of high stimulation reduction to follow. Finally, there is Fowler's (1965) suggestion that constant exposure to similar stimulation leads to boredom stimuli and that these are negative stimuli, which the organism is motivated to reduce in the same sense as hunger and pain stimuli. Behavior is motivated toward those directions where there is expectancy (a high K) of new stimulation, but still stimulation less than that resulting from boredom.

All of these explanations have problems. There is, as yet, little evidence to support the idea that low and high external stimulation have the same effects on RAS arousal, a research finding that also has implications for the usefulness of Fowler's assumption that boredom leads to greater internal stimulation than high external stimulation. In addition, a second problem with Fowler's argument is the use of the K variable, a type of construct that turns out, as we examine it closely, to be subject to the same dilemma and problems as the conditioned-stimulus and conditioned-reinforcer constructs we spoke of in Chapter 2. In fact, the K variable is really nothing but conditioned stimulation, deriving from the fact that the organism learns to associate his own movements to the consummatory response by a process of stimulus generalization from the goal box to the early parts of the maze to his own movement. Such movements, then, produce stimuli that he is motivated to reduce because they are frustrating. The dilemma, as we have pointed out, is that the procedures for developing K as a behavior incentive are exactly the same as those for developing the goal-box stimuli as secondary conditioned reinforcers and for defining frustration experimentally! Hence, when do the goal-box stimuli act as behavior incentives (i.e., stimuli that must be reduced)? When can they be called frustrating? When do they act as conditioned reinforcers, that is, when does the behavior that led to them cease? Any theory using K must be prepared to deal with this problem of having three different concepts defined by the same experimental operation, and unfortunately Hullian-type theorizing has not as yet done so.

As an example of the lack of coping with this dilemma, let us consider a recent proposal by Cofer and Appley (1964) for two incentivelike constructs, known as the *sensitization-integration mechanism* (SIM) and the *anticipation-invigoration mechanism* (AIM), as conceptual substitutes for the D construct. Berger and Lambert (1968) have described these mechanisms as follows:

The first mechanism (SIM) is posited to explain the invigorating effects on action of selective sensitization to certain stimuli. This effect is probably an innate one, but one that can be modified by learning. For example, under controlled conditions, activity increments which one would expect as a result of deprivation may not occur. However, these activity increments *do* occur when the relevant stimuli are introduced, in the sense that the deprived organism responds more vigorously than the non-deprived one. In sex behavior, as Beach (1956) has suggested, hormones are a necessary precondition for arousal of the male, but are not sufficient; usually a receptive female, plus physical or symbolic interaction, are also necessary for copulation to occur.

The parallel mechanism, AIM, carries the main weight of the Cofer and Appley analysis. Here invigoration of behavior is enhanced by learned anticipations. These may take several forms: the incentive cues (K) which "control" anticipation, working through such processes as the r_g mechanism; the energy released by the states of conflict between two or more anticipations; or (Cofer and Appley do not mention this) the *ee* mechanisms suggested by Sears (1951). According to Cofer and Appley, where anticipation is possible the usual effects of deprivation (or drive) merely invigorate behavior; furthermore, where deprivation does not appear to be operative, invigoration may occur through anticipation alone. Cofer and Appley stress the point (1964, p. 822) that "... stimuli, including any coming from internal features of the deprivation state, may have a double function: they come through learning to evoke anticipations (and thus arousal) and they serve (after learning) as cues for responses."[2]

The dilemma, from the point of view we are expressing, is that the problems we have seen in K do not seem to be overcome here either. That is, the conditions postulated for the development of SIM and AIM are the same as those postulated for the development of frustrating stimuli and secondary reinforcers!

There is one way of overcoming this problem in the physicalistic tradition, but the suggestion offered is (a) not really tested yet, and (b) not a Hullian solution. The mechanism we are referring to is that by Bindra (1969), whose basic proposal is that both internal stimuli (such as drive) and environmental-reinforcing stimuli (such as food, water, etc.) have similar effects on the organisms in that they lead to (or cause) a high state of general arousal, a condition that Bindra calls a *central motive state* (CMS). Once this arousal takes place, certain kinds of sensory-motor response connections are activated and take place, giving direction to behavior. Bindra's model, which we present in outline form in Figure 3.3 and which has strong similarities to the arousal theory frameworks we will discuss in Chapter 4, is based on the following considerations.

[2] Berger and Lambert, Stimulus-response theory in contemporary social psychology. *The handbook of social psychology,* 2nd ed., vol. 1, Lindzey and Aronson (eds.), 1968, p. 102.

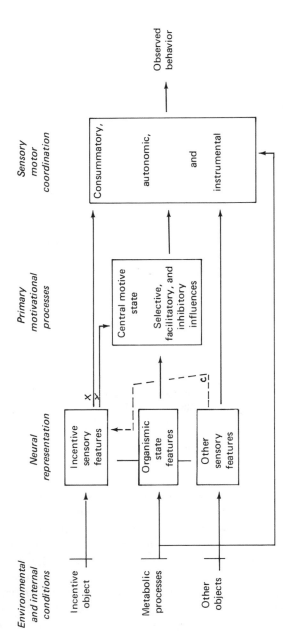

Figure 3.3 A hypothetical model of motivation showing (1) how the central motive state is generated by an interaction of neural representations of organismic-state features and incentive-stimulation features (Route Y), and (2) how the environmental (incentive and nonincentive) stimuli, together with the central motive state, influence response determination by selective effects (facilitation or inhibition) on sensory-motor coordinations. The stimulation arising from nonincentive environmental stimulation can, through conditioning (Route C), acquire the same properties as Route Y.

Source: D. Bindra, The interrelated mechanisms of reinforcement and motivation and the nature of their influence on response. *Nebraska symposium on motivation, 17,* 1969, 22. Copyright 1969 by the University of Nebraska Press.

1. The effect of a motivating influence such as hunger or a reinforcing variable such as hunger on a given type of behavior is determined by the *same set of experimental operations,* as the following paradigm shows:

Table 3.4 Experimental Procedures for Assessing Effects of Motivational Variables and Reinforcing Variables on Response Probability

	Antecedent Measurement	Experimental Procedures	Subsequent Measurement
Motivation	Measure Behavior A	Introduce Motivation (Hunger, thrist, pain, etc.)	Measure behavior A
Reinforcer	Measure Behavior A	Introduce Reinforcers (Food, water, sex, etc.)	Measure Behavior B

Table 3.4 indicates that you follow the same before-after measuring operations in both cases in assessing the effects of motivating and reinforcing stimuli on behavior. Thus, we can, if we wish, wipe out the distinction between motivators and reinforcers in terms of their effects on the organism, since both *could* act in the same way in influencing later behavior by stimulating the arousal of a central motive state (CMS) in the same fashion. (For our purposes, the reader will see that this approach, if it is a viable one, wipes out the operational confusion between conditioned stimuli, frustration, and conditioned reinforcers in Hull's system because these distinctions are irrelevant in Bindra's approach.)

2. Reinforcing events have their effects not just by strengthening (or weakening) specific responses, since organisms may learn without actually responding (cf. Solomon and Turner, 1962). Therefore, reinforcement may affect behavior by other mechanisms also, as for example, the creation of a central motive state that influences later behavior.

3. Motivating variables lead to general arousal as well as specific response.

Bindra's proposal is obviously an interesting one, but much work needs to be done to determine its viability. For example, how long do the effects of a reinforcement last? Do they remain as persisting as drive stimuli? How does the arousal of the CMS actively influence the occurrence of specific sensory-motor connections? Hull, we will recall, had some proposals in this area. On the other hand, Bindra doesn't really deal with this, suggesting at various points that these specific connections are built into and are part of the particular CMS being aroused. It is obvious, however, that most sensory-motor connections are learned, rather than innate, and questions need to be asked as to the manner in which a particular CMS can influence the occurrence of a learned sensory-motor connection.

Returning now to our discussion of the Hullian system, K as a construct has another problem, one previously mentioned in Chapter 2, and this is that the history of the organism (i.e., degree of reward in the past, etc.) determines the degree of responsiveness to later positive and/or negative incentives. Thus, the more the organism has been rewarded in the past, the more he will try to achieve positive incentives and avoid negative outcomes in the future. On the other hand, an organism punished in the past will be less motivated to achieve incentives and avoid negative outcomes. Hence, the introduction of K as an incentive variable, without any attempt to account for the fact that its actual behavioral effects will differ as a function of the previous history of the organism, means inadequate explanatory power, at best.

The heavy use of K has meant other problems, also. As we have stressed previously, the problem comes from the fact that K is postulated to arise as a result of the contiguity of certain physically defined stimuli (such as mazes, alleyways, etc.) and the physical movements of the organisms within situations where feeding has taken place. On the basis of such stimulus contiguity, it is hypothesized that organisms will make anticipatory conditioned responses, with the level of such responses being in part a function of how much eating has taken place in the goal box. According to the theoretical argument, the more eating has taken place, the greater the anticipatory behavior. The greater the anticipatory behavior, the more the tension and frustration involved (since eating is not actually taking place until the organism is in the goal box) and, it follows, the greater the motivation of the organism. In this way, theorists of the Hullian school attempted to account for such findings as the almost immediate effects of changes in incentives, either positive or negative, on behavior.

Despite the logic and ingenuity of this argument, we must again point out that, theoretically, it makes just as much sense to argue that the environmental stimuli associated with eating behavior acquire secondary reinforcing properties as a result of such contiguity. If they do have such reinforcing powers, then they should act like other reinforcers do in the Hullian system, that is, they should serve as a behavior decrement in that once having achieved such reinforcement, the organism should stop his anticipatory behavior and approach to the goal box, rather than increase it, as is predicted by the K variable. Now one may argue that the empirical data should guide us in deciding which alternatives we should adopt, that is, whether the environment is more likely to act as an incentive or as a conditioned reinforcer. This is all well and good. Certainly empirical data, rather than theoretical speculation, should guide our conclusions, *except* that both alternatives are equally logical and predictable. Hence, if one of them has not occurred (e.g., the tendency of contiguous environmental stimuli to serve as secondary reinforcers), then one cannot claim support for the system if the other occurs, since both are equally likely. Thus, either they both occur (and we then have the problem of differentiating them) or neither occurs. The first supports the approach but leads to other problems, while the second outcome does not support the framework. In brief, it strikes us as not theoretically useful to argue that variable A operates according to Principle One, when at the same time the same set of data points to the conclusion that variable B, which is equally likely according to Principle One, is not occurring at all. It is obvious that Hullian theorists are going to have to resolve this dilemma in their future work if the K approach to explaining expectancy behavior is to be considered a viable one.

In addition to these difficulties, there are some other problems in using the Hullian approach to motivational phenomena, as Howard Kendler, a psychologist who himself works within this framework, has recently noted (1965). The first of these problems is that the same experimental operations have been used to define and manipulate both arousal and directive determinants of behavior. As an example, food deprivation is supposed to lead to both increases in drive (D), the general arousal agent, and S_D, the distinctive physical stimuli associated with food deprivation. As the reader will recall, according to the logic of the approach, with increases in D, S_D also becomes more salient, and thus the responses learned in the past as a method of reducing food deprivation become activated and behavior takes place. However, as Kendler points out, D and S_D are separate variables and each should be manipulable experimentally, independent of the other. As these variables are currently defined and studied, this is now impossible to do.

Kendler's second criticism concerns the question of whether there is such a thing as a motivation unit of behavior in the same sense that there is a learning unit of behavior. We can fairly definitely say that something is learned or it is not learned. Can we also say, as it is implied by Hullian theory, that behavior can be viewed as a continuing series of stimulation-reduction episodes, that is, that behavior is aroused by whatever stimulation exists at the time and is directed toward whatever means will reduce it? Theoretically, this suggests an episodelike characteristic to behavior and a basic motivational unit of behavior that can be viewed somewhat as:

Yet, as Kendler points out, behavior can often be seen as a flowing, ongoing process, rather than the episodic pattern suggested by this approach. How useful, then, is a theoretical model that assumes this episodic characteristic?

Finally, Kendler also suggests that the old distinction between basic, primary sources of drive (e.g., hunger, thirst, sex, and pain) and secondary sources (e.g., anxiety) as being the difference between those sources that are primarily physiologically based and those that are not has outlived its usefulness, considering recent research findings. Since we have already discussed these and other difficulties in the various sources of D (drive) and how best to conceptualize this key construct in the Hullian system, we shall not bother to pursue this matter further here, except to agree with Kendler's criticism as relevant.

There is one last point worth noting concerning the Hullian system which illustrates the mixed success of this approach to motivational phenomena. This is that the introduction of the K variable had the effect of enabling the Hullian theoretical framework, which basically assumed behavior to be utility maximizing in the traditional economic sense, to predict behavior that is, in a sense, self-defeating. It is our personal belief that a theory of motivational process needs to be able to deal with such behavior since sometimes such behavior does occur. In fact, we will argue later that one of the reasons theories that do not posit utility maximizing (e.g., consistency theories) developed was because of the occurrence of self-defeating behavior and the need to account for it theoretically. Thus, it is significant to note that the introduction of K led to the basic prediction that organisms behave in a manner so as to reduce those drives they "expect" to reduce. However, if the expectancy of being able to reduce a certain kind of stimulation is low, then the probability of behavior decreases, i.e., even though there is available means for reducing stimulation (and thus maximizing utility), behavior designed to achieve these outcomes will not take place unless expectancy is high. It is because of this effect of expectancy that perhaps people do not always do the things that seem best for them, or so a Hullian might argue. In this way, then, a utility-maximizing theory can, to some degree, account for nonutility-maximizing behavior.

One problem, however, with the expectancy system of Hull and Spence is what to predict for low-expectancy people. Do they keep searching for the best alternative and pick that one? Does that mean that before we study the value of the theory we need to know the complete set of alternatives available for all people? Logically, this is what would seem necessary to provide an adequate test of the prediction that this, in effect, is what low-expectancy people do. Yet, it seems wholly unrealistic to expect us to know what the complete lists of alternatives are for all people in addition to their complete set of expectancies. Suppose, also, that a person has a low set of expectancies in general. Does that mean he is less likely to behave, in general, like a high-expectancy person? Will he "freeze"? If he is just as likely to behave, then what does the concept of expectancy mean? Questions such as these will provide continuing challenges in the future for those investigating motivational phenomena from the Hullian perspective.

SUMMARY

Our goal in this chapter has been to detail how the Hullian approach to motivational processes developed and changed in attempting to account for various problems. One major problem was the necessity to account for the fact that the direction of behavior is in part a function of the characteristics of the environment the person is in at the time, as well as his internal state. Basically, the problem was to show how those concepts we traditionally call expectancies of reinforcement, concepts inherently subjective in nature, could be represented by physicalistic, objective stimuli. The notion developed, represented by the symbol K, proposed that through a process of stimulus generalization, an individual learned a different anticipatory response to those stimuli associated with reinforcement as opposed to those stimuli associated with nonreinforcement. Such responses were also productive of different stimuli leading to further differentiating behavior, thus leading to different behaviors in environments with different expectancies of reinforcement (i.e., where reinforcement had been experienced at different levels previously).

K as a concept, however, did not work because it was logically possible to show that the same processes hypothesized to lead to K (i.e., behavior increase) would also lead to behavior reduction. In addition to this problem, other logical and empirical problems developed with the Hullian system, suggesting that Hull's goal of achieving an objective, physically oriented, natural-science approach to motivation did not succeed.

activation-arousal
theory

As a result of the problems that developed in the Hullian approach to the study of motivational process, laboratory investigators of a physicalistic, natural-science orientation became faced with the task of developing new ways of dealing with the psychology of motivation. These newer approaches needed to accomplish two goals. First, there was the need to eliminate some of the more significant problems of Hullian theory. Secondly, these changes needed to be achieved while still remaining within a relatively rigorous framework.

One result of this search has been the approach known as *activation* or *arousal* theory (both names have been used), an approach actually having two major interrelated components that reflect the interests of two different groups of investigators. However, we will discuss the general approach as a whole, starting first with its promise for overcoming problems noted in the Hullian tradition, such as (a) the weakness in the definition of D (drive); (b) the tendency of organisms to seek increased, as well as reduced, stimulation; and (c) the tendency of people to continue behaving and for behavior to show direction, even when people are not in an explicit state of need deprivation. In addition, we will deal with this framework independent of its relation to the Hullian theories, focusing here on its conceptual qualities, its susceptibility to research testing, its implications for contemporary interest in the physical environment, and similar types of questions.

THE OVERALL FRAMEWORK OF
ACTIVATION-AROUSAL THEORY

The essential logic of the activation-arousal framework, when viewed as an overall system for understanding motivational processes, can be summarized by the following statements:

1. Physical stimulation that affects an organism contributes to its physiological and psychological arousal level.

2. The impact of a stimulus in terms of its contribution to the arousal level of the organism is a positive function of such variables as its intensity, its meaningfulness, its complexity, the recency of its previous occurrence, the frequency of such occurrences, and the extent to which it provides variation from previous stimulation (Fiske and Maddi, 1961; Walker, 1964).

3. For a given organism at a given time of day (i.e., during the sleep-wakefulness cycle), there is a level of arousal that is normal and appropriate for it, and behavior is motivated toward achieving that normal arousal state for that given time of day; having attained that state of normal arousal, its behavior is also motivated toward maintaining that state, in that the organism will engage in behavior designed to increase its arousal level when it is too low and decrease it when it is too high.

4. Having attained such a state of normal arousal, the organism becomes more sensitive to other aspects of the environment and is more able to deal with them in an efficient manner. If his behavior does not have to be directed toward the achievement of optimal arousal, it can then be directed toward whatever external demands happen to be operating in the environment at the given time. Such increased attention to external environmental demands when an organism is at an optimal activation or arousal level should then lead, all other things being equal, to a U-shaped relationship between arousal level and task performance, since it is when he is in his optimal arousal state that he can pay most attention to task demands.

These statements as to the basic logic of the framework of activation-arousal theory are actually a composite of the work of a number of different investigators. This work can be considered to consist of two major components. In the first research cluster, there has been a concern with testing the basic idea that organisms are motivated to seek levels of stimulation that are not too high and not too low, but somewhere in the middle. Sometimes, the hypothetical framework proposed has been that the level being sought is some optimal level based on previous experience (cf. Fiske and Maddi, 1961; Walker, 1964). In other cases, it has been argued that, at least under some conditions, individuals seek levels slightly above the previous level (cf. Dember and Earl, 1957; Berlyne, 1960). Finally, there are others who argue that the level sought is either slightly higher or lower than previous experience, but not extremely different (cf. McClelland, 1955). What is common to all of these is that the level sought is some intermediate point between the levels of stimulation to which one may be exposed, and this is the reason they can all be classified under statement 3 above.

In the second research cluster that has defined activation-arousal theory the concern has been somewhat different, concentrating more on the effects of arousal on behavior. This group, which can be classified under statement 4, has its intellectual heritage in the Hullian group in that they have been interested in the effects of the *general-arousal* construct on behavior, a construct that the Hullians conceptualized as *D* but developed here somewhat differently. In addition, they have also been interested, as were the Hullians, in how such arousal interacts with other variables in influencing behavioral direction.

Even though these research clusters have developed somewhat independently over the years, our discussion here will attempt to integrate them and also point out how such integration is necessary in order to increase the value of future research.

"Activation Seeking" as a Type of Balance Theory

If we turn to the first research cluster, it is apparent that this is a balance, or homeostatic, formulation. The approach postulates that, at least in part, both the arousal and direction of behavior is due to the desire to achieve some kind of "balanced" outcome, that is, one in balance both with previous experience (either exact or relative) and what that individual desires for that time of day, and that rejects both too much stimulation and too little. The nature of the specific behavior that will actually be engaged in by the organism depends on his stimulation state at the time. If he is in too high a state, he is aroused to reduce the stimulation; if he is in too low a state, he is aroused to increase stimulation. Within this viewpoint, then, the same factor (i.e., the current arousal state of the organism) has both an arousal and directive influence on behavior. It determines to some degree the extent to which behavior will take place at all, and it influences whether the organism will attempt to increase or decrease stimulation. The degree of arousal and its direction is a function of the degree of deviation from the optimal level. The more the organism is in a deviation state from this level, the greater the behavior arousal, with the direction depending on the current state of activation relative to the optimum. (In addition, it may be that second sources of behavior direction at this time are those S-R habits stimulated by the lack of optimal-arousal stimuli, that is, those habitual behaviors that have been used in the past by the organism to achieve optimal stimulation. However, this latter source of direction has not been a systematic part of the approach, and precise statements as to how, why, and in what manner these habits are activated by the arousal level of the time have not been developed.)

A number of advantages, both theoretical and practical, seem worth noting about this balance-theoretical aspect of activation-arousal theory. For example, while deviation from optimal level is, in some respects, an arousal mechanism similar to Hull's *D,* in other respects it is not. In one sense it seems to constitute a significant advance as a theoretical construct since it is at least as well defined in a physiological sense as Hull's *D,* but its logic has not been based on a doubtful biological utility stemming from evolutionary consideration. Thus, while contributions to arousal level can include stimulation stemming from survival requirements (e.g., hunger deprivation, shock, etc.), other variables can and do contribute to arousal level and are equally important in a theoretical sense. For example, variables such as stimulus complexity, stimulus meaningfulness, and stimulus variability, which are of increasing interest in these days of designing meaningful satisfactory physical environments in both urban and rural settings, can be measured as contributors to arousal. In this way, as we will see later, a meeting ground seems both possible and desirable between those psychologists concerned with the nature of motivational processes and those concerned with our physical environment.

A second advantage of the approach is that it does not equate the "desirable" end state of behavior with need or stimulus reduction, a position we have found seriously deficient in previous chapters. Such findings of deficiency have not been unique with us, of course, and the literature has been replete with different attempts to develop a better theory in the area (cf. Eisenberger, 1972). The argument here is to propose behavior as oriented toward the achievement of a balanced state of activation. Is this an improvement? To some extent it is, since there are data supporting the hypothesis both from the physiological areas (cf. Grossman, 1967; Berlyne, 1967) and in the social-psychological literature (cf. Korman, 1971a). Since a considerable part of our discussion in later chapters will be directed to describing and analyzing the evidence relating to this proposition, we will not devote much space to it here except to indicate that this part of activation theory could be considered to constitute a physiological, natural-science analogue to the findings of a large number of other psychologists that balance is a sought-after property in a social-psychological sense, a property that brings pleasant affects once it is achieved. However, the advantages are balanced by some disadvantages also, particularly in testing a curvilinear theory. We will discuss this more a little later.

A third advantage to the activation approach is that balance theory, as stated, appears to be able to handle the frequent finding that, sometimes, behavior is engaged in in order to achieve increased as well as decreased stimulation. Hence, the research in "curiosity" and "exploration" leading to the frequent finding that organisms often try to achieve outcomes that result in increased stimulation becomes understandable and theoretically accounted for. However, we have used the phrase *appears to be able to* deliberately since it is in relation to this question that we find one of the major weaknesses of the approach thus far. This weakness concerns the fact that if this type of thinking is to be a viable and useful mechanism for understanding motivational processes, there must be some way of clarifying and measuring currently existing and desired arousal levels prior to the behavioral event under consideration. Once such classification and measurement has taken place, we can then (a) define what is meant by "low" and "high" arousal levels, (b) classify organisms into these "low" and "high" categories on the basis of some measurements as to the level of arousal they are currently subject to and the level of arousal they desire, and then (c) use such classifications for predicting whether an organism will act in a manner such as to increase or decrease stimulation in some given experimental situation, which we have also been able to measure for the arousal it stimulates. Clearly, unless this can be done, there is a danger of circular thinking. For example, suppose we did a study and found that behavior was performed in order to achieve more stimulation. We might interpret that as resulting from the fact that the environment must have stimulated a low state of arousal prior to the behavior. On the other hand, a study where behavior led to stimulus reduction might be interpreted in the opposite manner. The point is that in both cases we are reasoning in a circular fashion, and obviously such theorizing is not very useful in developing an adequate theory of motivational processes. Despite the necessity, however, for the development of such a measurement system for meaningful research, such requirements have, with rare exception (cf. Haber, 1958), not been met. Therefore, although there has been some work supportive of these aspects of activation-level theory, the degree of support, at this point, cannot be considered very strong, both for the above reasons and for other methodological and measurement problems we shall be discussing presently.

There is, at least ideally, a fourth major advantage to the approach in that it can be studied on both the physiological and psychological level. That is, although the arousal level of the organism can be assessed using physiological measurements (when developed) and, hence, can fit into a natural-science framework using physicalistically oriented variables, it does not have to be viewed in this fashion. Rather, the activation (or arousal) level of the organism can also, theoretically, be measured by purely psychological measurement, and behavioral predictions can be made on this basis. We can then measure the arousal level of an organism resulting from environmental stimulation using either physiological or psychological measurements. One advantage of this is that different levels of environmental stimulation could then be easily scaled, either on the basis of the degree of psychological arousal they elicit *or* the physiological state that results. Once this is done, it becomes relatively simple, at least conceptually, to manipulate exposure to these stimuli experimentally in order to test the various propositions of activation theory, using as independent variables the preferred arousal levels of the individual respondents, as these might be established by different measures. Consider, for example, Table 4.1, which illustrates that it is possible to classify environments either on the basis of the physiological arousal they stimulate or the psychological level of arousal perceived, using noise as an example of an environmental characteristic. Once

Table 4.1 Example of How Activation-arousal Theory May Be Tested Using Either Physiologically or Psychologically Measured Independent Variables (illustrative data only)

Physical Properties of the Environment	Physiological Measurements of Brain Activity	Psychological Measurements of Noise Level	Assigned Scale Value (on basis of subjective scale ranging from 0 to 100)
120 decibels	100	Very Loud (Earsplitting)	95
90 decibels	80	Loud	55
65 decibels	60	Moderate	23
35 decibels	40	Soft	11

individuals have been classified (either physiologically or psychologically) as to the level of noise they prefer, it would then be possible to predict what kinds of stimulus levels (environments) they would prefer as their optimum point, what kinds of environments might be substituted for one another since they fall within an acceptable range of optimum arousal levels, and so on. In addition to its theoretical interest, such measurements obviously would have value for such applied problems as the design of urban, work, and school environments.

Conceptually, then, the advantages here seem exciting. The problem is to achieve these advantages, and this has not been so easy, as our later discussion will indicate.

Behavior under Optimal Arousal

As we indicated earlier, one of the most significant aspects of the activation-theory framework is that it conceptually overcomes the weaknesses of the Hull/Freud approach in predicting that behavior ceases once the reduction of the stimulus is achieved. The argument of the arousal theorist, on the other hand, is that once optimum activation is achieved, organisms are more receptive and sensitive to the external stimuli extant in the environment at the time. Thus, if the organism is in a task situation that is making specific demands for a specific set of behaviors, the prediction of the activation-arousal framework is that there will be a U-shaped relationship between arousal and performance, such as is pictured in Figure 4.1.

In the intermediate case, the arousal and directedness of behavior is seen as stemming from the task demands of the situation, as well as whatever other specific motivational variables happen to be operating at the time (such as need for achievement). However, what is important is that one source of behavior variance, i.e., the seeking of optimum arousal, is not influencing performance in the optimum arousal situation. Hence, behavior is more controlled by the demands of the external environment and, thus, more effective, if it is a setting calling for task performance.

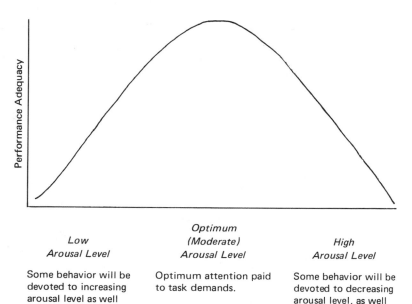

Figure 4.1 The inverted U-shaped relationship between arousal level and performance.

ACTIVATION-AROUSAL THEORY:
CONCEPTUAL AND METHODOLOGICAL ISSUES

Up to now we have been concentrating mainly on why activation-arousal theory developed and the conceptual advantages it brought to the understanding of the psychology of motivation. At the same time, however, that these conceptual benefits were being elucidated, implications began to be derived from various experimental studies and logical analyses that there were a number of methodological and measurement problems that had not heretofore been realized. It is these questions that we will discuss here.

The Physical Stimulus: How Does it Come to Have an Effect?

Let us assume for a moment that you are walking down Fifth Avenue in Manhattan on a Thursday afternoon in the spring, past the shopping crowds, past the brilliantly lit stores, past the skyscrapers, and in the midst of the noise and honking of automobiles. Clearly, there is a great deal of physical stimulation here, whatever measure of stimulation we use (i.e., intensity, variability, or meaningfulness). On the other hand, assume a week later you are walking along a deserted beach in Maine, where the only noise is the roar of the waves, where there are no crowds, and where there are no skyscrapers or brilliantly lit stores. The level of physical stimulation here obviously seems less. Taking both in context, then, the two environments should affect you differently. The question that concerns us here is the process by which these environments come to have their effect. Is it just a matter of the stimulus affecting the neurons of your body in a different manner? If so, then, clearly, all we would need to do to affect people's levels of arousal in the future would be to pay attention to the physical stimuli involved. Suppose, however, that it is more complex than this and that the effects of physical stimuli on arousal are a function also of the social-psychological characteristics of the situation and of the personality of the individuals being studied. Attempts, then, to develop a viable, optimal physical environment (i.e., one that would lead to optimum arousal) would be considerably more difficult since now we would have to consider the social and psychological variables involved, as well as the level of physical stimulation. Perhaps arousal is not involved at all, and physical stimuli have effect on people for reasons having nothing to do with arousal. In addition to theoretical interest then, there are important practical reasons for being interested in understanding the process by which different types of physical stimulation come to influence people differently.

As it turns out, this is a question that has interested a number of investigators working in both this and related areas. As a result, there are several different, but not always antithetical, hypotheses concerning the effects of physical stimulation on psychological processes. If we look at them, it becomes apparent that it is not difficult at all to propose different explanations for the effect of physical stimulation on psychological processes besides the framework we have called activation-arousal theory. Consider, for example, Table 4.2, where we have indicated several of the most important of these hypotheses and some of the research evidence attached to them.

With the possible exception of the second hypothesis in Table 4.2, and perhaps part of the sixth, it would be stretching it beyond a reasonable point, we think, to argue that the hypotheses and research listed in the table are just rewordings of the activation-arousal framework. Clearly, they are more than that, and therefore they raise doubts as to the necessity and importance of the arousal hypothesis. Since they suggest we have little reason to assume automatically that the way the physical environment affects behavior is only through its arousal properties, research needs to be done as to when and where the arousal hypothesis holds and when and where these other hypotheses hold. Once the research has been done, perhaps we will be able to understand why we get such conflicting research findings as the fact that sometimes high temperature leads to dislike (Griffitt and Veitch, 1971), and other times the same high temperature is *negatively* related to aggression (Baron, 1972). Similarly, we might also understand why we get a lack of correlation between crowding and performance over a range of different tasks (Freedman, Klevansky, and Ehrlich, 1971).

Table 4.2 Hypotheses Concerning Processes by which Physical Stimuli Come to Influence Psychological States and Related Behaviors

Hypothesis	Investigators
1. Crowding (i.e., increased number of people per unit of space) may affect the ability to control interaction with others (or increase the costs of doing so in a physiological and/or psychological sense).	Zlutnick and Altman (1972)
2. The psychological variable of unpredictablity, and the anxiety felt because of the lack of control, is more important than the physical parameter known as noise intensity in predicting adaptation to noise in task situations. The effect is the same over (a) different procedures for manipulating unpredictability; (b) different levels of physical noise; (c) both male and female subjects; (d) different laboratories.	Glass and Singer (1972)
3. The concept of relative deprivation may explain some of the effects of physical stimulation on behavior, in that people who are being exposed to stressful physical stimuli will find it even more intolerable if they are made conscious of the fact that others comparable to themselves are being exposed to stimuli less stressful.	Glass and Singer (1972)
4. The effect of noise on human performance may be understood in terms of its influence on the information-processing capacities of the individual and its tendency to utilize those processes in a manner that increases the capacity of the individual to respond adequately to other stress stimuli.	Finkelman and Glass (1970)
5. For people who are required to work under noisy conditions, high intensity has a negative influence; for people who choose to work under the poor conditions, the effects of high intensity are considerably lessened. Hence, the element of choice is crucial in affecting susceptibility to noise.	Glass and Singer (1972)
6. One's perception of the self as being in a state of a specific type of (or as feeling a particular emotional) arousal is a function of (a) the actual physiological arousal he is in (i.e., the stimulus to which he is subject) and (b) the cognitive and sound cues that are available in order to assist one in labeling the state of arousal (or emotion) one feels.	Goldstein, Fink, and Mettee (1972); Schacter and Singer (1962); Schacter and Wheeler (1962)
7. The effect of any specific type of physical stimulation on an individual is a function of his experience with stimuli of that nature, his expectancy for that situation, and the amount of time he has been in that situation.	Helson (1964); Zlutnick and Altman (1972)

Arousal: One Kind or Many?

If we examine the nature of what is being proposed by activation-arousal theory, one basic assumption seems clear: there is one kind of arousal that affects behavior the same way, no matter its source and how it is measured. In this sense it is very much like D in the Hullian system, in that it suggests that while arousal can take place as a result of an almost infinite variety of physical stimuli, it acts the same way once aroused, regardless of the source and measure of the arousal. It is clear that this is an important assumption, since if there is more than one kind of arousal (depending on how it is stimulated), then more than one kind of theoretical framework may be necessary. Similarly, if there is more than one arousal, then a research study where arousal theory is not supported may be due to the fact that different types of arousal, unknown as to nature and intensity, are involved.

There is some evidence relative to this question, but it lends itself to ambiguous interpretation. This evidence concerns the fact that the different measures typically used for assessing degree of physiological arousal (e.g., measures such as the degree of activity in the reticular formation, electrocortical activity, circulatory activity, vasomotor responses, respiratory activity, the electrical properties of the skin and skeletal tension) are positively correlated with one another, but not always at a very high level. As a result, some psychologists have cited the lack of very high correlations as indicating the presence of more than one type of arousal (cf. Lacey, 1950), whereas others see the positive relationships as supporting a general-arousal factor notion (cf. Berlyne, 1967; Appley, 1970). Which one is right? Like other arguments in psychology, there is no answer since it depends on what one wants to look at. In the meantime, until clearer data become available, some disagreement in interpretation will remain.

Testing a Curvilinear Hypothesis

A third methodological question in activation-arousal theory stems from the problems that are involved in testing a curvilinear, or U-shaped, hypothesis. Basically, the problems stem from two considerations. One is that the prediction of behavior at any specific time will be a function of two variables. The first of these is the degree of arousal that the person is used to and is predicted to desire in the future. The second is the degree of arousal that the person is subjected to at the time. It is only in knowing these two antecedent variables that a prediction of behavior is possible since it is clear that the following situation could easily occur:

Person's Typical Arousal Level	Contemporary Environment Arousal Level	Behavior Predicted
10	7	= Stimulus-Increasing Behavior
5	7	= Stimulus-Decreasing Behavior
5	3	= Stimulus-Increasing Behavior
1	3	= Stimulus-Decreasing Behavior

In other words, for any given level of each variable (person and environment), opposing behaviors would be predicted, depending on the level of the other.

The second problem stems also from the U-curve hypothesis and the fact that the relationships turn out to be far more complex than the simple linear relationships usually hypothesized. To begin with the latter case, a test of a relationship where variable A is postulated to be related to variable B is a relatively simple one, since only two levels of the independent (hypothesized causal) variable are needed. That is, the higher on one variable, the higher on the other, or so such a hypothesis would have it. However, the U-curve hypothesis is different and considerably more complex, since (a) a minimum of three levels of the independent (hypothesized causal) variable is needed, (b) the three levels used in a particular research study must be placed widely enough apart so that an adequate test of the U-shaped hypothesis may be made, and (c) the middle level used must be at the level of optimum performance. Thus, for example, if we utilize three levels of the independent variable and find a direct linear relationship with the dependent variable (either positive or negative), is this due to the fact that we have unknowingly chosen arousal levels too close together at the low (or high) point of the arousal continuum? Consider, for example, the illustrations in Table 4.3, from which it is clear that the testing of a U-shaped hypothesis can be very difficult. Thus, in Case A, three levels have been used in

Table 4.3 Different Alternate Situations when Testing U-shaped Hypothesis

Case	Individual's Desired Arousal Level	Arousal Levels Tested in Situation	Performance Levels	Conclusions
A	10	2, 4, 6	2 = 100 4 = 200 6 = 300	Positive linear relationship between arousal and performance
B	10	12, 14, 16	12 = 300 14 = 200 16 = 100	Negative linear relationship between arousal level and performance
C	10	8, 10, 12	8 = 300 10 = 400 12 = 300	U-shaped relationship

testing, but they are all on the lower end of the continuum. Hence, a positive linear relationship between arousal level and performance has been found. Conversely, just the reverse has occurred in Case B. In both cases, then, negative evidence for a U-shaped hypothesis has been found and would be reported, even though in actuality there has not been a true test of the theory. This has only occurred in Case C, where three levels of arousal have been used, the middle one of which is the desired optimal level. From the hypothetical data given there, a U-shaped relationship would then be reported quite properly. The point is that it is only in Case C that a true test of the hypothesis was possible, since it is only there that the desired level of arousal was actually included in the experimental situation. Thus, should the results have been

Arousal Level	Performance Level
8	300
10	300
12	300

the evidence would quite properly have been interpreted as negative for the U-shaped hypothesis in an appropriate test of the approach.

There is another point stemming from these considerations that further complicates the testing of a theoretical approach of this nature in addition to the fact that these methodological requirements for research be met. This consideration is that it is logically impossible to test a U-shaped hypothesis unless there is some preexisting theoretical or empirical reason for predicting at what level of the environment the optimum performance will take place. One might argue, and it can be easily illustrated, as we did in Table 4.3, that an obtained linear relationship might actually be either the ascending (Case A) or descending (Case B) part of a U-shaped hypothesis, which would have appeared had we included higher or lower levels of the independent variable. This problem means, the author would contend, that it is the obligation of those who propose the more complex U-shaped theories that they also provide us with a clear rationale for testing them. Integral to such a rationale would be theoretical and/or empirical reasons for predicting that optimum levels of performance should occur at certain levels of the environmental variable. If this is not forthcoming, it is clear that the possibilities for ambiguity of interpretation are great.

Given, then, all these difficulties, it is perhaps no wonder that, so far as this author is aware, there is no research program that meets the requirements for a full test of activation theory in all its facets.

The Measurement of Arousal: How Do We Do It? One of the advantages of the activation-arousal approach is the fact that, theoretically, we may study arousal by utilizing physiological measurements and/or psychological measurements. In each case, the antecedents and the consequences are supported to be the same. Hence, we can choose either one, according to our perferences and according to the adequacy of the measures available. Do we have any good measures now, in either the physiological or psychological areas? Clearly, the answer to this question depends on the criteria for what we call a "good" measure. In Chapter 6 we will discuss one set of criteria for measures. These criteria have come to be known as validity and reliability criteria.[1] If one uses these criteria, then the measures currently used to assess arousal show a varying pattern of results, depending on the area one is measuring in these findings. As

[1]There is some question about the reliability criterion in the measurement of motives. We will deal with these questions in Chapter 6.

we will see in a moment, this may have significant implications for activation-arousal theory in general.

Basically, the findings on the measurement of arousal states can be summarized as follows:

1. There are only moderate correlations at best between different measures of physiological arousal; this suggests that whatever each of these measures is measuring (e.g., respiratory activity, pupillary diameter, vasomotor responses, electrocortical activity, etc.), each one is measuring something separately from the others, in addition to the commonality that exists. The implications here are that while there may be a general-arousal state, there are also specific-arousal states (Lacey, 1950).

2. A simple self-report of arousal, either estimated in a general subjective sense (Dermer and Berscheid, 1972) or measured by an adjective checklist (Thayer, 1967), may correlate more highly with physiological measures than the physiological measures correlate with each other. In addition, such simple self-report measures seem to be able to meet fairly demanding construct-validity criteria of the type we shall be discussing in Chapter 6 (cf. Dermer and Berscheid, 1972; Thayer, 1967).

Do these results mean that activation-arousal theory, as we have discussed it here, is better thought of as a psychological theory than a physiological one? Does it mean that here, as in Hull's theory, the effort to tie psychological variables to a physiological base has not been successful and that we had best proceed, at least as of now, with a psychology of activation-arousal, rather than an approach based in both disciplines? With further development and testing of the psychological measures of arousal, answers to these questions may be forthcoming.

ACTIVATION-AROUSAL THEORY: THE RESEARCH EVIDENCE

This, then, is the activation-arousal theory framework for the understanding of motivational processes. Part of it is a consistency model, postulating behavior designed to achieve a level of arousal consistent with the level of arousal to which one is acclimated and that is in balance with one's previous experience. Part of it is a theory of a radically different type in that it utilizes both the arousal level of the organism and other conditions of the specific demands of the time, such as task expectancies and the like, in order to predict behavior. Together, a very intriguing system for predicting behavior under different environmental conditions appears to have been generated.

The dilemma, however, is that there are a considerable number of logical, methodological, theoretical, and measurement questions that can be raised about the approach, questions that need to be resolved if a better-articulated theory is to develop. The necessity for such development will become even clearer as we now turn to a review of the relevant research in this area. It is probably because these logical and methodological problems have not been resolved that the research findings are as inconclusive as we will show them to be.

One clearly obvious trend of evidence relating to the theory, which must be cited despite its relatively unsatisfactory nature, is all the research we have previously discussed in reference to Hullian theory. Thus, it is supportive of activation-arousal theory that, under some conditions, stimulus arousal (e.g., food deprivation, thirst, etc.) leads to efforts at stimulus reduction. Similarly, there is all the research we have cited as negative evidence for Hullian theory showing that under some conditions organisms will seek stimulus arousal. Both of these groups of experiments provide evidence of a sort for arousal theory, but it is evidence of a very poor nature since antecedent measurements were not used in order to classify the individuals involved into preferred states of arousal (i.e., high or low) prior to the behavior studied. Hence, there was no real prediction involved and the findings cannot be considered to be of very great value, pro or con, in assessing the usefulness of the activation-theory framework.

Evidence of a slightly better nature comes from those studies where organisms are placed in environments that can be considered to be extremely dull and lacking in stimulation by realistic social consensus. There is evidence, as Scott (1966) has pointed out, that the introduction of variety into these dull, repetitive environments has led to increased task performance, a finding that lends support to the lower part of the U-shaped curve hypothesis. In Table 4.4 we have listed some of the experiments that Scott cites in support of this derivation and others that have appeared since his paper. The problem, of course, is that these studies have not involved measuring the subjects as to their preferred arousal levels prior to the particular experimental induction. Hence, some ambiguity in any interpretation of these results must remain, particularly since there are no data indicating either support or rejection of the high part of the U-shaped curve.

A third line of research evidence relating to the arousal hypothesis, in this case to its theoretical balance aspects, concerns research relating to the desire and willingness to engage in creative forms of behavior. Thus, if we define creativity as engaging in a new, useful behavior (i.e., something that varies from previous behavior in such a manner that it has social utility), research findings on the antecedents of this behavior have relevance here. This research has indicated that, in general, there is considerable evidence to suggest that the motivation to be creative (i.e., to engage in varied forms of behavior) is, in part, a function of the extent to which one has engaged in varied forms of behavior in the past and the extent to which one has not been in a social-psychological environment that has encouraged routinization, specialization, and the "sameness" of behavior (Korman, 1971a). Thus, since one's normal activation level is, in part, a function

Table 4.4 Summary of Studies on the Effects of Introducing Some Variation into Environments that Can Be Classified as "Dull" by Social Consensus

Finding	Reference
A telephone message in the latter part of a clock-monitoring task leads to similar performance to that engaged in by fresh students.	Mackworth (1950)
Experimenter presence reduces the decrement in visual tasks of a prolonged task.	Fraser (1953)
There are fewer performance decrements when there are more signals to respond to.	Deese and Ormond (1953); Holland (1958); Jenkins (1958)
Performance decrements tend to occur more in simple vigilance tasks than in complex tasks with many stimuli to respond to.	Frankman and Adams (1962)
People engage in and complete their shopping tasks more quickly, with no loss in satisfaction, when noise is introduced in a real supermarket setting.	Smith and Curnow (1966)
Performance in monotonous tasks is increased by introducing noise and variety into the environment.	McBain (1961); McBain (1970)

of one's experience, such evidence can be considered in keeping with the general prediction that organisms seek outcomes in balance with one's normal arousal or activation level.

Fourth, there is a line of evidence supporting the idea that decreasing stimulation to virtually a zero level (i.e., below anybody's adaptation level) will lead to the development of hallucinations and self-stimulated increases in stimulation (Baxton, Heron, and Scott, 1954).

Fifth, there seems to be increasing evidence that individuals differ systematically and consistently in their preference for levels of stimulation. For example, there are data to support the conclusion that the stimulus-seeking scale (Zuckerman et al., 1964) predicts preference for visual complexity, drug and alcohol usage, varied forms of heterosexual activity for both sexes, and hallucinatory activity for females (Zuckerman, Neary, and Bustman, 1970). In addition, the fact that scores on the scale vary positively as a function of educational attainment would seem to support also the general conclusion that stimulus-seeking behavior is a balance process, reflecting the degree of stimulation to which one has been exposed in the past (Kish and Buisse, 1968). Other evidence supporting these conclusions is presented in Table 4.5.

Sixth, there is physiological support for the notion of general arousal in the work of Grossman (1967). Reviewing much of the research on the reticular and limbic functions in the brain, Grossman is led to suggest that the notion of drive state, as it has developed in psychological theory, may be, in essence, the deviation of some physiological process from its optimal point and that such

Table 4.5 Research Investigations Supporting Prediction that There Are Consistent Individual Differences in the Levels of Stimulation Sought

Summary	Investigator
Individuals who scored high on a need-for-stimulation test (a) preferred interesting stimuli, (b) paid attention to complex verbal communication, (c) talked a great deal in group interaction, and (d) showed high levels of activity in stimulus situations of high deprivation.	Sales (1971)
Individuals with previous training in music prefer tone sequences with larger amounts of stimulus variation than those with little previous training.	Vitz (1966b)
Organisms choose behaviors in terms of the psychological complexity of the alternatives, with the behavior being chosen that which is closest to its optimal level of complexity. Psychological complexity is a function of (a) the stimulus complexity of the behavior involved, (b) its arousal properties, (c) the frequency and recency in which it has been engaged, and (d) the selective readiness for the behavior involved.	Walker (1964)

deviation stimulates neural and/or chemical signals, which in turn affect behavior, general and specific. Grossman suggests that this line of thinking would account for such variables as thirst, hunger, anxiety, and man's need for a constant level of stimulation.

Seventh, as Table 4.6 indicates, there is research supporting the prediction that there is an inverted U-shaped relationship between stimulus complexity and

Table 4.6 Research Investigations Supporting Prediction that There Will Be an Inverted U-shaped Relationship Between Stimulus Complexity and Preference, Ignoring Individual Differences in Preferred Complexity

Summary	Investigator
The relationship between preference and stimulus-complexity ratings of slides of natural environments and representational modern art showed a curvilinear relationship, reaching a maximum at an intermediate point of complexity.	Wohlwill (1970)
The relationship between preference and black line drawings varying in stimulus complexity showed a curvilinear function.	Vitz (1966a)
The relationship between preference and tones varying in stimulus complexity showed a curvilinear function.	Vitz (1966b)

liking for the stimulus. This, of course, is support for the general framework if we assume that liking for a situation is directly related to the behavior in the situation. While this seems to be a reasonable assumption at first glance, it is by no means one that is easily supported. Thus, there is good evidence that such a relationship between liking and the adequacy of task behavior in a given situation may vary greatly as a function of such variables as the other alternatives available (March and Simon, 1958), the measure of performance used (Vroom, 1964; Korman, 1971b), and the self-esteem of the person involved (Korman, 1970).

Given all of these lines of different research bearing on activation theory, our rationale for our previous statement that the research is quite unsatisfactory becomes clearer. Basically, the problem has been that the research has tested only "high" or "low" parts of the activation dimension and its relationship to behavior, a procedure that only leads to ambiguity of interpretation. What is needed is a comprehensive research program that tests the theory in both its aspects within a integrated approach. As a bare minimum, it should provide antecedent measurements of individual differences in preferred arousal level, measurements of the arousal level of the various outcomes that organisms might be motivated to achieve, and some specific task variables that are presented at different levels of known arousal. Individuals could then be presented with either (a) tasks they wish for by choice and/or (b) tasks they would be required to perform. There is no program that has met all of these requirements known to the author at this time.[2] Admittedly, these research requirements and the other questions we spoke of earlier are not easy to resolve, both in an absolute sense and, as we have indicated, also in a conceptual sense. Yet they need to be dealt with, if the model is to be adequately tested and if activation-arousal theory is to actually achieve its promise in the study of motivational processes. Without such resolving, the unsatisfactory situations we have spoken of here will continue to persist.

SUMMARY

The goal of this chapter was to show that the failure of the Hullian approach did not deter those who operate in the natural-science, physicalistic, objective tradition from trying to develop a theory of motivational processes. The activation-arousal approach tries to account for (a) the fact that people sometimes try to increase as well as reduce stimulation and (b) the observation that people differ systematically as to what the desirable types of stimulation are. An additional advantage in its basic postulation (i.e., that there is an optimal level of stimulation that people seek, which, once attained, leads to more effective behaviors) is that the postulation of biological utility as a rationale for behavior is not assumed.

---

[2]The Vitz (1966b) study comes closest to this requirement, but even here, experience rather than measurement is used for inferring individual differences in preferred arousal level.

Despite these advantages, however, the activation-arousal model of motivation has problems of its own. One of these problems is that by the term *arousal,* it is not certain sometimes whether we are talking about psysiological arousal or a psychological variable. While the two are sometimes related, they do not have to be, since it is comparatively easy to show that the same experimental variables lead to different results as a function of psychological influences. Complicating this problem is that there are several types of physiological arousal and that, while related, they are not the same. Furthermore, until recently, there were few measures of physiological arousal that were known to be related to meaningful human behaviors; this, however, may be changing. Finally, the adoption of a curvilinear model (i.e., the postulation that there can be either too much or too little activation and that the optimal amount is somewhere in the middle) poses significant problems for research testing of the approach.

cognitive

approaches

to

motivation

THE EXPECTANCY - VALUE MODEL

We now turn to another approach to the study of motivation. It is similar to the work we have been discussing up to now in that the major motivational variables we will discuss here have also involved inferring individual characteristics as a result of certain specifiable antecedent operations that may be either experimental manipulations or life experiences, or both. Causative influence has then been attributed to these characteristics in the same theoretical sense as we attached causative characteristics to Hull's D and $_SH_R$.

However, there are also some important differences between what we have discussed previously and what will concern us here. Most important, many of the constructs used are of the type that Hull rejected. Thus, the frameworks we will discuss are of a cognitive, subjective nature, in that they include such types of variables as expectation, demands, values, and the like. A second difference is that the question as to the conditions under which the original impetus to or arousal of behavior develops was not, until recently, as great a source of interest and concern among the theorists we will discuss here as was the question of the direction of behavior. More recently, the primary concern with direction has remained, but arousal is now also treated in a systematic fashion. For example, one contemporary approach is to view the organism as always active, making behavioral-direction choices designed to achieve maximal outcomes. Behavior is viewed, therefore, as a continuing series of choices designed to obtain the best outcomes possible. Another difference is that in some of the cases the defining empirical operations for the psychological variables to which causal inferences are attributed have been psychological scale measurements, rather than experimental operations. This methodological difference is a significant one, since the problems of measuring motivational variables adequately are great indeed, and the basic methodological questions are different from those in experimental studies. This, as we will point out, has significant implications for the study of motivational processes.

EDWARD C. TOLMAN

About the same time as Clark Hull was developing his theoretical system at Yale University, a fellow psychologist at the University of California at Berkeley was developing an alternative approach to motivational phenomena, which for a good number of years served as a viable alternative to Hullian theorizing for many psychologists. In fact, it was the work of Edward Tolman that, probably more than any other single outside influence, served to spur the research that tested the various implications of Hull's theory, pinpointed the weakness in it, and led to the revisions of the 1950s. In addition to such tests of the Hullian notions, Tolman was also developing his own theory of motivational processes, a theory that had many of the characteristics to which we referred in the introduction to this chapter. We shall now turn to his work, and in addition, we will try to show how Tolman's approach led to the kinds of experiments that forced the revision of Hullian theorizing so that in terms of formal, logical properties, Tolman, Hull, and Spence were brought much closer together in their thinking. Nonetheless, some major differences continued to remain.

Tolman's approach toward motivational phenomena sees behavior as being initiated by various internal and external environmental cues and by disequilibrium situations of various kinds. These arousal conditions, though, are not further specified by Tolman since he is more interested in what happens next. Thus, the environmental cues then combine with other characteristics of the organism, such as his age, his previous training, his heredity, and his specific physical characteristics of the moment, to result in three major intervening variables. It is these intervening variables that are the major components of Tolman's theory, since it is to them that causality for the direction and persistence of behavior is attributed. The intervening variables to which he attributes importance are (a) demands for a specific goal, (b) the degree to which the goal is available or exists in the specific environment in which the organism finds itself, and (c) his expectancies of achieving the goal in the specific environment in which the organism finds himself. These three variables in turn determine an organism's direction and persistence of behavior until the goal is reached. Tolman's approach is outlined below in Table 5.1.

Table 5.1 Basic Framework of Tolman Model

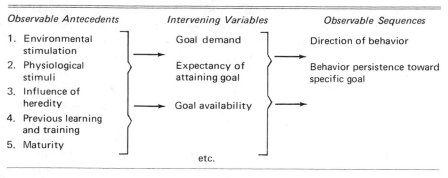

Observable Antecedents	Intervening Variables	Observable Sequences
1. Environmental stimulation	Goal demand	Direction of behavior
2. Physiological stimuli	Expectancy of attaining goal	Behavior persistence toward specific goal
3. Influence of heredity	Goal availability	
4. Previous learning and training		
5. Maturity	etc.	

At first glance, an examination of Tolman's major variables, such as demands and expectancies, connotes a much different point of view than a similar examination of Hull's work would yield. Terms such as these are not physicalistic and they are not palpable. Yet, Tolman was as much of an experimentalist as Hull and he followed the same procedures. He expended great effort in developing experimental procedures that would enable him to link his definitions of these concepts to physical operations that he could control as a experimenter. The more adequately he could do this, the more adequately he could test his theory, an argument the same as Hull's. How did he do it? One way was to suggest that, all other things being equal, demand for a goal could be inferred by the speed with which an organism attacked that specific goal. If we accept this statement, such goal behaviors (speed of attacking the goal) could be used as operational measures of demand for the goal. Once this was done, the hypothesized causal-agent variable (i.e., goal demand) could then be studied by manipulating the various antecedent conditions that determine goal demand. Such manipulations would then be studied for their effect on dependent (behavior) variables, which for Tolman were selectivity and persistence of performance of behavior. The H (heredity), A (age), and other variables outlined in the first column of Figure 5.1 are Tolman's antecedent variables, and once such antecedents had been mapped in terms of their effect on goal demands (i.e., speed of running in the specific experimental situation), they could be used in experiments as manipulable variables (or measured by psychological assessment techniques) because of their effect on goal demands. Hence, theoretical inferences could be made as to the significance of different goal demands on different kinds of behaviors. For example, Tolman argued that if you could show that level 3 of antecedent variable H led to twice as fast a response as level 5, you could then experimentally develop levels 3 and 5 in future groups and assume that the goal demand in the former is twice as great as the latter, all other things being equal. One could then look to see what effect goal demand would have on the selectivity and persistence of behavior.

Similarly, expectancies could be defined for Tolman in terms of the previous experiences of the individual. This simply meant that the more often an organism had engaged in a series of specific experiences, the more he built up a series of cognitive representations of what the world relating to those experiences was like. In addition, the more recently a person had engaged in a series of behaviors that had a certain set of outcomes, the greater the expectancy that behavior would lead to that outcome. To use the S-R language, Tolman argued that what an organism learned was that a given S-R led to a given S (i.e., he learned an expectancy). In this way, he could develop "high" and "low" expectancy groups on the basis of experimental operations and then determine the effects that differences in expectancy might have on the direction and persistence of behavior, all other things being equal. (That this process may not work the same way for all will be dealt with later in this chapter.)

Defined in this way, Tolman could lay claim to experimental rigor and, in fact, to a theory very similar to Hull's. In both cases, the theorizing involved the development of psychological constructs that were a result of certain antecedent, experimentally manipulable conditions to which they could be linked and which were in turn postulated to determine behavior. However, one difference was that Tolman brought into psychological theorizing such variables as demands, goals, and expectations, variables that Hull and those in his tradition had condemned as being mentalistic, nonrigorous, and not necessary for the scientific study of behavior. In addition, some of Tolman's intervening variables, which he suggested were reflected in behavioral choice and persistence, developed as a function of different life experience, not experimental operations. Despite the attacks that he was mentalistic and nonrigorous, however, it turned out that Tolman was right in his insistence that the persistence and selectivity of performance was both a function of the organism itself and its immediate environment (see Figure 5.1). Thus, if one wanted to understand behavior, one had to look at both antecedents, that is, the environment and the individual, and not just at the latter. It was precisely this mistake that Hull had made in 1943 and that he was forced to rectify in 1952 by the introduction of K. K is an incentive variable that reflects, in Hullian (and Spencian) terms, nothing more or less than the condition of the environment the organism is in at that particular time in terms of its reward potential characteristics (i.e., the expectancy of reward that the organism has there). However, expectancy in the two cases operates in somewhat different ways. For Hull and Spence, environmental expectancy arouses behavior by adding to drive (D) and directs behavior by providing specific stimuli that activate appropriate directional habits. For Tolman, environmental stimuli may steer and direct behavior by their presence as goals to be achieved in order to satisfy existing demands. In addition, environmental stimuli may also determine expectancies by the degree of their similarity to other environmental conditions whereby specific goals had been sought and achieved in the past. In neither case, however, do these environmental stimuli act as arousal mechanisms in the sense that K does in the Hullian system.

There were other very significant positive aspects to the Tolman approach. For example, the latent-learning experiments were no problem to him. In fact, the original work in the area had been done by one of his students (Blodgett, 1929) as a test of Tolman's notions that what organisms learned were not connections between stimuli and response that were strengthened on the basis of physiological-need reduction. Rather, what was learned, according to Tolman, was an S_1-R_1-S_2 environmental linkage, that is, an organism learned that if he made a given response (R_1) to a given stimulus (S_1), then another stimulus (S_2) could be expected to occur. Given such learning, according to Tolman, behavior was a function of the S_1-R_1-S_2 associations that an organism learned. Once these associations were learned (i.e., the S_1-R_1-S_2 connections), Tolman successfully predicted that behavior would not be expected to occur when the goals and/or incentives to be achieved in the situation by behaving (i.e., the S_2) were insufficient. Rewards affect performance, not learning, a position that Hull and Spence eventually adopted. Given these characteristics of Tolman's theory, he could explain the latent-learning experiment in the following manner, as summarized by Atkinson (1964).

> During the unrewarded trials, the animals develop cognitive expectations of the consequences of turning left or right at each of the various choice points. After several trials in the maze, these forward-pointing expectations constitute a kind of "cognitive map" of the maze that is "refined" during each run. In the very early trials the animals' performance is presumably guided by very general expectations carried over from earlier occasions when it had demanded food goal-objects. The initial explorations of the maze are guided, in other words, by preliminary "cognitive hunches" or "hypotheses" as to what might lead to what in this unfamiliar situation, such "hypotheses" being a function of previous experiences and learning in similar environments. In Tolman's view, a hungry animal is always actively trying to find food. After developing a more refined set of expectations concerning what does lead to what in the maze, the animal comes upon food, a demanded goal-object, in the end-box of the maze. The next day, as a result of this recent experience added to the cognitive expectations of what leads to what which had been built up without reward in earlier trials, the animal has both a demand for food and an expectation of a food object in the end box when placed in the starting box. The combination of these two determinants accounts for the sudden change in selectivity of performance at each choice point. The animal now selects the "correct" response, which is the one that it expects will lead most quickly to the demanded goal object.[1]

[1] J. W. Atkinson, *An Introduction to Motivation*, p. 144. © 1964 by Litton Educational Publishing, Inc. Reprinted by Permission of Van Nostrand Reinhold Company.

In addition to this basic latent-learning experiment, there were other related studies done during the same period by Tolman's students that provided support for his notions. Thus, Simmons (1924) found that maze performance was best for those animals offered bread and milk as an incentive. Second in performance were those who had been offered sunflower seeds, while last were those who had been offered no incentive at all. This finding was consistent with Tolman's notions that, holding physiological drive constant, (a) animals that expected to find some incentive would perform better than those that did not expect to find any, and (b) animals that expected to find a "good" incentive (e.g., bread and milk) would perform better than animals that expected to find only a "fair" incentive (e.g., sunflower seeds). In addition, this experiment supported Tolman's notions that demand for a specific goal object was a function both of the characteristics of the organism (held constant in this experiment) and the characteristics of the goal object itself.

Other experiments during this time that showed the effect of different incentives on performance were by Elliott (1928, 1929a and b) and Tolman and Honzik (1930). In all of these experiments the logic was the same, in that effects on performance were measured as functions of differing kinds and qualities of outcomes, and in all instances the results were as predicted. That is, performance increases either as a function of the level and quality of incentive being offered (holding physiological states constant) or as a function of the physiological state of the animal, holding incentives (or outcomes) constant.

Basically, then, all of these studies could be cited as support for the usefulness of two of Tolman's main assumptions. First, it supported his claim that behavior was a result both of what the organism wanted and what he expected to find. In addition, it also supported his argument that one could describe behavior by using common everyday language. It was not necessary to use the physiologically oriented language of Hull.

> A rat running a maze; a cat getting out of a puzzle box; a man riding home to dinner; a beast of prey stalking its quarry; a child hiding from a stranger; a woman doing her washing or gossiping over the phone; a pupil marking a mental test sheet; a psychologist reciting a list of nonsense syllables; myself and my friend telling one another our thoughts and feelings. These are *behaviors*. And it is to be noted that in mentioning no one of them have I referred to, or, I blush to confess it, for the most part even known, what were the exact muscles and glands, sensory nerves and motor nerves involved. For these responses somehow had other sufficiently identifying properties of their own. And it is these other properties in which, as a behaviorist, I am interested. (Tolman, 1932, pp. 353-54)

Tolman's attitude, then, was clearly different from that of Hull. Although no less an experimentalist, and an animal experimentalist at that, Tolman was not interested in reducing behavior to physically defined, physiologically oriented concepts in the sense that Hull was. Notions such as demands, expectancy, goals, and ideas were perfectly acceptable in a science of behavior, Tolman thought, as long as they could be tied to observable antecedents and specifiable consequences. There was no need to develop implicit physically defined mechanisms (such as K) that occurred between observable environmental variables and observable behaviors when one could use psychological, behavioral variables as well. To use his own term, Tolman was interested in *molar* behavior, that is, the accomplishment and adjustment of organisms in particular environments, and not in the "molecular" units of behavior that make it up. For him molar behavior was purposive, docile (teachable), and cognitive, and it could be studied experimentally. It was one of the most important achievements of Tolman that he was able to transmit these attitudes and beliefs to others and thus set the stage for the great growth in experimental investigations of other constructs like achievement, affiliation, and similar kinds of nonphysically defined concepts. For these later investigators, also, a psychological theory of motivation could be developed by first conceptualizing a meaningful set of variables hypothesized to be of causal influence. These could be psychological, not physiological, in nature. Once this was done, the theorist could clearly specify what the observable antecedents were of each psychological variable and how these antecedents came to influence them. It was in this conceptual insistence on keying each construct to observable antecedents and consequences that Tolman had his salutory effect on those who came later.

Another positive aspect of Tolman's work was his view of persisting individual-difference characteristics between organisms as important, systematic variables that would be included within his approach. The fact of individual differences between organisms as determinants of response, holding environmental variation constant, is, of course, one of the pervading characteristics of all forms of life, and Tolman felt that such recognition had to be included in any theory of motivation. In other words, Tolman felt that what an organism (animal or human) did in an experiment was not just a function of how the experimenter varied the environmental conditions. Rather, it was also a function of who and what the organism was genetically, what his previous learning experiences had been, and other such individual characteristics. Here, also, Tolman departed from the natural-science tradition in that his view of the subject to be sutdied was not that of an inert mass, stimulated and activated to some type of motor activity as a result of treatment by the experimenter, in the same sense that physical materials in the physical sciences were affected by the treatment of the physicist and the chemist. Rather he saw the organism as a living, breathing animal, carrying with it into the experimental condition certain genetic endowments and a previous learning history that, in combination, had endowed him with certain skills, knowledge, emotions, expectancies, and consistent ways of evaluating different environmental outcomes. It was this type of individual, Tolman felt, who interacted with the various conditions of the experiment, and it was the result of this interaction that determined the outcomes, not one or the other alone. Thus, while it was true that Hull had made some allowance in his system for genetic ($_S U_R$) and learned ($_S H_R$) differences, the notion of persisting individual differences as a determinant of the effects of different experimental conditions had never been developed systematically by him (although there is every indication that he intended to do it at a later date). It was Tolman, actually, who made the first systematic attempt to integrate into one theory the logic of contemporary environmental determinants of behavior (e.g., experimental operations) and the logic of persisting individual differences in the kinds of goals sought, independent of specific environmental variation of the time, as joint determinants of behavior.

There was one other characteristic of Tolman's theorizing that was different from Hull's and highly important in nature but that we have more or less previously glossed over. We refer specifically here to the fact that Tolman's constructs were purposive and goal seeking in nature. Briefly, the point is that using such terms as *expectancies, goals,* and the like meant that one was adopting the position that events that had not occurred (i.e., the incentives and goals) were causing or determining the behavior activity. To psychologists of the Hullian persuasion, such purposive constructs were a perversion of the nature of causal processes since they seemed to be indicating that the consequence was a cause of the antecedent. Their preference was much more strongly for a strict antecedent-consequent system, and it was because of this orientation that they preferred to build such constructs as D, $_S H_R$, and K, constructs that involved specifiable physical operations that occurred prior to the behavior being studied (e.g., eating, drinking, etc.). Tolman, however, could point to the mixed success of D and K and go on to propose that the theorist was perfectly free to develop any type of construct he wished, as long as he could anchor it to observable variables under the control of and able to be manipulated by the experimenter.

Tolman's use of purposive types of constructs such as expectancies and goal demands remained a controversial feature of his work despite his argument, because it invoked in many the memory of William McDougall's work in the early years of the twentieth century, an approach that had come into some disrepute. However, such a comparison was not quite accurate since Tolman's approach to the development and testing of his theory differed greatly from that of McDougall's. The difference can be seen clearly if we examine the latter's pioneering work in motivational theorizing.

Starting from the years prior to World War I, the theoretical position that purposiveness and goal seeking were what distinguished behavior was argued very strongly by William McDougall, a British psychologist. As support for his argument, McDougall cited the common observations that behavior is persistent, that it is variable in overcoming obstacles to reaching goals, that it terminates when a goal is achieved, and that it improves with repetition. For these reasons, McDougall adopted the word *hormic* (a Greek word meaning "vital impulses") as being descriptive of the psychology he was proposing, a psychology he carefully distinguished from the more mechanical study of stimulus-response linkages. This latter area was concerned more with *how* the goals and purposes of the individual were achieved, a less fundamental question, he believed, than the study of the purposiveness and goal-seeking nature of behavior in and of itself.

For McDougall, writing at the same time as Freud and being subject to similar Darwinian influences, conceptualizing the basic mainsprings of behavior as being primarily biologically determined also became a natural starting point. Purposive or goal-seeking behavior, as he viewed it, was primarily a function of innate instincts (or propensities, as he called them), which might be combined by learning experiences into sentiments. These sentiments, in turn, might arouse and direct behavior in order to be satisfied. In Table 5.2 we have one of the several different lists of basic instincts that McDougall proposed from time to time.

Table 5.2 Examples of the Types of Instincts that McDougall Proposed and How These Combined into Sentiments

Instincts	*Sentiments*
Food seeking	Love for a woman Combination of Sex ⎤
Avoidance of noxious stimuli	Protective ⊢ Instincts Comfort ⎦
Sex	
Fear	
Curiosity	
Protectiveness (parental)	
Gregariousness	
Self-assertiveness	
Submissiveness	Patriotism Combination of Protective ⎤
Anger	Self-assertiveness ⊢ Instincts Anger
Appeal	Appeal ⎦
Constructiveness	
Acquisitiveness	
Laughter	
Comfort	
Sleep	
Migration	
Simple body functions	

According to McDougall, instincts, such as those listed in Table 5.1, include at least three parts. First, each involves a receptivity to certain stimuli. Second, an instinct involves a disposition to behave in certain ways rather than others. Finally, it has an emotional component, a component that constitutes the core of the instinct. As evidence for the fact that the emotional aspect is the core of the instinct, McDougall argued that the first and second aspect of each instinct (i.e., the receptivity component and the behaving component) might change as a function of learning, but not the emotional component. Thus, as a person matures, an instinct might be activated by different sorts of stimuli, and once activated, it might be exhibited in increasingly different ways. However, the emotion involved remains the same.

McDougall's theory was a very important one for his time, but it eventually came under the very heavy criticism that shows McDougall's approach was very different from that of Tolman. One of these criticisms had to do with how McDougall conceptualized and defined his independent variable, that is, his innate instincts or propensities. Basically, the dilemma was with how these causal variables were to be either experimentally manipulated and/or measured and defined independent of the behavior they were designed to predict. As we will recall, Tolman was very careful to meet this necessary methodological requirement. Obviously, one could not explain aggressive behavior by appealing to a basic instinct of aggressiveness and then cite as an example of this instinct the fact that the organism engaged in aggressive behavior. This is a circular definition, trivial in nature, and to quote an old saw, "you can't hardly lose that way." Clearly, there are requirements if individual characteristics of organisms are to be attributed systematic status as causal determinants of the arousal and direction of behavior. First, they have to be susceptible to definition and either experimental manipulation and/or empirical measurement independent of the bahavior they are to predict. This is a requirement. Secondly, ideally, such measurement should take place before the behavior being studied. For example, while it is possible to measure an individual on a relevant motive either concurrently or after the behavior to which a relationship will be determined, there is possible contamination involved here in that behavior engaged in could affect scores on the measure of the motive. Therefore, a predictive study is the more desirable procedure when this can be obtained. In all cases, however, an independent measurement of the motive is the crucial necessity. It is only in this way that a clearer conceptualization of the influences of independent variables can be developed, their interrelationships studied over time, and their systematic importance assessed more clearly. If this is not done, the results are likely to lead to circular reasoning of the type described, confusion in the number and type of individual-difference variables proposed as explanatory concepts, lack of knowledge as to their importance, and an inability to develop meaningful predictive hypotheses. However, McDougall and other "instinct" theorists of his era never did develop such independent conceptualizations and measurements preferring instead to offer continually revised lists of "basic instincts" as the determinants of the arousal and direction of behavior. Since there was, as a result, no way to confirm whether these instinctive behaviors actually existed by manipulation and measurement procedures designed to affect and assess them, the sole criterion possible became the judgment of the psychologist that such an instinct was basic as a cause of behavior. As a result, the early 1920s saw increasing lists of these basic instincts, numbering eventually in the thousands. It was no surprise, then, that the whole approach fell into ridicule and disuse, with most psychologists turning to approaches that stressed experimenter control of presumed causal determinants of behavior, procedures of the kind we have seen associated with Hull and Tolman. It is in stressing the necessity for coordinating all independent variables to antecedent, independent, empirical operations under the control of the investigator that Tolman's use of individual difference (I.D.) variables as causal determinants differed from that of McDougall. Hence, the fact that McDougall developed several lists of basic instincts or propensities during his career while Tolman really never concerned himself with such specific lists is really not very important, since none of McDougall's instincts, as he developed them, were investigated empirically (although, theoretically, they could have been). Similarly, those later theorists who have attempted to incorporate measures of persisting individual differences with experimental variation in predicting behavior have generally accepted Tolman's requirement that all postulated independent variables, be they basic instincts, learned motives, or both, must be coordinated to antecedent observables under investigative control, or they are not utilizable in a science of behavior.

A second problem with McDougall's approach is very similar to the difficulties previously mentioned in our discussion of the 1943 Hullian system and that is the lack of accounting for environmental effects on behavior. As the latent-learning experiments showed conclusively, the arousal and direction of behavior is only partially a function of organismic characteristics. Environmental variables (e.g., the degree of goal appropriateness available in the environment, the available incentives, etc.) may be crucial in determining behavior at any specific time, and any comprehensive theory of motivation must include both organismic and environmental variables operative at the time of behavior. Otherwise, like the 1943 Hull postulates, the theory is doomed to incompleteness as a framework for understanding behavior, a fate also true of McDougall's approach and others like it. Thus, even if we look at a more contemporary individual-difference theory of motives, one that is not subject to our first criticism of McDougall's, this second problem sometimes still occurs.

Consider one of the most significant, more recent examples of this type of theorizing, the work of Abraham Maslow (1954). While we will discuss him more fully in a later chapter, some comments about his work are appropriate at this point. Maslow has postulated that human-need structures are organized in a hierarchical system and that needs lower in the hierarchy must be fulfilled before needs higher in the hierarchy become salient. Thus, the interrelationships between the needs are specified (a further weakness, incidentally, of McDougall's theory). According to Maslow, first the physiological needs (e.g., hunger, thirst) must be fulfilled. Once this has taken place, the security needs become relevant as determinants of behavior. This is followed in turn by the social needs, the self-esteem needs, and finally the self-actualization needs. Furthermore, measures of the most relevant needs for a given individual at a given point in time can be developed in order to provide an antecedent measure of organismic tendencies prior to the behavior to be predicted. Given, however, that these characteristics of the Maslow approach have overcome the circularity problem of the McDougall theory, the fact remains that in strict empirical tests of the theory, there has been little or no support (cf. Hall and Nougaim, 1968). Why is this? The answer may be that there has been little or no systematic account taken of environmental variation in the kind and nature of incentives available. The fact that individuals have a high amount of need A does not necessarily mean that behavior reflecting this need will be exhibited if there is little or no expectancy of fulfilling need A in that environment (e.g., no incentives) or if the incentives available are not very great. Thus, it is not clear whether or not the need hierarchy proposed by Maslow is a meaningful one since environmental variables have not been systematically incorporated into the theoretical approach.

An Historical Note.   Returning to Tolman's system, it is significant to note that his work was not subject to this criticism, at least in a conceptual sense, since it does show the recognition that both person and the environment have to be studied if we are to predict the arousal and direction of behavior at any given time. In this sense, Tolman was the person most responsible for implementing in an experimentally testable fashion the ideas and arguments of the German psychologist Kurt Lewin, a very dynamic person who influenced many others besides Tolman. Lewin had been very interested in how one builds theories in psychology (rather than building an explicit theory himself) and as a result had introduced into the psychology of motivation the distinction between Aristotelian modes of theorizing and Galilean modes of thinking. In the former case, Lewin pointed out, the search for determinant antecedents of phenomena (e.g., behavior) was made by looking for the intrinsic properties of objects, in and of themselves. For example, if one wanted to understand why a person was aggressive, the Aristotelian mode of thinking would encourage him to look at the person himself, his basic characteristics, and the factors that influenced him to become the person that he was at that time. Such an approach would lead the psychologist to examine the history of the individual, the factors that influenced him over time, and the general developmental experiences to which he had been subject. In terms of our discussion in this book, this type of thinking would characterize to a considerable extent the work of psychologists such as Freud, McDougall, and the early Hull. That is, it was the approach of these individuals to develop their motivational theorizing by looking at the properties of the specific objects (in this case, the people involved) and then attempt to develop causal explanations and theories based on the developmental experiences to which they had been exposed over time.

There was, however, another mode of theorizing, Lewin suggested, which the physical sciences had had to adopt and toward which the psychology of motivation might also move. This mode of theorizing he called Galilean, after Galileo, and it was marked by a belief that one understood and eventually predicted an event by studying all the influences that came to bear upon the event. Thus, in an instance of aggressive behavior, Lewin proposed, one looked not only at the characteristics of the person committing the aggressive behavior, but also at the environment in which the aggressive behavior was committed. The reason was that people were not always aggressive in all situations. Rather, it was only in some situations that aggressive behavior was likely to take place, as opposed to others. Therefore, if we wished to understand the likelihood of aggressive behavior as a behavioral choice, we had to look at both the characteristics of the person and the environment, since it was likely that some combination of these was determining the behavior that was taking place. An adequate theory of motivational phenomena, Lewin suggested, was one that showed how, given certain persons and certain environments at a given point in time, certain behaviors were more likely to take place than others. Historical factors were important in influencing the development and characteristics of people, but one did not need to deal with these factors in developing a theory of motivational processes. All that one needed to know was the contemporary situation, that is, the given organism and his needs, the environment and its characteristics, and a way of conceptualizing and categorizing these phenomena in some meaningful way. With this basic knowledge and the appropriate tools for conceptualization, one could build a motivational theory concerned with the prediction of behavioral choice and direction.

Lewin, himself, never really advanced to this latter step but spent most of his career working out procedures for conceptualizing characteristics of people and characteristics of environments as interrelated units of an overall system, or *field,* a term he used to describe his approach. Such conceptualizations had to be made, Lewin insisted, because behavior was a function of the field existing at the time (hence the term *field theory*), and it was the field that had to be developed as a conceptual construct if behavior was to be understood and eventually predicted. We shall not deal here with Lewin's actual procedures for conceptualizing psychological variables, such as the person, his tensions, or the perceived environment as a determinant of behavior, since these techniques did not last and his use of the branch of mathematics known as topology was inappropriate. However, it is vital for us to recognize that Lewin's importance as a figure in the psychology of motivation remains overwhelming. It was he who proposed the famous programmatic equation

$$B = F(Person, Environment)$$

and it was his insistence that both the person and environment had to be considered that led to the development of motivational theories that included both as influences on the arousal and direction of behavior. As a result of his work, for many psychologists the study of motivation involves studying the characteristics of people and the characteristics of the environment where the behavior takes place. The subject's motives and his perception of the environment are considerations to be studied, as are the incentives available and his expectancies of achieving them. We have already seen the influence of this way of thinking in Tolman's work, and we will be running into it frequently in the work of other famous motivational theorists such as Atkinson, McClelland, and Rotter. The major difference between these later motivational theorists and Lewin is not in the conceptual framework used, but rather in how to key the various psychological variables to specific empirical variables under the experimenter's control and in the need for predictive studies. Lewin also saw the necessity for such operational constructs and laboratory studies, but he, himself, never advanced to this stage in the development of a theory of motivational processes. It was up to these later individuals to take this step.

Tolman: A Summary

Given all the positive aspects of Tolman's work that we have indicated, however, it must be recognized that he by no means left a complete or perfect system. Far from it, for there were some very serious weaknesses that Tolman, himself, was among the first to recognize. One of these was that Tolman never did develop any clear statement of how his crucial antecedent variables were interrelated. Thus, if we assume that behavior at a choice point is a function of the demands of the organism, the values or goals available in the environment, and the expectancy of goal attainment, is the relationship multiplicative or additive? The differences may be crucial in predicting behavior. If the first were the case, it would suggest that no matter the ease of attainment, a nonvalued outcome would never be sought with relevant behaviors. In other words, if the value of the expected outcome equals zero, then no behavior would take place in an expectancy-value framework, whatever the level of the expectancy, if we assume a multiplicative model. In everyday terms, sometimes we do *not* "want what we can get." On the other hand, if the relationship were an additive one, the opposite would be true. That is, we would want and try to get whatever we could (or expect to) get, valued or not. Which is the more accurate model? Or, a more likely question, under what conditions does one model hold and under what conditions does the other hold? The question is an important one in understanding and predicting behavior. However, Tolman never explored this question very much. (It may be noted that while most of the later theorists have postulated a multiplicative relationship, not all have, and the question is still an open one.) In a related aspect of this problem of how experimental variables combine with one another, Tolman never developed any explanations of the forms of the relationships between the experimentally manipulable antecedent variables that presumably determined organismic demands. For example, how does hunger combine with age? Does increasing hunger mean the same thing for a teen-ager as for a person of forty? It seems doubtful. Does a three-month sexual deprivation mean the same to a twenty-three-year-old as to a seventy-five-year-old? This seems doubtful also. Yet, Tolman never really dealt with these questions. In this sense, Tolman's theory remained a programmatic one, rather than one where the relationships between the significant variables on both an experimental and conceptual level were carefully specified.

A second major problem with Tolman's work was that he never really worked very much on the individual differences in demands and needs that he had utilized as constructs in his system. He did not develop any systematic way of apportioning demands and needs to those instinctual in nature as opposed to those learned, as McDougall did. Similarly, he did little toward answering questions as to the existing number of significant individual determinants of goal-seeking behavior. How many instincts were there? How many learned goals were there? What kinds were there? Did this vary according to the kinds of individuals and/or organisms being studied? How could each of these determinants of behavior be measured and conceptualized in a manner independent of the behavior they were designed to predict? How did such individual differences in these determinants of behavior develop? All of these questions were relevant to Tolman's approach to theory building, yet few of them were dealt with by him. It was not until later years that these questions began to be answered in the work of the psychologists whom we will be discussing under the heading of contemporary expectancy-value theory.

Finally, Tolman never provided an explicit rationale for the arousal of behavior. The reader will recall that Hull postulated that behavior took place when biological utility demanded it or when some symbolic stimuli that elicited fear of biological difficulty occurred. Briefly, when the organism was in biological danger due to lack of food, drink, the occurrence of pain, or some symbolic representation of such situations, behavior designed to reduce the danger took place. Similarly, the arousal theorists viewed arousal as stemming from deviation from optimal-arousal level and task demands. Tolman, however, never had any such comparable concept, except for a disequilibrium notion never fully developed. The motivational concepts that underlie his rationale are directional in nature, for example, food deprivation leads to food seeking, pain leads to withdrawal from stimuli, desire for achievement leads to achieving behavior, affiliation desires lead to affiliative behavior, and so on. The problem is that Tolman never really made clear as to when and under what conditions these directional determinants became operative as arousers of behavior. For example, when a value is available and an expectancy is high, what are the conditions that will lead the demand or motive variable to be stimulated into action? Under what conditions will the actual behavior take place (e.g., when does affiliative orientation actually lead to behavior)? On the other hand, when will the organism be lost in thought, so to speak, so that behavior will not take place even though values and appropriate expectancies are available? How high does the affiliative motive have to be to kick off behavior? Or is the key arousal determinant the environment? If so, what are the key characteristics that actually stimulate the behavioral act? The closest Tolman came to dealing with these questions was his periodic proposal of an innate hedonistic tendency as the basic arousal mechanism, a postulation unsatisfactory on at least two counts. The first of these deficiencies centered around its failure to specify the conditions under which an organism is in a state of hedonistic distress and thus motivated to seek more satisfactory situations. Second, it did not define what was meant by "pleasant" and "unpleasant" situations in a hedonistic sense, independent of the behavior taking place (i.e., it did not specify why certain kinds of outcomes have "pleasant affect" and why others do not). It was not until a later time that theorists working in the expectancy-value framework began to deal with problems of this nature and came to be able to handle them within an expectancy-value tradition.

CONTEMPORARY EXPECTANCY-VALUE THEORY

Some Integrating Trends

During the last several decades, particularly since World War II, there have been a considerable number of theorists who have worked on expanding the logic of the expectancy-value approach to new areas and on overcoming some of the problems noted in our previous discussion. In all of this work, the basic position has been to argue that behavior is a function of both the characteristics of the person at the time (i.e., his needs and demands) and the characteristics of the particular environment of the time as it is perceived by the behaving individual; or restated, behavior is a function of the expectancy of value attainment at that time and in that particular environment and the actual degree of value (or incentive) that is available. In Table 5.3 we have listed the frameworks of some of these theorists. Upon examination one notes the resemblances between each of them and their relationships to both Tolman and Lewin's programmatic equation that B (behavior) results from or is a function of both P (person) and E (environment), a resemblance also noted by others (cf. Atkinson, 1964). With exception, all the theorists listed in Table 5.2 are really talking about the same thing and the same way of looking at motivational phenomena, even though the range of content they have studied has been quite broad. (The exception is Rotter's preference for an additive, rather than multiplicative, relationship, a question that is still an open one, as we noted earlier.) All of these are equivalent to one another in arguing that the likelihood of actually behaving in order to achieve values available in the environment is a function of the expectancy of achieving the valued goal, a relationship we can picture (see

Table 5.3 Summary Table of Expectancy-value Theorists

Theorist	Major Motivational Constructs			Resultant
Lewin et al. (1944)	Subjective probability of achieving desired outcome	X	(Valence) Value of desired outcome ⟶	Force
Tolman (1955)	Expectation of achieving desired outcome X	Demand level for given outcome X	Level of given outcome ⟶	Performance vector
Edwards (1955)	Subjective probability of achieving desired outcome	X	Utility of desired outcome ⟶	Behavior choice
Rotter (1954)	Expectancy of achieving desired reinforcement	X	Value of reinforcement ⟶	Behavior potential
Atkinson (1966)	Probability of achieving desired outcome X	Motive level for achieving desired outcome X	Incentive level of desired outcome ⟶	Resultant motivation
Vroom (1964)	Expectancy of achieving desired outcome	X	(Valence) Value of desired outcome ⟶	Force
Porter and Lawler (1968)	Probability of achieving desired reward	X	Value of reward ⟶	Effort

p. 108), if we assume that the degree of motivation for the value is the same for both individuals.

The reader might note in viewing this diagram that here, as with Hull, a theory that assumes a basic utility-maximizing rationale for behavior is still able to predict that, under at least some conditions, behavior will not be designed to achieve desired values and may, in fact, be self-defeating. The case in which this would take place, according to expectancy-value theory, is, as the figure indicates, the low-expectancy situation.

In addition to the fact that expectancy-value has proved popular among theory-oriented investigators, the logic of the approach has also been found valuable and is very popular with those psychologists whose interests have been

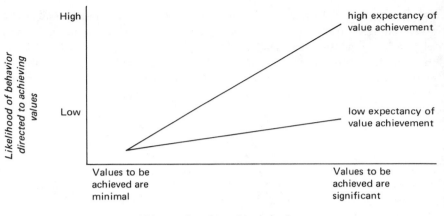

Values to be achieved by behaving

more in the content, applied areas. For example, Irwin Katz (1964, 1968) has found this approach of value in his research into the low-achievement behavior of minority-group members. He and others (cf. Clark, 1967) have argued that such behavior might be due to the prevailing low expectancies of value attainment inherent in the ghetto environment, rather than to differences in the value placed on achievement. These low expectancies, it is argued, are due to such factors as (a) the lack of successful models for children in ghetto areas to emulate in building up an expectancy system for themselves, (b) the increasingly technical and complex nature of employing organizations with its concomitant of increasing job difficulty, a situation for which the ghetto dweller particularly feels inadequate, and (c) the fact that most minority-group members live in urban areas of the country where the problems have become so overwhelming that low expectancies for value achievement are becoming very much the norm for all residents, regardless of group status (minority or other).

Similarly, as our inclusion of Vroom and Porter and Lawler in Table 5.3 implies, the expectancy-value framework has been found to be of value in explaining and understanding the commonly found lack of responsiveness to incentives offered by today's large work organizations. It is suggested that low expectancies and lack of value-oriented behavior have become increasingly the case because their large size, complexity, and pyramidal structure seems to encourage lower expectancies for success, the lower one goes in the organization. Thus, House (1971) has recently summarized data that indicate that managers who increase expectancies get increased responsiveness to incentives.

To return to theoretical considerations, it may be worthwhile for us to ask at this point whether this approach can in any way be coordinated to the Hullian and arousal-system frameworks we discussed earlier. Consider Table 5.4.

An examination of the above shows some convergence among the various frameworks, but also some differences. Thus, all of the frameworks view

Table 5.4 Personal and Environmental Determinants of Behavior in Different Motivational Frameworks

	Determinants of Behavior		
Theoretical Framework	Personal (Organismic) Characteristics	Form of Relationship Postulated	Environmental Characteristics
(1) Expectancy-value	(1) Personal motives or demands	X	(1) Expectancy of value achievement in given environment (as perceived by behaving organism)
	(2) Generalized expectancies for value attainment	X	(2) Level of value available in environment (i.e., incentive) (as perceived by behaving organism)
(2) Hull (1943)	Drive X Habit		
(3) Hull (1952)	Drive X Habit	X	K (incentive)
(4) Spence (1956)	[D (drive) + K] X Habit	X	[K (incentive) + D]
(5) Activation-arousal	Deviation from optimum arousal		Contemporary task and/or environmental demands

Note: Our reason for listing expectancy of goal achievement as both an environmental and personal variable reflects the fact that generalized expectancies for value attainment may be and are carried from situation to situation as a relatively enduring personality characteristic.

motivational processes as being a function of both the characteristics of an individual at the given time and the environmental situation that obtains at the time. Similarly, while all of the frameworks accept at least some physiological base for their conceptualizations, they are all psychological theories in that their constructs can be and are measured psychologically. Thus, we can investigate and evaluate the viability of these approaches from a purely psychological point of view, and not concern ourselves particularly with physiological or sociological aspects of motivation. As we have said, it is not that these latter questions are unimportant. It is just that these matters are not a focus of our concern here. (We might also note that finding support for physiological conceptions of motivational processes, crucial though it is at that level, may or may not be relevant or important at this time for an understanding of the psychology of motivation. The point is that the seeking of an adequate understanding of motivational processes may proceed at several different levels, and while one level should not deliberately ignore the knowledge of the other, neither is it the case at this level of our knowledge that any one level is any more important than any other.)

In a general sense, the frameworks show differing patterns and types of similarity to one another, depending upon which are being compared. For example, the expectancy notions and the *K* variable are highly similar to one another, in that they attempt to account for the fact that previous degree of value attainment in a particular environment influences the likelihood of behavior designed to achieve that value. On the other hand, while activation-arousal theory does not have an expectancy variable in its framework in any systematic fashion, it is similar to the Hullian notions in that it includes a general-arousal variable as the original stimulant to behavior. However, its general-arousal agent is somewhat different from Hull's *D* in that it may arouse behavior designed to increase stimulation in some situations and decrease stimulation in others, depending on whether contemporary arousal is above or below the optimal level. *D,* however, is hypothesized to activate only stimulus-reducing behavior. In another direction, the motive that has been aroused in expectancy-value theory has traditionally been directive in character, serving as a spur toward the achievement of specific kinds of goals, while responsibility for the direction of behavior in the Hullian system was given to stimulus-response habits activated by a general-arousal agent. It might be noted, however, that some increasing similarity is developing here also, in that while habit has not traditionally been part of expectancy-value theory, it has been suggested by Atkinson (1964) and Birch and Veroff (1965) as a concept that ought to be incorporated into this type of approach. Both of them have suggested that such a concept is necessary since, given a specific value and a specific expectancy in a given environment, certain behaviors are chosen as being more appropriate for achieving the value at that time than others. An example of this might be that the child who wishes to improve in his algebra and whose expectancy is fairly high that he can do so is more likely to open his book and study than he is to swing a baseball bat at that time. Thus, both have suggested that a concept such as habit as a partial determinant of behavior directedness is as desirable for a complete expectancy-value theory as it is for the other approaches. As a result, Atkinson (1964) has proposed the following equation:

Behavior is a function of (Motive X Expectancy X Value X Habit)

This, of course, has made the similarity to the Hullian approach even greater.

Some Theoretical Advances

In addition to the fact that contemporary expectancy-value theory has shown strong integrating trends within itself, it has also moved toward theoretically significant advances in at least two major areas. First, there has been a trend in expectancy-value theorizing to more clearly define the characteristics of individual needs and motives as systematic influences on behavior. This is particularly important if both needs and motives are to be fully specified, conceptualized, and measured as theoretical constructs. Secondly, the whole question of examining the arousal of behavior, a long-standing problem in expectancy-value theory, is now being dealt with in an increasingly satisfactory fashion. It is these advances that we will discuss here.

The manner in which contemporary conceptions of needs and motives have become developed as constructs in motivational theorizing can, like anything else, be traced to historical antecedents. Thus, while it is primarily the work of David McClelland that will concern us here, since it was through his efforts that the concept of motive first came to be brought under experimental control and then studied more completely for its influences on behavior. Our discussion would be incomplete without showing how McClelland's work stemmed from that of Henry Murray, a Harvard psychologist interested in the psychology of personality. In this way, it will become apparent what a major contribution Murray made and how McClelland has been able to add significantly to this earlier work.

Murray's arguments involved a number of both content and methodological considerations. In considering content, he started from the assumption that individuals had motives and these motives had to be studied as arousers and directors of behavior. Secondly, it was Murray's belief that the key to the understanding of human personality would not come from the biological, physiologically based theories of Hull or from insistence on experimental verification of hypotheses in laboratory settings. Rather, it was his feeling that much of what was important in human personality would manifest itself in everyday life. Hence, motivational processes could most profitably be viewed as a function of individual needs and motives[2] as observed in naturalistic and clinical settings, with the laboratory not being eliminated but no longer assigned the primary role. Given this belief, Murray devoted considerable effort to arguing and defending the theoretical position that individual needs and motives, as manifested in normal human activities, were useful constructs to utilize when studying the psychology of motivational processes. Since Murray's arguments for such a stance are as relevant today as they were when he made them in the 1930s, and since individual needs and motives as arousal and directional agents of behavior occur in almost all expectancy-value theories, it may be worthwhile to consider some of his points at this time. Following our discussion of his rationale as to why individual needs and drives are important for a theory of

[2]The reader will notice in this context that we are using the terms *needs, motives,* and *drives* interchangeably. Basically, as the discussion on the following pages will show, constructs that are more human in nature (e.g., achievement, affiliation, etc.) are typically called motives today. However, at the time of Murray's original writings, they were called needs or drives (despite their lack of similarity to Hull's theories). This is why we are using the terms interchangeably here, although we will try to limit our terminology to *motive* when our discussion becomes more contemporary.

motivation, we will examine how the concept of individual needs and motives as systematic factors in understanding motivational processes is being dealt with today.

According to Murray (1937), a need or drive has both (a) a directional aspect that differentiates it from other needs, and (b) an arousal component that actually kicks the behavior off and that can be activated in a number of ways. However, the conditions under which the arousal component actually becomes activated in Murray's theorizing are not at all clear, a not uncommon failing in this early era of motivational theory of a more cognitive nature. It is in response to this problem that McClelland was to make one of his most significant contributions. A need, to return to Murray, is an invisible link; it is a hypothetical construct that occurs between a stimulus and a resulting action pattern; it is a factor that (when active) directs behavior toward certain end effects rather than others. Furthermore, this concept of the end state of behavior being more important than the specific behaviors themselves is useful in developing an adequate conceptualization of motivation on the human level for the following reasons:[3]

1. Physical survival depends on achieving certain outcomes, not on what behaviors are used.
2. Certain effects are universally attained by living organisms, but the behaviors that attain them vary greatly.
3. During the life of a single individual, certain effects are regularly attained but the behaviors involved change.
4. When confronted by a novel situation, an organism persists in its efforts to bring about a certain result, but with frustration it is apt to change its mode of attack; hence, the trend is the constant feature and the behavioral mechanisms utilized are the inconstant.
5. There are some effects that can only be attained by entirely novel behaviors (e g., as a rule, laughter is only evoked by a new joke).
6. That specific behaviors are secondary is shown by the fact that many biologically necessary effects may be brought about by another person (e.g., when a nurse ministers to the wants of a sick child).
7. Complex action is characterized by muscular contractions in widely separate parts of the organism, contractions which manifest synchronous and consecutive coordination. Such organization of movement must be partially determined by a directional process, which is what a need, by definition, is.
8. Presenting a desired end state (e.g., food) during a behavior sequence should not stop behavior if external stimuli were the only determinants of behavior. However, behavior does end when these sudden presentations of desired end states are made, suggesting that need and desired end state are the crucial determinants of behavior.
9. When a need is not in a state of readiness, responses to specific stimuli do not occur (e.g., animals recently fed do not commonly respond to food).

[3]The items listed have been paraphrased from Murray, 1937.

10. When a particular need is active, common objects in the environment may evoke unusual responses, that is, responses that promote the progress of the active need. Thus, the usual S-R connections may not be exhibited (e.g., an angry boy may throw an apple at an antagonist instead of eating the apple).

11. When a need becomes active, characteristic behavior will usually ensue even in the absence of customary stimuli.

12. It is difficult to interpret without a concept of directional tension experimentally demonstrable phenomena such as the resumption of unpleasant work after interruption; the repetition of once-active trends with different movements; the increase of striving after opposition.

13. There are conscious correlates of desires (conscious feelings of goals, pathways, etc.).

14. Among the commonest subjective experiences is the feeling of conflict between desires.

15. Because of its close connection with happiness and distress, a need is more "important" than a behavior pattern (a need does not cease and is not "satisfied," until "pleasure is experienced").[4]

16. Experience seems to show that a certain desire may sometimes give rise to a dream or fantasy and at other times promote direct activity; without the concept of an underlying drive, one could not adequately represent the obvious relationship between fantasy and behavior. (There is a good deal of evidence to support the view that, under certain conditions, fantasy may partially relieve the tension of a need. That is, it may be the equivalent action.[5] We will talk of the implications of this for the measurement of individual differences in motives in the next chapter.)

17. Introspection and experiment demonstrate that a need may determine the direction of attention and markedly influence the perception and appreciation (interpretation) of external occurrences; to influence sensory and cognitive processes, a need must be some force in the brain region.

Given, then, the general argument that individual difference in needs (or motives) can be viewed as desirable and, if we accept Murray's argument, necessary constructs in developing an adequate theory of human motivational processes, a number of questions remained to be answered. It is these questions that more recent research has begun to resolve.

One of the most significant of these questions, given the assumption that there are individual differences in motives on a relatively complex human level, pertains to how these motives develop. Why, for example, do people develop

---

[4]As we will see, one of the great advances of contemporary need theories has been their attempt to define in a noncircular fashion the nature of pleasure.

[5]The reader will recall that this type of behavior was postulated by Freud as primary-process thinking, which he thought consisted of the attempt to reduce instinctual stimulation without reference to the external environment.

high motives for such goal outcomes as task achievement, or inflicting harm on others, or having an orderly world? Such individual motive differences in the degree to which such goals are desired constitute the essence of Murray's argument, and it is legitimate to ask why they develop differently in people, a question really not any different from the one Hull tried to answer when he postulated a biological explanation for the development of drive. A second issue stemming from the adoption of individual motives as useful constructs in the development of a theory of motivational processes relates to the question of what these motives are aimed at achieving. If we assume that a motive is a desire to behave in certain ways in order to achieve pleasure, what do we mean by *pleasure* and why can one outcome be pleasurable for one person and another outcome pleasurable for another? Is there a common basis for pleasure as a desired outcome of behavior that can be defined independent of the behaviors designed to achieve it in the same sense that Hull used physiological-need reduction and its derivatives as a basis for motivational behavior? That is, in Hull's system, hunger, thirst, and the like motivated behavior in order to achieve a common outcome (at least theoretically), the survival of the organism. This was the rationale for Hull, the survival of the organism, and this is what all these different motivations are aimed at achieving. But what about achievement? Affiliation? Order? Certainly motives like those are not necessary for survival. But what are they aimed at achieving then? What makes them motives?

Perhaps the most comprehensive theoretical answer to these questions has been made by McClelland (1955), the essence of whose position can be summed up in the following statements:

1. A hedonistic explanation for the arousal of behavior is assumed; that is, it is assumed that individuals are motivated to seek pleasant affect and to avoid negative affect.

2. The degree to which a given environmental situation has pleasant or negative affect, and thus will stimulate either approach behavior or avoidance behavior, is defined in a noncircular fashion and stems from a discrepancy hypothesis. This hypothesis states that moderate discrepancies along any dimension of experience, either a single dimension or some combination of several dimensions, will lead to positive affect and, it follows, approach behavior. Large discrepancies, conversely, will lead to negative affect, and thus avoidance of the stimulus situation. The actual predictions of the discrepancy hypothesis will show a distribution resembling a butterfly (see p. 115).

   In the example shown here, dimensions of stimulus experience that are different from previous experience up to a score of +1.5 (these scores are purely illustrative) will kick off or arouse behavior designed to stay in or approach that stimulus situation, while stimulus situations that show a greater difference will stimulate behavior designed to avoid that stimulus situation.

3. Given this conceptual way of looking at what arouses behavior (thus providing McClelland's analogue to Hull's drive), it follows logically

The "Butterfly" Hypothesis

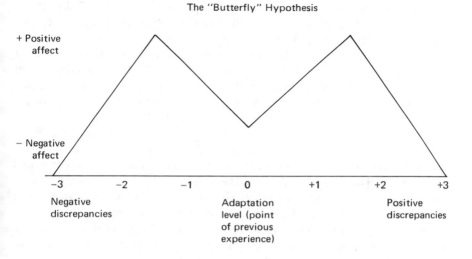

that humans are motivated to achieve end states that involve a moderate discrepancy from previous adaptation levels and to avoid end states that involve extreme discrepancies from previous adaptation levels.

If we define a motive, then, as a redintegration[6] by a stimulus cue of a change in the affect of a situation, we can summarize McClelland's argument by first making explicit his basic assumption that there is a desire to maximize positive affect and to minimize negative affect, and then stating his basic postulates that:

1. If the cue that is redintegrated in the specific situation has a positive-affect characteristic attached to it, in that the stimulus aspects evoked by the cue suggest moderate discrepancies from one's previous adaptation level, the behavior of the organism will be aroused and its direction will be to approach and stay in the given situation.
2. If the cue that is redintegrated in the specific situation has a negative-affect characteristic attached to it, in that the stimulus aspects evoked by the cue suggest extreme discrepancies from one's adaptation level, the response of the organism will be to avoid the given situation or leave it if one is already in it.

To use a concrete example, assume that it is possible to classify people as having differing levels of the achievement motive. According to this view, a

---

[6]The term *redintegration* in this context can best be defined as a reminder by a stimulus cue that a change in affect is going to take place. This type of arousal by a cue, as viewed by McClelland, and the ability by a stimulus to set it off, is a function of previous learning.

person with a high degree of achievement motive is one for whom achievement situations give off cues that suggest moderate discrepancies from his previous adaptation levels. He would, thus, be predicted to be motivated to approach, stay in, and, theoretically, behave more effectively in situations calling for achievement than those individuals with a lower degree of achievement motivation. These latter individuals would find such situations providing cues suggesting extreme discrepancies from previous adaptation levels and would therefore avoid and behave less effectively in them. Thus we can predict in a noncircular fashion (i.e., prior to the behavior taking place) that individuals with high-need achievement, as measured, will react differently to environments presenting opportunities for achievement than will individuals with low-need achievement. The reason is that for the former group, environments of such characteristics constitute low-discrepancy levels from previous environments and, hence, are sources of positive affect, a situation leading to approach behavior. On the other hand, such situations are sources of great discrepancy from previous environments for the latter group and thus stimulate negative affect, a situation leading to avoidance behavior.

Since we will, at a later point, be discussing the very considerable research relating to this hypothesis, we shall not spend any more time on it here. However, there is one more question for us to answer concerning McClelland and that concerns the development of motives. This question is a crucial one since, theoretically, there could be an infinite number of motives and since, according to the theory, anything that leads to affect, positive or negative, can become a motive. In order, then, to understand and eventually influence behavior, we should know how they develop. The major notion here, according to McClelland, is the contiguity principle. That is, stimuli that have been previously associated with positive affect come to stimulate approach behavior and those associated with negative affect lead to avoidance behavior.

In summary, then, considering its noncircular aspects and its consideration of the arousal problem, we can see how McClelland's theory is a major step, at least conceptually, in the development of an adequate expectancy-value theory of motivation. A further advantage is that McClelland's way of defining a motive does not have the problems we saw in Hull's K, in that here it is postulated that the stimuli associated with "affectual" outcomes only arouse behavior. They are not conceived of as reinforcers of behavior also, as they were in the Hullian system. The actual end goal of behavior here is defined differently and independently of the sources of behavioral arousal; the end goals are the attainment of moderate discrepancies from the previous stimulus adaptation level and the avoidance of extreme discrepancies. If, in fact, these end goals are achieved, then reinforcement (in the traditional sense) will occur, and only then. However, the likelihood of their achievement is a function of other variables such as environmental events and the like, as well as the person's motives and expectations. It is clear, then, that this type of conceptualization constitutes a theory of motivation that is noncircular in nature and that is, at least theoretically, experimentally manipulable and controllable by the experimenter. It is now theoretically possible in the expectancy-value approach to (a) control the development of a motive for a given type of outcome (e.g., achievement) by pairing stimulus cues from that outcome with moderate discrepancies from previous adaptation levels (e.g., by making achievement levels only a moderately discrepant mode of behavior from the environment that one is familiar with); (b) test whether a motive has developed or not by presenting the cue in a new context (e.g., put him in a new achievement situation by removing him from previous familiarity); and (c) change motives by pairing the relevant stimulus cues with different discrepancy levels from previous adaptation. The importance of these theoretical advances cannot be overestimated for socially significant purposes, as some of McClelland's recent work in increasing achievement motivation has indicated (McClelland, 1965).

Independently of McClelland, there has also been an attempt to account for the arousal of behavior by contemporary expectancy-value theorists in a manner that may have far-reaching implications for a wholly different view of motivation, if it develops significant research support. Hence, it needs to be very carefully studied. This view of behavior involves assuming organisms to be continually active, utility maximizing, and value seeking. In this view, the argument is that people are always seeking to get the most they can, given their rational expectancies about the world they know (Atkinson, 1964). Changing expectancies about the degree to which given goals may be attained by changing behavior leads to changes in behavioral direction, and so on. In addition, it is also postulated that the attainment of a goal reduces the value of that goal, thus increasing the likelihood that other behaviors will be engaged in since other incentives are now more valued (Birch and Veroff, 1965). The arousal problem is resolved in this view because, in essence, there is none. The view is that the organism is in a continuous state of arousal, and a theory of motivational processes becomes concerned solely with the prediction of behavior direction, as opposed to behavior arousal and direction. It then becomes necessary to understand the conditions under which a particular form of behavior will be persisted in and the factors that will lead to a change in the direction of that behavior.

It is very important to understand the implications of this view, as Atkinson (1964) has pointed out. For one thing, it means that the prediction of the likelihood of behavior of a given individual vis-à-vis a given environmental incentive has to include recognition of *all* of the influences on him at that time. If we view motivation as being concerned with predicting an organism's directive behavior, we have to predict both (a) when he will take off in a new direction, and (b) when he will not take off in a new direction (i.e., when he will persist in what he is doing). The prediction of his behavior then becomes one of inserting into our prediction equation all of the forces (i.e., motives, expectancies, and incentives) leading him to take a new direction, as opposed to all the forces leading him to persist in the old behaviors. While this would make a motivational theory more complex than what we have been dealing with up to now, this would not necessarily be a problem except for one other question, a question that may mean the theory is untestable at this point in our knowledge. This type of formulation means that the lack of support for a theory may mean either (a) that the theory is not supported, or (b) that we have failed to isolate all of the other motivational influences on the person that have led him to behave in a way we have not predicted. The only way we could choose between these alternatives is if we were sure we had isolated all of the other motivational influences on the individual, a conclusion we have no business making, considering the current state of psychological knowledge. It is for this reason that the approach may be untestable.

One other implication of the approach is that its view of the organism as constantly aroused and active means the concept of the stimulus (arousal) response unit as a behavior episode no longer makes any sense and would be dropped in motivational theorizing. This implication is a descriptive one and could easily be adapted if this new approach were a testable one and proved to be more fruitful.

Some Continuing Problems

Despite these advances in expectancy-value theory, a number of continuing problems with the approach have remained to this day, and it is in these areas that theoretical work will probably be concentrated in the future. In this section we will review briefly some of these continuing difficulties.

What is probably of most significance is the fact that there are simply too many cases where predictions generated by the theory are not supported. There are too many research studies in which people have been classified by their predominant motive pattern, have been provided an opportunity to achieve some significant values relative to their motives, and the resulting predicted positive behavior and affect has simply not occurred. As an example, Sheard (1970) has recently shown that preferences for work organizations were unrelated to the degree to which they provided work goals important to the individual. Similarly, Tosi (1970) has shown that satisfaction with a supervisor who emphasized participation in decision making on a job was unrelated to the degree to which a person desired this type of role. Since similar findings have been reported by Ewen (1965) and Wollack et al. (1971), it is clear that this is a serious problem for expectancy-value theory. To be more precise, this should not occur if expectancy-value theory is correct, and yet it does. Therefore, it must be accounted for in some way. One reason may be that people behave not only as a result of values they believe they can obtain from the situation, but also as a result of what they believe to be normal and appropriate for them at the time, independent of the personal values to be obtained. There are at least two theorists who have proposed such an extension (Dulaney, 1968; Fishbein, 1967), and research is now proceeding in order to test this approach. Another reason, not unrelated to this, may be that expectancy-value theory is useful only in those situations where the individual has control over his behavior. If he does not, then his expectancies of values to be obtained by different behaviors do not really matter. He can't behave in order to achieve these values anyway. Finally, in a later chapter we shall suggest a consistency model of behavior that, in essence, argues that at low levels of expectancy, personal values are neither motivators of behavior nor sources of satisfaction when attained.

A second continuing problem concerns the operational problems involved in testing the McClelland discrepancy hypothesis. Although it is, as we have pointed out, a major conceptual advance, there are some serious problems attached to it when we get down to the pragmatic business of doing research. One problem concerns that of testing a U-shaped hypothesis, in that Mc-Clelland's model predicts maximum behavior of approach at one point of the continuum and different behaviors at other points. For example, it is predicted that maximum approach is at one level (moderate discrepancy) and maximum avoidance at another level (extreme discrepancy). As we indicated in our discussion of arousal theory in Chapter 4, this type of hypothesis is untestable unless we have prior knowledge of the levels on the measuring operation we need to bring into the experiment. Thus, if the levels of discrepancy utilized are too high or too low, a proper test of the hypothesis cannot be made. This means that in addition to developing good conceptual predictions, we need good measurement of the key variables in the approach. However, measurement and operational specification of variables is a great problem here. Thus, there are many stimulus patterns (e.g., beautiful paintings, the smell of a skunk, etc.) that can and do produce affect within the organism. But along what dimensions can these affective experiences be scaled? To indicate the actual difficulty involved, consider the following:

> Actually, the discrepancy hypothesis deals with a relationship between affect and perceived discrepancies, not between affect and absolute intensities of stimuli even at the level of one sensory dimension. In other words, the perception of stimulus and its discrepancy from past stimulus events is what is called for by the hypothesis. A direct test of the discrepancy hypothesis as stated by McClelland demands psycho-physical scaling of the perception of differences along the perceptual dimension from some adaptation level. This scale forms the abscissa or independent variable in the typical schematic drawing of the discrepancy hypothesis. (deCharms, 1968, p. 129)

What this means is that the actual outcome being sought, that is, the moderate discrepancy (the source of pleasant affect, according to McClelland), is not measurable by any simple physical measure. Rather, the measurement procedure involved is to compute ratios of difference scores between current and past stimulation, an infinitely more complex procedure and one fraught with great potential for error.

In addition, there is also evidence that variations along simple physical stimuli may not produce affect, and that the discrepancy hypothesis applies only when each set of stimuli involve two or more dimensions (deCharms, 1968). This only makes testing the discrepancy hypothesis even more difficult in a measurement sense, since this means computing difference scores between multidimensional stimuli.

A third problem with expectancy-value theory is that much of it depends on the measurement of individual differences in motives so that systematic influences on behavior, if any, can be assessed. Since we will devote our entire next chapter to ways of measuring individual differences in motives, we will not dwell on these questions here except to point out that there are many difficulties in developing adequate measurement approaches for assessing motives and that these difficulties have meant severe problems for any theoretical system that must use such measurements in accounting for behavior.

A fourth continuing problem with expectancy-value theory concerns the fruitfulness of the expectancy construct as a key variable in the approach. If we assume that the fruitfulness of a construct is at least partially a function of the extent to which it is susceptible to experimental manipulation and control, the *internal-external control of reinforcement* hypothesis raised by Rotter (1966) some years back has some important implications in this context. Basically, the hypothesis, as originally proposed, suggests that people differ as to where they believe control of reinforcement is lodged. Thus for people high on internal control (IC), their belief system is that the attainment of reinforcement is due to their own efforts and under their control. On the other hand, for those high in external control (EC), their belief system is that the attainment of reinforcement is not due to their own efforts and not under their own control. In this latter situation, that is, when reinforcement is seen as based on chance forces over which the individual has no control, the person is predicted to learn less from reinforcement. In other words, if a person feels that success is determined by chance rather than by his own behavior, there is little rationale to utilize his outcome in a given situation in estimating his future expectancies of success in that given situation. Studies of people defined as holding internal, rather than external, beliefs have generally supported this hypothesis (cf. Rotter, 1966). For example, ICs are more likely to change expectancies more typically and realistically (i.e., increase expectancies after success and decrease them after failure), while ECs change their expectancies less, and less realistically, as a function of success and failure.

The question for us is how does one investigate expectancy-value theory and deal with external-control people, if they are not susceptible to feedback from their own behavior? One possible answer has been suggested by Gurin and Gurin (1970), an answer that is still not part of expectancy-value research:

The expectancy literature, the product of either social learning or cognitive psychologists, focuses too exclusively, perhaps, on schedules of reinforcement, task difficulty, feedback discrepancy, or cognitive aspects of personality as determinants of the course of expectancy change. Important as these factors may be, poverty programs concerned with expectancy change may also need to consider characteristics of the interpersonal situation in which the low-income, low skilled person begins to assess his chances for success. Opportunity changes generally are mediated by people – trainers in job training, employment counselors, teachers, job recruiters, political leaders, etc. Characteristics that make these people possible identification figures and credible to the poor may affect expectancy change as much as they affect permanance of other kinds of attitude change (Kelman, 1965), and as much as expectancy change follows from less interpersonal qualities of situations more typically examined in expectancy literature. This research direction connects with the conviction of many activities regarding the desirability, if not necessity, of involving community people as leaders and models in poverty intervention programs.[7]

As part of this general argument that expectation may change as a function of interpersonal evaluation as well as feedback from one's own behavior, these same authors have suggested (Gurin et al., 1969) that externally based expectancies may be as rationally predictable, understandable, and experimentally manipulable as internally controlled expectancies in that such perceptions of an externally controlled world may be highly veridical in nature. They cite the example of minority-group members who believe that their fates are controlled by power influences and not by themselves, a perception that is accurate in many instances. Viewing it in this way, then, expectancy-value theory might be able to handle the predictability of externally controlled people.

In another somewhat related direction, the expectancy construct is a difficult one to investigate empirically, in that there is good evidence to indicate that successful feedback from one's behavior may not affect expectancies of future success in similar tasks for reasons other than the internal-external control variable. Thus, the desire for consistent outcomes may lead one to regret and/or distrust and eventually ignore those outcomes inconsistent with one's prior cognition (Gurin and Gurin, 1970; Aaronson and Carlsmith, 1962).

In summary, the general point is that expectancy as a construct seems to be far more complex than was once originally thought, and much work seems to be necessary in order to uncover its antecedents and experimental determinants before it is brought under the kind of experimental control desirable in an adequate theory of motivational processes. Once this is done, more adequate tests can be made of its relationship to behavior, and we can then deal with

[7]G. Gurin and P. Gurin, Expectancy theory in the study of poverty. *Journal of social issues, 26,* 1970, 83-104.

other questions relating to the expectancy construct. For example, although some theorists see it as having a linear effect on behavior, others do not. An example of this is the need for achievement research, which we shall deal with in Chapter 8, where Atkinson states some conditions under which increasing expectancy decreases likelihood of performance.

Finally, there is a fifth problem with expectancy-value theory (and for that matter, with later versions of Hullian theory such as the Spence $[D + K] \times H$ model) and that is the nature of the "value" variable. As we have treated it here, the value of an outcome has been conceptualized as a function of the characteristics, needs, or motives of the individual and the amount of the value available in the given context.

However, there is possibly a very significant question involved here, and it stems from the implicit assumption in this statement that one value pretty much operates like any other in influencing behavior within an expectancy-value framework. That is, it is assumed here that there are really no differences between such values as money, achievement, social approval, and similar types of outcomes in influencing behavior. If this is true, however, is there nothing unique about money as an outcome? Achievement as an outcome? Social approval as an outcome? Are they the same in terms of methodological implications? Measurement? We shall explore these questions more completely in Chapter 8 where they are of particular relevance to expectancy-value theories of achievement.

SUMMARY

Expectancy-value theory is the name most psychologists use today for the psychological theory of motivation most closely approximating traditional "economic man" models. Basically, the idea behind it has been that man will make those behavioral choices that will maximize his outcomes given the value of the outcomes he sees available to him, the kinds of outcomes he desires, and his rational expectancy of achieving those outcomes in that given situation. This approach also reflects the thinking of those psychologists who accept the desirability of conducting experiments involving the careful manipulation of variables in order to observe their efforts on various motivational processes. They differ, however, from the Hullians in that (a) they are quite willing to use subjective concepts, as long as these are firmly tied to experimental or clear measurement procedures, (b) they are willing to accept the fact of individual differences between people as reasons for behavioral direction, as well as the influences of the environment of the moment, and (c) they see man as being motivated by other considerations than those motivational variables linked to and stemming from Darwinian evolutionary considerations.

Our concerns in this chapter have been to trace the evolution of expectancy-value theory from the programmatic work of Tolman and Lewin to the more recent theories of those psychologists who have been concerned with resolving some of the continuing questions within this general framework. Among these recent innovations and concerns has been the attempt to provide a firmer basis for why behavior arousal takes place (since it is assumed that evolutionary factors are only part of the answer). Particularly noteworthy here has been the work of McClelland and his "butterfly" hypothesis that the search for optimal discrepancy from previous stimulation constitutes the antecedent of behavior arousal. In addition, McClelland has used the same hypothesis in dealing with the question as to why some outcomes are sought (i.e., became approach motives) and some are avoided (i.e., became avoidance motives). However, methodological problems are involved in testing both this hypothesis and other recent work dealing with the same questions.

Despite these methodological questions, many psychologists in applied areas, such as educational, clinical, and organizational psychology, find this approach a useful one.

the
measurement
of
motives

SIX

In this chapter we will turn our attention to a different type of problem in the study of motivation than the kind we have been considering previously. The issues we will be concerned with here are the measurement of individual differences in motives and the procedures we can follow to assure such measurement is adequately done. There are a number of reasons why we will devote this amount of attention to the problem of measurement.

As we saw in Chapter 5, and as we will see later in our discussion of such matters as achievement and aggression, the concept of individual differences in motives as systematic influences on behavior is very much a part of the expectancy-value framework. (It has, in fact, recently been extended beyond human motivational considerations to the study of animal behavior [Birch and Veroff, 1965].) Similarly, the postulation of individual differences in anxiety as a negative motivational state influencing drive has, as we have seen, become very significant in experimental research testing the Hull-Spence motivational system with human subjects. Third, the idea that individuals differ in the kinds of goals and outcomes they are motivated to achieve has been very important in testing some kinds of consistency motivational theories, as our later discussion will show. Fourth, and perhaps the most important reason of all, it would be a denial of our sensory and perceptual experiences to say that people do not differ in motives and desired goals. For these reasons, then, at some point in time, an adequate theory of motivational processes must take individual differences in motives into account.

Our purpose here will be to discuss the measurement of individual differences in motives with our attention focusing on two major considerations. First, we will devote our attention to some of the important criteria developed in order to evaluate the adequacy of any specific measure of individual differences in some characteristic, motivational or otherwise. Following this, we will turn our focus to an analysis of the major types of measures of motivation developed, the degree to which they have met these criteria for adequacy in the past, and what the future may hold for the development of adequate measures of individual differences in motives.

THE MEASUREMENT OF INDIVIDUAL DIFFERENCES: BASIC FOUNDATIONS

A measure of some type of trait or characteristic, be it a motive or anything else, can be defined as an assessment of individual differences in behavior under relatively standardized conditions. Furthermore, such a measure, which might be an intelligence test, a personality inventory, or a prospective measure of motivation is obtained under such conditions and is observed in such a manner that the observations made can be coordinated in some manner to a number system in order to describe in numerical terms the types of observations made. There are basically four different types of number systems we can use to code observations of psychological phenomena, but, in essence, only two of these systems are normally used. The first is called a *nominal* system and is used to assign numbers to qualitatively different observed phenomena in such a manner that each number refers to one, and only one, of the qualitatively different phenomena. As an example, consider the uniform numbers assigned to members of basketball teams. These generally do not reflect any inherent differences between the players or any specific dimension and, in fact, constitute only identification systems to enable the observer to distinguish between qualitatively different phenomena (i.e., basketball players).

Suppose, however, that the numbers assigned were not purely for identification purposes but, rather, reflected team value, as judged by the group. That is, uniform No. 1 was assigned to that individual who was judged to have the greatest value to the team, uniform No. 2 to the second highest, and so forth. In this case you would have what we call an *ordinal* scale of measurement, that is, the numbers assigned would reflect some inherent difference between the phenomena being observed, in this case the individual's value to the team. Thus, if we now tell another person about uniform No. 1 as opposed to uniform No. 6, we are talking about phenomena that differ along some specified dimension (i.e., value to the team). This, of course, is a lot different than the nominal system approach where the assignment of numerals only involves identification of qualitatively different phenomena, with no "more" or "less" connotation being implied by differential number assignments.

In the measurement and assignment of numbers to reflect individual differences in motives on the basis of observations or some behavior sample, such as a test and/or inventory, the most common system used is the ordinal system, although there are some rare occasions where nominal assignments are made. What this means is that the motive measures usually used can generally reflect, at best, whether a person has more or less of a motive. They cannot, and the numbers assigned should not be used to, imply that equal differences between the assigned numerals reflect equal differences between observed phenomena. Specifically, in ordinal measurement, the difference in value between uniforms No. 1 and No. 2 does not equal the difference in value between uniforms No. 2 and No. 3, which does not equal the difference in value between uniforms No. 3 and No. 4, and so forth. If such equalities did occur, this would be considered an *interval scale* of measurement. Unfortunately, we generally cannot assign scores very accurately in the psychological measurement of motivational variables. Even more rarely achieved is the *ratio scale* that involves having the ability to assign measures in such a manner that uniform No. 1 has four times as much value as uniform No. 2, which in turn has twice as much value as No. 4, and so on. This level of precision in assigning numbers to phenomena in psychology is found in basic laboratory processes, if at all, and it will be a long time before we will be able to achieve this level in the measurement of motivational variables.

Given, then, that the common type of measurement achieved in the measurement of motives is at the level of ordinal measurement, the next question concerns the methods we may use for determining the adequacy of such measurement. To put it more simply, how do we know that the Taylor Manifest Anxiety Scale (MAS) is really measuring manifest anxiety? How do we know that the Thematic Apperception Test (TAT) of need for achievement, as used by McClelland as a measure of individual differences in the achievement motive, is really a measure of such a variable? How do we know that when a person responds on a questionnaire that his predominant motives are achievement and power, such responses do actually reflect his motives? It is clear that some criteria must be established for determining the adequacy of specific measuring instruments, and, in fact, psychologists have established such procedures. The key to assessing the adequacy of measuring instruments is determining their validity and reliability, and it is to a discussion of these notions that we now turn.

Determining the Validity of Measures

The validity of a measure is usually defined as the degree to which it measures that variable it claims to be measuring. Yet, despite the seeming clarity of such a definition, the actual procedures we can use in determining the degree of validity of any specific test have always been subject to some controversy. Of late, however, there has been considerable convergence as to the specific methodological procedures that can be followed in developing a good measure of, say, the motive to acquire power.

The key idea here is the procedure known as *construct validity,* or, to be more accurate, construct validating a measure. In essence, this first involves the development of a theory as to what the test or instrument measures, that is, the type of psychological construct hypothesized to determine differences in scores on the measure under consideration. Once this is done, we would then make derivations and predictions as to the relationships between scores on the instrument and other theoretically relevant variables. To the extent that the derivations are supported (i.e., the predicted relationships occur), the theory underlying the measurement procedure is supported and the construct validity of the instrument is supported. To the extent that the predicted relationships do not occur, questions are raised as to the interpretation to be placed on different scores of the measure, and the validity of the instrument is called into question. What could contaminate these relationships? There are a number of reasons why this might happen. There might be some other determinant of test performance besides the motive being measured, as, for example, anxiety. Many people are anxious in testing situations and if the questions being asked are threatening in any way, then, obviously, the possibility increases for anxiety to serve as a response determinant for either the whole group being studied or for part of the group.

A second factor that might negatively affect the construct validity of a measure is that the actual content of the test stimuli materials might have differential significance and meaningfulness for different subsamples of those being administered the test. As an example, many critics have argued that there is a middle-class bias in the usual verbal achievement tests. A similar problem may also be contributing to the lack of construct validity for measures of motives. There is good reason to argue that the nature of achievement motivation may manifest itself differently for groups from different ethnic and social-class backgrounds (cf. Katz, 1964). A third source of difficulty may be that the kinds of external variables to which achievement motivation, for example, might be related could be different for different groups. For example, an achievement-oriented individual from the ghetto areas might be greatly interested in social-welfare work, whereas the same type of person from a middle-class family might have strong business interests. This would, of course, foul up research studies testing the construct validity of these measures.

For these reasons, the need for establishing the construct validity of measures of individual differences in motives is great. But how might this be done? There are a number of ways.

Consider the problem of determining the construct validity of an instrument designed to measure the achievement motive. The research of McClelland in trying to develop his measure of the achievement motive, one that involved the projection of one's self into the stories one wrote, can illustrate one of the key ways by which construct validity may be established. The logic of this approach involves the prediction that scores on a specific measure should reflect experimental manipulations designed to vary levels of the relevant motive on a temporary basis. As an example, if we wanted to determine whether our measure of the achievement motive was actually measuring what it claimed, then the scores involved should differ as a function of experimental conditions designed to increase or decrease the value of achievement in the given instance. (This assumes that, all other things being equal, people will try to achieve "value" in a given situation.) But what are the kinds of experimental conditions? DeCharms has recently summarized McClelland's procedure, and we cite his discussion as describing one of the ways by which one might assess whether or not a measure of the achievement motive was really measuring this type of construct. Obviously, analagous but different experiments could be used for assessing the construct validity of measures of other motives.

> The instructional cues used in the achievement-oriented condition stress that the procedures in which the subjects are about to participate are used to select leaders, predict generalized success in a career and a high general level of intelligence. After mentioning that the tests to be taken were used to select officer candidates, the arousal instructions conclude: "In short, these tests demonstrate whether or not a person is suited to be a leader. The present research is being conducted under the auspices of the Office of Naval Research to determine just which individuals possess the leadership qualifications shown by superior performance on these tests (McClelland et al., 1953, p. 103)." The subjects were mostly ex-servicemen for whom this type of arousal would be particularly appropriate.
> By contrast, in the relaxed condition every effort was made to de-emphasize the importance of the tests by having them presented as of as yet unknown value that the experimenter, a graduate student, was trying out. He avoided any indication of involvement in the outcome and did not even require the subjects to sign their names to the protocol.
> Between the relaxed and the achievement-oriented condition along the dimension of arousal the experimenters created a neutral condition that stressed that the subjects had a task to perform but gave no indication of its purpose. The experimenter was serious and business-like, but did nothing to either emphasize or de-emphasize achievement orientation.
> One hundred and seventeen men participated in the experiment, thirty-nine under each condition of arousal. All of the categories described above were scored in the four scores from each subject and the frequency of all categories increased with increasing arousal. Highly significant increases were found for Achievement Imagery, Need, Instrumental Activity, Positive Anticipatory Goal state, Negative Anticipatory Goal state, Positive Affective state, and Achievement Thema. Nurturant Press, Personal and World Blocks, and Negative Affective states did not reach the criterion set for significance that was high (p. .004) to take into account the fact that the categories could not be considered independent of each other.

This step in the procedures for developing the measure of achievement motivation clearly shows that relevant indicators derived from a behavioral analysis of the instrumental sequence are affected by arousal techniques that stress intelligence, careers, and leadership.

In the above experiment, different subjects participated in the different arousal groups. Lowell (1950) has also demonstrated increases in all categories when the same male college subjects were first tested under neutral conditions and then a week later under achievement arousal conditions. A similar technique administered to 21 ninth-grade Navaho boys produced essentially similar results. (deCharms, 1968, pp. 186-87)

In this case, then, a measure of achievement motivation that was originally developed by coding of written stories in response to relatively ambiguous pictures could be found to have some degree of construct validity by the process of showing how it was sensitive to and reflected environmental (experimental) demands designed to increase this type of motive and make it more desirable to be concerned with at that point. A crucial assumption here is that the experimental manipulation would be in fact, a manipulation of what it was intended to affect. This is a highly complex condition involving certain questions that need to be tested before this assumption can be shown to be adequate. We shall not deal with the causes here (cf. Orne, 1962; Rosenthal, 1967). How else may one establish the construct validity of a measure? Another procedure appropriate for answering this question consists of an examination of the relationships between the proposed measure and other measures and variables with which it should and should not be related. Then, if the patterns of high and low correlations are consistent with the hypothesized characteristics of the relevant measure, it would be appropriate to infer that the measure is a measure of what it purports to measure, that is, it has construct validity. For example, a measure of academic motivation should be correlated with such variables as interest in school, grades, and attitudes toward educational improvement. On the other hand, it should be correlated at a much lower level with such variables as social interest, TV program interest, and ball-playing ability. If it were related to these latter variables at a higher level than the former, then we would have some basis for doubting whether the variable was measuring what we believed it to be measuring. Similarly, a measure of affiliative motivation should be related to such variables as number of groups joined, time spent in interaction with others, and degree of preference for group, as opposed to solitary, sports. On the other hand, it should be related, if at all, on a much lower level to such variables as school grades, ability to throw a football and the like.

Perhaps the most sophisticated manner of establishing the construct validity of a measure using this type of logic is the multitrait, multimethod matrix approach suggested by Campbell and Fiske (1959). The logic here stems directly from this rationale and can, perhaps, best be explained by an example.

Assume that a given sample of subjects have scores on a projective measure of achievement, affiliation, and aggression motivation and have also responded to objective measures of the same variables. According to the logic of the multitrait, multimethod matrix, construct validity may be claimed under the following conditions:

1. When the correlations between the two different measures of the same constructs are high and significant.
2. When the correlations between the two different measures of the same construct are higher than the correlations between measures of different constructs using the same method.
3. When the correlations between different measures of the same construct are higher than the correlations between measures of different constructs using different measures.

In Table 6.1 we have provided an example of a situation where the evidence for

Table 6.1 Example of Measures of Achievement, Affiliation, and Aggression Motivation which Show High Construct Validity

	Objective Measures			Projective Measures		
Objective Measures	Ach.	Affil.	Aggr.	Ach.	Affil.	Aggr.
Achievement	.79					
Affiliation	.24	.88				
Aggression	.29	.41	.87			
Projective Measures						
Achievement	.75			.81		
Affiliation	.18	.83		.43	.85	
Aggression	.10	.19	.81	.19	.36	.84

construct validity is highly favorable. Thus, the correlations between the different measures of the same constructs (.75 for achievement, .83 for affiliation, and .81 for aggression) are higher than any correlation between any other measures, with the exception of the correlation of each measure with itself.[1] However, we hasten to add that these data are purely imaginary and that such clear examples of the construct validity of measures are not this easy to come by in real life. Rather what is usually the case is that some statistical criterion must normally be applied in order to determine if construct validity has been established for the measure under consideration. Thus, for criterion (a) above, this may usually be done by the normal procedures of statistical significance, but for (b) and (c) the problem is a little more complex since this involves a continual comparison of one correlation against a number of others. For example, it would involve comparing, in the achievement case, the correlation of

---

[1]This correlation is called the reliability of the measure, a different but also important concept we shall be discussing later in this chapter.

.75 with .43 and .19 in order to meet criterion (b) for the projective measure, and .75 against .18 and .10 in order to meet criterion (c) for the same measures. Although such multiple comparisons play havoc with the logic of independent testing of statistical hypotheses, a useful approximation to a statistical test as to whether (b) and (c) have been met may be made by assuming that if there is no reason for the two measures of achievement to correlate higher with each other than with any other variable, then the number of times this correlation would actually be greater would be 50 percent or half the time. One would then keep count of the number of times the achievement-achievement correlation is actually greater than the correlations of each of these measures with other variables. The more that this percentage deviates from 50 percent, the more significance can be attached to the finding. In the example given above, the achievement-achievement correlation was compared with six other correlations and was higher than all. With such disproportionality it is safe to conclude that the two achievement measures have something in common with each other that they share with no other measure. Suppose, however, that the same correlation was only higher than three of the six against which it might be compared. We might seriously doubt, then, that the two measures were actually measuring something unique from the other measures.

A third way of determining the construct validity of a measure of individual differences in motives is to determine whether scores on the measure differentiate in the expected manner between groups of individuals already known to differ on the characteristic under consideration. As an example, let us assume that we are interested in developing a measure of the need for power. One way we might determine the construct validity of such a measure would be to administer it to a group of people in leadership positions and those in nonleadership positions who were satisfied with their roles. While there would undoubtedly be other differences between these groups of individuals, it would be very legitimate to seriously question a purported measure of power motivation that did not significantly distinguish between these two groups. Using similar reasoning, we would argue that a measure of need for order should distinguish between political conservatives and anarchists, and a measure of need for affiliation should distinguish between joiners and nonjoiners. Other examples will occur to the reader.

There are other ways of determining the construct validity of measures in addition to these. For example, we might examine whether the items that make up a particular motive scale correlate more with each other than with items from other need scales. Basically, the idea here would be to see whether the items group together or correlate with one another in the way they should if the scale is actually measuring the motive being claimed.

The procedure for grouping items on the basis of their correlations is known as factor analysis, a complex procedure we shall not discuss here. However, what is important for our purposes is that the conceptual idea is similar to that of the multitrait, multimethod matrix, in that we would like to see whether items that are purportedly measuring the same characteristic are more highly correlated with each other than they are with other items and thus more likely to group together. Similarly, since other techniques are also variants of the basic procedures we have already discussed, we will not examine them all here, but we will go on to other subjects. There is one important point to keep in mind, however, and that is that the establishment of the construct validity of an instrument is a never-ending one. We must continually be concerned with obtaining new information on the construct validity of the measure using different samples in different situations, since the more we know about the measure and its generality, the more we can have confidence that we are actually measuring what we claim we are measuring in specific situations. In this sense, then, the development of the construct validity of an instrument is similar to the testing of the utility of a theory.

Determining the Reliability of Measures

The reliability of a measure is the consistency with which it measures whatever it is that it does measure. There are a number of ways in which measures of such consistency may be obtained depending on the situation. Before reviewing these, however, it is important to point out that the concept of reliability is independent from that of validity. The reader can easily see that we may be measuring something very consistently, e.g., a variable we believe to be anxiety, whereas in actuality what we may be measuring consistently is something else, e.g., lack of education.

There are a number of ways of determining the reliability of a measure of motivation, and which is chosen depends a lot on the specific situation, since all have faults and all have values. If there is only one session with a group of subjects, a researcher may administer his measure to them, split the test into two parts on a random basis, and then correlate the two halves. Known as *split-half* reliability, this procedure assumes that if an instrument is measuring any trait consistently, it will be measuring it in all parts of the test. Hence, there should be a high correlation (i.e., high reliability) between any two random parts of the test. Although this procedure has the value of only requiring one session to determine reliability, it does have a couple of problems, only one of which is easily correctable. The one that is subject to remedy has to do with the fact that splitting a test in half means that each score is based on a smaller sample of behavior, thus building in unreliability. (As an extreme case, consider the difference between observing a person for an hour and observing him for a day. In the latter case, one can have much greater confidence that one has seen a true sample of behavior.) Since this split leads to an underestimate of the reliability for the whole test, a correction formula,[2] known as the Spearman-Brown

---

[2] The actual formula and examples of its usage may be found in any tests and measurement text (cf. Cronbach, 1970).

formula, is used to correct the underestimate. Not so easily solved, however, is another problem with split-half procedures, one that may lead to an over-estimate of reliability and which is not easily correctable by the simple applica-tion of a formula. This difficulty stems from the fact that only one period for testing is utilized. Hence, all influences on behavior occurring at that time will affect all parts of the test equally and thus increase the reliability level of the test, even though such influences may have nothing to do with the nature and quality of the test. As an example, the fact that a person may be feeling some-what ill on a particular day would affect his performance on all parts of the test and thus add to its reliability when computed by split-half methods, even though it is obvious that such influences on test behavior are irrelevant to the purposes of the test.

One traditional way of correcting for this problem is to use the *test-retest* approach to reliability, a method that involves administering the complete measure on two separate occasions and then correlating the two sets of results. In this case, the fact that a person is feeling ill on one occasion will not add to the reliability levels since he more than likely will be feeling well on the other, and any influence on test consistency resulting from feelings of well-being will be wiped out, as it should be if our interest is in determining the consistency characteristics of a measure of some motive. However, since the extent to which this technique is, in fact, applicable to the measurement of motives is a source of considerable controversy, and this controversy also has important implications for the study of theoretical processes in motivation generally, utilization of this approach to reliability cannot be recommended without some comment as to the questions involved.

Basically, the problem revolves around the definition of a motive and the conditions under which we would expect it to show behavioral manifestations. Is it a characteristic of an individual that is relatively invariant over different situations? Or is it a characteristic way of responding to some specific situation? If the first were the case, then we would expect and demand that a measure of some motive variable show high correlation over time, or, as we have used it, have high test-retest reliability. This type of expectation would be considered appropriate, since in this case we would be assuming that a motive reflects an intrinsic characteristic of the individual and the fact that he was in a different situation at the time of the second testing would be irrelevant. He should show the same motive score on the second test, or the motive measure is not reliable.

Suppose, however, that we do not make this assumption and assume instead, as Mischel (1968) has argued, that the manifestation of a motive is highly specific in nature and is, in fact, a function of the situation the person is in and the method of motive measurement used. Under these conditions there would be no reason to expect high test-retest reliabilities for motivation measures over time, unless the situation involved were similar and the methods of measuring the motive were similar. If these conditions did not obtain, then there would be no reason to expect high test-retest reliabilities over time. In a recent monograph, Mischel (1968) has, in fact, gathered an impressive body of evidence that does show low test-retest correlations over time for a considerable number of motive measures. It might be pointed out, however, that while these correlations are often low, they are quite often moderately high and almost uniformly positive. This latter aspect provides support for the first set of assumptions about motives we discussed above.

What does all this mean for us here? Perhaps we can resolve these questions and provide some integration by first defining how we consider a motive measure to be different from a measure of a personality trait or an attitude. Once we have stated such a definition, some directions for dealing with these questions will be developed.

Conceptually, we may consider a measure of a motive to be a measure of a variable that reflects differences in desired end states. They are measures of what a person tries to do or the behavioral point at which he wants to be. They are, therefore, different from personality measures and attitude measures, in that the personality measure is descriptive of what one does and the attitude measure is descriptive of what one likes (not necessarily what he does). This goal characteristic of the motive, and the measure, would then reflect two types of antecedent factors. The first would be those outcomes that the individual has found over time to be continually pleasant and that provide him with pleasant affect. Such positive affect may have been so frequent as to lead to a process of internalization over time whereby this type of outcome is now sought in most or all situations in which the person finds himself as a source of constant positive feeling. An example of how this type of phenomenon may be accounted for theoretically is the McClelland "butterfly" hypothesis we discussed in Chapter 5, although other hypotheses are possible.

The second antecedent factor determining the specific desired end state would, of course, be the situation stimuli of the moment. Generally, these add to preexisting motive states (such as in McClelland's manipulation of achievement motivation discussed earlier in this chapter) in leading to a resultant total motive state. This total motive state then reflects both relatively permanent desired end states and those that reflect the end states the environmental demands of the moment point to as being most appropriate.

Given both of these, the test-retest correlation for a motive measure becomes a function of four factors:

1. The strength of the permanent desire for a particular end state (which is a function of internalization and socialization processes)
2. The degree of environmental support for the desirability of a given goal state at Time 1
3. The degree of environmental support for the desirability of a given goal state at Time 2
4. The similarity of the environments at Time 1 and Time 2

What this conceptualization suggests is that we should generally expect a positive test-retest correlation for a measure of a motive over time but that we should not be too surprised if the measure is not always a high one. How high it will be in a given case is a function of the weight of these four factors, a function often very difficult to determine in an a priori fashion. For example, what do we mean by similarity between environments? Along what dimensions? How do we know beforehand when to expect a high test-retest correlation and when to expect a low one? The only answer to this latter question is that we must have a measure of each environment before we do the research. Otherwise, it is too easy to explain discrepant results post hoc by saying that the environment was more similar (or more different) than previously thought. Yet measures of environment are not easy to come by since we have little theory to guide us as to relevant dimensions of environments, the best type of measures to use, and similar questions.

Our conclusion is that test-retest reliability is important for a measure of a motive, since some consistency should always be expected (cf. Cronbach, 1970, p. 562). However the actual levels of correlation that should be expected to occur, even in a good measure, would more than likely be lower (e.g., r's = 40-50) than the levels that would be desirable using the other measures of reliability we have discussed here (e.g., r's = 80-90). It might be noted that one implication of this means that the prediction of behavior from measures of motives should not be expected to be too high unless environmental variables are also brought into account. The reason for this is that a measure that does not correlate too well with itself over time could not reasonably be expected to correlate with a measure of something else. In other words, significant prediction should be demanded, but perhaps the levels will not be too high without bringing in environmental variables also. Such a position is not too different from the kinds of suggestions we have made in Chapter 5.

A third method for establishing the reliability of a measure is to see whether two supposedly equivalent forms of the measure correlate highly enough with one another to warrant the inference that they are measuring similar properties known, not too surprisingly, as *equivalent-form* reliability. The procedure involves the psychologist developing two separate forms for measuring the same variable by utilizing similar methodological procedures, construct definition, and statistical analyses. Once such forms have been developed, the two are correlated with one another as a measure of the psychologist's success in developing two separate measures of the same variable. This approach can technically be a highly satisfactory one since it can overcome the various weaknesses of the split-half method and the two forms could be given one after the other to overcome the test-retest problems. However, its success and adequacy depend very heavily on the competency of the psychologist involved and his ability to conceptualize and define his construct adequately and carefully at the beginning since the adequacy of the test construction will depend on such definition. Unfortunately, this is not an easy thing to do, and questions along these dimensions have frequently been raised in specific instances, often quite appropriately.

Finally, a fourth approach to determining the reliability of measures of motivation stems from the fact that many of the instruments (e.g., the projective tests) encourage free, subjective responses on the part of the individuals involved, rather than requiring responding along objectively defined, predetermined categories. The procedure then followed is to code and interpret the free, essay-type responses. The reliability of the measure is determined by computing its *intercode r* reliability, that is, the correlation between coders as to how well they agree in the scores they assign a given set of responses. Such correlations may be between different coders at the same time or between the same coder's ratings over time, a less satisfactory procedure because of memory factors.

These, then, are the major criteria that have been developed for the assessment of the adequacy of motivation measures. The question for us now is how well those who have been concerned with the measurement of motives have been able to meet these criteria, the problems they have had, and what the future may hold in store. It is to these questions that we now turn.

MEASURING INDIVIDUAL DIFFERENCES IN MOTIVES: CONSCIOUS SELF-REPORT

A procedure used by many psychologists to measure motivation has been the method of conscious self-report. The oldest and most traditional form of this type of procedure has been described by Kleinmuntz (1967) as follows:

> The self-report inventory essentially is a standardized interview composed of items such as these:
>
> > Are your feelings easily hurt?
> > Do your interests change quickly?
> > Do you tend to get angry with people rather easily?
> > I daydream very little.
> > I enjoy detective or mystery stories.
>
> Instead of interviewing each person individually, the questions or statements of an inventory are printed in a booklet and administered to a group of subjects simultaneously. For any particular personality questionnaire, the items given each respondent are identical. This equivalence of items for all subjects, and the fact that administration and scoring procedures are uniform and standard, are the distinguishing features of the self-report inventory. These features serve to render scores obtained by any individual comparable to scores obtained by others, provided, of course, that norms are available.
>
> Because of the nature of mass test administration procedures, subjects' answers on inventories are limited to fixed alternative response categories

(e.g., "yes," "no," or "cannot say"). The disadvantage of these limited alternatives is that subjects are severely restricted in the freedom of their responding. The advantages of fixed response categories, however, are that they eliminate judgmental factors in scoring these tests and obviate the necessity of relying on memory to reconstruct a subject's responses.

Just as the type and content of the interviews are varied to suit their different purposes, so the item content of self-report inventories is modified to reflect their distinct uses. Therefore, if the purpose served in a particular test situation, let us say, is to assess respondents' attitudes toward authoritarian persons, then an inventory composed of one set of items might be used. If the intent, to take a second instance, of the test is the diagnosis of personality disorders, then an entirely different question-naire containing altogether different items is more appropriate. In the first instance, items might probe into subjects' feelings about prejudice, minority groups, democracy, and attitudes toward being ruled by others. Items designed for psychiatric diagnosis might concentrate more heavily on respondents' views about themselves, their ability to get on with others, and their attitudes toward their own habits and past experiences.[3]

There are many, many inventories of this nature (a sample is shown in Table 6.2), some of which are better than others in the degree to which they

Table 6.2 Items Similar to Those Appearing on the Maudsley Personality Inventory

Alternatives		Item
Yes	No	Do you have dizzy turns?
Yes	No	Do you find it difficult to get into conversation with strangers?
Yes	No	Are your feelings easily hurt?
Yes	No	Are you rather shy?
Yes	No	Have you sometimes walked in your sleep?
Yes	No	Do you often feel disgruntled?
Yes	No	Do you suffer from sleeplessness?
Yes	No	Are you troubled by aches and pains?
Yes	No	Do you lack self-confidence?
Yes	No	Are you touchy on various subjects?

Source: H. J. Eysenck, *The Maudsley Personality Inventory* (San Diego: Educational and Industrial Testing Service, 1952). Reproduced by permission.

have been construct validated and the general sophistication of the researchers involved. On an overall basis, however, the overwhelming trend of the evidence has been that measures based on simply asking people questions of obvious content relevant to specific motivational areas such as achievement, aggression, affiliation, and sex have been of limited value at best. Why is this? There are a number of reasons.

[3]Kleinmuntz, *Personality measurement* (Homewood, Ill.: The Dorsey Press, 1967), pp. 183-84. Reprinted by permission.

One problem is that often the measures and inventories that have been used have measured motivational constructs whose relevance might be great in one environmental context, but not in another. This limits the construct validity of the instrument in the latter context. As an example, some inventories have been developed by clinical psychologists who have been interested in dimensions of personality and motivation which can be generalized to nonclinical settings only with great difficulty, if at all. Briefly, the problem here is that if a motivational inventory is developed for clinical or counseling purposes, the behaviors looked at and assessed may not be particularly fruitful for theoretical and/or nonclinical assessment purposes. Similar logic would apply if we look at measures of motivation designed explicity for educational and/or work settings.

A second problem with the method of conscious self-report is that it is very difficult to write clear, unambiguous items reflecting meaningful kinds of motivational constructs. Consider the examples given at the introduction of this section and their clarity, or lack of it. What does "easily hurt" mean? 80 percent of the time? 70 percent? 30 percent? What does "changing interest quickly" mean? Does a change from being interested in baseball to basketball constitute a change? Or must it be out of the area of sports entirely? How quickly is "quickly"? How easily is "easily"? The point is that there is much ambiguity here and it is not a problem easily resolved, as the reader will see if he actually tries his hand at writing some items of the kind typically used in inventories of this nature.

A third major difficulty with these types of measures is their susceptibility to response sets of different types. The term *response set* is defined as a determinant of test behavior that is not due to the content of the question(s) being asked. Among those that have been studied within the context of the traditional conscious self-report inventory, two of particular interest are the "acquiescence" and the "extreme response style/central tendency" response sets. In the first case the hypothesis has been that some people will agree with virtually any type of statement, even those that are contradictory, as long as they are stated reasonably. The second hypothesized response set involves those individuals who show a consistent preference to be extreme about things. They never agree or disagree with a statement, but always strongly agree or strongly disagree, as opposed to those who mark moderate agreement and feelings about things, even though their degree of affective involvement with the object may be the same as the extreme case, and vice versa. How serious a problem are these response sets? There is considerable controversy as to exactly how serious some of these problems are (cf. Rorer, 1965; Kleinmuntz, 1967), so definitive statements are hard to make. Perhaps the fairest statement is to say that these response sets can be important influences on test behavior, at least under some conditions.

Much stronger conclusions can be made concerning another methodological problem with the self-report inventory. It is very easy to fake on a self-report inventory. Basically the individual respondent can and often does adjust his response to present whatever face he wishes to the world. This problem, found too many times and in too many studies to be doubted, looms of extreme significance in the psychology of motivation because, often, variables are dealt with that lend themselves to faking or putting one's self in a good light (e.g., sexual motivation).[4]

Given all these difficulties, psychologists interested in measuring motivational variables using the method of conscious self-report have devoted much attention over the years to developing procedures that will retain the values (i.e., the objectivity of scoring, the ease of administration, etc.) of the approach and yet overcome the difficulties we have described.

One approach that had a vogue for a considerable period of time and still has some adherents today is known as the criterion-groups procedure. The procedure is to first define and isolate groups known to differ from one another on the basis of the motive variable for which a measure is being developed. Once this is done, a group of items are administered to the various groups, and *any item* that is responded to in a significantly different fashion by the different groups is included in the makeup of that motive scale. The method calls for the inclusion in the scale of *any item,* whether it makes sense or not, looks relevant or not, is silly or not. The logic of the approach is that if it differentiates significantly between the groups in a statistical sense, it gets included in the scale. There are a number of very famous inventories that were originally developed this way, the most notable of which are the Strong Vocational Interest Blank and the Minnesota Multiphasic Personality Inventory. The reader can see that, at first glance, there are considerable advantages to this approach in overcoming the weaknesses we have spoken of. The behaviors that lead to the use of response sets such as acquiescence and central tendency and the major difficulty of faking drop out of the picture as problems, since neither the determinant of the response nor its veridicality matter. All that matters is the respondent's closeness to the specific criterion group, who, incidentally, may also have faked their responses. Similarly, the problems with clarity of wording and appropriateness of item content for the motive variable being measured become irrelevant. All that matters is assessing an individual in how close he is to a specific criterion group in the pattern of his responses. Does he answer in the same way as Group A, which is assumed to have a high amount of the motive? As Group B, which is assumed to have a low amount of the motive? The actual bases for the differentiation and classification into the appropriate group (i.e., the scale questions and items, their clarity, meaningfulness, etc.) are, logically, of no concern. This is how the method of criterion groups overcomes the problems we have mentioned above.

[4]On occasion, people will try to "fake down," particularly in clinical settings, perhaps to gain attention. This is relatively less common than "faking up" but the methodological problems remain the same.

Why, then, does it seem to be losing some vogue? The reason, simply, is that in the solving of these problems, it introduces other difficulties of a very serious nature. One of these problems stems from the fact that the usefulness of the criterion-groups approach depends on the adequacy of the criterion groups used. These must be (a) clearly defined, (b) relatively permanent in nature, and (c) not differing from one another on any other characteristic but the one under consideration. Can we find such groups in developing measurements of motives? Are there groups we can cite that differ from one another only on need for achievement and no other variable? Need for power? Need for order? It is extremely doubtful that such groups can be found. Yet it is clear that this is a basic requirement of this approach if it is, in fact, to be a measure of only that motive and nothing else. The significance of this as a problem is indicated by the fact that in scales constructed using the criterion-groups approach, the same items frequently appear on more than one scale. This suggests that the bases for differentiation between groups is not only the specific motive variable but rather a variety of dimensions, a confounding of which naturally leads to a decrease in the adequacy of the measurement. In addition, a third problem is that the method assumes that the basis for differentiating criterion groups remains constant over time. The validity of this assumption is doubtful at best (cf. Cronbach, 1970, p. 532).

A second procedure suggested for overcoming the faking problem in the measurement of motives has been to use subtle, rather than obvious and transparent, items in measuring the relevant variables. Presumably, the subtle items are equally as relevant to the variable under consideration as the obvious one, but they are more difficult to recognize as such. However, while the idea is interesting, there is little evidence as to whether scales of such a nature would meet validity and reliability criteria (cf. Cronbach, 1970, p. 500).

Still a third innovation in self-report methodology is also aimed at overcoming faking and this is the lie scale. This is an approach that seems to be quite intriguing on initial examination, but then problems start to manifest themselves. The idea is a simple one. Basically, an attempt is made to develop a group of items that are easily susceptible to faking and are very likely to be faked, *if one is faking*. Once this is done, the test scorer is able to use the person's score on the lie scale to see if he is faking, and this would then enable him to interpret his scores on the rest of the items more accurately. The procedure can be outlined in a series of steps as follows:

1. A series of items is administered to two separate groups, one of which is asked to answer honestly, the other of which is deliberately told to fake to look as good as possible.
2. Items are then analyzed to see which show the greatest difference between the two groups; those items that show the greatest difference are then combined into a lie scale.
3. The lie scale is then administered routinely along with any other measures in future administrations. In these later administrations, each

respondent is scored on the lie scale (as well as the other measures) to see how closely his responses approximate those of the group that had originally been told to "fake good."

4. If he scores low on the lie scale, the rest of his responses are analyzed since he has pobably answered truthfully. If he scores high on the lie scale, his answer sheet is either (a) discarded or (b) corrected by some formula for his tendency to "fake good."

This approach is an intriguing one, and yet it has never really worked very well in the limited number of cases that used it. One reason, perhaps, is its basic assumption that all people "faking good" will use the same items to fake. It is doubtful that this assumption holds. In addition, another problem, not inherent in the method but of significance to its usefulness, is that there has always been the practical problem of the measurement of those people found to be high in faking. What do we do with them? If we throw them out, we haven't measured them. If we keep them in, we can't trust their responses. It is not clear what the best procedure is.

Finally, there is a fourth procedure that has engaged the attention of those interested in overcoming the faking problem in the measurement of motives. This technique, known as the forced-choice method, differs from the others in that we do know a considerable amount about it since it has been subjected to considerable research. Unfortunately, the research has not been as favorable as we would like.

The underlying logic of the forced-choice technique can be outlined as based on the following assumptions:

1. There exists a variety of motives that one may have. Some are good and some are bad in that some will lead to positive reactions and outcomes from others and some will not.

2. Some of the good motives are highly relevant and true of the respondent as an individual, whereas some of the others are nice, but not really descriptive of him as an individual.

3. Some of the bad behaviors are highly relevant and true of him as a person, whereas the other bad behaviors are not desirable, but they are not really descriptive of him as a person.

Given these assumptions, one might set up an inventory in the following manner:

Type A — A rater might be asked to choose the most self-descriptive of a pair of behavior description items, each of which says something favorable about a person, with the degree of favorability being equal for the two alternatives.

Type B — A rater might be asked to choose the most self-descriptive of a pair of behavior description items, each of which says something unfavorable about a person, with the degree of unfavorability being equal for the two alternatives.

Given these pairs, then, the logic of the forced-choice method is that a person is more likely to tell the truth about himself since (a) in the first case he must say something favorable, no matter what he says, and (b) the reverse is true in the second case, that is, he must say something unfavorable no matter what he says. An example of one of the most famous of these types of scales is the Edwards Personal Preference Schedule (EPPS), illustrated in Table 6.3. The purpose of this scale is to provide a profile of the respondent's motive level for each of fifteen separate needs, with the needs utilized being those proposed by Henry Murray, the personality theorist discussed in Chapter 5.

Table 6.3 Items from the Edwards Personal Preference Schedule

Alternatives			Items
A	B	A.	I like to tell amusing stories and jokes at parties.
		B.	I would like to write a great novel or play.
A	B	A.	I like to say what I think about things.
		B.	I like to forgive my friends who may sometimes hurt me.
A	B	A.	I like to go out with attractive persons of the opposite sex.
		B.	I like to make as many friends as I can.

Source: Edwards, 1959a. Copyright 1953 by the Psychological Corporation, New York, N.Y. All rights reserved. Reprinted by permission.

Conceptually, each of the fifteen separate need or motive scores is supposed to indicate the degree to which that given area operates as a need in the manner proposed by Murray.[5] The way that measurement proceeds is by pairing alternative items that are supposedly equal in desirability of response, with the individual being asked to choose that which is most descriptive of the self.

There has been extensive work on forced-choice scales such as the Edwards during the last two decades with the results sometimes, but not always, favoring it over other conscious self-report methods. For one thing, the success of the forced-choice method in overcoming faking is still a matter of controversy. One reason is that the manner in which the alternatives are equated for equal favorability (and/or unfavorability) leaves considerable room for doubt as to how well these goals can be accomplished. Typically, the procedure has been to pair statements on the basis of their mean rated desirability, as these ratings are derived from some norm groups. There are two major problems with this. First, although the means of the two behaviors in terms of favorability may be equal when taking group mean ratings as a whole, some individuals may disagree as to this. That is, they may disagree with those "average ratings" in that to them one

[5]The fifteen needs measured by the EPPS are achievement, deference, order, exhibition, autonomy, affiliation, intraception, succorance, dominance, abasement, nurturance, change, endurance, heterosexuality, and aggression.

behavior may be more desirable than the other, with all the implications that this may have for faking, and so forth (Wiggins, 1966). Secondly, behaviors that are rated similarly when viewed singly may present differences when viewed as pairs. Consider, as an example, the favorability of (a) finding a new method for teaching disadvantaged students and (b) raising funds for the construction of schools. Each of these may be considered equally desirable when viewed singly, but if they are presented as a pair, significant difference might be seen between them by most people in terms of their desirability.

Probably the most serious drawback, however, in using the forced-choice technique is that those who must use it rarely like it and its have-you-stopped-beating-your-wife format. The feeling of many people in responding to scales of this nature is that its usage implies mistrust and belief in the evaluator's lack of competence to give an honest rating, a type of social evaluation that might tend to breed resentment and a general lack of cooperation.

With all these difficulties, the forced-choice method of assessment has come under increasing question. For example, in reference to the EPPS, recent separate reviews by Radcliff (1965) and Stricker (1965) have pointed to the lack of validity of the scales. In addition, a paper by Scott (1968) actually found little difference in either validity and/or reliability between forced-choice and the traditional type of scales. We must conclude, then, that the actual value of the forced-choice scale in overcoming the problems it was designed to correct is still an open question.

MEASURING INDIVIDUAL DIFFERENCES IN MOTIVES: PROJECTIVE TECHNIQUES

Projective techniques differ from the self-report measures mainly in that the test stimuli are deliberately made somewhat ambiguous in nature and the individual is generally free to give those responses he wishes, as opposed to having them structured along predetermined categories. Since the stimuli are ambiguous and may consist of inkblots, pictures, incomplete sentences, and ambiguous figures, it is argued that faking will be less of a problem since the test respondent doesn't know what kinds of demands are being made of him. For this reason, he will be more likely, in this kind of procedure, to project his own needs and motive structure onto his responses, at least according to the proponents of projective techniques.

A good example of this approach in motivational research is the Thematic Apperception Test (TAT), originally introduced by Morgan and Murray (1935), but since used by many others in both its original and revised forms as a way of measuring differences between people in their needs and motives. The TAT consists of the presentation of a series of ambiguous pictures to which the person is asked to write stories. These stories are then analyzed and coded as to the motives, needs, wishes, desires, and so forth, which are assumed to have been projected by the respondent onto the characters in the pictures and which then manifest themselves as he writes about these characters in the stories he develops.

Despite the fame of such projective instruments as the TAT and other such measures, however, the extent to which they are actually adequate measures of motives is still very much an open question, and many problems remain to be resolved before we can be overly optimistic about their potential fruitfulness in the study of motivational processes.

One major problem stems from the fact that when a projective test has been found to have construct validity in a given situation, there still remains serious doubt as to the cause of the validity. The reason for this is that it has been shown that projective-test responses may vary according to (a) the coding system used for analyzing the narrative-type responses,[6] (b) the person doing the coding, (c) the person actually administering the test, and (d) other such social influences. Hence, if a given set of scores happens to be correlated with another set of variables in a manner supporting construct validity, to what influences should the validity of the scores be attached? The test stimuli? The scorer? Is it because a psychoanalytic (or nonpsychoanalytic) coding scheme was used?

In addition, a second problem is that one of the original rationales for the projective test approach, that of its relative nonsusceptibility to faking, has not been as supported by research as early developers of the approach thought would occur.

Murstein (1963) has cited research that there is considerable evidence to indicate that what a person gives as his projective test response is controlled by him. If a respondent believes that the situation calls for a pleasant-type response, that is what he will tend to write as his test answer.

Perhaps most significantly, however, is that there is considerable doubt as to the whole theoretical structure and logic underlying projective tests. For this reason, even if the problems indicated above were to be resolved, the psychologist would still have many difficulties and few guidelines to develop a projective test of motivational processes. Murstein (1963) has pointed out that all of the assumptions listed below, assumptions that underlie the projective-test rationale, have come under attack in recent years for the reasons indicated.

Assumption One. The more ambiguous the stimulus properties of the projective technique, the more the response reflects the motivational characteristics of the respondent.

---

[6]For example, in the TAT alone, one can choose from Murray's coding scheme, McClelland's approach, or Aron's system (Kleinmuntz, 1967). All are different, yet all can be and are used. Similar problems exist with other projective measures.

This assumption underlying the logic of projective testing has *not* been supported by research data. Some studies have shown a curvilinear relationship, with medium ambiguity, eliciting the greatest projection of motivational characteristics. Other studies have found that the extremely ambiguous picture seems to lead to a lack of understanding on the part of the respondent as to what he is supposed to do. Not having such understanding, he winds up giving some superficially pleasant response.

Assumption Two.   Since the stimuli are supposed to be ambiguous and of little importance, it is of little significance what type of stimuli are used in projective tests.

There is little research support for this assumption and much against it. One strong line of evidence here is the continuing series of findings that the so-called ambiguous pictures of the Thematic Appreception Test differ greatly in their ability to elicit themes of aggression.

Assumption Three.   No projective test response is accidental; every response is meaningful for the analysis of personality.

There is little reason to think this to be an adequate assumption, either logically or empirically. Some responses in the projective test situation, as in any other test procedures, may be a function of chance error, whereas other responses certainly vary as a function of the intelligence and education of the respondents (Atkinson, 1964) and the particular stresses and environment of the moment (Mischel, 1968).

In addition to these problems, there are also other questions about the logic of projective testing that need to be better resolved than they are at this time. One of these is the confusion of the genesis of need expression. When is a need expressed in a projective test of the kind that will be reflected in overt behavior (thus suggesting a positive correlation between test and behavior)? When is a need expressed in a projective test of the kind a respondent is afraid to express overtly so projects into the test situation (thus suggesting a negative correlation)? Both are theoretically possible. Yet, although knowledge of which is relevant in a given test situation is of great significance for construct validity, we are only beginning to learn answers to this question. For one thing, it appears logical to suggest that such differential expression is a function of anticipated punishment for expression of the motive in overt behavior, and evidence for this does exist. Olweus (1969) found that TAT scores on aggression correlated positively with behavioral aggression for those low in inhibition but *negatively* for those high in inhibition. However, what we do not know is whether social-group expectancies, reference groups, and so on, also affect in some way whether the correlation between projective responses and behavior will be positive or negative. Research is greatly needed in these areas if projective tests are to fulfill their promise as theoretically useful, practically important tools.

MEASURING INDIVIDUAL DIFFERENCES IN MOTIVES:
UNOBTRUSIVE AND DISGUISED MEASURES

One of the recent developments in the measuring of motivational variables that seems to have considerable promise stems from the belief of an increasing number of psychologists that both self-report and projective measures, despite their differences, have certain common inherent structural weaknesses. These weaknesses, which are similar in nature for both types of measures, stem from the fact that in all of these cases the person *knows he is being measured.* Webb and his co-workers (Webb et al., 1966) have termed this type of measurement as reactive measurement and have suggested that such measures have the following characteristics:

1. The process of telling a person you are going to measure him introduces a foreign element into the social situation he is in, that is, there is an extraneous element.
2. Because there are extraneous elements in the situation, such processes might cause different sorts of motivation in the situation, as well as measure the motive variables of interest.
3. Since such measures constitute a definite extraneous element in the situation, they are linked as a means of measurement to that part of the sample willing to cooperate and be measured. Hence, for those who are not willing to cooperate, there is no way of measuring them.
4. Since the sample that does respond is different from that which does not, real questions develop as to what can be said about the results obtained and the population to which the results can be generalized.

Because of these problems, Webb and his co-workers have argued that psychologists should be devoting time to developing what they call unobtrusive measures, or ways of measuring people without their knowing they are being measured at all.

But how do you measure people without their knowing they are being measured? More particularly, how do you measure them on important variables of the kind we deal with in the study of motivational processes?

As one example of how an unobtrusive measure of achievement motivation may eventually be developed, we may begin with the Hand Skills Test reported by Kipnis and Glickman (1962). Their description of the test was as follows:

> The test sought to measure self-generated achievement motivation to "keep going" beyond minimum performance "quotas" on tiring tasks. The test consists of sequentially numbered boxes in which five Ss pencil five tallymarks. It is presented as a measure of how rapidly people can use their hands and fingers. There is a 1-minute practice session and three parts of 4-minutes each. A "passing score" is announced prior to each of the 4-minute parts. Pretesting had established that this score could be reached

by all examinees in the time allowed. The test seeks to discriminate between those who stop or slow down after the passing score has been reached and those who continue to strive for high performance. (Pp. 50-51)

In Table 6.4 are presented some correlations between this measure of achievement motivation and job performance evaluations, a pattern that shows that the test predicts job behaviors for the low-aptitude people, who need achievement motivation, but not for the high-aptitude people, who do not need it. While this study by Kipnis was not designed specifically as construct-validity research, the results reported in Table 6.4 are certainly consistent with the hypothesis of the test developers as to what the test measures.

Table 6.4 Phi Correlations between the Hand Skill Test and Performance Evaluations, by Aptitude Level and for Each Total Sample

Aptitude Level		Phi Correlation	N
High	AM	.03	63
	RM	.12	61
	NP	.04	56
	OC	.13	53
Low	AM	.43**	57
	RM	.47**	61
	NP	.39**	61
	OC	.26*	55
Totals	AM	.23*	120
	RM	.29*	122
	NP	.23*	117
	OC	.21*	108

*Significant beyond the .05 level.
**Significant beyond the .01 level.

Source: D. Kipnis, A noncognitive correlate of performance among lower-aptitude men. *Journal of applied psychology, 46,* 1962, 76-80. Copyright 1962 by the American Psychological Association. Reprinted by permission.

This test, however, is only part of the way toward an unobtrusive measure since the people knew they were in a measurement situation. They were just being measured on a variable different from the one they thought, a type of measurement known as disguised measurement. For it to be truly unobtrusive, we would have had to observe these behaviors as they occur in everyday life, without the person knowing he is being observed. Can we do such a thing? Consider each of the following: (a) observe the individuals who go to school at night even though their employers tell them they do not have to in order to get ahead; (b) observe the housewives who have little financial need, enjoy a meaningful and satisfying family life, and yet seek work experience; (c) observe the student who works harder in his courses after being accepted into graduate school than before such acceptance. Can we consider each of these unobtrusive measures of achievement motivation? Perhaps, but before we do so, two major potential problems need to be resolved.

The first stems from the relatively simple observation that some unobtrusive measures, which are obstensibly measuring the personality and motivational characteristics of the individual, are really measuring his behavior. Behavior is a function of other things besides motivational variables. In other words, we are always running a risk in inferring a single motivational cause from any observed bit of behavior. Consider the example of which book a person chooses to read out of a sample offered him. Suppose he has already read some of the books, and so chooses the book he hasn't read on this particular occasion. This doesn't necessarily mean that he specifically wants to read the chosen book more than the others. It may simply mean that he has read the others. Suppose, by accident, the seal on a chosen book (if new) is unusually resistant to tearing and he can't rip it open, so rather than continue trying, he picks up a second choice book.

Consider, also, the example of which choice the person makes in an experimental situation, an affiliative choice or nonaffiliative one. Has the experimenter provided him with some hint as to which he should choose? These hints might not be conscious in nature, such as word choice, a smile, a hand or body movement, and so forth.

The point, simply, is that behavior is not motivation. They are two different concepts and it is always dangerous to infer one from another without good reason. Hence, it is very necessary that unobtrusive measures be subject to vigorous construct-validating procedures in order to justify their use as measures of motivation variables, since the basis for incorrect inference is so great.[7]

There is a second drawback in the use of unobtrusive measures, and this concerns their ethics. If unobtrusive measures constitute observing a person without his knowledge or awareness of the basis upon which he is being observed (as in the disguised measure case), can it not be considered spying? Would it not also be considered unconstitutional, since a person might be bearing witness against himself without knowing it? We frankly do not know the answers to these questions since they involve legal, social, and other moral considerations in addition to the psychological, but we think they are quite complex and important. If we consider, for example, that unobtrusive observation violates the Fifth Amendment, it would then follow that all tests without perfect validity to measure what they are measuring would be unconstitutional. The reason for this

---

[7]The problem here is conceptually similar to the one in our discussion of the criterion-groups method of scale construction. In both cases we are generalizing from observed behavior to a single, underlying motive. This is, obviously, a very risky business, as we argued there.

is that they would be measuring something besides that which is claimed and which was overtly understood. Hence people would or might be giving evidence against themselves without knowing it. This would mean that all tests of less than perfect validity would have to be discarded and that any information a person provided about himself without his express intention to provide such self-incriminating evidence would be declared unconstitutional. Would this mean that an organization like a school, for example, would have no right to protect itself against those employees (teachers) who wish to destroy that school, but, who, on the other hand, disguise their intention during the selection process?

THE MEASUREMENT OF MOTIVES: A SUMMARY

What, then, can we conclude about these individual-differences measures of motivation? The problems and questions with each of them obviously continue to remain great. Have the outcomes been worth it? Can we use these measures in research? Should we continue to use them? The answer to these questions must be yes, even though we do not downgrade for a moment the enormous amount of work that still remains before these instruments can truly become effective measures of the constructs they are designed to measure and the urgent necessity that this work be done as soon as possible. Our reason for this recommendation stems from our belief that there really is no choice at this time but to utilize these measures, weak as they are, *if* one assumes that (a) motivated behavior of humans is worth investigating, (b) there are many kinds of motivational questions that do not lend themselves to experimentation with humans and for which animal experimentation cannot provide guidance, and (c) it is still an undecided question as to the theoretically most fruitful antecedent variables leading to the arousal and direction of behavior. Since all three of these assumptions appear to be reasonable to us, the rationale for our recommendation for continued usage, subject to urgently needed methodological improvement, becomes clear.

This does not mean that future technique research should not be methodologically more adequate than it has been up to now. Clearly, it needs to be if advances are to be made, and there are two suggestions we may make that would lead to more useful research. First, better measurement of motives will take place, we believe, only through the development of better theories of motives and motivational processes. Thus, the test developer must be a theorist as well as a developer of scales. Developing a measure of something without a clear conceptualization of what one is measuring is a waste of time, as Jackson (1971) has pointed out. The necessity for theory, then, is crucial. In addition, better measurement will occur only if we come to understand more fully the nature of the testing situation, the expectancies and attitudes that govern it, and the conditions under which certain motives will be expressed. There is a burgeoning research literature concerning various experimenter, situational, and testor influences on test responses (cf. Rosenthal, 1967; Mischel, 1968). The day is long past when we can view a test situation as reflecting only characteristics of an individual. It does do that. However, it is also an interpersonal situation and the behavioral outcomes (i.e., test responses) are also a function of interpersonal and other situational influences. It is these interpersonal and situational influences, as well as individual traits, that we must come to understand in the measurement of motives, both in terms of their implication for the reliability of motive measures over time and in terms of their implications for understanding behavior generally. In line with this point, Entwhistle (1972) has recently reviewed the dismal history of projective measures of the need for achievement in helping us to understand academic achievement. Her argument, essentially, is that this poor set of findings is due to the low reliability of projective measures of need for achievement, a claim she well documents in her paper. As we said earlier, such low reliability would limit the value of the measure in predicting academic performance, since a measure that does not correlate well with itself would not correlate well with anything else. Perhaps an understanding and utilization of Mischel's arguments (despite its difficulties), combined with better measures and more careful construct validation, will enable us to do better in the future.

SUMMARY

The adequate measurement of individual differences in such motives as achievement and aggression is crucial for theories of motivational processes and for various applied areas, such as clinical practice, school psychology, and organizational consulting. Because of these needs, psychologists have devoted much attention to the development of various methodological procedures to be followed in insuring the adequacy of such measurement. Two criteria are crucial, one being the construct-validity procedure. This, in essence, involves determining whether the test measures what it proposes to measure by determining its correlates with two types of variables. First, it is determined whether the test is correlated with what it should be correlated with, if it is measuring what it claims to be measuring. Second, it is determined if it is *not* related to those variables it should *not* be related to, if it is measuring what it claims to be measuring. To the extent that those situations occur, the measure can be assumed to have construct validity.

A second desirable aspect of a measure is its reliability or the consistency with which it measures whatever it does measure. A number of procedures exist for assessing the degree to which this is achieved. However, one persisting problem is that there is a real question as to whether individual motives can be thought to be greatly consistent over time and situations. Some recent work by

Mischel suggests that individual motives may be more variable than we have traditionally thought. Dispite this, however, it is reasonable to expect at least some consistency.

Given these criteria and even a lowered level of expectation as to how much can be achieved in the case of reliability, the blunt fact is that the required levels of adequacy have not been met. The evidence for the construct validity of most motive measures is slight at best and, frequently, even less than this. The only type of measurement that sometimes meets the reliability criterion is the objectively scored inventory, but the evidence for the construct validity of this type of measurement is no better than it is for projective tests. Unobtrusive and disguised tests of motives are intriguing but still in a raw, primitive state of development. Much remains to be done.

consistency
motivation

Up to now the approaches to motivation we have been discussing have been based on a similar basic view of man. As we have seen, this view is one that sees man as being utility-maximizing, hedonistic, and maximum-value seeking in his behavior choices, even though under some conditions (i.e., the low-expectancy situation) the behavior, at least on the surface, does not seem that way. The only exception to this general orienting approach is certain aspects of the activation-arousal framework discussed in Chapter 4. We now turn to a greatly expanded discussion of the basic balance framework introduced at that time. As we will see, this basic approach to understanding motivation has stimulated a great deal of interest over the years and has led many people to explore the ramifications of this view of man, a view radically different from those we have talked about up to now.

Our concern in this chapter will be with consistency and balance theory as a general orienting approach to the study of motivational processes. First we will discuss the historical aspects of this approach and then some of its current theoretical manifestations. Following this, we will concern ourselves with an examination of some of the major questions and problems that interest consistency theorists. Finally, we will conclude our discussion with some comments as to the logic of consistency motivation and why it continues to be a viable approach today.

THE HISTORICAL ANTECEDENTS:
HOMEOSTATIC THEORY

The idea that motivational processes may be described as being homeostatic in nature, that is, that they reflect the desire to restore one's equilibrium or balance when imbalance occurs, has a long tradition and can be found in the writings of a number of different fields besides psychology. Summer, a sociologist, wrote as far back as 1906 about a "strain toward consistency" in cultural norms and folkways (Summer, 1906). The term *homeostasis,* itself, was originally coined by Cannon (1939), a biologist, in order to describe the steady states the physiological processes were aimed at achieving, an observation that can be found in the work of Claude Bernard back in the early nineteenth century. From Cannon's point of view, the concept of homeostasis and homeostatic motivation relates to the need of the body to maintain a constant condition. However, the processes involved in such behavior choice and direction are not static but, rather, constitute an open system in constant interaction with the external environment. Thus, the physiological processes involved in the attaining of homeostasis and its maintenance differ as a function of changing stimulation. At one time this might involve food attainment, at another time liquid refreshment, at another time food and liquid refusal, and so forth. There is a continuous behavioral direction aimed at achieving equilibrium by the self as it interacts with the world, but there is *no* implication or assumption that this homeostatic process is always under the control of one specific set of elements. The need is to maintain a constant state, but the behaviors utilized in order to achieve this vary according to the current personal and environmental state of the organism.

There are a number of different kinds of data cited by Cofer and Appley (1964) in support of these original formulations by Cannon, prominent among which are the studies by Richter showing how imbalance resulting from temperature and diet changes leads to corrective behaviors designed to achieve a more balanced environment. In another direction, there is the area of psychophysical research that has dealt with the perceptual constancies and the routinely demonstrable finding that we perceive perceptual phenomena such as brightness, color, form, and size in a manner such as to achieve constancy of environmental stimulation. Stagner (1951), a noted exponent of homeostatic theory, has cited the perceptual constancies, in fact, as a prime example of our desire to maintain a steady state. Another type of research that can be cited in support of the general homeostatic formulation is the relatively commonplace finding that task and work behavior can be and often is kept at a steady level despite considerable variation in such environmental stimuli as noise and music (Korman, 1971b, chapter 16). In a related but somewhat different area, studies concerned with level of aspiration, or goal setting, in task situations can also be cited as being in support of the general homeostatic formulation. The finding that goal setting is positively influenced by task success (Festinger et al., 1941) constitutes support for a homeostatic model, because it stems from the assumption made by most homeostatic theories that the steady state desired incorporates the effects of previous experience. Differing life experiences (such as task success) result in changes in the organism, which in turn lead to differences in the equilibrium (or aspiration) levels sought. (In addition to experience, Cannon has also suggested aging and significant environmental changes as important influences on desired equilibrium levels.) Finally, in support of homeostatic formulations, there is the belief of many clinicians that the ego-defense mechanisms are primarily attempts to restore equilibrium after such equilibrium has been threatened by anxiety and frustration.

Despite this support, however, there have been some very active attacks on homeostatic theory over the years, some of which are still voiced today. Rather than deal with all of those right now, however, we will concern ourselves at this point only with two of these criticisms, reserving for later our discussion of some of the more general problems involved in any consistency or balance model.

The first of these criticisms we can deal with rather quickly, and this is the claim by Young (1949) that homeostatic theory cannot handle the observed data that organisms will sometimes seek nonnutritive substances, that is, those substances that cannot possibly restore homeostatic balance in a physiological sense. This is probably not a very serious criticism of the approach, however, since even though such choices occur, it does not negate the fact that the choice of balance-restoring outcomes may and could take place under unbalanced conditions if the organisms were given a choice between nutritive and nonnutritive substances. Perhaps, in the example that Young cites, the organisms were not in an unbalanced state, or the choice of a nutritive substance was not available, or both.

The second criticism is somewhat more difficult to deal with. This is the argument that homeostatic formulations cannot deal with or account for creativity, suicide, or self-sacrificing behavior. There are a number of questions involved in this criticism, each one of which probably should be dealt with separately. First, it would appear that one might argue against the criticism that consistency models cannot account for creativity by citing, for example, the activation theory hypothesis that we seek levels of activation in balance (or homeostatic) with previous levels of experience (Maddi, 1968). Since activation is, in part, a function of stimulus variability and change, it would appear that a homeostatic formulation may be able to handle creative behavior by arguing that such behavior is, in part, a function of the degree of exposure to and engagement in variable, changing behavior in the past. The more that one has engaged in or been exposed to such behavior in the past, the more likely that one will engage in such behavior in the future is the prediction that this type of homeostatic formulation would make, and the degree of its adequacy can only be determined empirically. (In Chapter 10 we will discuss the empirical data relevant to just such a proposition.)

In terms of accounting for suicide and/or self-defeating behavior, there is, first of all, nothing about a homeostatic formulation that necessarily precludes predicting such behavior *when* the primary units under analysis are psychological in nature, rather than physiological. It is this concentration on psychological imbalance that marks contemporary work in consistency motivation, and as we will see, there are a number of consistency theories that can well handle such nonadaptive behaviors as self-defeatism and suicide in a psychological sense. If the evidence that they do not handle physiological self-destruction as well is not as strong as it could be, perhaps one reply might be that at least they approach it by clearly predicting that some people would be more likely to commit suicide than others. Few other theories, with the possible exception of the Atkinson model we will discuss in Chapter 8, can do even this well. This is not to say that consistency theories do not have problems. They have many, as we will see. However, this particular problem happens not to be a very serious one.

CONSISTENCY MOTIVATION:
SOME CONTEMPORARY FORMULATIONS

A few years ago a psychologist named Albert Pepitone was moved to suggest at least three possible explanations for the explosive growth of consistency models of behavior in the social, interpersonal areas of psychology after World War II (Pepitone, 1966). The first of these reasons was the fact that the man to whom many social psychologists owed their debt, Kurt Lewin, had never really developed his theorizing past the descriptive stage into what was actually a predictive model of behavior. While in one sense this was not a good thing, it did have some beneficial effect in that there was no one theory (a la Hull) around which thinking was expected to be oriented. Thus, by the end of World War II, when his students and colleagues were ready to develop more predictive theories, the field was open, with the result that some of Lewin's followers developed expectancy-value approaches while others moved on to a consistency-model direction of the kind we will deal with in this chapter. A second factor, Pepitone argued, was that it was becoming apparent that it was most difficult to use Freudian psychoanalytic theory as a basis for social-psychological and cognitive research. It was just too murky, too cloudy, and too untestable. Therefore, there was a receptivity to other theoretical approaches by psychologists oriented in a cognitive, nonphysicalistic direction. Finally, there were also the increasing problems of Hullian theory that became apparent after World War II, problems we spoke of in Chapters 2 and 3.

Whatever the reasons, and there were probably others besides these, the years following World War II saw a great increase in the number of psychological theories of consistency motivation, an increase we will not attempt to cover in its entirety here. What we will do instead is outline and then analyze several of the more important and significant of these theories. In this way, the reader will be afforded a meaningful sample of the flavor of this type of approach to understanding motivational processes. As our first example, let us look at one of the first of the social-psychological theories of consistency motivation, that developed by Heider (1958).

Heider's Balance Theory

The basic framework of Heider's original theorizing can be explained as follows:

Let P = one person;

O = another person;

X = another social object (e.g., another person, a thing, etc.);

$+$ = a sign indicating a relationship of a positive nature between the source and the object of the arrow; the basis for this positive effect may be either likingness or belongingness;

$-$ = a sign indicating a relationship of a negative nature between the source and the object of the arrow; the basis for this negative effect may be either lack of likingness or lack of belongingness.

Given these definitions, a number of different types of relationships between the social objects from the viewpoint of P (the source of the arrow) are theoretically possible. Among these are:

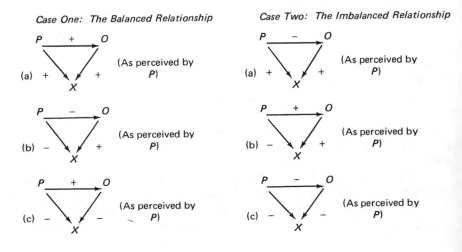

Case One: The Balanced Relationship

(a)   P + O   +   +   X   (As perceived by P)

(b)   P − O   −   +   X   (As perceived by P)

(c)   P + O   −   −   X   (As perceived by P)

Case Two: The Imbalanced Relationship

(a)   P − O   +   +   X   (As perceived by P)

(b)   P + O   −   +   X   (As perceived by P)

(c)   P − O   −   −   X   (As perceived by P)

By way of explanation, Case One (a) shows that P likes (or has some type of belonging relationship to) O, that he likes (or belongs to) X, and that he perceives that either O likes X, or that the two belong together in some way. As a concrete example of Case One (a), P might be Richard Nixon, O Spiro Agnew, and X the Republican Party. Richard Nixon, then, is shown as liking Spiro Agnew, liking the Republican Party, and perceiving that Agnew likes the Republican Party. This is a "balanced" perception in the Heider sense. For Case One (b), P might be Richard Nixon, O Ted Kennedy, and X the Democratic Party (i.e., Nixon dislikes Kennedy, dislikes the Democratic Party, and perceives that Kennedy likes the Democratic Party); while for Case One (c), P might be Richard Nixon, O Spiro Agnew and X the Democratic Party (i.e., Nixon likes Agnew, dislikes the Democratic Party, and perceives that Agnew also dislikes the Democratic Party). Both of these relationships are also what Heider has called balanced relationships, and these are the types of social systems that are satisfying and that a person (e.g., P) would be predicted to have no desire to change.

Suppose, on the other hand, that we define the persons and objects in the same way for all the examples under Case Two, but that the relationships that we have pictured also obtain. That is, in Case Two (a), Nixon likes (belongs to) the Republican Party, sees Agnew as liking (belonging to) the Republican Party, but finds that he neither likes nor sees any unit of belongingness or commonality between himself and Agnew. According to Heider, this would be an imbalanced situation, as would Cases Two (b) and (c), and imbalanced situations are defined by him as tension provoking. Hence, they are states that serve as motivating conditions in the sense that such imbalanced states operate to arouse behavior designed to reduce them. The direction of behavior is also theoretically determined by such imbalance in that the behavior that does take place is undertaken in order to reduce such felt imbalance. For example, in Case Two (a), Nixon might reduce his discomfort and achieve balance by increasing his liking for Agnew *or* decreasing his liking for the Republican Party *or* decreasing his belief that Agnew really likes (or belongs to) the Republican Party. Another possibility is that he may differentiate his perceptions in such a manner that he might come to see his dislike for Agnew as being based on reasons entirely different from either his liking for the Republican Party and/or his belief that Agnew and the Republican Party have some degree of positive interrelationship. These basic examples and predictions constitute the framework of the Heider balance theory, the first and perhaps most primitive of theories of consistency motivation. One reason we have used the term *primitive* in describing Heider's system is that the theory cannot predict which of these methods designed to restore balance will be chosen in a given situation. We know only that at least one of them will take place. Obviously, one real disadvantage of this ambiguity is that research tests of the theory become difficult to undertake since one does not know how to interpret the failure of a predicted method of balance restoration. Suppose we had predicted that Nixon, in the case cited above, would decrease his liking for the Republican Party and the prediction was not supported. Is it because there was no consistency motivation or because Nixon restored his balance in an unpredicted manner? The problem clearly is an important one if we are to adequately evaluate the approach, and yet it is not answerable by either Heider or, for that matter, other consistency theorists we will discuss later. A more unique problem with Heider, however, is that he really doesn't see imbalance as a high-tension state and as a behavior motivator (Zajonc, 1968). His predictions are stated as *tendencies* toward balance restoration, rather than specific behavioral predictions. Hence, failures of at least some balance-restoring behavior to take place as a result of being put in an imbalanced state could not technically be claimed to be failures of the theory (Shaw and Costanzo, 1970, p. 152). This is, of course, an undesirable position to take in any scientific theory, since it makes the theory empirically void and, thus, incapable of testing. In other words, either a specific behavior is being predicted or it isn't. If it is, then we can determine whether the prediction is supported. If it isn't, then there is no theoretical question with which to concern ourselves. For this reason, we will ignore this aspect of Heider's theory.

A third question relevant to Heider's work concerns his assumption of inconsistency as a motivator. Because of its importance, it may be worthwhile to take a slight detour here and devote some attention to this major assumption underlying the work of consistency theorists of a social-psychological bent. The problem is that while it appears to be logically and empirically valid to assume physiological imbalance as a sufficient antecedent condition to arouse and direct behavior (as in the arousal-theory framework and as the Hullians assumed for physiologically based needs), there is a question as to the justification of such a position where the imbalance stems from psychological, not physiological, considerations. A number of reasons have been offered for this assumption, and while we have little empirical basis at this time to evaluate them as to their comparative importance, it may be fruitful to keep them in mind as we discuss the work of Heider and others in the pages to come.

First, it may be that the reason for the importance of psychological imbalance stems from the stimulus-generalization processes. That is, individuals may find physiological-stimulus balance states more satisfying than an imbalanced condition. Since such physiological stimuli would then generalize to psychological stimuli by simple contiguity processes, we would therefore find balanced states, that is, where the pieces fit together and we can easily predict one phenomenon from knowledge of another, are far more satisfying for us. It should be noted that this argument is highly similar to the notions underlying a good Gestalt (i.e., it is regular and organized). In this sense, then, striving for consistency is similar to striving for a good Gestalt, a not unsurprising similarity considering the direct historical linkage between Gestalt psychology and much of contemporary social psychology. Secondly, balanced states may enable us to operate more effectively cognitively. Thus, an imbalanced state may stimulate behavior designed to reduce it, because imbalance may make the world more difficult for us to understand and predict. Consider, for example, how we would feel if Spiro Agnew had suddenly said he was in favor of amnesty for those who avoided the Army during the Vietnam conflict. Imbalances like this make the world more anxiety provoking and more frustrating, since not knowing how others will react and behave makes it difficult to satisfy our own desires and motives adequately. We, therefore, encourage and reward ourselves and others to act in a consistent fashion so that we may know and understand the world better and, thus, satisfy our own needs (Brehm and Cohen, 1962; Baron, 1968). Third, we may engage in consistent behavior because it makes us more credible and understandable in the eyes of others. Having such status then enables us to influence others in order to achieve our particular goals (Tedeschi, Schlenker, and Bonoma, 1971). Fourth, there is some evidence to support the hypothesis that imbalance may be considered as a secondary source of drive in a Hullian sense. However, evidence exists both for and against this proposition (Pallak and Pittman, 1972; Seudfeld and Epstein, 1971).

Whatever the reason, and all of the above as well as others may be involved, there is considerable support for the basic assumption that psychological imbalance is, at least under some conditions (as we will see), a sufficient condition for the arousal and direction of behavior aimed at reducing that imbalance.

Returning, then, to Heider and the research stimulated by his theorizing, supportive findings such as the following are available in the literature:

1. Jordan (1953) tested and supported the hypothesis that hypothetical imbalanced situations would be rated as more unpleasant than hypothetical balanced situations.[1]

2. Zajonc and Burnstein (1965) found that triads about relevant issues that were balanced were learned more rapidly than those that were imbalanced; for irrelevant issues, balance did not have an influence on learning.

3. People who interact frequently (i.e., are more likely to be seen as "belonging" to one another) are more likely to like one another, according to Homans (1950) and Festinger, Schacter, and Back (1950).

4. Knowledge that one had been assigned somebody else as a partner increased the attractiveness of the other person even before personal contact with the individual (Darley and Berscheid, 1967).

5. Using the galvanic skin response (GSR) as a measure of emotionality in balanced and unbalanced situations, Burdick and Byrnes (1958) found

[1]It should be noted that Jordan also found support for the hypothesis that positive situations are more pleasant than negative ones, independently of balance. In addition, Whitney (1971) has failed to replicate Jordan's research.

that (a) the GSR differed depending on whether the subjects agreed or disagreed with a well-liked experimenter, and (b) subjects who liked an experimenter tended to change their opinions toward greater agreement with him, while those who disliked him tended to change their opinions toward greater disagreement.

In addition to these studies, Heider's work has also served as the basic paradigm for a theory of communications behavior suggested by Newcomb (1956) known as the *A-B-X* model, and research relating to this theory is relevant to any evaluation of Heider. The essential logic of the *A-B-X* model is to apply the notion of a drive toward balance as being the basic motivating force underlying the directiveness of the communicative act between people. Starting from the basic postulation of a strain toward symmetry that leads to a communality of attitudes of two people (*A* and *B*) concerning a third social object (*X*), Newcomb argues that this strain toward symmetry influences communication between *A* and *B* so as to bring such attitudes toward *X* into congruence. There are a number of research findings consistent with the *A-B-X* model. One of the most important of these is Newcomb's own field study of the acquaintance process (Newcomb, 1961). In this study two separate groups of freshmen at the University of Michigan who had not previously known one another were invited to live at a rent-free house in return for their willingness to serve as experimental subjects. In line with his theoretical expectations, Newcomb found that individuals who were attracted to one another tended to increasingly agree over time on such things as the way they perceive their real selves, their ideal selves, and their attractions toward other group members. In other words, using the abstract symbols we used earlier, if *P* likes *O,* the tendency will be for both to think alike about *X*. Moreover, also in line with predictions, these findings occurred for both real and perceived similarities.

In addition to Newcomb's own work, there are a considerable number of other findings that support the general predictions that can be made from his theory. For example, there are many studies showing that attitudes toward a communicator (e.g., his prestige and/or his competence) are a determinant of the degree to which the communicator's message will have an effect on the recipient (Hovland, Janis, and Kelley, 1953). The fact that this effect is transitory is usually accounted for by the fact that, over time, the source is disassociated from the message. When the subject is reminded reminded later about the nature of the communicator, the prestige effect shows up again (Kelman and Hovland, 1953). This seems to justify the conclusion that if the association between the source (*O*) and the message (*X*) can be kept in the cognitive structure of the recipient, then a direct positive relationship results between source prestige and message effectiveness.

Despite these affirmations of direct support for the Heider model and its indirect support through the research upholding Newcomb's *A-B-X* theory, it has long been apparent that the major value of the Heider approach lies in its historical importance as the forerunner of later, more sophisticated balance models. When viewed in and of itself, however, the Heider theory has a number of significant flaws, in addition to those stemming from the preference to state predictions in terms of tendencies rather than behaviors (Shaw and Costanzo, 1970). One flaw is that the Heider model does not account for the fact that differences in degree of liking are both possible and likely. Taking account of these differences may be crucial in any given case of balance restoration as, for example, when P likes O a little, dislikes X a lot, and perceives that O likes X a lot. In this case, he may change his attitudes toward O. On the other hand, if the differences in degree were reversed, he might change his attitudes toward X. The point is that differences in degree of liking could be very important. A second flaw is that Heider's approach does not tell us how we may know when the degree of imbalance has reached the point that behavior is aroused. What is needed is both the theoretical basis for predicting when behavior will be aroused and a method of measuring whether that point has been reached. Heider's approach never provided us with either.

More recently, however, Newcomb (1968) has attempted to deal with these difficulties in the Heider model and to take the general approach (which he has also followed) to higher levels of theoretical and empirical sophistication. Basically, what he has done is to suggest a number of revisions of the basic Heider framework that he feels are justified on the basis of empirical data and that seem to have substantive theoretical significance.

One of these suggestions is that the perceived relationships between the various cognitive units (i.e., P-O-X) that are the basic units of the theory might be best thought of as attitudinal relationships only, rather than either attitudinal or unit (belongingness) linkages. The latter type of linkage apparently is not as meaningful to the individuals involved, in that imbalances of this type do not seem to elicit responses consistent with the theory.

Second, Newcomb suggests and cites evidence that the balance principle may not hold when P does not like O, that is, when $P \underrightarrow{=} O$. The reason for this is that if $P \underrightarrow{=} O$, then he would not care particularly what O thought about X or any other social object. Thus, a balanced situation when $P \underrightarrow{=} O$ is no more pleasant in affect to the individual than an imbalanced situation where $P \underrightarrow{=} O$. In diagram form, this would mean that

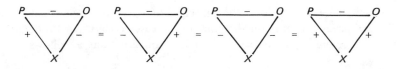

in degree of positive affect.

Finally, Newcomb suggests that balance-seeking behaviors are most likely to take place when people are actively engaged in situations and the objects involved are highly important to the individual. If the situation is not important and not significant to the person, then the person is not likely to be aroused to any form of behavior. He will just be apathetic.

Despite these suggestions by Newcomb, however, it should be noted by the reader that the other problems we cited with the Heider theory still remain.

Osgood and Tannenbaum's Congruity Theory

Although congruity, as developed by Osgood and Tannenbaum (1955), is in its basic orientation a special case of balance theory as developed by Heider, the identity is in some respects a misleading one. The reason it is misleading is that congruity theory is far more sophisticated in terms of its measurement aspects and the preciseness of its predictions. In this way, it overcomes, at least to some degree, the very real measurement problems of the Heider approach to consistency motivation that we spoke of earlier. However, its advances in measurement are limited, as we will see, and the advances it does make are at a cost. The cost is that congruity theory is considerably more limited in scope than other theories, concerning itself only with two major phenomena. First, it deals with the problem of predicting the direction of attitude change as a function of the nature and characteristics of attitude-change messages. Second, it deals with the prediction of how complex stimuli will be evaluated as a function of the simple stimuli out of which they are constructed (Tannenbaum, 1968). Since it is the former case that has received the most attention, this is the area we will discuss here. There are two basic assumptions of Osgood and Tannenbaum's congruity theory:

1. Evaluative judgments tend toward maximal simplicity. Since "black or white," "all or nothing," or "you're with us or against us" evaluative judgments are easier to make than more refined, differentiated ones, there is continuing pressure within the cognitive structure toward judgments of this nature, and, therefore, toward the polarization of one's opinions.
2. Since seeing two things as being identical is less complex than seeing them as being finely discriminated from one another, related concepts will tend to be brought together within one's cognitive structure and related to one another in a similar manner.

Given these assumptions, the principle of congruity argues that attitude change will always occur in the direction of increased congruity with the prevailing frame of reference. This may occur in different situations, as follows:

1. When the recipient's attitude toward a communicator is positive and the object about which he is talking is also positive, but the statement the communicator makes about the object is a negative (disassociative) one. (For example, if a supporter of Richard Nixon and free enterprise

should hear a speech in which Nixon attacks the capitalist system, this would be an incongruous situation that would initiate attitude change processes.)

2. When the recipient's attitude toward a communicator is positive, the object about which he is talking is also positive, and the statement is a positive (associative) one. (This would happen if the same person heard Nixon defend capitalism. Here there would be no incongruity and, hence, no attitude change processes.)

3. When the recipient's attitude toward a communicator is positive (negative) and the object about which he is talking is negative (positive), but the statement is a positive (associative) one. (This situation is one in which the same person and his neighbor, a member of left-oriented political groups, might both hear Nixon defend state socialism. For both of these people, there is an incongruity in perception, and attitude-change processes are instituted.)

4. When the recipient's attitude toward a communicator is positive (negative), and the object about which he is talking is negative (positive), and the statement is a negative (disassociative) one. (This, of course, is if the man and his neighbor hear Nixon denounce state socialism. Here there is no incongruity and no behavior is aroused.)

It is the basic prediction of congruity theory that when sources of statements and objects of statements are linked (or associated) by an assertion in an incongruous fashion, there will be a tendency to change attitudes toward both the source and the object in the direction of increased congruency. The change that will take place will, first of all, depend on whether the assertion is positive or negative in terms of how it links the person making the assertion (i.e., the source) and the object of the assertion (i.e., what the statement is being made about). Second, it depends on how the person feels about the source and object and the strength of these original feelings. Finally, the degree of change will also depend on how discrepant these attitudes are to begin with. These three factors then combine (with two other minor factors we will mention in a moment) to influence behavior in the following ways:

1. If a highly positive source makes an associative statement about a less positive object, then congruity would be achieved by evaluating' the highly positive source a little less positively (since he has been associated with a less positive object) and the less positive object more positively (since it has been linked with a highly positive source). Thus, a person who liked Richard Nixon very much and Nelson Rockefeller a little, would, upon hearing Nixon making a speech praising Rockefeller, like Nixon a little less and like Rockefeller a little more.

2. If a somewhat positive source (for example, Rockefeller, in the example above) says something in an associative fashion about a somewhat negative object (the Democratic Party), the source (Rockefeller) becomes viewed more negatively and the object (the Democratic Party) more positively.

3. If a slightly positive source (Rockefeller) says something in a disassociative fashion about a slightly negative object (George McGovern), a polarization process takes place that leads to the source (Rockefeller) being viewed as highly positive and the object (McGovern) as highly negative.

Osgood and Tannenbaum are able to make such specific directional predictions as these, and even more, as we will see, because from the beginning their theorizing has been keyed around and coordinated with the measurement procedure known as the semantic differential technique. The purpose of this technique is to determine the meaning that concepts and stimuli have for individuals, and its essential logic is to ask people to check off on seven-point bipolar adjective scales the types of associations they make to a given concept. Consider the following example:

The Democratic Party

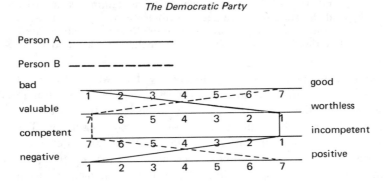

In this case, Person A sees the Democratic Party in a pretty negative light, checking those points on the scale quite close to the negative adjectives; whereas Person B sees the same concept (i.e., the Democratic Party) in pretty much the opposite fashion in that he checks the higher, more positive portions of each scale. In Osgood and Tannenbaum's terminology, such profiles constitute the meaning of a concept to an individual, and a highly significant component of such meaning is the person's general evaluation of the concept. In fact, it has been found that such evaluative judgments are by far the most significant components in the meaning of a variable, and those scales that measure this component correlate highly with the concept as measured by regular attitude scales. Osgood and Tannenbaum have used such semantic differential measures as their way of operationalizing actual attitudes toward other peoples and things, and it is because of such coordination that they are able to make the precise predictions they do.

The advantages of such precision may be illustrated, if we assume first, from our above example, that a person's attitude toward an object is an average of his evaluative ratings. In the above example, Person A's attitude toward the Democratic Party would be 1.00 (1 + 1 + 1 + 1 divided by 4) while

B's would be 7.0 (7 + 7 + 7 + 7 divided by 4). Predictions might then be made as follows:

1. If somebody highly valued by both A and B (e.g., somebody rated at 7.0) makes an associative statement about the Democratic Party, then Person A would achieve congruity by changing his rating of the person to be more negative and his rating of the Democratic Party to be more positive. On the other hand, Person B would not change his attitudes at all on hearing the same statement.

2. If a person who is valued somewhat positively (5) by both A and B says something positive about the Democratic Party, he would go down in the estimation of Person A and up in the estimation of Person B. On the other hand, changes in the evaluation of the Democratic Party would show a reverse process, in that A would come to see it more positively and B would come to evaluate it more negatively.

3. If the same person had said something in a disassociative fashion about the Democratic Party, the reverse process would have taken place. That is, he would have gone down in the estimate of Person B since he was disassociating himself from a highly positive concept. On the other hand, he would have gone up in the view of Person A since, for that person, the Democratic Party is quite negative and he was disassociating himself from it. Similar reasoning would be used if the statement were associative.

How much change actually takes place? Do the attitudes toward both the source and object change equally, or does one change more than the other? In addition to their major advance in predicting the direction in which the congruity will be resolved, Osgood and Tannenbaum actually go even further and predict that the actual movement of attitudes after the communicative assertion is made will be in inverse proportion to the original polarization (i.e., the original extremity of the attitude). Thus, they argue that attitudes originally rated at 7 or 1 will be less likely to change than those originally scaled at 3, 4, or 5. Hence, an assertion linking a source rated at 7 and an object rated at 5 will see a greater positive change for the latter than a negative change for the former. (Formulas actually predicting the degrees of such change have been developed by Osgood and his co-workers and are available [1957].) The point to which the change process gravitates is predicted to be that point at which objects linked together associatively are viewed similarly as measured by the semantic differential, and objects disassociated from one another are viewed and evaluated in an opposite manner. An associative connection between Nixon (when rated 7) and the Republican Party (when rated 4) would lead to an eventual reevaluation of both at approximately 6. A disassociative connection between Nixon (when rated 5) and the Democratic Party (when rated 3) would lead to the former being rated 7 and the latter rated 1. This would be the state of congruity to which the change process would gravitate, or at least so the theory predicts, with one exception.

This exception occurs because of two theoretical innovations in the congruity model, innovations that operate in conjunction with the three factors we mentioned previously in affecting the degree of change that takes place. One innovation is the correction for incredulity that is applied to all assertions between sources and objects and that, in essence, states the condition under which all of the facts stated previously will not operate. Thus, if the assertion is too discrepant with one's preexisting cognitive structure, incongruity is reduced by just not believing the statement. For example, if a statement were published claiming that the prime minister of Israel had asserted that Adolf Hitler had been correct in his attitudes toward Jews, nobody would believe it. The effect of this correction for incredulity is that no behavior-change prediction is made in extreme cases, that is, when a source rated 7 asserts positive statements about objects rated 1, or when a 7 source acts in a negative fashion toward objects rated 7 also.

A second innovation proposed by Osgood and Tannenbaum is a correction based on the assumption that attitudes toward objects will change more than attitudes toward sources. This second correction, formulas for which are also available, is a significant aid in predicting which attitudes will change in the achieving of congruity.

There are a number of studies that provide fairly strong support for the congruity principle (Tannenbaum, 1968). Of these, perhaps the following are among the most worthy of being cited:

1. Paragraphs of different passages of merit (all written by Robert Louis Stevenson) correlated +.33 to +.53 with the merit of the author to whom attached (Sherif, 1935).
2. Tannenbaum and Gengel (1966) showed that attitudes experimentally controlled could be changed in a manner consistent with congruity theory.

Overall, however, it cannot be said that congruity theory has generated a great amount of research, a fact somewhat surprising considering its general sophistication and the preciseness of its predictions. Thus, while it does have such weaknesses as not providing means for assessing the strength of assertions or for the fact that incongruity reduction may take place in ways not specified by the theory, these weaknesses are relatively common to all consistency theories, while the others do not have the strengths of the congruity approach. It is somewhat puzzling, then, that the amount of research it has generated has been small when compared to other consistency theories, in particular the theory of cognitive dissonance to which we now turn.

Festinger's Theory of Cognitive Dissonance

No discussion of consistency motivation would be complete without mention of the theory of cognitive dissonance, the giant of theories of this nature if we use as a criterion the degree of research and controversy stimulated.

The logic of dissonance theory as originally expounded by Festinger (1957) is really quite simple at first glance and one wonders why it has stirred up the fuss it has. However, this wonder soon ends as the implications of the theory are explored and tested. The basic postulates of the theory are as follows:

1. Man has cognitions about the world and about himself (cognitions are bits of knowledge, attitudes, and perceptions).
2. These cognitions may have three forms of relationship with one another within the individual's cognitive apparatus.
3. One relationship is that any two cognitions may be consonant with one another. By consonant, Festinger means that one cognition follows from the other, for example, when a person who enjoys watching a baseball game goes to a baseball game.
4. A second type of relationship between any two cognitions is that they may be irrelevant to one another. For example, a person who enjoys watching baseball games decides to have ham and eggs for supper.
5. A third type of relationship between any two cognitions may be that they are dissonant with one another in that considering the two cognitions alone, the obverse of one would follow from the other. For example, a dissonant relationship would be that the person who like watching baseball games goes to the opera even though there is a game being played that he could attend.

Dissonance, according to Festinger, is a negative motivational state that one wishes to reduce when it occurs. Thus, in terms of our interest here, the occurrence of dissonance is postulated to serve as an antecedent condition leading to the arousal of behavior, and direction is a function of choosing those behavioral alternatives that will reduce the dissonance. In addition, dissonance will also be avoided, according to Festinger, through such processes as selective information seeking and the like.

Why does dissonance occur and what determines its magnitude? When does it occur? There are a number of reasons why dissonance could occur, according to Festinger, with the first of these being expectancy disconfirmation. For example, a person may expect, on the basis of physical knowledge, that water will turn to gas when it is exposed to certain high temperatures. If he were to see water being boiled at high temperatures and yet remaining in a liquid state, he would be in a state of dissonance. Secondly, dissonance may arise because one's cognitions are inconsistent with cultural mores. For example, one may see himself as being a respected member of the community and yet know also that he is attracted to socially disvalued behaviors of various types, such as alcoholism. A third source of dissonance may arise because, without any clear justification, one may engage in specific behaviors that are at variance with one's general attitudinal system, such as being a Democrat and voting Republican. Whatever the original reason that dissonance may arise or be anticipated, it can also come from a combination of these determinants. Festinger postulates that the total amount of dissonance a person feels is a function of the total number of units that are in a dissonant relationship with one another, weighted by the importance of the cognitive elements involved. The basic behavioral prediction is that the greater the amount of dissonance, the more likely behavior will be undertaken in order to reduce the dissonance.

This, then, is the theory as Festinger originally postulated it, that is, this is where dissonance comes from, the factors that affect its degree of occurrence, and its predicted behavioral effects. Why has it had such importance in the study of motivational processes of behavior? Perhaps the best way to answer this question is to examine some of the behavioral situations in which it has been applied and the kinds of predictions it makes in each situation. Given such predictions, we will concurrently examine the degree to which such predictions have actually received support in the research literature. Following this discussion, we will turn to an examination of the current state of consistency-motivation theory in general, the questions with which it is currently dealing, the problems it is facing, and some of the ways in which such problems are being resolved. Within the context of such a discussion we will examine the questions and problems of dissonance theory in particular, since to a great extent the problems of dissonance theory are the problems of consistency-motivation theory in general.

Postdecisional Behavior.   One of the most crucial and most intriguing derivations from dissonance theory concerns the kinds of behaviors people will go through *after* they have made a decision of some sort. Suppose, for example, you had just purchased a Chevrolet after considering a Ford. According to Festinger, the making of a choice between alternatives A and B leaves a person with two sets of cognitions. One of these is composed of the reasons he had for making whatever choice he did make (i.e., the reasons he had for buying the Chevrolet), and the second set is composed of all the reasons he had for making the choice he did not make (i.e., the reasons for not buying the Ford). According to Festinger, dissonance will occur in the individual as a result of decision making under the following conditions:

1. The more there are negative aspects in the chosen alternative (the Chevrolet) and positive aspects in the unchosen alternative (the Ford).
2. The importance of the decision.
3. The more the two alternatives are cognitively distinct from one another and cannot be substituted for one another.

The more these conditions occur, according to Festinger, the more he would predict such postdecisional behaviors as (a) the seeking of cognitions that are consonant with the decision (i.e., the buying of the Chevrolet), (b) increased confidence in one's decision after having made it, (c) increased discrepancy in the evaluative rating of the decision alternatives (Ford and Chevrolet) in favor of the choice that was made, and (d) increased difficulty in reversing a decision once it is made.

There are a considerable number of studies that have dealt with these predictions, predictions that suggest reading of Chevy ads more than Ford ads and higher ratings for Chevys than Fords after the purchase of the Chevrolet. Generally, the outcomes of choice studies of this nature have been highly supportive of dissonance theory in a variety of different areas (Zajonc, 1968). The fact that this proposition has received empirical support, therefore, provides evidence for the frequent observation that the less rational a reason you had for doing something, the more you will defend and justify the fact that you did it. This type of nonobvious prediction is, incidentally, one of the reasons for the popularity of dissonance theory.

To take a slight detour for a moment, one other aspect of this dissonance theory derivation is that it also provides an interesting theoretical explanation of how attitudes may develop. It is clearly proposed here that at least some attitudes develop as a function of behaviors, reversing the usual hypothesized causal relationship. Such a reversal sets the stage for a whole variety of other questions, since it leads to some direct implications of great social and theoretical import. It seems to imply that administrative changes (e.g., in civil rights areas) can be introduced without preparation of supportive attitudes to any great extent, since such supportive attitudes will develop as a function of being forced to engage in the behavior. In fact, according to Festinger, all that you would need and want is enough supportive attitudes to just barely pass the legislation, since this would lead to the maximum level of dissonance and, it follows, the greatest amount of attitude change supporting the decision. Anything more than that would be undesirable, since reevaluation of one's previous attitudes would not be necessary in order to justify the new behavior being engaged in, if there was reason to engage in the behavior originally.

However, the support for dissonance theory suggested here is not unequivocal. In a later section of this chapter, we will explore some questions that have been raised about this aspect of dissonance theory and the work of Darryl Bem in proposing an alternative theoretical interpretation of these findings.

Forced Compliance. In this derivation, the logic is based very much on the rationale indicated above, in that it is proposed that dissonance and consequent attitudinal and behavioral realignment to justify behavior occurs when a person publicly acts in a way contrary to his private opinion. Also, the level of dissonance increases when the reasons for so acting are not great, that is, the rewards for doing so are small and/or the punishments for *not* doing so are also small.

There is a great variety of research developed relative to this prediction, some of which is supportive and some of which is not. At one time it was argued that forced compliance would have an effect on behavior in the manner predicted by dissonance theory only if the person felt he had free choice to act in an inconsistent, contrary manner (Brehm and Cohen, 1962). However, this explanation turned out not to be a very satisfactory one since it was difficult to establish experimentally that people would willingly act (e.g., of their own free choice) in a way contrary to their own opinions, and such free choice of behaviors may be necessary for the arousal of dissonance (Brehm and Cohen, 1962). Yet, there is some research that suggests that the choice of behavior not congruent with one's opinions is demonstrable in a research sense (cf. Chapter 10). Perhaps the most meaningful summary one can make at this time is that the evidence for this derivation is, at most, mixed.

Selective Exposure to Information.   Although this is probably the most complex of the dissonance derivations, the results of the research it has stimulated have not been positive for dissonance theory proponents. More specifically, this is the area in which research has been weakest in upholding support of the theory.

The derivation itself has been described by Shaw and Costanzo (1970) as follows:

> As stated earlier, dissonance results in selective exposure to information: the individual will seek consonance-producing information and avoid dissonance-producing information. Festinger hypothesized that active information seeking is curvilinearly related to the magnitude of dissonance. If there is little or no dissonance, the person will neither seek consonant nor avoid dissonant information. Moderate amounts of dissonance lead to maximum information-seeking/avoidance behavior. With near maximum dissonance there is again a decrease in selective exposure, and the person may actually seek out dissonance-producing information. This latter is based upon the assumption that the person will try to increase the dissonance to an intolerable level that will bring about a change in some aspect of the situation, and, ultimately, dissonance reduction. (P. 212)

In 1965, a literature review was published by Freedman and Sears that concluded that this dissonance-theory prediction was clearly not supported. Considering the fact that the dissonance approach has received considerable support in many of the other areas to which it has been applied, why did this happen? A psychologist named R. J. Rhine (1967a, b) has recently suggested that there were methodological flaws in previous tests of this derivation and has outlined a different way of approaching the question. Rhine's argument is essentially quite similar to the one we developed in Chapter 4 in our discussion of the various problems involved in testing the activation-theory framework. He argues that this derivation cannot be tested using only two levels of dissonance because curvilinear relationships are being postulated. According to Rhine (1967a), the derivation leads to behavioral predictions of the form indicated in Figure 7.1, a form that means at least *three* levels of dissonance must occur in order for an adequate test of the hypothesis to occur. Although it is not

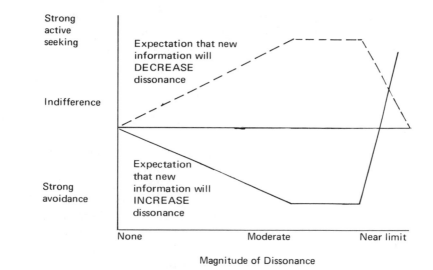

Figure 7.1 Relation between magnitude of dissonance and active seeking of new information. *Source:* R. J. Rhine, Some problems in dissonance theory research on information-selectivity. *Psychological Bulletin, 68,* 1967, 21-28. Copyright 1967 by the American Psychological Association. Reprinted by permission.

emphasized by Rhine, the reader will recall from our previous discussion that the various levels must occur at sufficiently spaced points along the continuum or the predicted curvilinear relationship will not occur. In addition, a really adequate test of the model, in the sense of giving the investigator an opportunity of finding positive results, should have some prior basis for predicting where the high points of the curve should occur.

Using a more methodologically adequate approach, Rhine (1967b) has reported the results of a study that gave greater support for the dissonance-theory framework than previous research had indicated. It may be, then, that a greater degree of support for this dissonance-theory prediction will be forthcoming. But before we get too optimistic, it is essential that we realize that such improvement will have to rest on advances in the adequacy of measuring the degree to which the person is in a dissonant state, since this will allow more precise prediction as to when the most information seeking will take place. As we will point out later in this chapter, however, there have been almost no improvements at all in the direct measurement of dissonance since the early days of the theory. In addition, it may also be that other theoretical frameworks will be more useful in enabling us to understand information-seeking behavior. As an example, Feather (1967) has proposed and offered support for a model of information-seeking behavior that is an integration of both the consistency and expectancy-value frameworks. The major principle underlying his argument is that information seeking is a function of the values expected to be gained by the information, with his assumptions being that values can be either extrinsic or intrinsic in nature. In addition, the psychological state of consistency can be a value worth attaining under certain conditions, in and of itself. Such an approach, Feather suggests, may eventually account for information-seeking behavior more satisfactorily than the dissonance model has been able to do up to now.

Partial Reinforcement. Perhaps one of the most intriguing derivations made by dissonance theory is its predictions concerning the problem of partial reinforcement spoken of in Chapters 2 and 3 in our discussion of Hullian theory. The problem, the reader will recall, is that there is clear behavioral data that organisms reinforced for learning on a partial-reinforcement schedule (i.e., on fewer than 100 percent of the trials) will persist in the learned behavior longer after reinforcement has been totally withdrawn (i.e., during extinction) than those reinforced more often (i.e., for 100 percent of the learning trials). As we saw, this has been a particularly difficult finding to account for within a mechanistic, natural-science framework of the type expounded by Hull and his followers. In a series of animal experiments, however, Festinger and another psychologist at Stanford University, D. H. Lawrence, proposed to account for these findings by arguing that the partial-reinforcement effect is, in essence, nothing but a manifestation of the forced compliance predictions we have spoken of earlier (Lawrence and Festinger, 1962). Thus, the organism who learns something for less reward (i.e., those on a partial-reinforcement schedule) is in a more dissonant state than the organism who has learned the same behavior for more reward (i.e., those on a full-reinforcement schedule). Being in a dissonant state, he is motivated to reduce the inconsistent cognitions that (a) he has engaged in work (i.e., he has learned something), and (b) he has not gotten much for it (i.e., he has only been partially reinforced). How does he reduce such dissonance? Since he cannot deny the fact that he has engaged in behavior, this can most easily be done by convincing oneself that there are intrinsic values in the behavior over and above any reinforced reason for engaging in behavior. Such attitudinal reevaluation and enhancement of the behaviors involved take place in the partially reinforced group and serve as a reason for behavior arousal and direction (since the behavior is now desirable) after all reinforcement has been withdrawn, both full and partial. In this way, then, dissonance theory is proposed as a way of accounting for the partial-reinforcement phenomenon.

The argument is an ingenious one and it has become a major contender in explanations of the partial-reinforcement phenomenon. It has one weakness, which is that the argument being proposed is a cognitive one, even though all the data to date, so far as this author is aware, is based on animal research. While work based on the latter type of subject is of great value for any motivational theory, it would appear that findings with human subjects need to be obtained before a full evaluation of this particular hypothesis can be made.

This, then, is the logic of dissonance theory and some of the major areas in which it has been applied. It is an intriguing approach, particularly in its capacity to generate subtle, nonobvious predictions that are frequently supported when empirical data are obtained. However, the predictions are not always supported, and even when they are, problems sometimes emerge as to the nature of the interpretations that can safely be made. Since these problems are very often the problems of consistency theory in general, however, we shall bring these out during the course of such a general discussion, a discussion to which we shall now turn.

CONSISTENCY MOTIVATION:
SOME CONTINUING QUESTIONS

In this section we shall examine the current status of consistency theories, the logical and empirical problems they face, and the manner in which such problems are being attacked. These questions have been examined in extensive papers by McGuire (1966) and Pepitone (1966), and we shall be relying heavily on their thinking in the following pages.

Perhaps the best place to start is with this question: If consistency is such an important motivational variable, why are there inconsistencies in our cognitions at all? In a sense, this question points out a very important limitation to all our discussions in this chapter. This is that whatever the value of consistency motivation, it will always be an incomplete theory of motivation since, clearly, inconsistencies exist in the cognitions of all of us at one time or another. In addition, it may even be, as Bem (1970) has suggested, that consistency may not be important for some people, e.g., those who are not intellectually oriented and who do not care particularly about the degree to which they present a logical, coherent, consistent picture to the world. However, even granting that such limitations do exist, all this means is that consistency motivation will not account for all behavior. Since such a position has not been adopted by any consistency theorist we know of, this argument is not greatly relevant as far as we can see. What is relevant, however, is that consistency motivation does seem to be an important influence on behavior. Hence, it warrants the attention we shall devote to it here.

Turning to more content-oriented questions, one of the most significant has centered on the different modes for resolving cognitive inconsistencies. What are the different modes of resolving imbalance in one's cognitions and what are the factors that determine one's choice as to how to reduce such inconsistencies? Unless these questions are resolved, it is clear that we will have difficulty in understanding the results of experiments and in designing them properly to begin with. It may be that in experiments where the consistency model doesn't work, the inconsistency was resolved in ways not thought of by the experimenter, ways more appropriate to the given experimental situation.

To indicate the complexity involved and the possibility for inappropriate inferences to occur, it is possible to distinguish at least nine different ways of resolving cognitive inconsistencies. For example, it is possible to just repress the inconsistency and not allow it to reach consciousness. This is a procedure that therapists have argued to be of considerable clinical significance from the time of Freud. Secondly, a process of bolstering may be used whereby a person, when confronted with an inconsistency, will develop a great deal of evidence supporting one of the beliefs. This will bolster it and, at the same time, submerge (although probably not entirely eliminate) the conflicting cognition. A third method involves the "mote" method, whereby a person resolves his inconsistency by pointing out that others are even worse than he. Fourth, and slightly more complex than this, there is the procedure known as differentiation, a procedure best illustrated by the situation in which a person believes in the theory of evolution, but also is religious and has positive feelings toward the Bible. The manner in which he might resolve this inconsistency is by first differentiating between the literal Bible and the figurative Bible, and then claiming to love the latter rather than the former. This would lead to a cognitive structure involving positive feelings toward the figurative Bible and evolution and a lack of positive feelings toward the literal Bible, a not inconsistent situation. A fifth way of resolving inconsistency, which is also a little complex, is the procedure known as transcendence, a process by which the person decides that the Bible and evolution are two faces of a higher reality that has led to both. He can, therefore, have positive affect toward both since they have both been created by a higher power, and it is this higher power toward which he has the overall positive feeling. Sixth, cognitive inconsistencies may be resolved by psychologically changing one's self-definition of one of the cognitions causing the imbalance. For example, suppose a person sees himself as an ethical human being on the one hand and on the other spends some of his spare time scalping tickets to sold-out theatrical and sporting events.[2] There are at least two ways that such a person might resolve this inconsistency. First, he might claim that he is making tickets available to people who would otherwise be shut out. Second, he could argue that he is doing a favor for the person who cannot get a good ticket to a game (or theater) because he is not rich enough to buy a season ticket and it is the people (or corporations) who buy season tickets who get the choice locations. The reader may, of course, question the ethicality of scalping despite such cognitive redefinitions, but the point is that such a process could easily be used, particularly in those states where the person is helped by the fact that scalping is

[2]Scalping tickets involves obtaining tickets at regular, listed prices and then reselling them at whatever the traffic will bear right before the event. Depending on the event, such resales might go at 5 to 10 times the listed price, although this is unusual. More often the increased price is less than this. In rare cases, tickets may go at less than the listed prices if demand for the event has suddenly lessened for some reason.

not illegal.[3] A seventh way of resolving cognitive inconsistency is to just downgrade and devalue the importance of the whole area in question. Festinger (1957) cited this as a very significant alternative that might be used in resolving dissonance, but unfortunately, he never provided any procedures by which to predict the conditions under which this method would be used. An eighth procedure for overcoming inconsistency stems from the assumption in all consistency theories that inconsistency is a state of dissatisfaction that humans are motivated to reduce. One way of reducing such dissatisfaction might be to see what kinds of satisfactions are available in the environment at the time and attempt to achieve these, whether or not they are related to the original inconsistency. In this way, overall satisfaction would be increased and the tension resulting from the inconsistency would be reduced in its overall salience for the individual. A good example of this is a study by Goodman and Friedman (1969) in which subjects were manipulated to believe they were receiving financial outcomes too high for their qualifications. The manner in which they resolved their problems depended on the kinds of satisfactions made available to them by the experimenter, even though in at least one case the method of achieving satisfactions may have increased the feelings of imbalance by increasing income even more. In this case, the rationale essentially was that the experimenter allowed them to make even more money (value) to overcome feelings of dissatisfaction related to inconsistency, and the subjects did behave in the way predicted. (These results, incidentally, led these researchers to suggest expectancy X value theory as a better overall framework for understanding motivational processes, with inequity reduction being only one source of value.) Finally, a ninth way of reducing inconsistency, which is somewhat related to our earlier discussion is that people may just learn to tolerate the inconsistency. All of us have to do this to some extent and it is just part of life, this argument goes. There seems to be little doubt that this argument must have some validity, since we must be able to tolerate inconsistency to some extent in our lives.

One clear implication of there being so many different ways to reduce inconsistency is that the failure of an experiment to evidence dissonance reduction may be due to another method of dissonance reduction being used without the experimenter's knowledge. This is only one aspect of the question, however. There are other aspects to be considered. One of these other factors is that these different approaches are probably complementary to one another, rather than mutually exclusive. Hence, an added problem is that it is at least theoretically possible that a person may be resolving inconsistency at a given

---

[3]The argument here is one that is reminiscent of the logic underlying Machiavellianism, a type of behavior viewed as the using of others in order to achieve one's personal ends. Indeed, there are research data that support the conclusions that high Machiavellians do not engage in dissonance-reduction processes after engaging in behavior some would consider unethical (Burgoon, Miller, and Tubbs, 1972).

time in a specific situation by using two (or more) processes in that particular instance. When we also add other factors, such as the fact that it is likely that people differ both among themselves and over time in the processes they favor using, it is perhaps no wonder that the question of how people choose the method of dissonance reduction they will use is one of the major ones concerning contemporary investigators of consistency motivation (Steiner and Johnson, 1965; Campbell et al., 1970).

To cite a concrete example of the significance of this question, one continuing controversy has stemmed from the fact that the dissonance formulation has been tested primarily by experimentally manipulating the dissonance levels of Ss cognitions and then allowing such dissonance to be reduced only (supposedly) by means controlled by the experimenter. However, such manipulations and their adequacy have come under very severe attack in recent years, and at least one of the kinds of questions that have arisen has important implications for the general problem of determining how people choose their means of dissonance reduction. We are referring to the fact that in many cases individuals have been eliminated from the experiment because they didn't respond to the manipulation (Chapanis and Chapanis, 1964). Is this due to experimenter inadequacy, or the fact that these people are not dissonant prone, or the fact that they immediately reduce dissonance by depreciating the value of the experiment and not responding appropriately to the experimenter's question? We don't know. Similarly, we don't know when a dissonance (or other inconsistency) experiment fails, whether this is due to (a) the S resolving inconsistency by a method not known or controlled by the experimenter, (b) a failure of the manipulation, (c) the inadequacy of the theory, or (d) some combination of these. It seems clear that the only way we can answer such questions, at least partially, as Aronson (1968) has proposed, is to understand more about how people prefer to reduce dissonance in given situations and the various parameters that influence such preferences for given situations. Work is only beginning in this area, but illustrative of some of the ways in which this problem has been dealt with is some of Aronson's (1968) own work concerning preferences for modes of dissonance reduction following an unsuccessful expenditure of effort (e.g., the partial-reinforcement situation). Thus, Aronson suggests that if the task effort has been of a relatively short duration, dissonance will be reduced by depreciating the goal (e.g., the "sour grapes" phenomenon). On the other hand, if the task has involved an effort of long duration, the individual is more likely to argue that the task has heretofore unknown values and benefits, since it is only in this way that he can justify the amount of time he spent on it. Similarly, Aronson quotes research supporting the hypothesis that people will choose that mode of dissonance reduction least likely to be challenged by future events. Another illustration is a recent study by Leventhal and Lane (1970) that supports the idea that expected cultural norms for men and women can influence the mode of dissonance reduction.

Another question in the consistency-theory approach of particular importance involves the problem of measurement. How do we measure (a) the relevance and importance of cognitions to an individual, (b) his degree of dissonance, and (c) his degree of self-perception, either consciously or unconsciously, to determine that he is in a state of inconsistency? As Pepitone (1966) has pointed out, these questions are crucial for consistency theory since behavior predictions would depend on answers to them. Yet, little research has been forthcoming, and what there is is not very encouraging (Farley, 1969).

Another problem category of particular significance in discussing methods of inconsistency reduction concerns those aspects of the cognitive system most likely to be changed as a result of the desire to achieve consistency. As we have mentioned earlier, Osgood and Tannenbaum (1955) predict that those cognitions less polarized in value and affect are most likely to change, a view with which some others have agreed (Abelson and Rosenberg, 1958). However, McGuire (1966) makes a prediction opposite from this, in that he argues that those cognitions most distorted by wishful thinking (e.g., have the most affect) will change the most. Unfortunately, research testing these opposing predictions has not been done, nor is there any data available using adequate methodological procedures testing some of the other suggestions made in response to this question. Of these other hypotheses concerning elements of the cognitive structure most susceptible to change, those that seem particularly fruitful for research purposes and investigation might include the following:

1. Cognitions about objects change more than cognitions about people (Osgood and Tannenbaum, 1955).
2. Cognitions that stand alone and are not supported by other cognitions are most likely to change (Festinger, 1957).
3. Inconsistent cognitions that can be made consistent by changing minus to positive are more likely to be changed than those where positive signs have to be made negative (Newcomb, 1968).

It is clear that such topics as the various modes of dissonance reduction, measurement problems, and differential resistance to change by the various segments of the cognitive apparatus are only some of the questions concerning consistency theorists. Another major theoretical problem stems from some research we briefly mentioned previously. This is the work of Darryl Bem (1966, 1970), a psychologist who has developed an alternative explanation to the famous dissonance experiments showing that people who are paid less to perform an unpleasant task will describe themselves as liking it more than those who are paid more for performing the same task. According to Bem, such descriptions of "liking for the task" merely result from the tendency to describe oneself and one's characteristics as a function of surrounding environmental cues, and that a dissonant state need not be postulated in order to explain why people who have been paid $1 for performing a negative task claim to like it more than those who have been paid $20. According to Bem the individual looks at himself and what he is doing, looks at the fee ($1), and consequently says to himself "I must really like this task – I'm doing it for only $1!" As support for his notions, Bem has shown that when he presents the situation to onlookers and asks them to predict ratings, they also predict higher ratings for the $1 group than those paid $20. In other words, they also use, as he predicts, the environmental cues to argue "he must really like what he is doing; he is only being paid $1 for it." This appears to corroborate the argument by Bem that dissonance does not have to be involved, since the onlookers are not behaving!

The implications of Bem's work are to throw open the whole question of the necessity of a dissonance explanation and to lead us to ask whether other dissonance-theory findings might also be subject to different explanations. (It might be noted, incidentally, that there is little reason to think, as yet, that Bem's proposals are necessarily the best alternative. One possible limitation has been suggested by Leventhal, Klemp, and Brown (1972) who have found that the type of explanation suggested by Bem holds only when the person doesn't have personal subjective experience to guide him in rating how the person likes the task. If he has had personal experience with the task, the objective cues suggested by Bem do not have great influence, or so Leventhal and his co-workers suggest.)

In other directions, other questions currently being investigated by consistency theorists, or suggested as needing research, include the following:

1. How is the degree of inconsistency in the cognitive system to be defined by measurement? Shall it be the ratio of inconsistent to consistent cognitions? Or shall it be the strength of the weakest set of cognitions (consistent or inconsistent)? There is some evidence for the former (Glass, 1968), but it may be that under some conditions the latter can be used to define the degree of inconsistency.

2. What are the individual and situational determinants of degree of tolerance for inconsistency?

3. What are the necessary conditions for inconsistency arousal? Can we experience inconsistency without being aware of it? Most data suggest awareness is not necessary, but perhaps awareness of the elements that make up the cognitive structure is necessary. One factor suggested as being necessary for dissonance arousal for which some evidence does exist is that of commitment to a specific action or point of view (Brehm and Cohen, 1962). Glass (1968) has cited some of the evidence supporting the significance of commitment to a specific behavior as very important for dissonance arousal, suggesting that it works primarily by influencing which cognitions are relevant to a person, and thus potentially dissonance arousing.

   In addition, as we mentioned earlier in our discussion of the forced compliance paradigm in dissonance research, free choice of behavior seems to be important as a prerequisite to the arousal of dissonance as a determinant of behavior (Brehm and Cohen, 1962). The rationale here is that free choice implies commitment, commitment leads to relevance, and relevance is necessary for dissonance arousal.

4. What is the role of external cues in the environment in determining the nature of inconsistency reduction? Is there some systematic relationship between the nature of the external environment and the nature of the inconsistency that together account for the arousal and direction of behavior?

SOME COMMENTS AND CONCLUSIONS
ON CONSISTENCY MOTIVATION

In a very real sense the immediately preceding section should justifiably cause the reader to ask why consistency motivation has remained so popular and so viable, considering the very many real questions that can be, have been, and continue to be raised about the approach (and we have not dealt with them all here). There is no easy answer to this, partially because of the very legitimacy of the question. However, there are some reasons why the popularity of the approach has remained so great, even considering these problems.

One of the reasons has to do with the capacity of some of the theories involved, particularly dissonance theory, to generate frequently supported subtle, nonobvious predictions. Psychologists often like to argue that human behavior is far more complex than common sense and that it involves more than the homilies and bromides many of us learned as children. Perhaps it is in a theory such as dissonance theory that the field has developed a relatively coherent approach for explaining, at least to some degree, those perversities of human behavior that the layman finds so puzzling and at the same time so fascinating.

Second, consistency theorists of the cognitive era (post-World War II) have dealt to a great extent with very real-life, human problems. As we will point out in the rest of this book, the general consistency approach has been of considerable value in dealing with such pragmatic questions as value development, receptiveness to financial incentives, achievement, aggression, and the like. Hence, it has had great appeal to those psychologists who want to investigate questions of a more human, as opposed to animal, bent but who still want to be relatively rigorous and experimentally oriented in their thinking and research.

Finally, and what is perhaps most significant, the consistency approach remains viable today for the same reason as the other theories of which we have spoken. Those who use it as a basic framework have shown themselves to be responsive to data in the same way as the Hullians, for example, and to be willing to revise their constructs and approaches as they go along. As an example, in Chapter 10 we shall present a consistency model of motivation that is an attempt to overcome some of the major problems of consistency theories listed here by attempting to link its arguments to measurement operations and to specify directional behavior as a function of different kinds of discrepancies. Thus, although it does not deal with all of the problems of a general theory of motivation, it is an attempt to overcome some of the weaknesses listed here in a somewhat circumscribed area. Similarly, as we go along, we shall have other occasions to indicate the responsiveness of consistency theories to the implications of their data.

SUMMARY

In this chapter we have reviewed a conception of motivational processes radically different from the belief that man is a rational, utility-seeking organism, a belief that has traditionally had strong support in our society. The view of man we have discussed here is that he seeks outcomes that are consistent with some previously defined standard. Perhaps the major innovation of this approach is that, sometimes, this involves choosing to engage in a set of behaviors that is, at least overtly, less desirable than other behaviors that could be engaged in.

Three major types of consistency theory were dealt with. The first, developed by Heider, has considerable historical interest and continues to show considerable ability to predict behavior choice, as revised by Newcomb. The second theory, proposed by Osgood and Tannenbaum, is formally similar to that of Heider in that it also predicts that individuals try to balance their perceptions by either liking or disliking those objects that are linked together in their perceptions, and by differentiating their likes and dislikes for those objects that are not linked. However, the Osgood and Tannenbaum model is a far more specific model, making considerably more precise predictions than the Heider approach. Finally, we discussed the theory of cognitive dissonance, a theory that has had influence because of its ability to predict a wide range of behaviors from its basic argument that people attempt to develop rationales and justifications for behaviors they have engaged in which cannot be justified by the amount of reward involved.

Despite the usefulness and innovativeness of the consistency view of motivation, it is clear that serious problems exist with the approach. Most specifically, it is clear that if the consistency framework is to remain a viable one, attention will have to be paid to such questions as (a) the measured degree of inconsistency in a person at a given time, (b) individual differences in the type of inconsistency reduction preferred, and (c) the conditions under which inconsistency leads to behaviors designed to reduce it and the conditions under which it will not (i.e., the inconsistency is tolerated as a "fact of life").

the
motivation
toward
achievement

EIGHT

Why do some people try to achieve success on a task? Why are some people highly motivated to perform well when they are given a problem to solve, a test in school, or an assignment on the job? Why do others not care at all about performing well? Why are they unwilling to undertake the behaviors designed to achieve a task-success experience and why are they willing to accept, or at least not fight, failure?

Questions such as these comprise the core of the study of achievement motivational processes, an area which has long been of significant interest among psychologists. The reasons for such interest are not hard to find. Its practical importance for the understanding of school and work behavior is obvious. Anyone interested in the effective functioning of a society, school, organization, and/or the individuals in them must inevitably deal with the question of achievement motivation and its determinants. Psychologists interested in mental health and life satisfaction have become interested in the study of achievement motivation because, for many individuals, the act of achieving is highly important for satisfaction with the self (Korman, 1971b). If we know the conditions that determine the arousal and direction of behavior for these achievement-seeking individuals, it enables us to plan the nature of therapeutic intervention to increase the likelihood of achievement. Also, it has long been apparent, as the reader will see in this chapter, that the decision to try to achieve may be a highly complex one and not simply a matter of the rewards and punishments that may accompany different levels of task performance. While there is no question that under certain conditions the opportunity to achieve rewards and avoid punishments has worked quite well as a stimulant to performance, often it has not. It is partially because of puzzling findings such as these that interest has been so great in the question of why some people achieve and others do not.

Our concern in this chapter will first be to examine the range and type of theoretical frameworks that have been developed as a way of understanding the specific psychological processes we call achievement motivation. Some of these ideas consist mainly of applying general motivation frameworks to specific instances of achievement-oriented behavior. Others, however, are somewhat more concerned with achievement motivation specifically and are not designed to provide an overall systematic approach to motivational processes. Each has its proponents and opponents, and each has advantages and disadvantages, depending on where one chooses to focus. Finally, we shall conclude the chapter by discussing some continuing questions in the field of achievement motivation that current theoretical frameworks do not seem able to account for and that, in essence, serve as challenges for students of achievement motivation in the future.

ACHIEVEMENT MOTIVATION:
THE CONSISTENCY-THEORY APPROACH

Let us begin our discussion by looking at how some psychologists working in the consistency or balance theory tradition have attempted to deal with the question of achievement motivation.

Suppose you were given a series of tasks to do, all of them highly similar to one another, and you found that you were relatively incompetent in all of them. This would undoubtedly lead you to a good assessment of your abilities concerning those tasks, if you were a relatively rational person with some degree of intelligence who was able to distinguish between failure and success. Having established this opinion of yourself, if you then performed another task of the same type and did it well, what would your reaction be? Would you think there was something wrong with the last task experience, so that if given the opportunity, you would change your behavior to be consistent with your previous cognitions, even though such consistency was at the expense of task success? Or would you be glad for the fact of achievement and try to repeat it, given the opportunity again, even though such achievement was inconsistent with the previous set of experiences? In this case we can see why the theory of cognitive dissonance (Festinger, 1957) can serve as a good example of how the consistency approach to motivation can be used as a base for predicting the conditions under which people will be motivated to achieve and the conditions under which they will not. For example, consider the study that directly tested the questions that opened this chapter (Aronson and Carlsmith, 1962). It will be seen that the theory of cognitive dissonance would predict that, given such a situation, the individual would do poorly on a retrial in order to be consistent with the cognitions of incompetency that he developed. Aronson and Carlsmith tested this prediction in a laboratory situation where the subjects were manipulated in such a manner as to think they had either done well or poorly on a succession of four tasks similar in nature. On the fifth task the individuals were differentially treated in a way ensuring that two of the groups would perform in a manner consistent with their expectations (i.e., "high" or "low"), while the two others were given an experience different from their expectations. That is, those who were used to doing well were told they failed, while those who were used to failing were told they passed. This is a dissonant experience, and according to the theory dissonance is to be reduced by changing one's cognitions and/or the behavior leading to the cognitions. The reasoning of the authors, then, was that the previous experience (involving four tasks) was stronger than the last experience (based on only one task), and that given the opportunity, the subjects would try to change their behavior on the last task in order to match their expectancy based on their self-competence. Using a ruse, then, the authors had the subjects respond to the fifth task again, predicting that there would be a greater number of changes in the dissonant than in the consonant groups. Table 8.1 shows that this is exactly what happened, even for group C. This was the crucial group since it was these subjects who needed to change their good responses in order to be consistent with their bad self-image in relation to the task. In other words, they gave up an achievement experience in order to be consistent with themselves.

Table 8.1 Number of Responses Changed on Repeat of Lask Task

Group	Expectancy On Last Task	Actual On Lask Task	Number of Responses Changed
A	High	High	3.9
B	High	Low	11.1
C	Low	High	10.2
D	Low	Low	6.7

Source: E. Aronson and J. M. Carlsmith, Performance expectancy as a determinant of actual performance. *Journal of Abnormal and Social Psychology, 65,* 1962, 178-82. Copyright 1962 by the American Psychological Association. Reproduced by permission.

Is this a freak finding that could occur only by chance? The answer is that while this type of result has not always occurred in experiments of this nature (cf. Brock, 1968), it has occurred often enough to indicate that it is not just a chance happening. Dissonance theory has actually turned out to be highly useful for understanding achievement motivation, as we indicate in Table 8.2, in which we have listed the basic findings of some of the studies done by those working in

Table 8.2 Summary of Dissonance Studies Supporting a Consistency Approach to the Understanding of Work Motivation

General Findings	Investigators
1. When a person is paid by piecework,* his productivity will be greater when he perceives his piecework rate as deserved than when he feels it is not deserved.	Adams and Rosenbaum (1962)
2. Subjects who perceive they do not have the qualifications to earn a given piecework rate will produce better quality work and less quantity work than those individuals who perceive they have the qualifications to earn a given piecework rate.	Adams and Jacobsen (1964)
3. Women of high self-esteem who want to go to college are more likely to engage in behaviors designed to achieve that goal than women who want to go to college who have low self-esteem.	Denmark and Guttentag (1967)
4. Subjects who perceive that they are getting a higher piecework rate than they deserve, based on previous experience, decrease their performance, while individuals getting less than they perceive they deserve increase their performance.	Andrews (1967)
5. People who expect that they will have to do something unpleasant on the basis of previous experience choose to perform the unpleasant task, even when they could have chosen a more pleasant one.	Aronson, Carlsmith, and Darley (1963)
6. People who anticipate an unpleasant experience voluntarily endure more shock than those anticipating a pleasant or unspecified experience.	Walster, Aronson, and Brown (1966); Rosekraus (1967)

*By piecework it is meant that the person's income is a function of the quantity of units produced. Hence, a person who deliberately decreases his performance in terms of quantity is reducing his organizational reward (income).

a dissonance framework. If we look at these studies as a total group, they provide impressive support for the notion of consistency as an important motivating influence in achievement behavior. It appears clear that under some conditions, we achieve at a level that will achieve a just, or equitable, or balanced outcome, even though such consistency may have to be achieved at the cost of various kinds of external rewards.

In summary, then, this cognitive dissonance research provides one bit of evidence for the fruitfulness of the consistency rationale in understanding some of the conditions that lead to achievement motivation. Further evidence to support this conclusion is provided by the considerable body of literature that has developed around the "equity" hypothesis presented by Adams (1963, 1965). This framework, originally developed for the study of organizational compensation practice, also illustrates the value of this approach.

According to Adams (1965), inequity can be defined as follows:

> Inequity exists for Person whenever he perceives that the ratio of his outcomes to inputs and the ratio of Other's outcomes to Other's inputs are unequal. This may happen either (a) when he and Other are in a direct exchange relationship or (b) when both are in an exchange relationship with a third party and Person compares himself to Other. (P. 280)

The basic paradigm can be diagrammed as follows:

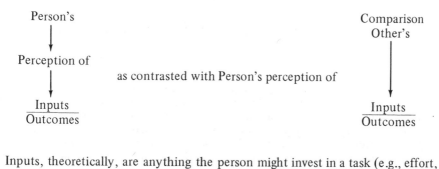

Person's
↓
Perception of   as contrasted with Person's perception of
↓
Inputs
Outcomes

Comparison
Other's
↓
↓
Inputs
Outcomes

Inputs, theoretically, are anything the person might invest in a task (e.g., effort, education, or time) and outcomes are anything he might receive (e.g., money, recognition, etc.). The cognitive elements, as in dissonance theory, are weighed by their importance. The basic motivational hypothesis is, as in dissonance theory, that unequal ratios lead to negative motivational states (e.g., tension, etc.), which the person tries to reduce. The way in which he tries to reduce the tension may vary from person to person and for a particular person over time, but can include any (or a combination) of the following: (a) cognitive distortion of one's own inputs and/or outcomes, (b) withdrawal from the situation, (c) a real or perceived change of the inputs and/or outcomes of the comparison person, (d) an actual change of his own inputs or outcomes, or (e) a change of the comparison person against whom he compares his input-outcome ratio. Which method will he choose? A minimal-cost hypothesis is proposed in that the person will do those things that are easiest for him, that is, he will be more likely to change his perception of the comparison person's input-output ratio than his own.

The relevance of Adams's notions for achievement behavior can be seen by examining the various contexts in which most of the studies testing the theory have taken place. There have been four separate types of studies undertaken and these can be classified as follows:

Case 1. Overpaid, hourly rate — This case involves the situation in which people are paid on an hourly or weekly basis, but the rate (outcome) is higher than they believe their qualifications (inputs) warrant.

Case 2. Underpaid, hourly rate — This is the same situation as Case 1, but the rate is lower than they believe their inputs warrant.

Case 3. Overpaid, piecework rate — In this case, the rate of pay is based on the number of work units (pieces) achieved, as opposed to the amount of time put in, with the rate being higher than the person believes his inputs warrant.

Case 4. Underpaid, piecework rate — This is the same as Case 3, with the difference being that the piecework rate is lower than the subject believes the perceived inputs warrant.

According to Adams, the following behaviors should, therefore, take place:

Case 1: Achievement effort (input) behaviors should increase as a way of justifying the high outcomes.

Case 2: Achievement effort (input) behaviors should decrease since the outcomes are so low.

Case 3: Achievement effort (input) behaviors should decrease in terms of quantity, since increasing input would increase the dissonance of getting too high an outcome for each unit of work produced and too high an outcome overall. Achievement effort should increase in terms of quality since each unit is worth more (i.e., the piecework rate is very high).

Case 4: Achievement effort (input) behaviors should increase since this is a way of getting equitable outcomes overall, considering one's inputs. Achievement effort should decrease in terms of quality since each unit is worth less.

How well have Adams's predictions worked out? Do people actually lower their achievement-oriented behavior in a way that will result in less financial reward (Case 3)? Do the other predictions hold up? There have been several reviews of the large number of studies stimulated by Adams's theory, and the answer to these questions depends to some extent on the review being read (cf. Lawler, 1968; Pritchard, 1969; Campbell et al., 1970; Goodman and Friedman, 1971). However, the reviews do seem to be in agreement on several conclusions important for our purposes. These are listed below.

1. There are different implications for achievement-oriented behavior when one is overrewarded on a piecework-rate basis as opposed to being overrewarded on an hourly-rate basis.

2. Similarly, there are different implications for achievement-oriented behavior when one is underrewarded on a piecework-rate basis as opposed to being underrewarded on an hourly-rate basis.

3. In general, the various predictions for the separate situations have received a considerable degree of support (cf. Lawler, 1968; Pritchard, 1969; Campbell et al., 1970); however, there are cases where theoretical predictions have been weakly supported. Most strongly supported is the prediction that underpaid piecework-rate subjects produce more than equitably paid subjects (Goodman and Friedman, 1971). Less strongly supported, but still receiving some support, are the predictions that overpaid, hourly workers produce more than those who are equitably paid; overpaid piecework-rate subjects produce lower quantity and higher quality than those who are equitably paid; and underpaid hourly subjects invest less input than those who are equitably paid (Goodman and Friedman, 1971).

In addition to these conclusions, more recent research has added to the fruitfulness of the approach by reporting that people actually do decrease their achievement-oriented behavior in piecework-rate overpayment (Case 3) situations (Wood and Lawler, 1971). Similarly, a comprehensive field experiment under natural employment conditions in which the people did not know they were being studied found considerable support for equity-theory predictions in both the overpaid and underpaid situations (Pritchard, Dunnette, and Jorgenson, 1972).

Generally, then, there seems to be good reason why Adams's model has remained as viable as it has, and there is good reason to expect that it will continue to remain an important theoretical contribution to the understanding of achievement motivation in the future. In order for this future research to achieve its maximum promise, however, some methodological questions involving measurement and conceptual issues will have to be resolved.

One problem is that input and outcome variables as separate, clearly distinguishable variables are nowhere near as distinct as they seem at first glance. Tornow (1971), for example, has pointed out that such variables as making use of abilities, making many decisions, keeping up on a variety of subjects, bearing sole responsibility, learning a new system, and working on complex tasks may be perceived by some individuals as inputs to a job. On the other hand, others may see these as outcomes or values to be derived from a good job. It is Tornow's argument that how one will perceive these variables (i.e., as inputs or outputs) will depend on the personal characteristics of the individual. Such individual differences have to be incorporated into the theoretical framework if we are to make accurate predictions, a process Tornow (1971) has begun, but which clearly needs to be expanded on.

A second problem concerns the factors that determine those individuals chosen for comparison. Which individuals choose which comparison others? Does this change over time? If so, how? Andrews and Henry (1964) and Lawler (1965) have made some preliminary steps toward resolving this question, but much remains to be done when we consider how complex this question can be. As an example of such complexity, Weick and Nesset (1968) have suggested that there are at least six different ways that the comparison process can result in an inequitable outcome. These are as follows:

	Person			Other	
Comparison	Self-Perceived Inputs	Self-Perceived Outcomes		Perceived Other's Inputs	Perceived Other's Outcomes
1	Low	Low	as compared to	High	Low
2	Low	Low	as compared to	Low	High
3	Low	High	as compared to	Low	Low
4	High	Low	as compared to	Low	Low
5	High	High	as compared to	High	Low
6	High	High	as compared to	Low	High

For each of these comparisons (or various subgroups of them) it is possible that different people would be chosen for comparison, with the resulting perceived feelings of inequity a function of such choices.

To add to the complexity, there is an increasing amount of evidence that the basis for feelings of inequity is not only the comparison person chosen, but one's internal standard as to what is an appropriate level of income for the self Pritchard, 1969; Lane and Messè, 1972). In other words, the causes of inequity may be not only the current comparisons but also the socialization history of the individual, since this is what determines one's concept of a fair standard of pay in large part. This makes the theory a lot more complex than originally hypothesized by Adams, if this argument holds up. We will, in fact, suggest a theory in Chapter 10 that has considerable similarity to this expanded version of the equity hypothesis.

ACHIEVEMENT MOTIVATION:
THE EXPECTANCY-VALUE APPROACH

In our society it is quite common to hear the argument that people are motivated to achieve as a function of the value one expects to obtain by this behavior. This argument is, in essence, nothing more or less than the application of the expectancy-value framework we developed in Chapter 5 to the understanding of achievement motivation and achievement-oriented behavior. In fact, the acceptance of the expectancy-value approach to achievement motivation is so embedded within us that to a great extent it provides the theoretical basis upon which most of the administrative practices commonly found in our formal organizations have traditionally rested. In these organizations the controlling influence, usually the administration, decides that there are certain gratifications that most people want from school and/or their jobs which the administration has the power to control. Typical of these may be such rewards as good grades in the school situation and promotion or security and good working conditions on the job. According to this line of thought, the administration controls and increases achievement by making the attainment of these rewards contingent upon effective performance. Thus, it is believed, the promise of such value attainment will result in increased performance, i.e., these possible outcomes will serve as incentives for better performance provided the individual involved believes the rewards actually are attainable on the basis of his efforts. If he believes that such rewards are not contingent on his performance, he will not react to them as incentives.

An example of this type of expectancy-value approach in the study of work achievement is given in a study by Lawler and Porter (1967). Their research was concerned with testing the hypothesis that the amount of effort a person expended on his job (as judged by his superior and peers) was related to the extent to which he perceived he could achieve desired outcomes by engaging in such effort. They also predicted that his overall performance would be related to such perceptions of rewards to be attained by performance, although at a somewhat lower level. (His overall performance would also be affected by such things as his ability and the accuracy of his perceptions concerning the role he is supposed to perform, whereas his degree of effort would not be.) The sample used in testing these hypotheses consisted of 154 managers in five organizations, ranging from a large manufacturing firm to a local Y.M.C.A. In Table 8.3 we have summarized some of the results of this study, indicating significant support for their hypotheses.

Table 8.3 Correlations Between Extent to Which a Person Perceives Valued Rewards Are Dependent Upon Work Performance and Various Measures of Work Performance

Work Performance Measures	Correlations
Superior's rankings on:	
Job performance	.18
Effort	.27[a]
Peers' rankings on:	
Job performance	.21
Effort	.30[b]
Self-ratings on:	
Job performance	.38[c]
Effort	.44[c]

[a] $p < .10$.
[b] $p < .05$.
[c] $p < .01$.

Source: E. Lawler and L. Porter, Antecedent attitudes of effective managerial performance. *Organizational Behavior and Human Performance, 2,* 1967, 122-42.

Since there are a number of other studies with highly similar results (cf. Georgopoulos, Mahoney, and Jones, 1957; Hackman and Porter, 1968; Gailbreath and Cummings, 1967; Goodman, Rose, and Furcon, 1970), it has generally been concluded that the adequacy of this type of expectancy-value theory can be fairly useful in accounting for performance variation in achievement situations. However, for the most part, the correlations tend to be of a low to moderate level at best (Hineman and Schwab, 1972; House and Wahba, 1972), and sometimes they are even insignificant despite the rationality of the approach (Arvey and Mussio,1972).

The Porter-Lawler type of approach is, however, only one way in which the expectancy x value framework has been applied to the study of achievement-oriented behavior. There are others starting from the same perspective but differing from it in that instead of proposing that people are motivated to achieve in order to obtain certain extrinsic values (e.g., money, recognition, promotion, etc.), they are motivated toward achievement in and of itself. For these people, an achieved outcome is a valued or desirable state in and of itself, and people are distinguishable from one another on the basis of their need for achievement, that is, the degree to which an outcome they have achieved is a desirable state independent of any extrinsic values that might have been attained. For this kind of theorizing, in order to predict behavior, one would need to know (a) the person's motive or need for achievement (i.e., some people have more of this motive than others), and (b) his expectancy of being able to achieve in the given situation. The problem is that these two variables may interact with one another in a very special way, as we shall see when we discuss the work of the two psychologists most identified with this approach, David McClelland and John Atkinson.

The first and older of these, McClelland, is of importance here for two reasons. First, he has provided a theoretical base by arguing that achievement motivation develops in some people more than in others because for some people achievement outcomes have positive affect, that is, these outcomes are only of moderate discrepancy from what has been previously experienced. On the other hand, for others, these outcomes are of great discrepancy and thus have negative, avoidance effects on the individual. Such a conceptualization, as we argued earlier, enables (a) measurement of people's achievement motivation, (b) possible specification of who will develop achievement motivation and who will not, and (c) predictions as to who will act in an achievement-oriented fashion in a given situation and who will not.

McClelland's second contribution is more in the area of content, in that he has used these basic laboratory hypotheses as a framework for understanding the rise and fall of nations and societies. The basic rationale underlying this argument can be outlined as follows:

1. Individuals differ in the degree to which they find achievement a satisfying experience.
2. Individuals with a high need for Achievement (n Ach) tend to prefer the following situations and will work harder in them than individuals of low n Ach:
   a. Situations of moderate risk — the rationale for this is that feelings of achievement will be minimal in cases of little risk and achievement will probably not occur in cases of great risk.
   b. Situations in which knowledge of results is provided — the rationale for this is that a person with a high achievement motive will want to know whether he has achieved or not.
   c. Situations in which individual responsibility is provided — the rationale here is that a person oriented toward achievement will want to make sure that he, and not somebody else, gets the credit for it.
3. Since the business entrepreneurial role has the characteristics outlined

in 2a, b, and c, individuals of high need for achievement will be attracted to the entrepreneurial role as a lifetime occupation.

Assuming, then, that the economic growth of a nation depends on successful fulfillment of the entrepreneurial role, it would follow that the success of a society depends on the number of people attracted to the entrepreneurial function. McClelland then goes on to argue that this is a function of the level of concern for achievement in that society and of the number of individuals who find achievement situations pleasantly effective. The prediction for economic growth is a clear one, that is, the greater the achievement motivation in a society, the better the economic performance of the society.

How good is this hypothesis? How much of such a vast set of complex behaviors as societal growth (and decline) can be attributed to the effects of a psychological variable of this nature? How can we even test it? A necessary requirement is that we be able to measure the relative concern with achievement in given civilizations, on the assumption that the number of people who would be achievement oriented in a civilization would be directly related to the concern of that civilization with achievement in general. After deriving these measures, we would then follow the procedure of (1) measuring a society's concern with achievement and (2) measuring its economic growth and/or decline subsequent to the measurement of achievement, perhaps for the following twenty-five or fifty years. (This measurement of change would have to be made subsequent to the achievement measurement, since a causative relationship is being hypothesized here.)

Surprisingly, despite the enormous methodological difficulties involved, McClelland has been able to perform just such a set of operations, and part of the reason he has been able to do so is traceable to the way he and his co-workers have traditionally measured n Ach. In most of the individual research performed, n Ach has been assessed by making judgments about the extent of achievement concern in the stories an individual writes. In its most common form, this measurement procedure has involved presenting the individual with a TAT-type picture and asking the person to write a story about the picture, according to a somewhat structured outline. The more these stories are rated as containing achievement-related topics, the greater the n Ach that is inferred.

The logic then follows that if one can assess n Ach in an individual by studying his literary output in a situation, then why could one not assess the level of n Ach in a nation by the same method, namely, by studying its literary output? Essentially, this is what McClelland did. His basic procedure was to study the dominant themes in childhood stories and folktales in different nations at different times (on the assumption that the dominant characteristics of a society are most likely to show up in this area of literature). He then derived scores for that nation on n Ach and related these scores to the subsequent economic growth and/or decline of that country, with economic growth being measured in two basic ways: electrical power and national income in international units. The reader may have some doubts as to whether such a research scheme is advisable at all, considering how hard it is to control for the contaminating influences of wars, weather, national resources, and so on. Yet, despite all this, McClelland's results were intriguing and promising. Relationships were found between these sets of variables, and they were generally in the direction hypothesized; economic growth followed rises in *n* Ach, rather than these being concurrent relationships (McClelland, 1961, pp. 83-103). Table 8.4

Table 8.4 National Economic Development from 1925 to 1950 (approximately) as Related to *n* Ach Levels in 1925

Country	Level of n Ach in 1925[a]	Gain in Income Levels Over Randomly Expected Values[b]	Gain in Electricity Produced Over Randomly Expected Values
Sweden	2.19	+2.35	+3.17
United States	1.90	+1.28	+1.86
New Zealand	1.48	+ .63	+1.73
Canada	2.67	− .04	+1.73
Great Britain	2.10	−1.71	+1.65
Australia	2.81	+ .61	+1.13
Finland	1.24	+1.10	+ .74
South Africa	1.05	+ .70	+ .69
Ireland	3.19	+ .14	+ .33
Denmark	2.00	−1.23	+ .14
Norway	1.33	+ .44	− .03
Netherlands	.29	− .78	− .10
Austria	1.57	−1.02	− .12
Hungary	1.29	− .47	− .26
Chile	1.29	− .47	− .26
Greece	.38	−1.28	− .52
France	.81	− .92	− .55
Argentina	1.86	− .50	− .61
Uruguay	1.48		− .62
Spain	.81	−1.93	− .63
Belgium	1.00	+1.57	− .75
Germany	1.38	− .51	− .79
Russia	.95	+ .39	

Note: Not all data are available for all countries.

[a]Achievement level is the sum of *n* Ach scores per story divided by the number of stories per country.

[b]From C. Clark, *The Conditions of Economic Progress,* 3rd ed. (London: Macmillan, 1957).

Source: David C. McClelland, *The Achieving Society,* pp. 90-91. Copyright 1961 by Litton Educational Publishing, Inc. Reprinted by permission of Van Nostrand Reinhold Company.

shows some of these findings, and the consistency of the patterns found is impressive, considering the relatively gross and crude nature of the variables involved. In addition, McClelland has attempted to construct a generalized model of how *n* Ach develops and to which variables it is related. In Table 8.5 we have reconstructed portions of his generalized approach so that the reader may obtain the full flavor of McClelland's approach and, perhaps, be stimulated to read further (e.g., McClelland, 1961) in order to evaluate on his own the adequacy, degree of support, and so on.

Table 8.5 Need for Achievement

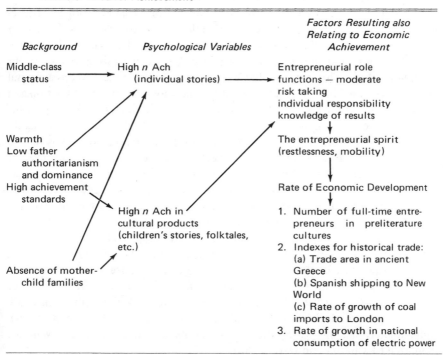

Background	Psychological Variables	Factors Resulting also Relating to Economic Achievement
Middle-class status	High *n* Ach (individual stories)	Entrepreneurial role functions — moderate risk taking individual responsibility knowledge of results
Warmth Low father authoritarianism and dominance High achievement standards		The entrepreneurial spirit (restlessness, mobility)
	High *n* Ach in cultural products (children's stories, folktales, etc.)	Rate of Economic Development
Absence of mother-child families		1. Number of full-time entrepreneurs in preliterature cultures 2. Indexes for historical trade: (a) Trade area in ancient Greece (b) Spanish shipping to New World (c) Rate of growth of coal imports to London 3. Rate of growth in national consumption of electric power

Source: David C. McClelland, *The Achieving Society*, p. 438. Copyright 1961 by Litton Educational Publishing, Inc. Reprinted by permission of Van Nostrand Reinhold Company.

Despite the fact that this approach seems to have been supported in McClelland's research and has recently been replicated in studies of entrepreneurs in India (Hundal, 1971) and the rise and decline of Minoan civilization in Crete (Davies, 1969), the reader should be aware of some problems associated with the *n* Ach research that need to be resolved. For example, one problem is that there are cases in which the theory, as developed by McClelland, simply has not been supported. While these studies vary in quality and relevance, the large number of negative findings leaves room for pause and considerable doubt (Klinger, 1966).

A second problem is that the theory not only may not predict in cases in which it should, but it may predict in cases in which it should not. For example, if positive affect toward achievement is the key notion, then positive relationships should not occur in chance situations, because feelings of achievement cannot be attributed to the chance nature of the activity. Yet such relationships do occur, and the theory cannot explain why. One way of accounting for this is hypothesizing that chance situations (such as dice) take on characteristics of skill situations in a psychological sense. However, such changes in the meaning of a situation are not part of the theory.

Similarly, it is hypothesized, according to McClelland's original framework, that *n* Ach should not have much relationship to achievement-oriented behavior in situations that do not have the parameters of moderate risk taking, quick feedback, and individual responsibility. Yet, such relationships do occur (Cummin, 1967). This suggests that what is actually being measured is a general performance capability in real-life situations and not performance variation as a function of different kinds of task and risk situations. In fact, most support for the moderate risk-taking notion, a key aspect of the theory, is highly controversial at best (Kogan and Wallach, 1967). The reason for this is that in experimental studies in which this aspect has been supported, the level of difficulty has been defined by the experimenter, that is, he is the one who has decided what should be labeled a hard task, a moderate task, and an easy task. To illustrate, in a ringtoss experiment (Atkinson and Litwin, 1960), the researchers marked off distances from the goal object and assumed that the middle distance would be the moderate risk for the subjects. However, it is quite obvious that what is difficult for one individual may not be difficult for another; thus, a proper test of the hypothesis is that individual differences in perceived risk must be controlled for. After this is done, we can test to see whether preferences for moderate risk taking is related to *n* Ach (as these risks are perceived by the decision-making subject rather than by the experimenter). Unfortunately in one case where this has been done, the theory was not supported (deCharms and Davé, 1965).

As a result of these problems, some alternative theories have begun to appear that have been designed to account for what McClelland found and what he did not find. One of these has been proposed by Klinger and McNeily (1969), who have hypothesized that people will achieve because such role behavior is believed to be consistent with their self-perceived status in life. Similarly, the writing of achievement-oriented stories in TAT-type tasks occurs for the same reasons. Thus, it is because (a) writing achievement stories in ambiguous situations, and (b) engaging in achievement behaviors in life are both consonant with higher social status in life that we find a correlation between the two, and not because (a) causes (b). In this way, Klinger can account for the fact that in his research the correlation between TAT measures and achieved social status is greater when the latter is measured prior to the former as opposed to when the former is measured prior to the latter. McClelland's theory, on the other hand, is based on opposing findings. We shall meet Klinger's hypothesis again in

Chapter 10 when we shall propose a model somewhat related to Klinger's and in which we shall also indicate how this type of theory can account for the rise and fall of societies. Suffice it to say at this point that Klinger's hypothesis is basically a consistency model and, thus, may suggest one mechanism whereby the findings of the expectancy-value theorists can be reconciled with those working in a consistency framework.

We now turn to the second major research program in achievement motivation, the work of John Atkinson and his collaborators. As it has developed over the years, it has had several features that distinguish it from McClelland's program. First, it has been more laboratory oriented, concentrating more on manipulable experimental variables as opposed to real-life complex social variables. Second, his work has constituted an explicit attempt to integrate the concerns of personality theory and the concerns of experimental psychology, in that his basic procedure all along has been to first classify and measure people according to their dominant persisting motivational characteristics and then see how the behavior of differently classified people differs according to different environments (i.e., experimental conditions).

Thus, for Atkinson, in the most recent of his theoretical statements (Atkinson and Feather, 1966), there are basically two types of people in a theoretical sense, and each will act in an achievement-oriented fashion under different conditions. However, the environments in which the motivation to achieve will be greatest will differ for the two kinds of individuals. These two major theoretical types are (a) the person for whom the need to achieve is greater than the fear of failure, and (b) the person for whom the fear of failure is greater than the need to achieve. Each of these individuals is motivated by the desire to achieve certain pleasant affect, with the difference being that for the former the pleasant affect is in achieving, whereas for the latter the pleasant affect is in avoiding a sense of failure.

These are the two major kinds of persisting motivational characteristics that Atkinson uses to classify people, with his bases for classification the respondent's scores on a need for achievement measure and a fear of failure (or anxiety) measure. In his typical procedure, Atkinson and/or his students compute the median of the distribution for each of the two sets of scores and then categorize all individuals above the median on the n Ach measure and below the median on the fear of failure measure as a high n Ach person. An analogous procedure is then used to classify the high FF (fear of failure) person, and, normally, these are the two groups then studied. The reader will, of course, note that this approach leaves out half of the sample population, namely, those high on both measures and those low on both. Theoretically, these groups are assumed to show behaviors in between the two sets of differential behaviors that are predicted for the extreme groups. However, an even greater problem than this has been the nature of the different measures used for classifying individuals in different studies and their conceptual and empirical equivalence. We shall discuss at a later point that such equivalence, demanded by the approach, has been dubious at best.

Before doing so, let us complete our discussion of Atkinson's model. Having classified people according to their predominant motivational tendencies, these then interact with the characteristics of the environmental demands at the time to determine actual behaviors. Behavior, for Atkinson as well as for the other expectancy-value theorists we have discussed, is a function of both the person and the environment. However, Atkinson has a very specific conception of environmental variation and its effects on behavior, one that differentiates him from those we have discussed previously. For him, the task environment (remember this is an explicit theory of achievement) can be conceptualized in terms of the difficulty of the task involved. That is, some tasks have a high probability of being achieved successfully, for example, P (probability of success) = .90, whereas for other cases the probability of successful achievement is quite low, P = .10. *Furthermore, it is an explicit theoretical assumption of Atkinson's that the incentive value of success* (i.e., the pleasure one gets from success) *is a negative function of P* (probability of success), that is, we get more pleasure out of succeeding at hard tasks than at easy tasks. *Similarly, it is also an explicit assumption that the negative incentive of failure* (i.e., the shame one gets from failing) *is a positive function of P,* that is, we get more shame from failing on easy tasks than hard ones. Thus, *the expectancy of task success and the pleasure derived from succeeding* (or the shame from failing) *are not experimentally independent of one another in Atkinson's framework.* Manipulate one variable experimentally (and these are generally among the variables Atkinson manipulates experimentally in his research), and the other is also affected. Hence, this is different from the work of others we have spoken of previously and should be recognized as such. (The various approaches are not antagonistic to one another, however, as we will see later in this chapter.)

Atkinson's major constructs are the predominant motivational characteristics of the individual, the probability of task success in the given situation, and the incentive value for success. They are then combined by him into the behavioral prediction model depicted in Table 8.6.

In looking at Table 8.6, there are a number of factors to be kept in mind. First, it is important to realize that, in both cases, achievement-oriented behavior that is a function of both individual and environmental variation is being predicted. It is very clear that Atkinson predicts that both kinds of people will try to achieve. However, and this is crucial, the model predicts that the level of achievement behavior that will take place and how this will vary as a function of the environmental context is different for parts A and B of Figure 8.2.

Thus, looking at part A first, where the people have been classified as scoring 1 (or high) on n Ach,[1] these people are predicted to approach task

---

[1] Arbitrary numbers have been used throughout Table 8.6 for pedagogical purposes.

Table 8.6 Outline of Atkinson Model of Achievement Motivation

A. For People Classified as High n Ach Individuals

Score on n Ach		P (Probability of Task Success)		I Incentive for Task Success Assumed to be = (1−P)		Behavior Designed to Achieve in Given Environmental Context (Approach to Task Behavior)
1	X	.9	X	.1	=	.09
1	X	.8	X	.2	=	.16
1	X	.7	X	.3	=	.21
1	X	.6	X	.4	=	.24
1	X	.5	X	.5	=	.25
1	X	.4	X	.6	=	.24
1	X	.3	X	.7	=	.21
1	X	.2	X	.8	=	.16
1	X	.1	X	.9	=	.09

B. For People Classified as High Fear of Failure Individuals

Score on FF		P (Probability of Task Failure)		I Negative Incentive for Task Failure Assumed to be = 1−(1−P)		Behavior Designed to Avoid Failure in Given Environmental Context (Avoidance of) Task Behavior
1	X	.1	X	−.9	=	−.09
1	X	.2	X	−.8	=	−.16
1	X	.3	X	−.7	=	−.21
1	X	.4	X	−.6	=	−.24
1	X	.5	X	−.5	=	−.25
1	X	.6	X	−.4	=	−.24
1	X	.7	X	−.3	=	−.21
1	X	.8	X	−.2	=	−.16
1	X	.9	X	−.1	=	−.09

situations because they like to achieve (that is, they find pleasant affect in task achievement (notice the similarity to McClelland). However, the extent of their approach and performance will vary as a function of the task, in that it is predicted that the behavior will be greatest where the probability of success is medium (i.e., where $P = .50$). (Again notice the similarity to McClelland's medium risk-taking hypothesis for entrepreneurs.) This comes, Atkinson argues, from his theoretical assumption that

Behavior is a function of (Motive X Probability of Task Success X Incentive of Task Success)

$$B \quad = \quad M \ X \quad P \quad X \quad I$$

Given, then, his assumption that $I = (1-P)$, one generates the prediction, as shown in part A of Table 8.6, that the motivational tendency to perform the task will be greatest when $P = .5$.

If we take the same approach as Atkinson does and apply it to people whose dominant motivational tendency is to *avoid* task situations because of their fear of failure, as is done in part B of Table 8.6, some interesting paradoxical predictions are generated. The behaviors being postulated here are *avoidance* behaviors (hence, the minus sign), with the specific prediction being that the situation to be avoided most here is precisely the one the high n Ach people will approach most, that is, the medium-risk situation ($P = .50$). The theoretical rationale here is that the high *FF* people would avoid all task-achievement situations if they could because of the negative affect they associate with failing. However, if they must remain in a task-achievement situation (and Atkinson assumes that for these people there is always some other motivational force operating to keep them in the task-achievement environment), the ones they will avoid most, Figure 8.2 predicts, are the medium-risk cases. This is explained by the rationale that if one fails in a high-risk situation (i.e., where $P = .05$), one will not feel like a failure since few people would be expected to succeed in these cases. On the other hand, in cases where the probability of success is very high (i.e., $P = .98$), failure and the accompanying negative feelings are not likely to occur. It is important to stress, therefore, that for Atkinson's model, it is not the objective probability of failure that the high *FF* person seeks to avoid. Rather, it is the negative affect associated with the feeling of failure that he seeks to avoid, a postulation in keeping with the McClelland theory of motivation that it is affect states (defined as extreme discrepancies from previous experiences) that are the key motivational influences, both approach and avoidance. In this way, then, Atkinson is able to develop at one and the same time an explanation for the often-noted actual failure-seeking behavior of people, at least in an objective sense, within a subjective value-seeking framework. This is to be distinguished from the low-expectancy notions of Hull, Spence, Tolman, and the like, which account for nonvalue-seeking behavior to some extent. In this case we are talking about actual failure-seeking behavior.

These, then, are the differential predictions.[2] How well does the theory work?

Tables 8.7 and 8.8 provide the answer, and it is in many respects a contradictory one. Thus, Table 8.7 provides a summary of a relatively consistent set of positive empirical findings supporting the predictions of the model relating to risk preference in general experimental situations. On the other hand, Table

---

[2]It should be noted that Atkinson's model is thus able to handle the observation by Allport (1937) that succeeding (and presumably being reinforced) on a task would not lead to the choice of the same task again. This has long been a problem for reinforcement theories. Atkinson provides us here with a way of predicting the direction of such choices.

8.8 shows that the various instruments used to measure *n* Ach and *FF* do not show anything like the patterns of intercorrelations that they should, if they were all measuring what they claim to be measuring. To use our previous defined terms, there is little construct validity being evidenced here as we discussed it in Chapter 6. How, then, can there be strong behavioral predictions when the measures do not evidence construct validity? We, frankly, along with others

Table 8.7 Summary of Studies of *n* Ach Research and Risk Preference Behavior

Investigator	Measure Used	Type of Sample	Support or Nonsupport for Hypothesized Relationship Between n Ach and Intermediate Risk
Littig (1963)	Thematic Apperception [a] Test (TAT) and Test Anxiety Questionnaire (TAQ)	College	Supported
Mahone (1960)	TAT & TAQ	College	Supported
Burnstein (1963)	TAT & TAQ	College	Supported
Raynor and Smith (1966)	TAT & TAQ	College	Not Supported
Morris (1965)	TAT & TAQ	High School	Supported
Litwin (1958)	TAT & TAQ	College	Supported
Moulton (1965)	TAT & TAQ	High School	Supported
deCharms and Davé (1965)	TAT & TAQ	Grammar School	Not Supported
Atkinson and O'Connors (1966)	TAT & TAQ and Achievement Risk Preference Scale (ARPS)		Supported
Hancock and Teevan (1964)	TAT	High School	Supported
Meyer, Walker, and Litwin (1961)	TAT	Noncollege adults	Supported
Scodel, Rutoosh, and Minas (1969)	TAT	Noncollege adults	Supported
Crockett (1962)	TAT	Noncollege adults	Supported
Atkinson (et al.) (1960)	French Test of Insight (FTI) [b]	College	Supported
Atkinson and Litwin (1960)	FTI & TAQ	College	Supported
Isaacson (1964)	FTI & TAQ	College	Supported
McClelland (1958)	Doodles	College	Supported

[a]This is a measure of need achievement motivation based on graphic expression.
[b]This is a measure of need achievement motivation based on sentence completion.

Source: M. S. Weinstein, Achievement motivation and risk preference. *Journal of Personality and Social Psychology, 13,* 1969, 153-72. Copyright 1969 by the American Psychological Association. Reprinted by permission.

(Weinstein, 1969), are puzzled. It seems clear that something is being studied that is of behavioral significance, but is it what Atkinson claims it to be? Clearly, the correlations shown in Table 8.8 are highly negative in their implications for this hypothesis, as is a recent comprehensive study by Weinstein (1969). Is the alternative of the consistency model suggested by Klinger, or some variant of it, a more viable approach? We do not know.

It seems apparent that despite the tremendous amount of work and supportive empirical findings, much remains to be done in evaluating the explanatory fruitfulness of Atkinson's hypotheses because of the serious doubts

Table 8.8 Summary of Intercorrelations Between Need Achievement Measures and Fear of Failure (Anxiety) Measures

Variables Being Correlated	Range of Correlations	Number of Studies
1. TAT need achievement[1] and Test Anxiety Questionnaire[2]	−.43 to + .11	7
2. TAT need achievement[1] and French Test of Insight[1]	−.07 to + .25	4
3. TAT need achievement[1] and Doodles[1]	+.27 to + .51	2
4. TAT need achievement[1] and EPPS need achievement scale	−.05 to + .20	7
5. TAT need achievement[1] and value for achievement	.23	1
6. French Test of Insight[1] and EPPS need achievement scale	+.02 to + .51	4
7. TAT need achievement[1] and Sherwood achievement scale	+.29 to + .42	3
8. EPPS need achievement[1] scale and Test Anxiety Questionnaire[2]	.11	1
9. Test Anxiety Questionnaire[2] and Debilitating Anxiety Scale[2]	.79	1

[1] All measures followed by superscript 1 have been used by Atkinson and/or his collaborators in research tests of his model as a measure of n Ach.
[2] All measures followed by superscript 2 have been used by Atkinson and/or his collaborators in research tests of his model as a measure of FF.

Source: M. S. Weinstein, Achievement motivation and risk preference. *Journal of Personality and Social Psychology, 13,* 1969, 153-72. Copyright 1969 by the American Psychological Association. Reprinted by permission.

that have been placed on the validity of the measurement procedures used.

A somewhat similar statement needs also to be made when we look at expectancy-value theory in terms of its overall framework, both in its extrinsic version (e.g., Porter and Lawler approach) and its intrinsic versions (e.g., the McClelland and Atkinson approaches). Briefly, there are still numerous questions associated with this approach, problems we have not mentioned yet. It may also be because of these problems, which we will now discuss, that some of the inconsistent results noted previously tend to occur as often as they do.

One of the major, persisting dilemmas is the nature of "value" and what we mean by it. Clearly, it is an assumption of the approach that the more of a given value, all other things being equal, the more it will influence behavior. All well and good *except* that dissonance theory predicts that, at least under some conditions, just the opposite will occur. As we saw earlier, while there are many problems with dissonance theory, it has been supported frequently enough to suggest that there is something substantive involved in a psychological sense. When, then, is value as an incentive to behavior positively correlated with the quantity of the value and when is it negatively related? We are really just beginning to find out as a result of dissonance-theory research. However, dissonance theory is far from the whole answer and until better answers are forthcoming, we may continue to have inconsistent findings from expectancy-value theory.

A second problem involving the concept of value is the independence of values and the possible interactions between them in influencing behavior. Briefly, the logic of expectancy-value theory is that the more values a person can achieve by a given form of behavior, the more he will engage in that behavior. Yet, it may not be quite that simple if we use some recent research by Deci (1972) as a guide. In this research Deci has found that the more we obtain an extrinsic type of reinforcement (e.g., money) for performing a task, the more likely we are to lose our intrinsic motivation to perform that task. On the other hand, the more we receive verbal reinforcements, the more we come to develop intrinsic motivations to perform the task. Clearly, then, money and verbal reinforcements are not the same in their effects and in their relationships with other reinforcers, that is, adding money and verbal reinforcements is not the same as just adding money reinforcements and/or verbal reinforcements alone. If we wanted to use expectancy-value theory for influencing the achievement-oriented behavior of schoolchildren, this problem would be a very meaningful one in trying to decide on a strategy for exercising such influence.

A third problem of expectancy-value theory in its intrinsic version concerns its degree of generalizability to females. It has long been known that the basic McClelland formulations are not applicable to females and that whatever motivates women and girls to success in a task-oriented sense, the factors are not the same as those for men. But what are these factors? One much-publicized proposal has been made by Horner (1968) who has suggested that the woman of high ability and high need for achievement must contend with an additional motivational variable that a man does not. This additional variable she has termed the "motive to avoid success," a motive that she proposes is encouraged in women by the socialization processes of our society. According to Horner, the woman who is encouraged to think of high achievement as being mildly discrepant, and thus, a source of positive affect, is also, in our society, taught that high achievement is a source of great discrepancy according to other dimensions and is something "unladylike," "not feminine," and so forth. Hence, the same possible outcome, high achievement, is both an approach and avoidance incentive for the high *n* Ach woman, *at one and the same time.* These are the reasons that predicting the achievement behavior for women is a lot harder than for men within an expectancy-value intrinsic framework, since what needs to be done is to determine the relative weights of these two motives, as well as, perhaps, the fear-of-failure motive. Horner's proposals are quite interesting and, as we have said, have been the subject of much publicity. Yet, intriguing though they are, replicating her findings has proved quite difficult, as a recent study by Karabenick (1972) has shown. In this research, Karabenick found that females actually did better when competing against males than when competing against females, a finding directly opposite to Horner's hypotheses. How come? Does society legitimatize achievement more for women now? Was this a uniquely different group than the one Horner dealt with? We don't know, nor do we know why, given McClelland's findings and Horner's research, a research finding appears that supports the conclusion that the familial antecedents of high *n* Ach may be the same for boys and girls (Berens, 1972). Clearly, there is much to be learned about the factors leading to achievement motivation among women.

Finally, there has recently appeared a major challenge to the logic of the entire structure underlying achievement-motivation theory as proposed by the McClelland-Atkinson framework. This challenge, developed by Weiner and his co-workers (1971), is not necessarily antithetical to the more traditional framework but does constitute a major elaboration and major revision of its rationale. Basically, it is the argument of Weiner and his co-workers that cognitive processes occur between the outcomes of a given behavioral act and later behaviors, which affect the directionality and likelihood of these later behaviors by affecting the expectancy of successfully engaging in these later acts and the degree of positive affect to be attached to them. In a formal sense, it is suggested that:

(from Weiner et al., 1972)

In the area of achievement motivation itself as a specific content question, it is proposed that several kinds of cognitive activities can take place as a result of a behavior that has led to achievement (Weiner et al., 1972). These cognitive activities and their hypothesized outcomes are diagrammed as shown at the top of page 203.

Relevant to our consideration here, it is Weiner's (1972) basic argument that the high and low need achievement individuals differ significantly in that the high *n* Ach person is more likely to attribute success to his own efforts. This

	Possible Cognitive Responses	Hypothesized Cognitive + Emotional Outcomes	Hypothesized Behavioral Effects
Successful Achievement Behavior	1. Attribute reason for success to personal effort, as opposed to environmental factors (like task difficulty) →	1a. Magnifies positive affect attached to achievement 1b. Magnifies negative affect attached to failure →	Increased achievement-oriented behavior
	2. Attribute reason for success to low task difficulty and/or high ability →	2a. Increase in expectancy of task success	
Failure in Achievement Behavior	3. Attribute reason for failure to luck or lack of effort →	3a. Lack of decrease in expectancy of task success →	No change in achievement-oriented behavior
	4. Attribute reason for failure to low ability and/or high task difficulty →	4a. Decrease in expectancy of task success →	Decrease in achievement-oriented behavior

would, in turn, be more likely to lead to achievement behavior in the following manner:

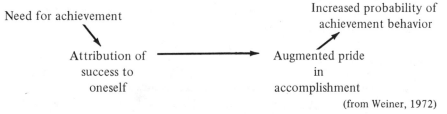

Need for achievement

Attribution of success to oneself ⟶ Augmented pride in accomplishment

Increased probability of achievement behavior

(from Weiner, 1972)

How well does Weiner's new approach account for the data we have? How well can it make new predictions of the kind not made by other theories? These are two criteria by which we evaluate any theory, Weiner's or anybody else's. Obviously, it is too early to make any definitive judgment about it but there is some support for it in existing data. Otherwise, it would not have received the serious consideration it has. What is needed now is to see how well it accounts for the new data it generates. Then we may be able to make a judgment.

ACHIEVEMENT MOTIVATION: AN INTEGRATED APPROACH

It is clear from all we have been discussing that achievement motivation can be approached in a number of different ways ranging from a simple application of a general motivational framework to the derivation of specific achievement-related hypotheses. Thus, as examples of the former, we have the balance approaches previously cited, and the expectancy-value approaches of the type suggested by Porter and Lawler. Similarly, it is also possible to cite here as illustrations the Spence-Taylor, Hullian-type theory of performance discussed in Chapter 3 and the U-shaped hypothesis of performance that has been associated with the activation-arousal theorists. On the other hand, there are also the specific hypotheses of Adams, McClelland, and Atkinson. Can any integration be made of these various approaches? We will suggest an attempt of our own in Chapter 10 to provide at least some integration, but it may also be of some value to present here an alternative integration proposed by Graen (1969).

Graen's approach is essentially in the expectancy-value tradition, but it also includes other characteristics such as suggesting that achievement behavior is, in part, a desire to avoid negative punishment by authority figures. This is, as is Atkinson's *FF* proposition, in the Hullian $D \times H$ tradition. In addition, he differentiates between Case A in the expectancy-value approach, which is the situation where the value to be achieved is some extrinsic value, and Case B, which is the intrinsic value of achievement. Graen's differentiating between these two is of value experimentally, since in Case A the extrinsic outcome can be defined and varied independently of probability of task achievement, whereas in Case B, as in Atkinson's model, it cannot. Integrating all of these ideas leads him to propose that gain in work performance (achievement) for a particular individual is a function of the following.

1. a. His preferences for various role outcomes
   b. His beliefs that the attainment of the work role of effective performer will lead to these various role outcomes
   c. His belief that increased effort in the performance of the act will lead to more effective performance (expectancy)
2. a. His perceptions of what others expect him to do (perceived role)
   b. His perceptions of the amount of pressure these other persons would apply to influence his compliance (perceived pressure)
3. a. His preference for various intrinsic consequences of the act
   b. His beliefs that the act will lead to these various intrinsic consequences

The first hypothesis is, of course, the expectancy-value (extrinsic) case, the second category stems from the Hull D (anxiety) $\times H$ (habit) tradition, and the third is the expectancy value (intrinsic value of outcome) approach. How well does Graen's integration work as a total approach? We have little data from him, but there is a converging line of evidence from other researchers that suggests his attempt at integration is aimed in a fruitful direction. Thus, in his research on the achievement behavior of black children in desegregated schools, Katz (1968) found significant influences to be threat in both a social and performance sense *and* the child's expectancy of task success. Considering that Graen has been primarily concerned with working adults, the degree of convergence between his proposals and Katz's findings are quite strong. Apparently, both threat (anxiety?) and cognitive expectancies, as well as other factors, are important if we are to understand achievement motivation, and integrating arguments of the kind suggested by Graen and Katz are feasible and, perhaps, necessary.

ACHIEVEMENT MOTIVATION: SOCIAL INFLUENCE

As our final example of how a specific process such as achievement-oriented behavior can take place as a derivative of a more general form of motivational process, it may be useful to cite some findings from general social psychology.

It has long been apparent that people frequently are influenced by other people in terms of level of aspiration and behavior engaged in, with such influence often defying the "laws" of common sense in a good many instances. A famous experiment in psychology by Asch (1956) revealed that substantial numbers of individuals, although not a majority, publicly stated that a physically shorter line was longer than one that was in fact physically longer, with such statements being made, for the most part, when the individual was confronted by the unanimous, though wrong, opinions of others. However, this conformity dropped drastically if the subject was joined by at least one other person who made a correct statement as to the physical state of affairs. Similarly, Milgram (1965) has recently shown that individuals can be influenced by high-status experimenters to administer physical shock punishment to other individuals, even though these other individuals object violently to such punishment. The reader of such experimental research investigations cannot help but be impressed by the degree to which we are subject to other people's definitions of how to evaluate and behave in given situations, whether we are referring to a laboratory situation on a college campus or to everyday task environments. This generalization was recognized as far back as the late 1920s and early 1930s during the course of the famous Hawthorne investigations that began as a study of the effects of physical factors, such as lighting, on performance. The studies ended up illustrating the influence on behavior of such social, interpersonal influences as peer-group approval, democratic as opposed to authoritarian-oriented leadership styles, and peer expectancies on performance. Although quite controversial in nature because of relatively poor methodological procedures (cf. Landsberger, 1958) these studies have often been cited as examples of how achievement motivation may be determined by social peer influences, which may work for either better or worse performance (Roethlisberger and Dickson, 1939; Vroom, 1964), depending on the given situation.

Given these findings and the continued ability to demonstrate the influence of social factors on task and work achievement in the psychology laboratory, recent theory construction has attempted to concentrate on three major questions. First, why do these opinions and differing social environments influence achievement behavior? Second, what kinds of social environments are associated with differential motivation to perform? Third, under which conditions will social environments have their greatest influence on the motivation to achieve?

Looking at the first question, we might ask why the tendency to conform to social demands should be so powerful in determining behavior. There seems to be at least two major reasons. First, somewhat related to our previous discussion on consistency, it is clear that groups and group opinions provide definitions of reality for us as individuals, particularly when no other measures of reality are available. They tell us how good we are, how able we are, and what is just and proper in the given case. They give us definitions and meaning for the world. Given similar definitions it then seems likely that we should expect similarity in performance. In this sense, our groups provide us with the sense of social reality we need, and we are motivated to perform in a way that is consistent with that reality.

Second, it is also the case that groups may affect the means by which we attain the various levels of performance we feel are best and the rewards we want. In this sense, we go along with the group because the group is the mechanism by which we hope to achieve the outcomes we want.

Different levels of achievement motivation (i.e., the levels of performance the group deems appropriate) appear to develop as a function of the kinds of people in the groups, how they view themselves, and so on. The reasons why high achievement norms develop are also a function of specific environments and the self-evaluations they cultivate (Festinger, 1954), matters already discussed briefly in reference to the need for achievement research and also implied in the relay-room experiments in the Hawthorne studies (Roethlisberger and Dickson, 1939). In the latter case, decreasing leader authoritarianism, as one example, was associated with higher achievement norms.

As to the question of the conditions under which the influence of social environments on achievement motivation is greatest, one major hypothesis is that group influence is greatest when the individuals involved are highly attracted to one another. It would be predicted, then, that variability of performance would be less in groups of people who are highly attracted to one another. Conversely, in the indifferent-to-one-another groups, individuals would be less likely to conform to one another and would show a more variable distribution of task-achieving behaviors. This tendency would make them more average in nature than the highly cohesive groups, since it would reflect individual differences in ability and motivation, and most people tend to be average. There are a number of findings which support this notion quite clearly (cf. Schachter et al., 1951; Berkowitz, 1954; Seashore, 1954).

Another point which these studies emphasize is that cohesiveness (i.e., degree of liking for one another) bears little relationship to performance per se, as we have suggested. Rather, it operates as a determinant of whether or not the person will go along with the group as to level of performance, whatever those levels of performance happen to be.

There are some other things that we know about the conditions under which individuals will use group- and leader-defined goals as a basis for their own level of achievement motivation in a given situation, based to a great extent on the research of Walker and Heyns (1962). According to these researchers, we should expect susceptibility to a social norm as a determinant of achievement motivation to increase with (1) the ambiguity of the situation, (2) the necessity of going along with the group for goal achievement, (3) the decreased self-confidence of the individual, and (4) the appropriateness of the goals being offered the individual (i.e., whether he thinks the goals are correct for himself). Taken in essence, these findings generally fit with our expectations in that they seem to indicate that we are most likely to use group definitions of reality as guides to our own behavior when (1) no other reality is available to us, (2) we do not trust these other definitions of reality (i.e., low self-confidence), and (3) our going along with the group supports our other definitions of reality (i.e., self-defined appropriateness of the goal being offered for conforming).

There is, however, one major question for which we do not as yet have information. Except perhaps for the "liking" variable, the mechanism of how we choose the social groups (and/or influences) whose definitions we shall accept, particularly when two groups are vying for a person's claim, is still an open question. As Pettigrew (1967) has pointed out, the whole problem of how we choose our reference groups is still an unanswered question.

SOME STATEMENTS ON ACHIEVEMENT MOTIVATION
FOR A FUTURE THEORY

Despite the usefulness of the theories we have presented in this chapter and elsewhere, it is necessary to remind the reader that theories are not permanently valid mechanisms. Basically, they are tentative summarizing devices for current states of knowledge. However, knowledge accumulation goes on without regard to theory, eventually forcing the development of new systems. Accordingly, we present below some summary statements of contemporary research findings on achievement motivation, which are fairly well substantiated and which do not seem to be accounted for by contemporary theoretical frameworks. These findings may serve as possible spurs for the development of new theories of achievement motivation in the years to come. These new theories will need to be able to account both for the data already explained by our existing frameworks *and* for the findings we present here.

1. Zajonc's (1965) findings that the presence of others facilitates performance on easy tasks and hurts it on hard ones is a persisting dilemma in a theoretical sense. While he has preferred to interpret his data within a $D \times H$ framework, viewing the presence of others as anxiety elicitors, it is clear from what we have said previously that there is much wrong with the $D \times H$ system. The research question here is to account for these findings with an alternative theoretical scheme. None has as yet been offered.

2. What gives a social object "value" so that groups and people will work to achieve it? In addition to the quantity problems we spoke of earlier, there are at least three other explanations in the literature and they are all difficult to reconcile with one another. The first is that objects gain value the more they are associated with primary reinforcing events (e.g., drive reduction of various types). This is the process we previously called secondary reinforcement. Secondly, there is the research stemming from dissonance theory that seems almost to suggest a self-destructive process in what we come to value. This is the prediction that we come to value objects to which we are committed and which we have, with such value increasing the *less* it has served as a reinforcer in the past. Finally, there is McClelland's hypothesis that moderate discrepancy from previous adaptation levels leads to positive affect for a stimulus. How do we reconcile these and the quantity questions we mentioned earlier? There is little guidance as yet in the literature.

3. There is some evidence that different motivational processes may be involved in achieving as an individual and achieving within a group. Thus, a strong ego is seen to be of considerable value for achievement as an individual (cf. Korman, 1971b; McClelland, 1961). On the other hand, it may be detrimental when trying to achieve within a group where sublimation of the self may be necessary (Collins and Guetzkow, 1962). Are the two sets of findings reconcilable? Under what conditions?

The answers to these questions are unclear at this time.

SUMMARY

Achievement motivation is obviously a phenomenon of great significance to our society, and psychologists have spent a great deal of time trying to understand the factors that influence it. This interest has involved two major approaches, with one of these being the application of general motivational theories to specific achievement motivational processes. The second has been the development of more limited theories specifically oriented to achievement motivation in and of itself.

As examples of the first approach, we discussed the work of expectancy-value theorists, such as Porter and Lawler, who have applied this approach to understanding the behavior of people in work situations and have found it quite fruitful. Similarly, consistency theory as an aid to understanding achievement motivation was illustrated by the work of J. S. Adams who has applied a dissonance theory approach to understanding achievement-oriented motivation. In addition, we also mentioned briefly our discussion earlier in this book on the usefulness of the Hullian model and activation-arousal theory for understanding achievement motivational processes.

As examples of the second approach, we discussed the work of McClelland, Atkinson, and those who have worked along with them in understanding how individual differences in the need for achievement and the fear of failure interact with the expectancy of task success in a given situation in affecting one's desire to achieve at that given time. Particularly notable among more recent work in this tradition has been Horner's work on "fear of success" among women and Weiner's concern with attribution for success and failure as a behavior influence.

Despite the values of these approaches, there are some remaining questions in understanding achievement motivation that are *not* accounted for. Hence, they remain as challenges for the future.

the
motivation
toward
aggression

In addition to the process we have called achievement motivation, there are other specific forms of motivated behavior that are frequently studied because of their significance for societal and/or personal functioning. Of these other behaviors, one of considerable interest to many psychologists is the motivation to hurt others, or the motivation toward aggression, a type of behavior that obviously has importance at a number of levels in both a theoretical and practical sense. In this chapter we will deal with this work in aggression motivation, both for the significance this work has had for the study of motivational processes in general and also for the light it has shed on this specific type of socially important behavior.

Our procedure will be to first discuss the research relating to the frustration-aggression hypothesis, probably the most popular of psychological theories of aggression, and how it fits with other, more general motivational theories of the types we have been discussing. Following this, we will turn to other theoretical and research approaches to the area of aggressive behavior, detailing at that time how they are similar and/or different from the overall motivational frameworks that have concerned us in this book and how they may provide unique understanding in and of themselves.

THE FRUSTRATION-AGGRESSION HYPOTHESIS

In 1939 a book called *Frustration and Aggression* was published by Dollard, Doob, Miller, Mowrer and Sears. Its main thesis was cited clearly and unequivocably at the very beginning: "Aggression is always a consequence of frustration," and "occurrence of aggressive behavior always presupposes the existence of frustration and, contrariwise, the existence of frustration always leads to some form of aggression." Therefore, a one-to-one relationship between frustration and aggression is postulated. The authors then carefully define "frustration" as follows: "Frustration is defined as a condition which exists when a goal response suffers interference [p. 11]." Whenever any type of aggressive act occurs, such an act, according to the hypothesis, is always due to some frustration or interference with a goal response the organism has suffered, and conversely, whenever an organism suffers any kind of thwarting or frustration, it will aggress. (Kaufman, 1970, pp. 24-25)

In looking at this hypothesis, it is perhaps easy to see why it had the original appeal it did, particularly during the era when it was offered. Thus, its attempt to state these complex behaviors in experimental terms with operational definitions fits in very well with the Hullian behavioristic natural-science emphasis of the times. (All five authors were either students of Hull or faculty associates at Yale.)

Unfortunately, however, the goal of these authors was never achieved, and the years since the original publication of the hypothesis have seen such continuing revisions and reformulations that the current status of the proposal bears little resemblance to the automatic linkages originally postulated. The first of these revisions was only two years after publication when one of the authors agreed that the original propositions had been too baldly stated and that instead of arguing that frustration leads to observable aggression, it would be better to assume that frustration leads to an instigation to aggression (Miller, 1941). The likelihood that the aggression would actually take place in an observable sense was now assumed to be a function of other behavior habits. While it was not recognized at the time, we will see that such a revision leads inevitably to a recasting of the hypothesis into terms more congruent with general motivational frameworks such as the Hullian and expectancy-value theories discussed earlier.

As the years went on, other weaknesses of the frustration-aggression hypothesis started to become apparent. It was quickly pointed out, for example, that often goal-directed responses were interfered with, yet aggression did not take place. Similarly, considerable aggression did often take place despite frustration of a relatively minor nature (e.g., the Nazi persecution of the Jews). These findings and other questions relating to the theory were eventually used in a monograph by Berkowitz (1962) as the basis for a revised formulation of the hypothesis, and it is his revisions that we now consider.

Berkowitz began his review of the frustration-aggression hypothesis by suggesting that it leads to three specific types of prediction. The first is that the greater the frustration, the greater the instinct to aggression. Second, there is the prediction that the stronger the behavioral motive being frustrated, the greater the frustration and, hence, the greater the impulse to aggression. Third, the hypothesis predicts that the greater the number of frustrations, the greater the aggressive response. Reviewing the research findings, Berkowitz comes to the conclusion that only the first two of these hypotheses are supported, but that the third is not. Rather, the data on the third suggest not a linear relationship as proposed but, rather, a curvilinear one, in that aggression as a response to frustration will increase with the number of frustrations up to a point, and then it will decrease, as indicated in the following figure:

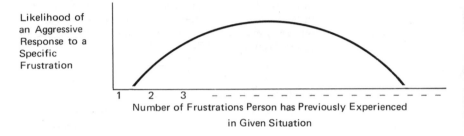

Likelihood of
an Aggressive
Response to a
Specific
Frustration

Number of Frustrations Person has Previously Experienced
in Given Situation

Why does such a relationship develop? Expectancies seem to be the major answer, in that as the number of frustrations increase, a person comes to expect them. Hence, when a frustration does occur, the reaction is not as negative, or so the literature seems to indicate.

> In general, expected frustrations produce less intense emotional reactions than do unanticipated frustrations. Two reasons are suggested: (1) through anticipating interference with his activity, the individual may alter his actions, or even his goals, so that he actually experiences less frustration; (2) expected frustrations may be judged as less severe. (Berkowitz, 1962, p. 72)

Whether or not these are the reasons that expected frustrations are not as likely to lead to aggression as those that are unexpected, aggressive behavior, clearly, is not the automatic process implied in the original frustration-aggression theory. Rather, it is apparent that expectations, cognitions, and the previous history of the behaving organism interact with the environmental characteristics of the moment in determining behavior, a conceptualization that brings us closer to the expectancy-value and other motivational frameworks previously discussed.

There is, however, one more step needed before we can simply integrate aggression motivation into a general expectancy-value (or $D \times K \times H$) framework whereby it is viewed as a form of behavior to be engaged in when certain values can be expected to be achieved by it. This step should show that the likelihood of aggressive behavior increases as a function of the expectancy that extrinsic values can be achieved by it, and negative outcomes can be avoided by such behaviors. It turns out that such evidence does exist from a number of different studies and conceptualizations. Thus, each of the following statements is based on research findings, and when taken in context, they all lend support to the conclusion that the motivation to aggress against others can be viewed, if we wish, as a form of behavior engaged in as a result of (a) being in a nonvalue-attained state at the time (i.e., being frustrated), and (b) expecting to achieve desired values as outcomes by so doing. Similarly, we can coordinate the frustration state to a nonoptimal, high D (drive) situation and postulate a K (expectancy) variable, and this also would serve as a relatively useful framework. The research evidence for such an integration is as follows:

1. Aggressive behavior as a response to frustration is inhibited when punishment for such behavior is expected.
2. Hostile behavior is inhibited the greater the degree of punishment that is expected.
3. High-status people are usually less likely to be aggressed against than low-status individuals. (This supports our general principle because high-status people are more likely to control the likelihood of obtaining other desired goals.)
4. The groups and individuals who are usually chosen as scapegoats and as targets of aggressive behavior are usually weaker individuals who have not the strength (economic, psychological, social) to fight back at the aggression; hence, this makes the aggression more likely to be successful.
5. The likelihood of revolution as a function of frustration is more apt to take place after a period of rising expectations (Davies, 1962). One explanation for this, which Wallace (1971) has pointed out and which is consistent with our general point, is that it may be true that during periods of rising expectations rigid controls over people are progressively relaxed, protests are increasingly tolerated, and the inhibitions of downtrodden peoples to engage in violent protest are gradually lowered. In this sense, the expectancy that aggression will lead to greater value is increased, thus making it more likely that aggression will be engaged in when frustration does occur.

When we consider all of these findings, we discover that the frustration-aggression hypothesis has come a long way from its original formulation. It is now more cognitive, it incorporates the previous history of the organism as an explanatory mechanism in order to aid in the interpretation of contemporary environmental manipulations, and in fact, it is not greatly different in its major orientation from some of the motivational frameworks to which we have referred in our earlier discussions of major contructs and approaches.

As further support for this conclusion, there is one more major body of research literature, which we have not mentioned up to now but which is quite relevant. The studies, known under the general heading of *modeling*, investigate the effects of watching the behavior of others on one's own behavior. Basically, this research has focused on the conditions under which models and modeling may be used as a mechanism for changing the behavior of the observer (cf. Bandura and Walters, 1963). What is relevant for us here is that one of the findings of this literature is that the observation of aggression in others that leads to some reward or the cessation of some punishment is more likely to be repeated by the observer than if the behavior is punished (Bandura, Ross, and Ross, 1963; Berkowitz and Rawlings, 1963). If we make the rather simple assumption that people learn about attainable values by their observation, then this type of finding certainly fits in with our general conclusion that aggression is more likely to be engaged in if there is some type of value to be attained by it.

We should mention, however, that this general conclusion as to the effects of observing successful aggression in others on one's own aggression has been based mostly on laboratory research, and that when the same notion has been tested in the field, just the reverse has occurred. A field study by Feshbach and Singer (1971) has recently found that boys who watched aggressive behavior on television were less likely to be aggressive than those who did not watch television violence, a finding directly opposite from the modeling studies and, in fact, from the general expectancy-value framework. As a matter of fact, the best theoretical explanation for the Feshbach and Singer research is the previously thought-to-be discredited "catharsis" hypothesis of Freud, which postulates that people have an inbred capacity to aggress against others as a result of displacing the aggression against the self (cf. Chapter 2). Hence, the more aggression is exhibited harmlessly, as in television watching or in games, the less it will be displaced against others. Despite the adequacy of this explanation, however, the utilization of the Freudian framework is probably not an optimal way to proceed, considering all the problems we have noted with Freud's hypotheses. What really should be done is to integrate the Feshbach and Singer findings with those of the modeling researchers, an integration that does not seem readily available right now.

Until this integration occurs and until we can better understand the significance of the Feshbach and Singer research, perhaps the most meaningful integration we can suggest at this time is that offered by Kaufman (1970) in his recent review of the literature. It is this model that we present below:

$$\text{Potential for Behavior} = f(a_i A_{ijk} + V_{ijk} + H_{ijk})$$

where A_{ijk} = Persisting aggression motive of the individual or the extent to which the situation calls for aggressive behavior

V_{ijk} = Perceived value expected from aggressive behavior in the situation

H_{ijk} = Aggressive habits of the individual

a_i = Extent to which person customarily acts in accordance with his values and motives

The similarity to the Spence, Hull, and other models we have discussed is, of course, great, but the readers should notice there are differences. First, additive, rather than multiplicative, relationships are postulated, an approach completely different from Hull and partially different from Spence. Is it a better one? As we indicated earlier, this is still an unresolved question. Secondly, there is another variable being postulated here, a_i, and this is the degree to which people customarily act in accordance with their motives. This is a very important difference from the previous motivational frameworks we have been discussing since, as we will see in Chapter 10, such differences do definitely exist and may be significant in understanding the motivation of behavior.

A CONSISTENCY THEORY APPROACH TO AGGRESSION

If we look at our discussion of the frustration-aggression hypothesis, where it started, and where it wound up, we can see in capsule form a process that, in some respects, underlies the whole field of motivation. This process, in brief, is one in which an attempt is first made to understand complex psychological processes by physicalistic, natural-science means of the kind Hull and psychologists working in the same tradition valued. Eventually, however, the approach falls down and cognitive, nonphysicalistic concepts have to be introduced if we are to understand the complex behaviors under consideration. In some cases, the result is the development of approaches that are sometimes in the expectancy-value tradition and sometimes in the consistency tradition. In both cases, however, the emphasis is on accepting and somehow incorporating the nonphysical, psychological concept into a theoretical framework that is rigorous and experimentally testable and yet still does justice to the complexity of the process involved.

All of this is really just a way of introducing the fact that as the expectancy-value formulation has turned out to be viable and useful in understanding aggressive behavior, so has the consistency-theory framework. Most prominent here has been the work of Elaine and William Walster and Ellen Berscheid, all three of whom have used the consistency formulation in building an understanding of certain types of aggressive behavior. Recently they have attempted to integrate their findings in an explicit fashion. If we look at this integration carefully, we can see how this type of thinking can add to our understanding of some aspects of aggressive behavior.

The approach proposed by the Walsters and Berscheid (1972) starts from the same point as that of the Adams inequity theory in that for them:

$$\text{Equity} = \frac{\text{Outcomes A}}{\text{Inputs A}} = \frac{\text{Outcomes B}}{\text{Inputs B}}$$

$$\text{Inequity} = \frac{\text{Outcomes A}}{\text{Inputs A}} \neq \frac{\text{Outcomes B}}{\text{Inputs B}}$$

Starting from the same point, then, and from the same assumption that inequity is a negative tension state that we wish to reduce, the Walsters go on to propose and cite research support for the following propositions:

1. Under some conditions, a person will feel inequity because he receives outcomes higher than he perceives he deserves (such tension may result because this would violate the societal norms of equity that underlie the basic equity assumption and because of a fear of retaliation for this equity violation).

2. A person may reduce his feelings of inequity, under certain conditions, by (a) derogating the other person in terms of the value of the other person's inputs into the system (thus reducing the necessity for higher outputs); (b) minimizing the other person's inputs (thus increasing relative output); and (c) denying the fact of one's responsibilities for the lack of value (or outputs) that the other person receives.

What is being argued here is that a person who sees himself in an inequitable relationship, in which he gets too much as compared to another person's input-output ratio, may try to reduce his feelings of inequity by behaving toward the other person in a manner to justify the perception that the person *deserves less.* Since the best way, or at least the easiest way, that this can be done is to make the other person appear like a "negative" individual, aggressive behavior toward that person is therefore initiated with that goal in mind, that is, to make the other person look like a "negative" person who is not deserving of valuable outcomes for his behavior.

When is this deprecation of the victim likely to take place? The behavior is more likely to take place when it is less costly, less difficult, when it is more likely to be adequate in reducing inequity, when it requires little distortion of reality, and when it is most likely to maximize the person's outcomes. This proposal is similar to the one made by Adams. It is obvious that the Walsters see people as being motivated to achieve both equity and maximal value and argue that the two are both operative. In this way, their work on the conditions under which the aggression is most likely to take place constitutes a tentative bridge between the expectancy-value and consistency theorists.

As we have indicated, there is considerable support for these basic ideas of the Walsters and Berscheid, both in their own research and that of others working in the consistency tradition (cf. Lerner and Simmons, 1966). This is also quite evident in the writings of those interested in aggression on a societal level. It has been argued that race prejudice, certainly a form of aggression, is nothing but the development and exhibition of negative behaviors toward groups felt to be inferior in a societal sense in order to justify the superior status of the perpetrating group (Wrightsman, 1972; Jones, 1972). This extension of the consistency-theory approach to societal phenomena is also seen in the recent research by Campbell and LeVine (1968). Working primarily at the group, intergroup, and intersocietal levels, they have found support for *both* the predictions of the Heider approach to consistency theory *and* the predictions of dissonance theory. Thus, in support of Heider, Campbell and LeVine were able to cite the following results:

1. The more similar an outgroup is in customs, values, beliefs, and general culture, the more liked it will be.
2. Regional patterns of intergroup relations will be balanced as follows:

> an ally of an ally will be an ally;
> an enemy of an ally will be an enemy;
> an ally of an enemy will be an enemy;
> an enemy of an enemy will be an ally.

On the other hand, in support of dissonance theory, Campbell and LeVine report that the more suffering, cost, and effort that members have endured in association with their group membership, the more loyalty and ingroup esteem there will be and the greater the relative hostility toward outsiders.

In reviewing this literature, then, it is very clear that the logic of balance theory can be valuable in enabling us to understand aggressive motivation (Pepitone, 1964). However, it is also clear from our previous discussions of consistency theory that many questions remain to be answered about the viability of this approach, and that a complete motivational theory of aggression will have to include more than the predictions of the consistency theories.

AUTHORITARIANISM, DOGMATISM, AND AGGRESSION

In 1950 a book was published that proved to be a landmark for social scientists interested in the study of such problems as racial hatred, interpersonal and intergroup aggression, and similar types of variables. The book, *The Authoritarian Personality* (Adorno et al., 1950), has been a major source of controversy and research since that time, but in the main, despite its methodological difficulties and a relative lack of sophistication, the reported findings have held up fairly well (Kirscht and Dillehay, 1967). It is these findings that are of most relevance to our study of motivational processes.

Basically, there are three major questions that interest us here. First, what did *The Authoritarian Personality* researchers find, empirically, that has proved to be relatively stable in later investigations? Two, what types of motivational constructs did they use in order to explain their findings? Three, are other interpretations of their findings possible? We will deal with each of these in turn.

It is, perhaps, best to deal with the first question by citing the historical background of the research. Basically, the research that led to the publication of *The Authoritarian Personality* had its origins in the holocaust that the Jews of Europe suffered at the hands of Nazi Germany during World War II. As a result of this horror, a Jewish philanthropic organization provided financial support to a team of psychiatrists, sociologists, psychoanalysts, and psychologists at the University of California to investigate the causes of anti-Semitism, where it came from, what kinds of people were anti-Semites, and similar types of questions. The eventual hope was that the insights gained by such research might lead to remedial actions of various kinds.

The results of the investigation were, as we have said, controversial in nature, with the controversy stemming from such varied considerations as the methods used, the political ideologies of the investigators, and the representativeness of the samples. As a result, the past twenty years have seen continuing reeaximination and questioning of the findings at a level almost unparalleled anywhere else in social psychology. Yet, despite the questioning, testing, and the possible improvements in some aspects of the conceptualization and methods used, it appears that the basic findings of the study remain firm and supported (Brown, 1965; Kirscht and Dillehay, 1967). These findings are listed below:

1. Individuals who are anti-Semitic tend also to be anti-other minorities and groups outside the prevailing social norm. More specifically defined, this means that people who are anti-Semitic tend to be anti-any other deviate group such as blacks, Catholics, physically disabled, the blind, and so on. There tends, generally, to be a cluster of "anti-deviate-from-the-majority-norm" feelings and people who are high on one tend to be high on others.
2. Relationships between such anti-feelings and such demographic variables as education, status, and so on, do exist, but they are relatively minor in terms of their level of correlation with such feelings.

These, then, were the basic findings. First, anti-Semitism was not an isolated phenomenon but, rather, seemed to be part of an interwoven web of generalized anti-other and generalized anti-anything but the prevailing majority group. Secondly, demographic correlates were only part, and only a small part at best, of the answer. Why then did such a pattern of anti-other, or ethnocentric, behavior develop? What were the motivational dynamics involved? In attempting to develop a theoretical explanation of their findings, these researchers leaned heavily on the concepts of psychoanalytic theory:

> As a first approximation, one might say that in the highly ethnocentric person the superego is strict, rigid and relatively externalized, the id is strong, primitive and ego-alien, while the ego is weak and can manage the superego-id conflict only by resorting to rather desperate defenses. (Sanford, 1965, p. 275)

In essence, what the researchers proposed was that the anti-other person was a person with relatively strong drives (the id) that had been and continued to be prevented from expressing themselves directly by strong authority figures to which the individual was subject and who did not wish to see such drives expressed. As a result of such fear of punishment, it was hypothesized that such drives would then express themselves in ways that would be acceptable to the authority figures, allow the individual to release his tension, and still allow him to keep his ego intact.[1] It is these hypothesized means of drive expression, which constitute in Freudian terminology a type of ego-defense mechanism, that were used as a base upon which to build the famous F- (or Fascist) scale. It was this scale that *The Authoritarian Personality* investigators built to reflect what would be the characteristics of a person who would be ethnocentric and anti-others *if* their psychoanalytic thinking was correct, that is, if the highly ethnocentric individual was one who had both strong drives of a Freudian nature (i.e., mostly sexual in nature) and who was also fearful of expressing them because of fear of punishment from some authority figure. The characteristics the F-scale was designed to measure were:

1. *Conventionalism* — rigid adherence to conventional middle-class values;
2. *Authoritarian Submission* — submissive, uncritical attitude toward idealized moral authorities of the ingroup;
3. *Authoritarian Aggression* — tendency to be on the lookout for, and to condemn, reject, and punish people who violate conventional values;
4. *Anti-Intraception* — opposition to the subjective, the imaginative, the tender-minded;
5. *Superstition and Stereotype* — the belief in mystical determinants of the individual's fate and the disposition to think in rigid categories;
6. *Power and Toughness* — identification with power figures and exaggerated assertion of strength and toughness;
7. *Destructiveness and Cynicism* — generalized hostility and vilification of the human;
8. *Projectivity* — the disposition to believe that wild and dangerous things go on in the world and the projection outward of unconscious emotional impulses;
9. *Sex* — ego-alien sexuality, an exaggerated concern with sexual goings-on, and punitiveness toward violators of sex mores.

These were developed as the components of the F-scale, a set the investigators felt reflected the kinds of thinking processes that would result if a person (a) found himself in the grip of strong, instinctual desires, (b) knew he could not express them because he would be punished, and (c) had outgroups available upon whom he could project these forbidden impulses with a high expectancy of success since they were too weak to fight back (a function of their being an outgroup). Once having projected these negative behaviors onto

---

[1]The reader will notice here how this use of ego-defense mechanism is conceptually similar to the expectancy-value paradigm since, in essence, the mechanism is one whereby the ego seeks out a situation where the expectancy of a successful instinctual drive reduction is greatest.

others, he could then identify with the feared authority figure and attack these "bad" outsiders (i.e., those who had the "bad" instincts and traits).

The logic underlying the F-scale demanded that scores on it be correlated with aggression toward outgroups and such a correlation has, with rare exception, been found in a wide variety of different investigations (Brown, 1965; Kirscht and Dillehay, 1967). In this sense, the investigators were theoretically correct and their psychoanalytic hypothesis as to the cause of this type of aggression has been a useful one. However, it is conceivable, as one of the original investigators himself has pointed out (Sanford, 1956, p. 277), that other hypotheses might be developed to account for these feelings of hostility and aggression toward outgroups, which are not psychoanalytically based. In the next chapter we shall offer a hypothesis that attempts to account for the findings of *The Authoritarian Personality* investigators within a balance-theory framework, rather than within the psychoanalytic model proposed here. Here we shall be making use of the finding that high authoritarians (i.e. high F-scale people) tend to come from homes that are highly hierarchical in nature, stress impersonality and rule orientation, and emphasize strict, physical punishment for rule violation.

In addition, it may also be noted that dissonance theory has been used to account for behaviors such as these. Bramel (1962) found that individuals who were experimentally manipulated to have high self-esteem and provided feedback indicating possible homosexual feelings were more likely to project homosexuality onto others than those experimentally manipulated to have low self-esteem.

RAPIDITY OF SOCIETAL CHANGE AND AGGRESSIVE BEHAVIOR

Among the highly stable phenomena that we can count on in our rapidly changing world is that the level of unplanned and random violence in our society seems to be increasing. Thus, any casual observer of the day's events cannot help but be struck by the crime on the streets, the senseless murders and beatings of innocent people, and other similar events. The question for the psychologist is why? Unfortunately, only the first steps at answering this question have been made. In this final section of Chapter 9, we will review the work of one psychologist, Philip Zimbardo, who has made some attempts at developing some answers to these questions, the motivational hypothesis he has suggested for integrating his findings, and a possible alternative suggestion to his formulations. However, as we will see, despite the relative newness of the problem, general motivational frameworks of the kind we have been dealing with in this book may have some degree of fruitfulness here also.

Zimbardo's major hypotheses can be summarized as follows and in Table 9.1.

Table 9.1 Outline of Zimbardo Model of Deindividuation and Aggression

Input Variables ⟶	Inferred Subjective Changes ⟶	Output Behaviors
A. Anonymity B. Responsibility: shared, diffused, given up C. Group size, activity D. Altered temporal perspective: present expanded, future and past distanced E. Arousal F. Sensory-input overload G. Physical involvement in the act H. Reliance upon noncognitive interactions and feedback I. Novel or unstructured situation J. Altered states of consciousness, drugs, alcohol, sleep, etc.	Minimization of: 1. Self-observation evaluation 2. Concern for social evaluation Weakening of controls based upon guilt, shame, fear, and commitment Lowered threshold for expressing inhibited behaviors	a. Behavior emitted is emotional, impulsive, irrational, regressive, with high intensity b. Not under the controlling influence of usual external discriminative stimuli c. Behavior is self-reinforcing and is intensified, amplified with repeated expressions of it d. Difficult to terminate e. Possible memory impairments; some amnesia for act f. Perceptual distortion — insensitive to incidental stimuli and to relating actions to other actors g. Hyperresponsiveness — "contagious plasticity" to behavior of proximal, active others h. Unresponsiveness to distal reference groups i. Greater liking for group or situation associated with "released" behavior j. At extreme levels, the group dissolves as its members become autistic in their impulse gratification k. Destruction of traditional forms and structures

Source: P. G. Zimbardo, The human choice: individuation, reason, and order versus deindividuation, impulse, and chaos. *Nebraska symposium on motivation, 17,* 1969, 237-307. Copyright 1969 by the University of Nebraska Press. Reprinted by permission.

Deindividuation is a complex, hypothesized process in which a series of antecedent social conditions lead to changes in perception of self and others, and thereby to a lowered threshold of normally restrained behavior. Under appropriate conditions what results is the "release of behavior in violation of established norms of appropriateness."

Such conditions permit overt expression of antisocial behavior, characterized as selfish, greedy, power-seeking, hostile, lustful, and destructive. However, they also allow a range of "positive" behaviors which we normally do not express overtly, such as intense feelings of happiness or sorrow, and open love for others. *Thus, emotions and impulses usually under cognitive control are more likely to be expressed when the input conditions minimize self-observation and evaluation as well as concern over evaluation by others* [italics mine].

> We may speak loosely of: conditions of deindividuation (conditions stimulating it), the feelings or state of deindividuation (the experiential aspect of the input variables together with the inferred subjective changes), and deindividuated behaviors (characterized by several specific output behaviors). Deindividuation refers to the entire process and only then becomes a unique psychological construct.[2]

This is an attempt by one psychologist to account for the increasing amount of unbridled violence in our society. It has some degree of empirical support, but much more evidence is needed, as Zimbardo himself suggests (Zimbardo, 1969). What is of most importance for us here, however, is Zimbardo's motivational hypothesis as to why deindividuation results in greater aggression. His hypothesis is basically an instinctual general drive or energy one, arguing in essence that man has a desire to throw off all controls and do what his nature tells him to do.

> We must then posit a "universal need" to shatter all formal controls, albeit temporarily, as occurs in every person through dreaming. This fact is the basis of society's institutionalization of revelous behavior — harvest festivals in agrarian societies and carnivals in religious ones — where an "unproductive waster of energy" is encouraged. Functionally, such festivals serve to siphon off destructive energy, prevent unpredictable individually initiated release of impulses, and enable the deindividuated reveler to experience both the pleasure of his revels and the satisfaction of becoming reindividuated following their termination.[3]

It is not necessary, however, to adopt this interpretation to make use of Zimbardo's findings. We might, for example, just argue that increasing change leads to increasing frustration due to lack of predictability of behavior outcomes. Such increasing frustration then leads to increased propensity to aggression, an aggression more likely to occur because external controls inhibiting the aggression (i.e., possible punishment) have decreased in salience due to the rapid change. In this way, then, we may use a general motivational framework of the kind discussed earlier to account for Zimbardo's findings.

SUMMARY

Aggression motivation is like achievement motivation, a process very important for our society to understand. Hence, a great deal of attention has been devoted to this question. Much of this interest has stemmed from the frustration-

---

[2]P. G. Zimbardo, The human choice: inviduation, reason, and order versus de-individuation, impulse, and chaos. *Nebraska symposium on motivation, 17,* 1969, 251. Copyright 1969 by the University of Nebraska Press. Reprinted by permission.
[3]Ibid., p. 254.

aggression hypothesis, a proposal originally made some thirty years ago that suggested an automatic linkage between frustration and aggression. However, it soon became clear that this was much too simplistic a proposal and that the relationships were far more complex than this. Increasingly, the research over the past several decades has pointed to the conclusion that aggression as a response to frustration is much more likely to take place when the expectancy that it will succeed in reducing frustration is high. Another source of research in the area of aggression has been the hypothesis stemming from the research on the authoritarian personality and the central role it assigns to fear of power figures as a source of aggression against weaker others.

More recently, alternative theories of aggression have begun to appear. Thus, Walster and her co-workers have shown how the consistency model is useful in understanding aggression. In addition, Zimbardo has postulated the existence of a general drive for freedom from restraint as underlying such aggressive behavior. While the Walster model has considerable empirical support, research is necessary for the evaluation of the Zimbardo proposal, particularly since alternative explanations of his arguments seem feasible.

a motivational theory
of
achievement,
aggression,
and
receptivity to change

The discussion in this chapter links the two major approaches to studying motivational processes utilized in this book. As the reader may recall, we have indicated that one way of understanding motivational processes is to develop comprehensive theoretical frameworks and then to derive from such frameworks specific instances of motivated behavior. Thus, our discussion in Chapters 2 through 6 was centered around such overall frameworks, their logic, and some indication of their adequacy and their weaknesses. We then turned in Chapters 8 and 9 to a discussion of their success in accounting for such specific forms of motivated behavior as achievement and aggression.

These latter discussions also served to illustrate the second major way in which motivational processes can be studied. This latter approach, as we indicated, is to focus on a particular phenomenon of interest (e.g., aggression) and then develop theoretical frameworks and research approaches centered around a particular type of behavior.

Our goal in this chapter is to present a theoretical framework that is somewhat midway between these two major approaches. We will discuss a theoretical model that is not designed to be a comprehensive overall theory of motivational processes but, nevertheless, attempts to account for a number of different motivational phenomena within one framework. We have several reasons for presenting this theory. First, it serves as an illustration that such midway theories are possible in the area of motivation. Second, the theory we will present is a consistency model, which suggests that some of the weaknesses mentioned in Chapter 7 are not inherent in the consistency approach. Thus, in the theory we shall present here, an attempt has been made to (a) incorporate variables that are subject to measurement procedures (e.g., self-esteem, esteem for others), (b) utilize measurement procedures in such a way that degree and direction of discrepancies can be systematically incorporated into the framework, and (c) develop constructs that allow directional predictions. Third, the theory is presented here because there are considerable data to indicate that it is useful in accounting for some of the varied sorts of research we have discussed in previous chapters within one relatively systematic framework. Therefore, we will have reason, from time to time, to refer to some of the ideas and research findings discussed in earlier chapters.

ACHIEVEMENT, AGGRESSION, AND CREATIVITY: AN INTEGRATED THEORETICAL APPROACH

In a basic sense, one may argue that in our society people must do at least three things if they are to be effective.[1] First, one must achieve on tasks, whatever those tasks might be. Second, he or she must keep interpersonal conflict and aggression toward others under sufficient control so that such behavior will not become debilitating and consume so much time and effort that one's goals cannot be achieved. Finally, a person must have the capacity to be creative and change if the environment calls for it. Since the latter seems to be clearly the case in today's dynamic society, it would seem defensible to argue that a major goal of psychology should be the development of a theory that will allow an understanding of the antecedent conditions under which various levels of these motivational processes will be more likely to occur. Basically, the goal should be to develop a theory that specifies that under condition A, various types and levels of achievement, aggression, and creativity will occur; whereas under condition B, other behaviors will occur. Furthermore, it is also desired that the conditions and characteristics studied be of the nature that lend themselves to meaningful research control and eventual practical application.

It was as a step toward this eventual outcome that the theoretical model we are presenting in this chapter was developed.[2] We have two goals. First, we will try to show how the proposed theory can account for research findings relating to behavioral variation on the three major motivational processes of

---

[1] We have chosen the term *effective* to connote being satisfied with oneself, having high self-esteem, having positive mental helath, and the like.

[2] Since the framework we will propose constitutes an elaboration and extension of models previously suggested by the author (Korman, 1971a, 1970), the reader might wish to refer to these papers.

achievement, creativity, and aggression. Secondly, we will indicate how such variation in motivation is subject to influence by environmental variables that are susceptible to experimental manipulation and practical control. There are two reasons for this second goal: (1) it will provide us with a means for predicting and understanding the *direction* of behavior, a major goal of a motivational theory and one on which some other consistency theories are weak; and (2) our presentation may then be of value for those readers with applied interests and careers.

Our procedure will be to propose that the motivational processes known as achievement, creativity, and aggression are a function of certain belief systems about the self, others, and the world. Following the presentation of evidence relating to the propositions, we will suggest that these varying belief systems are a function of exposure to sociopsychological environments and that environmental characteristics that are more likely to be associated with one set of belief systems than another can be identified. To support this argument we will present two further types of evidence. First, we will present evidence that the relevant belief systems are a direct function of these environments. Such evidence is important for our model because it provides data supporting our postulated mediating processes between environment and behavior, a matter of great psychological importance, as we saw in our discussion of Tolman. Second, we will present data that support direct relationships between these types of environments and our dependent variables of achievement, creativity, and aggression. This evidence is of value for us because such a direct relationship between environment and behavior is predicted from our previous postulations that the motivational processes relative to these behaviors are a function of certain belief systems and that these belief systems are in turn a function of certain kinds of environments. Hence, the obtained relationship constitutes support for our notions. The direct relationship between environments and behavior has additional value, in that it specifically directs the attention of practitioners to those aspects of the environment that need to be changed in order to have the motivational and behavioral effects one desires.

As a result of these discussions, we will propose an integrated theory of motivational processes that will hypothesize that:

1. Motivational processes are a function of the drive to be consistent with belief systems about the nature of the self, others, and the world.
2. Belief systems leading to differing levels of achievement, creativity, and aggression are a function of and develop in the same types of environments.
3. Changing environments in certain directions specified by the theoretical model will result in changes in achievement, creativity, and aggression.

The model makes two basic assumptions. The first is that man is motivated to achieve outcomes that are consistent with his evaluative beliefs about himself, his evaluative beliefs about others, and the degree to which he believes that there is one set of values (whatever they may be) to guide behavior in this world. Second, man learns about himself, others, and the world, in part, as a function of the actual and symbolically stated opinions of others. Thus, holding other learning experiences about the self and others constant, the more the individual interacts with a world that encourages a certain system of beliefs about the self, others, and the world, the more these beliefs become part of the individual.

The rationale for these assumptions stems from two considerations. First, it is argued that man is motivated to achieve outcomes consistent with what he has learned to believe about the nature of the self, others, and the world because inconsistent worlds, that is, those that do not conform to his beliefs about the nature of the world (self, others, etc.), are anxiety provoking and dissatisfying. It should be noted here that this assumption does not demand that it is an unvarying world that is sought. For example, what might be sought as a consistent outcome is a world of change, expectancies of independent behavior, and variability, since this is consistent with one's belief about the nature of the world. In this case what might be rejected is a world of nonchange, nonindependence, and nonvariability, since this is inconsistent with the world one knows. As we pointed out earlier in this book, Fiske and Maddi (1961) have suggested a concept very similar to this. They have argued that individuals are motivated to achieve an optimal activation level (i.e., one consistent with the world as one knows it), with activation level being a function of the variability, meaningfulness, and intensity of the internal and external stimuli to which an organism is now exposed, with the level that defines optimality for the given individual at least in part a function of previous experience.

A second consideration underlying these assumptions about man's motivations is that man is motivated to learn about himself and others and establish a socially real world (Festinger, 1954). In the world of social behavior, since there is no physical reality, the only way for a person to establish a system of evaluative beliefs about the self and others and the variability of the world is to interact with others, both overtly and symbolically.

Given these assumptions, the following predictions can be made:

1. People of high self-perceived competence and positive self-image should be more likely to achieve on task performance than those who have low self-perceived competence, low success expectancy and low self-image concerning the task or job at hand, since such differential task achievement would be consistent with their self-cognitions. This assumes that task performance is seen as valued. (We will discuss at a later time the implications for achievement motivation when the task is seen as not valued.)

2. People who have beliefs that there is one set of rules to guide behavior in this world and that there is one way of looking at the world are more likely to be opposed to creative change, change in general, and to those people or things that are different or constitute a change from

themselves, since such change would be inconsistent with their belief systems.

3. People who have beliefs that people, in general, are not desirable, cannot be trusted, and must be controlled by threats and punishments are more likely to develop aggressiveness toward others and are more likely to engage in generally hostile interpersonal behavior, since such types of behavior would be consistent with their belief systems about people.

In Tables 10.1, 10.2, and 10.3 we present evidence relevant to these propositions. Table 10.1 provides summaries of studies concerned with the relationship between the favorability of self-image and various kinds of task performance. While the measures used in these studies have differed, the unifying element among them has been that in each case there has been some kind of direct measurement of the self-image along such dimensions as

Table 10.1 Summary of Studies Relating Self-Esteem and Self-Evaluation to Achievement Behaviors

Basic Findings	Investigators
1. Women of high self-esteem who want to go to college are more likely to engage in behavior designed to achieve that goal than women who want to go to college who have low self-esteem.	Denmark and Guttentag (1967)
2. People who expect that they will have to do something unpleasant on the basis of previous experience choose to perform the unpleasant task even when they could have chosen a more pleasant one.	Aronson, Carlsmith, and Darley (1963)
3. Individuals who have high social reinforcement standards (i.e., degree to which they have been rewarded previously) are more likely to perform in a manner designed to achieve high rewards than those who have low social-reinforcement standards.	Baron (1966)
4. Self-perceived ability on a task based on previous task performance is positively related to later task performance.	Kaufman (1963); Feather (1965)
5. Individuals of high self-esteem are more likely to choose occupations in which they perceive themselves to have a great degree of ability than those of low self-esteem.	Korman (1967a); Korman (1967b)
6. Individuals who are told they are incompetent to achieve a specific goal on a task, even though they have had no previous experience with the task, will perform worse than those who are told they are competent to achieve the goals.	Korman (1968a)
7. Academic achievers have a more positive self-concept than underachievers.	Shaw (1968)
8. There is a significant positive relationship between self-concept and grade-point average.	Brookover and Thomas (1963-64)
9. Individuals of high self-esteem are more likely to perform a task successfully when qualifications are challenged than individuals of low self-esteem.	Finkelman (1970)

self-perceived competence, self-perceived abilities, and expectancy of success, all variables that are logically subsumable under the general overall self-esteem variable. In addition, one further reason for treating these measures as psychologically similar is that there is good evidence that measures of self-esteem are highly related to one another (Silber and Tippett, 1965).

Tables 10.2 and 10.3, which report data relevant to our second and third predictions, differ from Table 10.1 in that in both of these latter cases the measures of individual differences in belief systems utilized were the F-scale (authoritarianism) (Adorno et al., 1950) and D-scale (dogmatism) (Rokeach,

Table 10.2 Summary of Findings on the Relationship Between the F-Scale and: (a) Reactions to Newness, Difference, and Change; (b) Aggressiveness and Hostility Exhibited Toward Others

Basic Findings	*Invesitgators*
1. Authoritarianism is negatively correlated with attitudes toward (a) the blind and (b) the deaf.	(a) Cowen, Underberg, and Verrilo (1958); (b) Cowen et al. (1967)
2. Authoritarianism is positively correlated with the tendency to keep social distance from others in Germany, Japan, and the United States.	Triandis, Davis, and Takezawa (1965)
3. High authoritarians are more likely to be aggressive toward groups different from oneself across different situations; they are more likely to exhibit more generalized hostility toward such groups.	Epstein (1966)
4. Task groups led by leaders low in authoritarianism were more likely to adjust to changing demands of situation and to be more flexible in meeting these new requirements.	Ziller (1958)
5. In an experimental game situation, authoritarianism scores were positively correlated with the tendency not to trust the other side and to act in an untrustworthy manner toward the other side.	Deutsch (1960)
6. Authoritarianism is positively related to the tendency to use physical punishment and ridicule in controlling children.	Hart (1957)
7. Authoritarianism is positively related to the use of negative (hostile) sanctions (e.g., penalties, negative evaluations) and the use of sanctions, in general, in controlling the behavior of others.	Dustin and Davis (1967)
8. Attitudes toward minority (or perceived different) groups are all highly correlated with one another, and these generalized attitudes are negatively correlated with authoritarianism.	Adorno et al. (1950)
9. Authoritarianism is highly correlated with militaristic attitudes and an aggressive foreign policy.	Eckhardt and Newcombe (1969)
10. High F-scale people are more likely to act in a hostile fashion toward others at the behest of an authority figure.	Elms and Milgram (1966)
11. High F-scale people were less likely to have demonstrated against the Vietnam war in 1969.	Izzett (1971)

1960). Neither of these scales is as desirable for our purposes as they could be, since each is a composite measure of a number of different beliefs and values rather than being a clear measure of either belief in the values of other people in general, or belief in the existence of a set of rules and procedures with which to guide behavior in this world. However, both of these scales have strong components of each of these two beliefs as significant contributors to their overall scores, beliefs we have postulated to be negatively related to one another, which are scored as such on both scales. Thus, for example, Nevitt Sanford, one of the original developers of the F-scale, has emphasized that the scale was designed to measure such variables as (a) belief in authority, conventionality, and general rules as guides to behavior, (b) opposition to reliance on imagination, subjectivity, and individually determined guides to behavior, and (c) generalized hostility and vilification of people in general (Sanford, 1956). Similarly, Rokeach (1960) has viewed his D-scale as measuring very much the

Table 10.3 Summary of Findings on the Relationship Between the D-Scale and: (a) Reactions to Newness, Innovation, and Difference; (b) Aggressiveness and Hostility Exhibited Toward Others

Basic Findings	Investigators
1. Dogmatism is negatively correlated with the ability to learn new beliefs and to change old beliefs.	Ehrlich and Lee (1969); Torcivia and Laughlin (1968)
2. High dogmatic individuals are more likely to learn problems involving the simple following of authority, while low dogmatists are more likely to do well on problems involving the learning of new principles.	Restle, Andrews, and Rokeach (1964)
3. Resistance to compromise with the other side during collective bargaining (simulated) and the tendency to use unilateral planning (as opposed to bilateral discussion) is positively correlated with dogmatism scores.	Druckman (1967)
4. Dogmatism loads heavily on the same factor with authoritarianism and a belief in militarism and an aggressive foreign policy.	Eckhardt and Newcombe (1969)
5. Dogmatism is negatively related to the likelihood of rejecting standard operating procedures and developing new procedures into a working system.	Fillenbaum and Jackman (1961)
6. Dogmatism is negatively related to liking for new approaches in music, art, and films.	Vacchiano et al. (1969)
7. Dogmatism is negatively related to acceptance of liturgical change among Catholics and acceptance of technological change in a factory.	Vacchiano et al. (1969)
8. Dogmatism is positively correlated with dislike of dissimilar religions.	Berkowitz (1962)

*It should be noted here, however, that the correlation between militarism and dogmatism, while positive, was not significant.

same types of variables. The advantage of his scale, as he sees it, is that the D-scale is more psychologically based and is not confounded with agreement with rightist political ideologies, a problem he views as very much a part of F-scale measurement. As support for these conceptualizations, research has consistently shown a high positive correlation between the two scales, but not as high as the individual scale reliabilities (cf. Kerlinger and Rokeach, 1966).

It is because these conceptualizations are so similar to ours and the scoring systems of the scales conform to our hypotheses that we present in Table 10.2 and Table 10.3 summaries of research studies involving these scales that are relevant to our propositions. For clarification purposes we present in Table 10.2 the relationships between the F-scale and change and aggression, and in Table 10.3 the relationships between the D-scale and similar motivational processes.

Taken in total, Tables 10.1, 10.2, and 10.3 can be considered to provide some of the basic research evidence that can be cited in support of our propositions. However, it would be extremely desirable if research were undertaken that used as predictor variables clear measures of (a) belief in the value of others, and (b) belief in the existence of rules as guides to behavior in this world.

Given this theoretical base, let us go a bit further and assume two types of environments, oversimplified a bit, but theoretically useful. Environment A is one of a high hierarchical orientation (i.e., one in which high authority control of behavior is emphasized). Low-status individuals in such environments are required to obtain superior approval before any variety in activity from that ordered by such superiors is undertaken, and it is demanded that all follow to the letter the rules and procedures specified by those high in the hierarchy. Let us assume further that not only does Environment A demand that all pay attention to the rules, but that most of the activities are likely to be rule specified and programmed. That is, the ratio of the

$$\frac{\text{Number of activities that are programmed and rule specified}}{\text{Total number of activities}}$$

is high. Finally, assume also that these externally controlled, rule-specified, programmed activities are increasingly specialized the lower one ranks in the environment. Rephrased this would mean that the variety of activities performed increases greatly the higher one's status in the environment.[3]

[3]Conceptualizing environments by assuming positive relationships between these variables has received considerable empirical support in the literature (cf. Argyris, 1964; Hinings and Lee, 1971).

Contrast this with Environment B, which has characteristics that are at the other end of the continuum from those of Environment A. This means that B has a low hierarchical orientation, in that great stress is placed on self-control of one's activities once overall objectives have been designed. In addition, it has a low degree of programmed activities in that the ratio of the

$$\frac{\text{Number of activities that are programmed and rule specified}}{\text{Total number of activities}}$$

is low, and there is variety and change in everyday behavior even for those at low status levels. As a final characteristic of Environment B, the overall development of objectives for the environment (be it family, organization, or society) stems from the participation of many at all levels, rather than just a few at the top.

Of what behavioral significance are these two different types of social-psychological environments? Our hypothesized answer is given in Figure 10.1 and Tables 10.4, 10.5, 10.6, and 10.7, all of which propose and support the conclusion that environments such as A are the types of social-psychological environments that cultivate and encourage the growth and development of low self-esteem, low esteem for others, and a belief that there is a set of rules and procedures to guide behavior as a function of the natural order of things and the nature of the world. On the other hand, Environment B encourages the development of high esteem for the self and others, beliefs that the self and others are valuable, and a belief that the world is a changing, developing, dynamic system.

Thus, from environments of high hierarchical orientation, we would expect the growth of belief systems that would be consonant with the basic mistrust of people implicit in such control systems, that is, we would predict the growth of low self-esteem and low esteem for others as a function of such authoritarian control systems. On the other hand, from democratic self-control environments, we would predict high self-esteem and esteem for others. Similarly, we would predict the growth of low esteem for self and others as a function of the high number of programmed activities, since programming and high rule specification implies a symbolic mistrust in the ability and willingness of people to complete their tasks without direction and control of others. High self-esteem and esteem for others would develop where there is low programming of activities because this symbolizes faith in people's ability to control themselves. Finally, we would also predict the growth of a belief system in which there are universal rules and procedures to guide behavior and keep it in line with the nature of the world in hierarchical-oriented environments for two reasons. First, the high reliance by authority figures on programming and rule specification implies that the world is stable and unchanging enough to permit the utilization of and reliance on hierarchical-oriented rules and programming. Second, the reliance on a relatively permanent specialization of activities, as opposed to variation, encourages a belief system that rules and routine are the order of things, while variations, difference, and lack of rules as guides are not. If we look at a nonhierarchical world, on the other hand, we would expect a belief in a variable, changing world to develop because the lack of a hierarchical authority would be taken to mean that the world is too variable and dynamic to make hierarchically specified rules of behavior of value. In Table 10.4, we summarize those investigations supporting our argument that environments differing in these characteristics cultivate the development of the types of belief systems we have hypothesized to be crucial as determinants of different types of motivated behavior.

Table 10.4 Summary of Studies Relating Environmental Variables to Belief Systems Concerning: (a) the Value and Competence of the Self; (b) the Value and Competence of Others; (c) Belief in the Existence of a Set of General Rules and Order as a Guide for Perceiving the World

Basic Findings	Investigators
1. High self-esteem is positively related to low father dominance in childhood, low previous external control, and the setting of high achievement standards.	McClelland (1961)
2. High scorers on the F-scale (authoritarianism) are likely to have come from homes that stressed great reliance on formally stated external control and rigidity of behavior.	Adorno et al. (1950); Kirscht and Dillehay (1967)
3. Self-perceived competence (expectation of task success) is a positive function of extent to which parents have encouraged independence of thought and action, self versus external control, and participation in family decision making.	Rehberg, Sinclair, and Schaefer (1970)
4. Level of educational attainment that one expects to achieve is positively correlated with the degree to which the family was democratic as opposed to being hierarchically controlled.	Bowerman and Elder (1964)
5. Feelings of power and control over one's fate increase when poor people are given roles of influence and responsibility.	Gottesfeld and Dozier (1966)

In Tables 10.5, 10.6, and 10.7 we have listed those investigations basically concerned with the influence of hierarchically structured, programmed environments on achievement, creativity, and aggression, respectively. Given the findings listed in Table 10.4 that these environments do, indeed, lead to the belief systems we have hypothesized, it seems clear that the findings of Tables 10.5, 10.6, and 10.7 can be considered highly supportive of the basic assumptions of our theoretical model.

Table 10.5 Summary of Studies Relating Hierarchical Environments to Achievement Behavior

Basic Findings	Investigators
1. Those who had their jobs redesigned to decrease specialization and enlarge responsibilities and authority increased their performance.	Davis and Valper (1968); *Business Week* (1969)
2. The more individuals feel they have control over their work activities, the higher their performance.	Bachman, Smith, and Slesinger (1966); Bucklow (1966); Tannenbaum and Kahn (1958); Smith and Brown (1964); Bowers (1964); Tannenbaum (1962)
3. Situations where individuals appraise themselves result in less defensiveness and greater performance increment.	Bassett and Meyer (1968)
4. The more that is expected of an individual in terms of goals to be achieved or the amount of time allocated for achievement, the better he will perform.	Berlew and Hall (1966); Stedry and Kay (1966); Aronson and Gerard (1966); Locke (1967); Bryan and Locke (1967); Korman (1970)
5. Participation in decision making and planning by those not used to it increases performance and productivity.	Farris (1969); Puckett (1958)
6. Choosing one's own work partners increases performance.	Van Zelst (1952)
7. The more individuals are allowed to choose their work activities, the higher they will perform on them.	Pallak, Brock, and Kiesler (1967)
8. The more an individual comes from a background of repression of independence and an overemphasis on one's own "special world" as opposed to "others," the lower is their test achievement performance.	Vernon (1965)
9. The more the person has been encouraged to think independently, take part in decision making and attain high achievement standards, the higher the achievement.	Rosen (1959); Rosen and D'Andrade (1959); McClelland (1961)

Table 10.6 Summary of Studies Relating Environmental Variables to Creativity, Change, and Receptivity to Change

Basic Findings	Investigators
1. Mothers of creative high-school males value autonomy and independence, prefer change and lack structure, and exhibit great self-assurance; the mothers of a control group scored lower on all of these variables.	Domino (1969)
2. The creation of an experimental atmosphere with decreased evaluation by others and perception of control and evaluation by others resulted in higher scores on tests of creative thinking.	Adams (1968)
3. Innovativeness in organizations is negatively related to hierarchical centralization of authority and positively related to lack of programming and rule orientation.	Guetzkow (1965)
4. Decreasing hierarchy, external control, and task specialization during a "change" program increases receptivity to the goals of that "change."	Coch and French (1948); Sarason (1967)
5. Middle-class subjects are more likely to engage in alternation behavior than those from lower-class backgrounds. (Middle-class environments are generally less hierarchical than lower-class.)	Strain, Unikel, and Adams (1969)
6. Individuals in college environments where hierarchical control, programming, and specialization have been deemphasized are more likely to accept continuing changes in the university and its functioning.	Korman (1970)
7. Individuals in specialized roles and occupations are likely not to be in sympathy with people different from themselves and are less likely to communicate with such different individuals on an informal basis.	Korman (1963); Sutton and Porter (1968)
8. Individuals who have been employed in hierarchical organizations do more poorly on creative tasks than those who have not been employed by such organizations.	Maier and Hoffman (1961)
9. Creativity is positively related to the degree to which the person is in a "strong" position vis-à-vis his superior (i.e., is in a less hierarchical system of authority).	Hoffman, Harburg, and Maier (1962)
10. Groups that experience changes in membership are more creative than those that are stable.	Ziller, Behringer, and Goldstein (1962)
11. Organizations that hire unusual, different types are more likely to be creative organizations.	Steiner (1965)
12. Creative children come from homes (a) marked by lack of parental dominance and structures, and (b) where individual divergence is permitted and risk is accepted.	Watson (1960); Getzels and Jackson (1962)

Table 10.7 Summary of Studies Relating Environmental Variables to Aggression and Hostility Toward Others

Basic Findings	Investigators
1. Exposure to sensitivity-training group with its emphasis on non-hierarchy and nonprogramming increases acceptance of self and reduces prejudice toward others.	Rubin (1967)
2. Hostility between labor and management groups decreased when they were both part of a larger group where nonhierarchy, non-programming, and nonspecialization of activities were stressed (i.e., they met on an equal status basis and goals were developed for all groups on an equal basis).	Blake et al. (1964); Blake, Mouton, and Sloma (1965)
3. Generalized support for finding number 2 above in a variety of laboratory studies.	Deutsch (1969)
4. German Communists during the pre-Hitler era were more concerned with fighting those with a democratic ideology (i.e., the Social Democrats) than they were in fighting the rightist authoritarian (Nazi) group.	Draper (1969)
5. The more society legitimates differences between two groups along various hierarchical status dimensions and the more it says the two are different, the more likely it is that conflict will result between the two groups.	Triandis (1959); Lindgren (1969); McDavid and Hararri (1969)
6. The less people are committed as belong to one specific group and being specialized to it and the more people move from group to group, the less the hostility between groups.	Deutsch (1969)
7. Work groups that are (a) homogeneous, (b) isolated from other different groups, (c) rarely interact with them, and (d) view themselves as highly specialized and different from others are more likely to engage in strikes than groups with differing characteristics.	Kerr and Siegel (1954)
8. Children having more positive affect toward other children and being less likely to be aggressive and hostile are more likely to come from homes that are marked by (a) a lack of parental dominance and structures, and (b) flexibility.	Watson (1960)

As a result we are led to suggest in Table 10.8 an integrated theoretical system that is able to relate specific forms of antecedent environmental variables to intervening belief systems. In turn, given our theoretical assumption of a motivation toward consistent outcomes, this results in different forms and levels of socially significant behavior consistent with the behavior originating cognitive systems. This behavior, in turn, leads to the development of a consequent authority system that reflects the differential performance outcomes (i.e., external control and hierarchical leadership systems [Farris, 1969]). We are suggesting that motivated behavior of the type we have been discussing here is, to a great extent, a closed-loop system, as the arrows in Table 10.8 indicate. The way in which the loop must therefore be broken, if it is a malfunctioning system, is by intervening to break down and change the belief system, a matter that involves considerations we will not discuss here. This, then, is the theory and some of the support upon which it is based. One may ask how the proposed framework relates to the motivational frameworks we have discussed earlier in this book. Where does it fit in with them? Where are the disagreements? What are the directions in which future research needs to go? These are the matters that will concern us now.

Table 10.8 Summary of Model Relating Environmental Antecedents to Motivational Processes

A. Basic Theoretical Assumptions

1. Man is motivated to seek a stable world; hence, he will attempt to seek outcomes consistent with belief systems.
2. Man's belief systems are a function of environmental experience and learning.

B. Consequences of Different Environments for Behavior

Environmental Characteristics → *Consequent Belief Systems* → *Behavior*

Environmental Characteristics	Consequent Belief Systems	Behavior
1. High hierarchical control of behavior →	1. Men (both the self and others) are undesirable (since they must be controlled). →	1. Low achievement
		2. High aggression toward the self and others
2. High programming and routinization of activities	2. There are universal rules and principles that one should use as a guide to behavior; these principles are universal, perma-	3. Hostility toward change and varia- tion
3. High specialization and non- variability of activities →	nent, and apply to everyone as guides to behavior. →	4. Noncreative prob- lem solving and behavior

1. Low hierarchical control of behavior		
2. Low programming and routinization of activities		
3. Low specialization and → variability of activities	Opposing predictions to above	

RELATIONSHIPS WITH HULLIAN, AROUSAL, AND EXPECTANCY-VALUE FRAMEWORKS

In beginning our examination of the relationships between the theory presented in this chapter and the various frameworks and research presented earlier in this book, it may be best to begin with the Hullian, arousal, and expectancy-value frameworks that have occupied so much of our attention. Upon close examination, there is considerable (although not complete) correspondence to be noted. We have already noted the convergence between the theory presented here and the Fiske and Maddi (1961) postulation of a sought-for optimal arousal level that is a function of stimulus variability, change, and meaningfulness. In terms of the degree of correspondence with the Hullian and expectancy-value frameworks, the following points may be worth noting:

1. Both expectancy-value theory and the later Hullian-Spence models, including the K (incentive) variable, predict, as we have noted, that behaviors actually oriented to fulfilling one's needs and values are a postive function of one's success in fulfilling one's needs and values in the past; that is, those who have a low K or expectancy for achieving a given value do not behave in a way designed to achieve that need or value fulfillment. In the theory proposed here the same prediction is made, if we make the reasonable assumptions that (a) high self-esteem is a function of one's previous success in fulfilling and achieving needs and value satisfactions, and (b) fulfilling one's needs and values is a symbol of competence.

2. Following this line of thinking, it also seems reasonable to assume, on a human level, that positive reinforcement up to some level generally constitutes an increment to a person's self-esteem. Similarly, we might also assume that punishment and/or lack of positive reinforcement operates in the same manner to constitute a decrement to self-esteem. Building on these assumptions, we would then derive the following predictions from the theory we have presented in this chapter:

   a. The less a person has been positively reinforced for performing a specific type of behavior in the past, the more he will be willing to perform the behavior in the future without receiving any positive reinforcement.

   b. The more the person has been punished in the past, the less he will work toward achieving rewards in the future and the less he will change his behavior to maximize the possibility of achieving such rewards in the future.

   c. The more an individual has a high degree of competence relative to a given task, the more that putting him in a state of anxiety (or frustration) will lead him to perform well in order to achieve and thus reduce his frustration and increase his satisfaction; the less his degree of self-perceived competence relative to the task, the less he will view task performance as a way of achieving satisfaction in order to reduce frustration and anxiety.

The reader will notice that the first example is the partial-reinforcement effect, the second constitutes a summary of the research on punishment we spoke of earlier, and the third is the Spence-Taylor prediction that anxiety facilitates performance when the task is easy for a given individual but debilitates performance when the task is hard. Thus, we have used the framework described in this chapter to account for three of the more interesting established findings in the psychology of motivational processes.

However, as we have said earlier, our theory here is a limited one and is not designed as a general approach to overall motivational processes in the same sense as the Hull-Spence or expectancy-value approaches are. Comparisons of overall or limited theories should not be taken too far or made too much of, since they involve, to some extent, an attempt to assess apples and oranges along the same dimensions for both. For this reason we will end this discussion by noting these similarities between the different theories and then turn our attention to other matters.

RELATIONSHIPS WITH OTHER CONSISTENCY THEORIES

Since the theory we have presented in this chapter is a consistency model, it is by definition similar to many of the other consistency models discussed in Chapter 7. Among these areas of similarity are (a) the postulation of inconsistency as a negative tension state that we desire to reduce, (b) similar assumptions about why inconsistency is a negative tension state, and (c) the prediction that directionality of behavior is determined by the desire to reduce dissonance.

However, there are some different aspects to the approach presented here, as we have seen. These may, hopefully, overcome some of the difficulties of consistency models outlined in Chapter 7. As an example, one value of this approach is that the self-concept and the evaluation of the self is explicitly postulated as part of the cognitive structure, and this level of self-evaluation is therefore argued to be a key determinant of what is and what is not consistent. In other words, such specification of the self-concept as part of the cognitive structure has the additional value of determining how the inconsistency will be reduced; that is, it will be reduced in a manner that will bring the evaluation of outcomes relative to feelings about the self into balance. (As we have seen, this type of evaluation has been suggested as a possible means of revising Adams's equity model by Pritchard (1969), among others. However, such a formal integration has not yet taken place. Perhaps, eventually, there will be an integration of the "self" emphasis discussed here and the "other" emphasis of the Adams approach.)

RELATIONSHIP TO THEORIES OF SOCIETAL ACHIEVEMENT AND SOCIETAL AGGRESSION

In Chapters 8 and 9, we reviewed the various theories about the types of social-psychological environments that are likely to lead to high task-oriented achievement (Chapter 8) and aggression toward others (Chapter 9). In Chapter 8 we reviewed McClelland's work on the need for achievement variable, its significance in determining the rise of societies, and the environmental and family conditions that encourage the development of the achievement motive.

Similarly, in Chapter 9 we discussed the research on authoritarianism, its significance as a contributor toward hostility toward others, and the kinds of environmental and family conditions under which the authoritarian personality develops.

In both these cases very similar conclusions came to be made, in that it seemed clear that while the relationships between the environmental variables and the behaviors evidenced were as predicted, the theoretical explanations for the findings were tentative at best. For example, the variable "need for achievement," as measured by the McClelland-Atkinson TAT procedures, leaves much to be desired psychometrically, and because of this severe lack of construct validity of the procedure, doubt is cast on the entire explanatory framework offered by McClelland. Similarly, there have been few competitors to psychoanalytic theory to date who attempt to explain the findings of the authoritarian researchers concerning the type of family and home environments that give rise to hostile and aggressive behavior toward people different from the self. We suggest that this situation is not at all desirable because of the difficulties of using psychoanalytic theory as an explanatory framework for motivational processes.

How, then, can we account for the findings that show relations between these environmental variables and these behaviors, if we can account for them at all in a theoretical sense? It turns out that the model we have proposed here may be able to do so, if we consider the fact that the environments proposed by McClelland as leading to high achievement seem to be the same as those we proposed as leading to low authoritarianism *and* the same as those we have called a high self-esteem environment. That is, these are environments marked by high valuation of independence, low obeisance to authority figures and tradition, and low degrees of control by others. If we assume a drive toward consistent outcomes, we would generate the type of societies and the nature of changes in these societies as those we have pictured in Figures 10.1 and 10.2. Thus in both of these, we find that societies that are structured along hierarchical, authoritarian dimensions are likely to lead to outcomes of a low achievement and high aggression. Furthermore, continuing changes are pictured in these societies as a result of these outcomes, with cyclic behavior being predicted unless external interventions are made to change the cycles.[4]

Is this theoretical explanation any better than those offered by the achievement and the authoritarian personality researchers? One trend of

[4] Although we did not discuss it in Chapter 8, it should be noted that McClelland has also postulated that the factors that lead to societal failure develop as a function of success. His approach may be described as a cyclical system of the kind described in Figure 10.2. The difference is that McClelland assigns significance to different explanatory variables. According to McClelland the decline of the society is due to the wealthy families assigning child-rearing duties to servants who do not demand competence and independent behavior from children. This, in turn, leads to low-achievement orientation when these children grow up.

LSE Environment

1. High valuation of authority figures and traditions
2. Low feelings of independence

Low *n* Ach scores in projective materials and books on both individual and societal levels. Low achievement concern is consistent with LSE environments.

Low performance, low production of goods because:
(a) LSE environments encourage low opinions of self and a consistency model of motivation is posited.
(b) Authority figures were functional at one time, but their demands became less functional as the world changed from the time when their authority was originally established, and their authority originally developed at a time different from the current time (i.e., the authority originally developed because they were able to satisfy needs that were not being satisfied).

High valuation of tradition, traditional behaviors, and figures associated with authority in the past. Low feelings of independence from tradition.

Increasingly high respect for these individuals, traditions, and specific behaviors that have been associated with high performance, high production of goods

High performance, high production of goods

Satisfactions derived from environment sink below minimum levels

HSE Environment

1. Rejection of authority figures
2. High feelings of independence from previous traditions

High *n* Ach scores in projective materials and books on both individual and societal level. High achievement concern is consistent with HSE environments.

Figure 10.1 Hypothesized model of societal achievement based on Korman consistency model.

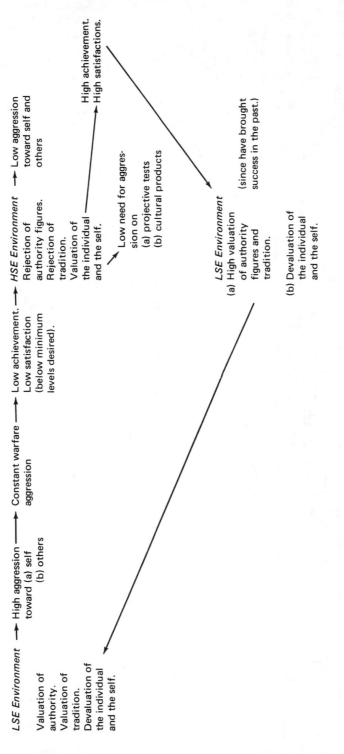

Figure 10.2 Hypothesized model of societal aggression based on Korman consistency model.

evidence comes from the work of Klinger (1966; Klinger and McNelly, 1969), who has offered a model very similar to that we have depicted in Figure 10.1. It is Klinger's argument that McClelland's supposition that high high-achievement need predicts growth in occupational status is unable to account for a considerable amount of data (not McClelland's). According to Klinger, the correlation between occupational status and need achievement, as measured, is greater when they are measured in this order rather than the other way around, that is, the r is greater when occupational status precedes the achievement measure in time instead of measuring achievement prior to occupational status. Such a finding leads Klinger to propose what is essentially a consistency theory of motivation. Basically it is that performance on (a) behavioral achievement and (b) a projective measurement of achievement are both performed in a manner consistent with one's social status in life. Klinger proposes that the higher the social status, the higher the score on both. He has considerable data to support his argument that it is this common background in social status that accounts for the correlation between the TAT measure and achievement, and not that the former leads to the latter. Klinger's approach is very similar to our own and much of his thinking is incorporated into the relationships we have postulated in Figure 10.1.

In addition to Klinger's research, some other data are available that support the models postulated in Figure 10.2. For example, unpublished research by the author shows that nations high in achievement, according to McClelland, were those found to be low in aggression in independent research by Fieraband and Fieraband (1966). In addition, some of the research proposed in support of the theory outlined in Figure 10.1 might also be generalized and cited as support for the proposals made here. However, most of this evidence cited (including that by Klinger) cannot really be considered to be firm data in support of the dynamic relationship we have postulated in Figures 10.1 and 10.2. Only longitudinal studies can provide the needed evidence and such studies have not as yet been done. Until that time, perhaps the most appropriate conclusion for us to make is that Figures 10.1 and 10.2 do provide alternatives to the explanations proposed by McClelland and the authoritarian personality researchers, alternatives that are consistent with the theory proposed here and that might be worth research investigation in the future.

RELATIONSHIPS TO THEORIES
OF MOTIVE DEVELOPMENT

Our discussion in Chapter 6 devoted considerable attention to the significance of McClelland's achievement in developing a firm theoretical base for how significant human motives such as the need for achievement and the need for aggression develop. Basically, such motives develop as relatively persisting characteristics of the individual because (1) such anticipated outcomes come to be accounted for and viewed as moderate discrepancies from one's adaptation level; (2) moderate discrepancies from previous adaptation levels are hypothesized to have positive affect for the individual; and (3) individuals are assumed to be motivated to attain positive affect in their behavior. It is also predicted that individuals will be motivated to avoid such outcomes as achievement and aggression if these constitute extreme discrepancies from previous adaptation levels, since extreme discrepancies constitute negative affect and it is predicted that people are motivated to avoid negative affect.

The theory proposed in this chapter predicts the development of individual motives in a way somewhat analogous to that of McClelland. The approach suggested here would predict that individual motives, such as achievement, aggression, and the like, would develop in individuals to the extent that they have used these behaviors in order to achieve consistent outcomes. For example, the more an individual uses achievement in order to achieve consistency, the more he comes to value achievement in and of itself and be motivated to achieve it in the future. The more he uses aggression to achieve consistency, the more he comes to value aggression in and of itself and be motivated to achieve it in the future. Finally, the more he is creative and change oriented in order to achieve consistency, the more he comes to value and be motivated to achieve creativity and change in the future. This process suggests that individual differences in the desire to achieve certain outcomes (or motives) develop because these outcomes have been of functional value in the past when the individual was engaging in behavior for other purposes and, through such contiguity, have come to assume value in and of themselves. If we substitute consistency for that of moderate discrepancy, our proposed process is similar to McClelland's and to one recently made by Kagan (1972).

There is, however, one question that is relevant. It applies both to McClelland's proposals and the theory advanced here. The question concerns the conditions under which the greatest values will come to be attached to the contiguous stimuli that are proposed to eventually develop into individual motives (e.g., achieving behavior, aggressive behavior, etc.). Will greater value be attached to them if they are associated with great amounts of consistency (or moderate discrepancy) achievement? This, obviously, is the prediction that would be made by reinforcement theory, in that the more stimuli become associated with primary reinforcers, the more power they assume. There is evidence for this argument (cf. Breer and Locke, 1965). However, there is also the argument made by dissonance theorists (Festinger, 1957) that value for the behavior engaged in (and its contiguous stimuli) may be negatively related to the reinforcement received. There is also evidence for such a proposition, as our discussion in Chapter 7 indicated. How do we reconcile these conflicting propositions? One way of doing so is suggested by Kiesler's (1969) research suggesting that the dissonance prediction holds when the person has been committed to the behavior, but it does not hold when he is not committed. Motive development, then, would be more likely to occur as a function of the behavior that has achieved desired outcomes in the past for the person who feels "free," but may develop in an opposite manner for those who are not free. The idea is an interesting one and deserves further investigation.

One final point worth mentioning, which differentiates the approach developed here from McClelland's, is that while it is predicted that individuals do develop motives such as achievement, the significance of such motives for behavior is not the same for all individuals. Thus, the theory would predict that only high self-esteem individuals would use their individual motives and their desires to satisfy them as guides and cues to their behavior, since motive satisfaction would be consistent only with high self-esteem and not with low. This prediction has been upheld in a number of different studies (cf. Korman, 1966, 1970).

RELATIONSHIPS TO THEORIES OF SELF-ACTUALIZATION AND HUMANISTIC PSYCHOLOGY

There is one additional type of motivational theorizing quite popular today to which we will now turn our attention. The approach, previously mentioned briefly, is known by such names as self-actualization theory, humanistic psychology, third-world psychology, and the like. It is a highly important movement among many psychologists interested in such problems as personal and social growth, institutional and organizational change and development, and similar areas. We have chosen to postpone our major discussion of this movement in this book until this time because, as will become apparent, its significance as a unique theoretical framework for the understanding of motivational processes is not clear at the current time. Our procedure here will be to first discuss the basic logic of this movement and the major theory of motivation upon which it rests. Following this, we will discuss the nature of the research evidence for the approach. Finally, we will make some summary statements concerning the fruitfulness of the approach at this time and investigate some possible pathways for future work.

Self-actualization theory has some of its philosophical base in the work of the existential philosophers. Basically, self-actualization theory argues that man has a capability for a meaningful, viable, potential-filling existence, that he has the properties and the nature to implement a meaningful existence, but that he has been prevented from engaging and behaving in this meaningful, self-actualizing manner by the conditions and environments in which he lives. Instead, he has been forced to behave in some suboptimal manner in which he is not able to fulfill himself (or self-actualize) because of the nature of the environmental forces that surround him. The role of the therapist (change agent) is to understand the factors and conditions that are preventing man from reaching his self-actualizing state and that state in which his motivational processes will be toward self-actualization. He then tries to change these conditions so that man can reach this state in which his motivational processes will be toward self-actualization, rather than toward some suboptimal motivation, since man does have this capacity for self-actualization.

On what basis, that is, from what theory of motivational processes, does the self-actualization theorist assume that man does have these potentialities and desires for self-actualization, growth, and development? A number of motivational theories of this type have been proposed, but the most significant one, which has served as the base for the self-actualization movement, is the one by Maslow (1954, 1968). The reader will recall that we introduced Maslow's work briefly in Chapter 5, and that basically, his theory proposed that man's strivings and the directionality of his behavior were organized around a hierarchy of motives with the lowest being the physiological needs such as hunger and thirst. Once these were satisfied, the security needs become paramount as influences on behavior (or become prepotent, in Maslow's terms), with these being followed in the hierarchy by social needs, self-esteem needs, and self-actualization needs as motivators of behavior.[5] In all cases, Maslow argues, the prepotency of the higher needs increases as a function of the satisfaction of the need immediately lower in the hierarchy.[6] This basic framework does not, however, give full justice to Maslow's approach or explain why so many therapists and change agents have adopted the goal of trying to move people to a point where they and their environmental conditions will allow them to be motivated to self-actualization rather than be motivated to achieve the lower-level needs. The real flavor of Maslow's theory, and the basic reason that self-actualization motivation is better than being motivated by the lower-level needs, can be seen by looking at how Maslow contrasts the differences in behavior between those people who are primarily motivated by the lower-level needs as opposed to those who are motivated by the desire for self-actualization. Table 10.9 summarizes how Maslow would expect a person who was growth motivated (i.e., by self-actualization needs) to behave, as opposed to a person who was deficiency motivated (i.e., motivated by the lower-level needs). Examination of this table does indicate very clearly why self-actualization as a goal to be attained by change methods has become accepted by so many people concerned with the optimal development of individuals and/or organizations and institutions.

[5] In some publications, Maslow has postulated higher needs than self-actualization. Among these are needs for understanding and cognition. It is not clear, however, how much significance Maslow attached to these cognitive needs, and most discussions of Maslow's work do not deal with them.

[6] In some of Maslow's writing, it is argued that residues of basic needs always remain and these may sometimes influence behavior in unpredictable ways. We see this as a basic flaw in his system with which we will not deal, concentrating instead on the major thrusts of his argument.

Table 10.9 Maslow's Proposed Behavioral Differences Between Deficiency-Oriented and Growth-Oriented Individuals

The person who is deficiency oriented is the person whose basic needs have not as yet been satisfied and who is oriented toward achieving these satisfactions. His behavioral characteristics are likely to be the following:	The person who is growth oriented is the person whose basic needs have been satisfied and who is motivated toward self-actualization. His behavioral characteristics are likely to be the following:
1. Rejecting of one's own impulses.	1. Accepting of one's own impulses.
2. Satisfying a need or achieving gratification leads to tension reduction.	2. Satisfying a need or achieving gratification leads to excitement, growth, and change.
3. Gratifications achieved are relatively short, stable, and temporary in nature.	3. Gratifications achieved tend to influence and change the person in a relatively permanent way.
4. The goals sought are species-wide in nature.	4. The goals sought are individualistic and unique to the individual.
5. Behavior is dependent on environmental cues.	5. Behavior is relatively independent of environmental cues.
6. Others are viewed primarily in terms of their ability to satisfy one's own basic needs.	6. Others are viewed objectively for what they are, rather than in terms of their ability to satisfy one's own basic needs.
7. Tends to be ego-centered, concerned with self, and the satisfaction of basic needs.	7. Tends to be ego-transcendent, not as concerned with the self as with the nature of the world.

The question for us, here, however, is the adequacy of the Maslow framework as a theory of motivational processes. How much support does the Maslow model receive from systematic research? Is the hierarchy of motives supported in the way that Maslow proposed? As incredible as it may seem, considering the popularity of his arguments, there is little research support for it anywhere in the literature with which this author is acquainted. Of four studies that have directly tested his propositions, three found little or no support for them (Hall and Nougaim, 1968; Alderfer, 1969; Lawler and Suttle, 1972), while one found moderate support (Trexler and Schuh, 1971). In addition, factor analyses of questionnaires aimed at measuring the Maslow needs have resulted in conflicting findings; some found that the items did not group together in the manner proposed by the theory (Payne, 1970), whereas others have found the predicted relationships (Beer, 1966).

There is evidence for the theory in the work of the large numbers of writers who have proposed that if we decrease hierarchy, external control, and specialization, and if we allow people to control their own fates more, we will get a greater degree of what Maslow and others have called self-actualizing behavior (cf. Argyris, 1964; McGregor, 1960; May, 1953; Fromm, 1941). This evidence is, unfortunately for Maslow's theory, very weak at best, since such behavioral effects from this type of environmental manipulation can be derived from other theories as well. One does not need Maslow to predict that the decrease of hierarchical control by others will lead to the greater seeking of values and favorable outcomes. This is also predictable from expectancy-value theory if we make the reasonable assumption that throwing off controls by others leads to a greater sense of one's own value as a person and, hence, a greater expectancy that one will be able to achieve the values he desires. Similarly, the same kinds of predictions as to the kinds of behavioral outcomes to be achieved by decreasing hierarchical control are made by the theory proposed in this chapter. Thus, if one looks at the kinds of behaviors predicted by Maslow for the self-actualizing person and the kinds of behavioral outcomes with which the consistency model proposed here is concerned, it becomes apparent that (a) similar kinds of independent variables are used, and (b) similar kinds of dependent variables are used. The behaviors predicted by self-actualization theorists can therefore be derived by this theory also.

What, then, can we say of the Maslow hierarchy of motives as a motivational theory? At this point, very little. There is little direct research of a systematic nature that it has stimulated, and what has been done is generally negative. For these reasons, then, despite its almost intuitive common-sense approach and its great popularity, the value of humanistic psychology and self-actualization theory for the development of an adequate theory of motivational processes remains a promise for the future.

SOME LIMITATIONS TO THE THEORY

Despite the general tone of this chapter thus far, we must make it clear that there is no intent here to claim that *the theory* has been found. Clearly, this is not so. For one thing, the approach we have suggested here is a consistency model, and as we said in Chapter 7, any consistency model cannot be a complete answer. Secondly, the theory we have proposed is perhaps overly optimistic and, maybe, overly naive. There are people who are high achievers and who are not creative, people who are high achievers and who are also highly aggressive, and people who are very creative but also aggressive. Leonardo da Vinci painted the *Mona Lisa,* but also developed instruments of war. Similarly, as further evidence that "not all good things go together all the time," a good accountant does not have to be creative, a good soldier is not always creative, and a great salesman may in fact be highly aggressive toward others, using his manipulative skills to express such aggression. It is obvious, then, that our approach is not the complete answer. Other factors that lead to achievement, aggression, and creativity must be studied and examined in a research sense.

Similarly, the actual evidence relating to the approach is still limited. Much of the evidence is favorable, but there is no guarantee this will continue. Negative evidence for the hypothesis will no doubt be forthcoming.

Perhaps the best way to look upon our discussion, then, is that we have suggested an integrated way of looking at achievement, aggression, and creativity motivation that seems useful at this time. The length of time for which it will remain so will be determined by the research it stimulates.

SUMMARY

Our purpose in this chapter has been to present a limited consistency model of motivational processes. The basic proposal is that environmental events lead to belief systems, which in turn dictate the types of outcomes people seek as being consistent with their beliefs. As to content, the proposal centers around the hypothesis that situations of a centralized, hierarchical nature lead to low self-esteem for self and others and low tolerance for change. Situations of a noncentralized, nonhierarchical nature are predicted, conversely, to lead to high achievement motivation (consistent with high self-esteem), high creativity motivation (consistent with high tolerance for change), and low aggression motivation (consistent with high esteem for others).

Evidence has been presented that suggests some support for the basic model being proposed as well as its degree of overlap with other theories and proposals discussed in this book. However, like any theory, more research is needed in showing where the theory is adequate and, just as important, where it is inadequate. This latter type of information is particularly crucial if we are to build better theories of motivation in the future.

some
concluding
comments

ELEVEN

We have now come to the end of our survey of the various ways in which psychologists have viewed the psychology of motivation. Our purpose has been to deal with some of the major frameworks that have been developed, the logic that underlies them, the evidence that has been brought together in their support, and their possible fruitfulness for further research and theory in motivational psychology. What conclusions can we draw from our discussions? What implications do these conclusions have for further research and theory in the psychology of motivational processes? In this final chapter we shall review the directions to which our discussions have led us. Following our listing of these implications, we shall conclude with some comments about what we perceive to be needed research approaches in the future study of the psychology of motivation.

1. *Any theory of motivational processes will have to include the relatively permanent characteristics of the organism, both innate and learned, as a significant variable affecting behavior arousal and direction.*

Our reasons for making this statement stem from a number of the phenomena discussed earlier in this book, most obviously the fact that such a requirement has already been incorporated into the theorizing of people such as Atkinson and McClelland. However, it is also clear that those working in a physicalistic activation-arousal tradition must also incorporate this point (see Chapter 4), as have the Hullians, particularly in their development of K as an influence on behavior. Basically, there is no way to explain the partial-reinforcement effect and/or the lack of responsiveness to external reward systems by those with a history of punishment unless systematic, relatively permanent individual differences in the organisms being studied are taken into account. Finally, there seems to be no way of dealing with some of the problems of consistency motives as to the choice of a method of inconsistency reduction unless the characteristics of the organisms involved are considered. The theory presented in Chapter 10 is one such attempt, but clearly other approaches are both desirable and necessary.

2. *Attempts to link behavioral arousal and direction to biological survival needs are not necessary to the development of a physicalistic, experimentally oriented theory of motivational processes.*

This comment stems directly from our discussions in Chapters 2 through 4 concerning the more recent Hullian approaches and the activation-arousal model. Both approaches remain active and viable today and both can lead to meaningful knowledge, despite the problems to which we pointed, even though the logic of biological survival is not now an integral part of either framework.

3. *Despite different approaches, different assumptions, and different approaches to research, there is considerable convergence between the various types of motivational frameworks. However, strong differences do remain.*

This statement is, in essence, a reiteration of much of the theme of this book. Thus, it reflects (a) the degrees of convergence we have noted between the later Hullian theories, expectancy-value theory, and activation-arousal theory; (b) the similarities between the theory we have presented in Chapter 10 and other themes discussed throughout the book; and (c) the fact that similar concepts (e.g., expectancy) appear in different theories.

4. *The measurement and conceptualization of persisting individual differences in motives remain highly unsatisfactory and highly primitive. Hence, future research on how individual motives combine with environmental variables in influencing behavior will depend on advances in these areas.*

The basis for this statement comes from our discussions in Chapter 6 as to the relatively poor construct validity that most measures of motives have and our uncertainty as to exactly how important they are. It is clear that future attention will have to be paid to these questions.

5. *There is no necessary relationship between the degree to which the concepts used in a theory are physicalistic in nature and the degree to which the theory is experimentally testable.*

The basis for this statement stems from the operational confusion we noted earlier between Hull's definitions of D and S_d, and between his definition of conditioned stimuli and conditioned reinforcers. In both cases, the two concepts involved could not be defined and measured independent of one another, despite their physicalistic basis. This does not mean that concepts such as these are worse than nonphysicalistic ones. It just means that using them does not guarantee an adequate, operationally testable theory.

6. *There is no evidence at this time that the assumption that we can understand complex human behavior by first understanding more basic motivational processes on the animal level is any more fruitful than studying complex human behavior directly.*

This statement reflects the serious problems that Hull ran into in his theorizing. It does not claim that the approach cannot be fruitful. It just says that the claims of those who make this assumption have not been supported up to now by the research data available.

7. *Whether it is more fruitful to view behavioral arousal as coming from a general state or a specific desire does not seem to be capable of resolution at this time.*

The major point reflected here is that there is little reason at this point to decide whether behavior can best be viewed as aroused by a general state with direction due to other variables (such as habits), or whether it is better viewed as being aroused and directed by a specific need. Hence, theories reflecting both these approaches, and others, should be encouraged.

8. *Any theory of motivational processes will have to deal with anticipation and expectancy of outcome as an influence on behavioral directionality. This poses problems for any theory developed within a physicalistic framework.*

This statement merely reflects the fact that Hull, Tolman, and their students all found it necessary to use such a variable in their formulations, and that consistency theory will need to do so also in order to overcome some of its problems. Once having said this, it is also apparent that the Hullian attempt at the development of an expectancy variable, K, was not very successful and that it is not at all clear how well physicalistically oriented theorists will be able to solve this problem.

A DUAL RESEARCH STRATEGY

Of the many possible implications of our analyses of motivational processes, there is one that stands out most importantly to us. There seems little reason to think that future advances in the study of motivation are more likely to come from one specific sort of methodology as opposed to another. It has been traditionally assumed that laboratory research is the epitome of scientific research because of its emphasis on experimental control of variables and rigor of design. Yet, it is apparent from our discussions of the Hullian system, the most laboratory oriented of the motivational theories, that such supposed advantages have not in fact been translated into theoretical developments. Eventually, they may be. But certainly the experimental confusions we have noticed in Hull's definitions of D and S_d, and in the confounding of conditioned stimulation, conditioned reinforcement, and frustration, suggest very serious difficulties in the approach. Hence, there is much work to be done before a laboratory-oriented approach to motivational processes will result in the rigorous, experimentally testable theory that its adherents have generally claimed for it. In addition, not only has rigorous theory been more difficult to develop than was previously thought, but serious doubt must still remain as to whether a physicalistically oriented theory that hopes to account for complex behavior by first understanding simple units of behavior and then building on these basic units can actually achieve its goals. One must wonder how such concepts as expectancy and incentive will be explained, considering the difficulties we noticed with K, as the Hullians developed it.

All this should not be taken to mean that we should ignore laboratory work in the future in favor of field research. Far from it. Our purpose is not to limit the future, but to open it up to a broader spectrum of research activity. Field research in real-life situations has as definite a place in theoretical research in motivational processes as does laboratory study. We need to test our motivational theories in real situations, such as in schools, clinics, and work organizations, as well as in laboratories, if we are to build meaningful concepts that have some degree of generality for different samples and different situations. The concepts we develop in such field situations will be cognitive in nature, but this, it seems to us, is inevitable at this stage of our knowledge. As far as we can see, constructs such as expectancy and motive are inevitably part of a motivation theory today and we see no way of accounting for them in any manner but cognitively. One major disadvantage is the relative lack of control over the variables in the field as opposed to the laboratory. Certainly this is a problem, but it is not a complete negative, considering the gain in realism.

In essence, then, what is needed is both kinds of research, planned in conjunction with each other and integrated in such a manner as to maximize the advantages of each and to minimize their disadvantages. In this way, meaningful advances in the study of motivational processes are most likely to be made.

bibliography

Abelson, R. P. and M. J. Rosenberg. Symbolic psycho-logic: A model of attitudinal cognition. *Behavioral Science,* 1958, *3,* 1-13.

Adams, J. C., Jr. The relative effects of various testing atmospheres on spontaneous flexibility, a factor of divergent thinking. *Journal of Creative Behavior,* 1968, *2,* 187-93.

Adams, J. S. Toward an understanding of inequity. *Journal of Abnormal and Social Psychology,* 1963, *47,* 421-36.

————. Inequity in social exchange. In L. Berkowitz (Ed.), *Advances in experimental social psychology,* Vol. II. New York: Academic Press, 1965, pp. 267-99.

————. Effects of overpayment: Two comments on Lawler's paper. *Journal of Personality and Social Psychology,* 1968, *10,* 315-16.

———— and P. R. Jacobsen. Effects of wage inequities on work quality. *Journal of Abnormal and Social Psychology,* 1964, *69,* 19-25.

Adams, J. S. and N. E. Rosenbaum. The relationship of worker productivity to cognitive dissonance about wage inequities. *Journal of Applied Psychology,* 1962, *46,* 161-64.

Adorno, T. W., E. Frenkel-Brunswick, D. J. Levinson, and R. N. Sanford. *The authoritarian personality.* New York: Harper & Row, 1950.

Alderfer, C. P. An empirical test of a new theory of human needs. *Organizational Behavior and Human Performance,* 1969, *4,* 142-75.

Allport, G. *Personality: A psychological interpretation.* New York: Holt, Rinehart & Winston, 1937.

Amsel, A. The role of frustrative nonreward in noncontinuous reward situations. *Psychological Bulletin,* 1958, *55,* 102-19.

——. Frustrative nonreward in partial reinforcement and discrimination learning: Some recent history and a theoretical extension. *Psychological Review,* 1962, *69,* 306-28.

Andrews, I. R. Wage inequity and job performance: An experimental study. *Journal of Applied Psychology,* 1967, *51,* 39-49.

—— and M. M. Henry. Management attitudes toward pay. *Industrial Relations,* 1963, *3,* 29-39.

Appley, M. H. Derived motives. *Annual Review of Psychology,* 1970, *21,* 485-518.

Argyris, C. *Integrating the individual with the organization.* New York: John Wiley, 1964.

Aronson, E. Dissonance theory: progress and problems. In R. B. Abelson, E. Aronson, W. J. McGuire, T. M. Newcomb, M. J. Rosenberg, and P. H. Tannenbaum (Eds.), *Theories of cognitive consistency: A sourcebook.* Chicago: Rand McNally, 1968, pp. 5-27.

—— and J. M. Carlsmith. Performance expectancy as a determinant of actual performance. *Journal of Abnormal and Social Psychology,* 1962, *65,* 178-82.

—— and J. M. Darley. The effects of expectancy on volunteering for an unpleasant experience. *Journal of Abnormal and Social Psychology,* 1963, *66,* 220-24.

Aronson, E. and E. Gerard. Beyond Parkinson's Law: the effect of excess time on subsequent performance. *Journal of Applied Psychology,* 1966, *3,* 336-39.

Aronson, E. and J. Mills. The effects of severity of initiation on liking for a group. *Journal of Abnormal and Social Psychology,* 1959, *59,* 177-81.

Arvey, R. D. and F. Mussio. A test of the expectancy-value theory of work performance. *Journal of Vocational Behavior,* in press.

Asch, S. Studies of independence and conformity: I. A minority of one against a unanimous majority. *Psychological Monographs,* 1956, *70,* Whole No. 416.

Atkinson, J. W. *An introduction to motivation.* Princeton, N.J.: Van Nostrand, 1964.

—— and D. Birch. *A dynamic theory of action.* New York: John Wiley, 1970.

Atkinson, J. W. and D. Cartwright. Some neglected variables in contemporary conceptions of decision and performance. *Psychological Reports,* 1964, *14,* 575-90.

Atkinson, J. W. and N. T. Feather (Eds.). *A theory of achievement motivation.* New York: John Wiley, 1966.

Atkinson, J. W. and G. H. Litwin. Achievement motive and test anxiety conceived of as a motive to approach success and to avoid failure. *Journal of Abnormal and Social Psychology,* 1960, *60,* 52-63.

Bachman, J., C. Smith, and J. Slesinger. Control, performance, and satisfaction: An analysis of structural and individual effects. *Journal of Personality and Social Psychology,* 1966, *4,* 127-36.

Bandura, A., D. Ross, and S. A. Ross. Imitation of film-mediated aggressive models. *Journal of Abnormal and Social Psychology,* 1963, *66,* 3-11.

Bandura, A. and R. H. Walters. *Social learning and personality development.* New York: Holt, Rinehart & Winston, 1963.

Barber, R. G., T. Dembo, and K. Lewin. Frustration and regression: An experiment with young children. *University of Iowa Studies in Child Welfare,* 1941, *18,* No. 1, 1-314.

Bare, J. K. Hunger, deprivation and the day night cycle. *Journal of Comparative and Physiological Psychology,* 1959, *52,* 129-31.

Baron, R. A. Aggression as a function of ambient temperature and prior anger arousal. *Journal of Personality and Social Psychology,* 1972, *21,* 183-89.

Baron, R. M. Social reinforcement effects as a function of social reinforcement history. *Psychological Review,* 1966, *73,* 527-39.

_____. Attitude change through discrepant action: A functional analysis. In A. G. Greenwald, T. C. Brock, and R. H. Ostrow (Eds.), *Psychological Foundations of Attitudes.* New York: Academic Press, 1968, 109-45.

_____. The SRS model as a predictor of Negro responsiveness to reinforcement. *Journal of Social Issues,* 1970, *26,* 61-81.

Bassett, G. A. and H. H. Meyer. Performance appraisal based on self-review. *Personnel Psychology,* 1968, *21,* 421-43.

Beer, M. *Leadership, employee needs, and motivation.* Columbus: Ohio State University, Bureau of Business Research, 1966.

Bem, D. J. Inducing belief in false confessions. *Journal of Personality and Social Psychology,* 1966, *3,* 707-19.

_____. Self-perception: An alternative interpretation of cognitive dissonance phenomena. *Psychological Review,* 1967, *74,* 183-200.

_____. *Beliefs, values and human affairs.* Wadsworth, Calif.: Brooks-Cole, 1970.

Berens, A. E. The socialization of need for achievement in boys and girls. *Proceedings of the Annual Convention of the American Psychological Association,* 1972, *7,* 273-74.

Berger, S. and W. W. Lambert. Stimulus-response theory in contemporary social psychology. In G. Lindzey and E. Aronson (Eds.), *Handbook of Social Psychology,* Vol. 1, 2nd Ed. Reading, Mass.: Addison-Wesley, 1968.

Berkowitz, L. The study of urban violence: Some implications of laboratory studies of frustration and aggression. *American Behavioral Scientist,* 1968, *11,* 14-17.

————. Group standards, cohesiveness and productivity. *Human Relations,* 1954, *7,* 509-17.

————. *Aggression: A social psychological analysis.* New York: McGraw-Hill, 1962.

————and E. Rawlings. Effects of film violence on inhibition against subsequent aggression. *Journal of Abnormal and Social Psychology,* 1963, *66,* 405-12.

Berlew, D. E. and D. T. Hall. The socialization of managers: Effects of expectations on performance. *Administrative Science Quarterly,* 1966, *11,* 207-23.

Berlyne, D. *Conflict, arousal and curiosity.* New York: McGraw-Hill, 1960.

————. Arousal and reinforcement. In D. Levine (Ed.), *Nebraska Symposium on Motivation.* Lincoln: University of Nebraska Press, pp. 1-96.

Bernard, L. L. *Instinct: A study in social psychology.* New York: Holt, Rinehart & Winston, 1924.

Bexton, W. H., W. Heron, and T. Scott. Effects of decreased variation in the environment. *Canadian Journal of Psychology,* 1954, *8,* 70-76.

Bindra, D. The interrelated mechanisms of reinforcement and motivation and the nature of their influence on response. In *Nebraska Symposium on Motivation.* Lincoln: University of Nebraska Press, 1969, pp. 1-33.

Birch, D. Motivation shift in a complex learning task. *Journal of Experimental Psychology,* 1958, *56,* 507-15.

————and J. Veroff. *Motivation: The study of action.* Wadsworth, Calif.: Brooks-Cole, 1965.

Blake, R., J. S. Mouton, C. B. Barnes, and L. E. Greiner. Breakthrough in organization development. *Harvard Business Review,* 1964, *42,* 133-55.

Blake, R., J. S. Mouton, and R. L. Sloma. The union management intergroup laboratory: Strategy for resolving intergroup conflict. *Journal of Applied Behavioral Science,* 1965, *1,* 25-57.

Blodgett, H. C. The effect of the introduction of reward upon the maze performance of rats. *University of California Publications in Psychology,* 1929, *4,* 113-34.

Bolles, R. C. *Theory of motivation.* New York: Harper & Row, 1967.

Bowerman, C. and G. Elder, Jr. Variations in adolescent perceptions of family power structure. *American Sociological Review,* 1964, *29,* 551-67.

Bowers, D. G. Organization control in an insurance company. *Sociometry,* 1964, *27,* 230-44.

Bramel, D. A dissonance theory approach to defensive projection. *Journal of Abnormal and Social Psychology*, 1962, *64*, 121-29.

Breer, P. and E. A. Locke. *Task experience as a source of attitudes.* Homewood, Ill.: Dorsey, 1965.

Brehm, J. W. and A. R. Cohen. *Explorations in cognitive dissonance.* New York: John Wiley, 1962.

Brock, T. Relative efficacy of volition and justification in arousing dissonance. *Journal of Personality*, 1968, *36*, 49-66.

Brookover, W. B. and S. Thomas. Self-concept of ability and school achievement. *Sociology of Education*, 1963-64, *37*, 27-28.

Brown, J. A. C. *Freud and the post-Freudians.* Baltimore: Penguin Books, 1961.

Brown, J. S. and I. E. Farber. Emotions conceptualized as intervening variables — with suggestions toward a theory of frustration. *Psychological Bulletin*, 1951, *48*, 465-95.

Brown, J. S. and A. Jacobs. The role of fear in the motivation and acquisition of responses. *Journal of Experimental Psychology*, 1949, *39*, 747-59.

Brown, J. S., H. I. Lakish, and I. E. Farber. Conditioned fear as revealed by magnitude of startle response to an auditory stimulus. *Journal of Experimental Psychology*, 1951, *41*, 317-28.

Brown, J. S. Problems presented by the concept of acquired drive. *Current theory and research in motivation*, 1952, Lincoln, Nebraska: University of Nebraska Press, 1-21.

————. *The motivation of behavior.* New York: McGraw-Hill, 1961.

Brown, R. *Social psychology.* New York: Free Press, 1965.

Bryan, J. and E. Locke. Parkinson's law as a goal setting phenomenon. *Organizational Behavior and Human Performance*, 1967, *2*, 258-75.

Bucklow, M. A. A new role for the work group. *Administrative Science Quarterly*, 1966, *11*, 59-78.

Bugelski, B. R. Extinction with and without sub-goal reinforcement. *Journal of Comparative Psychology*, 1938, *26*, 121-33.

Burdick, H. A. and A. J. Byrnes. A test of "strain" toward "symmetry" theories. *Journal of Abnormal and Social Psychology*, 1958, *57*, 367-70.

Burgoon, M., G. Miller, and S. Tubbs. Machiavellianism, justification and attitude change following counterattitudinal advocacy. *Journal of Personality and Social Psychology*, 1972, *22*, 366-71.

Business Week, April 19, 1969, pp. 88-89.

Campbell, D. and D. Fiske. Convergent and discriminant validation by the multitrait-multimethod matrix. *Psychological Bulletin*, 1959, *56*, 81-105.

Campbell, D. and R. A. LeVine. Ethnocentrism and intergroup relations. In R. A. Abelson et al. (Eds.), *Theories of cognitive consistency: A sourcebook.* Chicago: Rand McNally, 1968, 551-64.

Campbell, J. P., M. D. Dunnette, E. E. Lawler, and K. E. Weick. *Managerial behavior, performance and effectiveness.* New York: McGraw-Hill, 1970.

Cannon, W. B. *The wisdom of the body.* New York: Norton, 1939.

Chapanis, N. P. and A. Chapanis. Cognitive dissonance: Five years later. *Psychological Bulletin,* 1964, *61,* 1-22.

Clark, K. B. Explosion in the ghetto. *Psychology Today,* 1967, *1,* 30-39.

Coch, L. and J. R. P. French. Overcoming resistance to change. *Human Relations,* 1948, *1,* 512-32.

Cofer, C. N. and M. H. Appley. *Motivation: Theory and research.* New York: John Wiley, 1964.

Cohen, J. *Secondary motivation.* Chicago: Rand McNally, 1969.

Collins, B. E. and H. Guetzkow. *A social psychology of group processes for decision making.* New York: John Wiley, 1964.

Costello, T. W. and S. Z. Zalkind. *Psychology in administration: A research orientation.* Englewood Cliffs, N.J.: Prentice-Hall, 1963.

Cottrell, N., B. Rittle, and E. Wack. The presence of an audience and list type (competitional or noncompetitional) as joint determinants of performance in paired-associate learning. *Journal of Personality,* 1967, *35,* 425-34.

Cowen, E. L., P. Botrove, A. Rockway, and J. Stevenson. Development and evaluation of an attitude to deafness scale. *Journal of Personality and Social Psychology,* 1967, *6,* 183-91.

Cowen, E. L., R. P. Underberg, and R. T. Verillo. The development and testing of an attitude to blindness scale. *Journal of Social Psychology,* 1958, *48,* 297-304.

Cowles, J. T. Food tokens as incentives for learning by chimpanzees. *Comparative Psychological Monographs,* 1937, *14,* No. 5, Whole No. 71.

Cravens, R. V. and K. E. Renner. Conditioned hunger. *Journal of Experimental Psychology,* 1969, *81,* 312-16.

Crespi, L. P. Quantitative variation of incentive and performance in the white rat. *American Journal of Psychology,* 1942, *55,* 467-517.

Cronbach, L. J. *Essentials of psychological testing,* 3rd Ed. New York: Harper & Row, 1970.

——— and P. E. Meehl. Content validity in psychological tests. *Psychological Bulletin,* 1955, *52,* 281-302.

Cummin, P. TAT correlates of executive performance. *Journal of Applied Psychology,* 1967, *51,* 78-81.

Darley, J. M. and E. Berscheid. Increased liking as a result of the anticipation of personal contact. *Human Relations,* 1967, *20,* 29-40.

Darwin, C. *Origin of species.* New York: Modern Library (1936 Edition), 1859.

Davies, E. This is the way Crete went. *Psychology Today,* 1969, *3,* 42-47.

Davies, J. Toward a theory of revolution. *American Sociological Review*, 1967, *27*, 5-19.

Davis, L. E. and E. S. Valper. Studies in supervisory job designs. *Human Relations*, 1968, *19*, 339-47.

deCharms, R. *Personal causation: The internal affective determinant of behavior.* New York: Academic Press, 1968.

_____ and R. Davé. Hope of success, fear of failure, subjective probability, and risk-taking behavior. *Journal of Personality and Social Psychology*, 1965, *1*, 558-68.

Deci, E. L. Effects of externally mediated rewards on intrinsic motivation. *Journal of Personality and Social Psychology*, 1971, *18*, 105-15.

_____ . Intrinsic motivation, extrinsic reinforcement, and inequity. *Journal of Personality and Social Psychology*, 1972, *22*, 113-20.

Deese, J. Some problems in the theory of vigilance. *Psychological Review*, 1955, *62*, 359-68.

_____ and E. Ormond. Studies of detectability during continuous visual search. NADC Tech. Rep., 1953, pp. 53-58.

Dember, W. N. and R. W. Earl. Analysis of exploratory, manipulatory and curiosity behaviors. *Psychological Review*, 1957, *64*, 91-96.

Denmark, F. and M. Guttening. Dissonance in the self-concepts and educational concepts of college and non-college oriented women. *Journal of Counseling Psychology*, 1967, *14*, 113-15.

Dermer, M. and E. Berscheid. Self-report of arousal as an indicant of activation level. *Behavioral Science*, 1972, *17*, 420-29.

Deutsch, M. Trust, trustworthiness and F-scale. *Journal of Abnormal and Social Psychology*, 1960, *61*, 138-40.

_____ . Conflicts: Productive and destructive. *Journal of Social Issues*, 1969, *25*, 7-41.

Dollard, J., L. W. Doob, N. E. Miller, O. H. Mowrer, and R. R. Sears. *Frustration and aggression.* New Haven: Yale University Press, 1939.

Domino, G. Maternal personality correlates of sons' creativity. *Journal of Consulting and Clinical Psychology*, 1969, *33*, 180-83.

Draper, T. The ghost of social fascism. *Commentary*, 1969, *47*, 29-42.

Druckman, D. Dogmatism, prenegotiation experience and simulated group representation as determinants of dyadic behavior in a bargaining situation. *Journal of Personality and Social Psychology*, 1967, *6*, 279-90.

Dulaney, D. E., Jr. Awareness, rules and propositional control: A confrontation with S-R behavior theory. In D. Horton and T. Dixon (Eds.), *Verbal behavior and general behavior theory.* Englewood Cliffs, N.J.: Prentice-Hall, 1968, pp. 340-88.

Dustin, D. and H. P. Davis. Authoritarianism and sanctioning behavior. *Journal of Personality and Social Psychology*, 1967, *6*, 279-90.

Easterbrook, J. A. The effect of emotion on cue utilization and the organization of behavior. *Psychological Review*, 1959, *66*, 183-201.

Eckhardt, W. and A. G. Newcombe. Militarism, personality, and other social attitudes. *Journal of Conflict Resolution*, 1969, *13*, 210-19.

Edwards, A. E. *Edwards personal preference schedule*. New York: The Psychological Corporation, 1959.

Edwards, W. The theory of decision making. *Psychological Bulletin*, 1954, *51*, 380-417.

————. The prediction of decision among bets. *Journal of Experimental Psychology*, 1955, *50*, 201-14.

Ehrlich, H. and D. Lee. Dogmatism, learning, and resistance to change: A new paradigm. *Psychological Bulletin*, 1969, *71*, 249-65.

Eisenberger, R. Explanation of rewards that do not reduce tissue needs. *Psychological Bulletin*, 1972, *77*, 319-39.

Elliott, M. H. The effect of change of reward on the maze performance of rats. *University of California Publications in Psychology*, 1928, *4*, 19-30.

————. The effect of change of "drive" on maze performance. *University of California Publications in Psychology*, 1929, *4*, 185-88 (a).

————. The effect of appropriateness of reward and of complex incentives on maze performance. *University of California Publications in Psychology*, 1929, *4*, 91-98 (b).

Elms, A. and S. Milgram. Personality characteristics associated with obedience and defiance toward authoritative command. *Journal of Experimental Research in Personality*, 1966, *1*, 282-89.

Entwhistle, D. To dispel fantasies about fantasy-based measures of achievement motivation. *Psychological Bulletin*, 1972, *77*, 377-91.

Epstein, R. Aggression toward outgroups as a function of authoritarianism and imitation of aggressive models. *Journal of Personality and Social Psychology*, 1966, *3*, 574-79.

Estes, W. K. Stimulus-response theory of drive. In M. R. Jones (Ed.), *Nebraska Symposium on Motivation*. Lincoln: University of Nebraska Press, 1958, pp. 35-69.

Ewen, R. B. Weighting components of job satisfaction. Unpublished Ph.D. Dissertation, University of Illinois, 1965.

Eysenck, H. J. *The Maudsley personality inventory*. San Diego, Calif.: Educational and Industrial Testing Service.

Farley, F. H. Two putative measures of cognitive dissonance. *Acta Psychologica*, 1969, *31*, 176-81.

Farris, G. Organizational factors and individual performance: A longitudinal study. *Journal of Applied Psychology,* 1969, *53,* 87-91.

Feather, N. T. An expectancy-value model of information-seeking behavior. *Psychological Review,* 1967, *74,* 342-60.

————. The relationship of expectation of success to need achievement and test anxiety. *Journal of Personality and Social Psychology,* 1965, *1,* 118-26.

Feshbach, S. and R. D. Singer. *Television and aggression.* San Francisco: Jossey-Bass, 1971.

Festinger, L. A theory of social comparison processes. *Human Relations,* 1954, *7,* 117-40.

————. *Theory of cognitive dissonance.* Evanston, Ill.: Row, Peterson & Co., 1957.

————, S. Schacter, and K. Back. *Social pressures in informal groups: A study of human factors in housing.* New York: Harper & Row, 1950.

Fierabend, I. and R. Fierabend. Aggressive behavior within politics, 1948–1962. A cross-national study. *Journal of Conflict Resolution,* 1966, *10,* 249-71.

Fillenbaum, S. and A. Jackman. Dogmatism and anxiety in relation to problem solving: An extension of Rokeach's results. *Journal of Abnormal and Social Psychology,* 1961, *63,* 212-14.

Finkelman, J. An investigation of the relationship between self-esteem and risk-taking behavior, preference for heterogenous environment and academic achievement. Unpublished term paper, New York University, 1970.

Finkelman, J. M. and D. C. Glass. Reappraisal of the relationship between noise and human performance by means of a subsidiary task measure. *Journal of Applied Psychology,* 1970, *54,* 211-13.

Fishbein, M. A behavior theory approach to the relations between beliefs about an object and the attitude toward that object. In M. Fishbein (Ed.), *Readings in attitude theory and measurement.* New York: John Wiley, 1967, pp. 389-400.

Fiske, D. W. and S. R. Maddi. *The functions of varied experience.* Homewood, Ill.: Dorsey, 1961.

Fowler, H. *Curiosity and exploratory behavior.* New York: Macmillan, 1965.

Frankman, J. P. and J. A. Adams. Theories of vigilance. *Psychological Bulletin,* 1962, *59,* 257-72.

Fraser, D. C. The relation of an environmental variable to performance in a prolonged visual task. *Quarterly Journal of Experimental Psychology,* 1953, *5,* 31-32.

Freedman, J., S. Klevansky, and P. R. Ehrlich. The effects of crowding on human task performance. *Journal of Applied Social Psychology,* 1971, *1,* 7-25.

Freedman, J. L. and D. O. Sears. Selective exposure. In L. Berkowitz (Ed.), *Advances in experimental social psychology*. New York: Academic Press, 1965, 57-97.

French, E. G. Some characteristics of achievement motivation. *Journal of Experimental Psychology*, 1955, *50*, 232-36.

_____. Development of a measure of complex motivation. In J. W. Atkinson (Ed.), *Motives in fantasy, action, and society*. Princeton, N.J.: Van Nostrand, 1958.

Frenkel-Brunswick, E. Intolerance of ambiguity as an emotional and perceptual personality variable. In J. S. Bruner and D. Kuch (Eds.), *Perception and personality: A symposium*. Durham, N.C.: Duke University Press, 1950, pp. 108-43.

Freud, S. *New introductory lectures on psychoanalysis*. New York: Norton, 1933.

Fromm, E. *Escape from freedom*. New York: Farrar and Reinhart, 1941.

Gailbreath, J. and L. Cummings. An empirical investigation of the determinants of task performance: Interactive effects between instrumentality-valence and motivation-ability. *Organizational Behavior and Human Performance*, 1967, *2*, 237-57.

Georgopoulos, B. S., G. M. Mahoney, and N. W. Jones. A path-goal approach to productivity. *Journal of Applied Psychology*, 1957, *41*, 345-53.

Getzels, J. W. and P. W. Jackson. *Creativity and intelligence*. New York: John Wiley, 1962.

Ghiselli, E. Traits differentiating management personnel. *Personnel Psychology*, 1959, *12*, 535-44.

Glanzer, M. The role of stimulus satiation in spontaneous alternation. *Journal of Experimental Psychology*, 1953, *45*, 387-93.

Glass, D. C. Theories of consistency and the study of personality. In E. F. Borgatta and W. W. Lambert (Eds.), *Handbook of personality theory and research*. Chicago: Rand McNally, 1968.

_____ and J. E. Singer. *Urban stress*. New York: Academic Press, 1972.

Goldstein, D., D. Fink, and D. R. Mettee. Cognition of arousal and actual arousal as determinants of emotion. *Journal of Personality and Social Psychology*, 1972, *21*, 41-51.

Goodman, P. and A. Friedman. An examination of quantity and quality of performance under conditions of overpayment in piecerate. *Organizational Behavior and Human Performance*, 1969, *4*, 365-74.

_____. An examination of Adams's theory of inequity. *Administrative Science Quarterly*, 1971, *16*, 271-86.

Goodman, P., J. H. Rose, and J. E. Furcon. Comparison of motivational antecedents of the work performance of scientists and engineers. *Journal of Applied Psychology*, 1970, *54*, 491-95.

Goodrich, K. P. Performance in different segments of an instrumental response chain as a function of reinforcement schedule. *Journal of Experimental Psychology*, 1959, *57*, 57-63.

Gottesfeld, H. and G. Dozier. Changes in feelings of powerlessness in a community action program. *Psychological Reports*, 1966, *19*, 987.

Graen, G. B. Instrumentality theory of work motivation: Some experimental results and suggested modifications. *Journal of Applied Psychology Monographs*, 1969, *53*, Part 2, 25 pages.

Griffitt, W. and R. Veitch. Hot and crowded: Influence of population density and temperature on interpersonal affective behavior. *Journal of Personality and Social Psychology*, 1971, *19*, 92-98.

Grossman, S. P. *A textbook of physiological psychology*. New York: John Wiley, 1967.

Guetzkow, H. The creative person in organizations. In G. Steiner (Ed.), *The creative organization*. Chicago: University of Chicago Press, 1965, pp. 35-45.

Gurin, G. and P. Gurin. Expectancy theory in the study of poverty. *Journal of Social Issues*, 1970, *26*, 83-104.

Gurin, P., G. Gurin, R. C. Hao, and M. Beattie. Internal-external control in the motivational dynamics of Negro youth. *Journal of Social Issues*, 1969, *25*, 29-53.

Haber, R. N. Discrepancy from adaptation level as a source of affect. *Journal of Experimental Psychology*, 1958, *56*, 370-75.

Haber, R. N. and R. Alpert. The role of situation and picture cues in projective measurement of the achievement motive. In J. W. Atkinson (Ed.), *Motives in fantasy, action and society*. New York: Van Nostrand Reinhold, pp. 644-63.

Hackman, J. R. and L. Porter. Expectancy theory predictions of work effectiveness. *Organizational Behavior and Human Performance*, 1968, *3*, 417-26.

Haggard, D. F. Acquisition of a simple running response as a function of partial and continuous schedules of reinforcement. *Psychological Record*, 1959, *9*, 11-18.

Hall, D. T. and K. E. Nougaim. An examination of Maslow's need hierarchy in an organizational setting. *Organizational Behavior and Human Performance*, 1968, *3*, 12-35.

Harlow, H. Motivation as a factor in the acquisition of new responses. In J. S. Brown et al., *Current theory and research in motivation: A symposium*. Lincoln: University of Nebraska Press, 1952, pp. 24-59.

————— and R. R. Zimmerman. Affectional responses in the infant monkey. *Science*, 1959, *130*, 421-32.

Hart, I. Maternal child-rearing practices and authoritarian ideology. *Journal of Abnormal and Social Psychology*, 1957, *55*, 232-37.

Hebb, D. O. Drives and the c.n.s. (conceptual nervous system). *Psychological Review*, 1955, *62*, 243-54.

Heider, F. *The psychology of interpersonal relations*. New York: John Wiley, 1968.

Helson, H. *Adaptation-level theory: An experimental and systematic approach to behavior*. New York: Harper & Row, 1964.

Heneman, H. G., III and D. P. Schwab. Evaluation of research on expectancy-theory predictions of employee performance. *Psychological Bulletin*, 1972, *78*, 1-9.

Heron, W. The pathology of boredom. *Scientific American*, 1957, *199*, No. 1.

Hilgard, E. R. *Theories of learning*. New York: Appleton-Century-Crofts, 1956.

Hill, W. F. An attempted clarification of frustration theory. *Psychological Review*, 1968, *75*, 173-76.

Hinings, C. R. and G. L. Lee. Dimensions of organization structure and their context: A replication. *Sociology*, 1971, *5*, 83-93.

Hoffman, L. R., E. Harburg, and N. R. F. Maier. Differences and disagreement in creative group problem-solving. *Journal of Abnormal and Social Psychology*, 1962, *64*, 206-14.

Holland, J. G. Human vigilance. *Science*, 1958, *128*, 61-67.

Holt, E. B. *Animal drive and the learning process: An essay toward radical empiricism, Vol. 1*. New York: Holt, Rinehart & Winston, 1931.

Holz, W. C. and N. Azrin. Discriminative properties of punishment. *Journal of Experimental Analysis of Behavior*, 1961, *4*, 225-32.

Homans, G. *The human group*. New York: Harcourt Brace Jovanovich, 1950.

Horner, M. S. *Sex differences in achievement motivation and performance in competitive and noncompetitive situations*. Unpublished doctoral dissertation, University of Michigan, 1968.

House, R. J. A path goal theory of leader effectiveness. *Administrative Science Quarterly*, 1971, *16*, 321-28.

——— and M. A. Wahba. Expectancy theory in industrial and organizational psychology: An integrative model and a review of literature. *Proceedings of the Annual Convention of the American Psychological Association*, 1972, *7*, 465-66.

Hovland, C. I., I. L. Janis, and H. H. Kelley. *Communication and persuasion: Psychological studies of opinion change*. New Haven: Yale University Press, 1953.

Hull, C. L. Simple trial-and-error learning: A study in psychological theory. *Psychological Review*, 1930, *37*, 241-56.

————. Goal attraction and directing ideas conceived as habit phenomena. *Psychological Review,* 1931, *38,* 487-506.

————. Knowledge and purpose as habit mechanisms. *Psychological Review,* 1930, *37,* 511-25.

————. *Principles of behavior.* New York: Appleton-Century-Crofts, Inc., 1943.

————. *Essentials of behavior.* New Haven: Yale University Press, 1951.

————. *A behavior system: An introduction to behavior theory covering the individual organism.* New Haven: Yale University Press, 1952.

Hundal, R. S. A study of entrepreneurial motivation: Comparison of fast-and-slow progressing small-scale industrial entrepreneurs in Punjab, India. *Journal of Applied Psychology,* 1971, *55,* 317-23.

Humphrey, G. *An introduction to thinking: Its experimental psychology.* London: Methuen, 1951.

Isaacson, R., M. Hutt, and M. L. Blum. *Psychology: The science of behavior.* New York: Harper & Row, 1965.

Izzett, R. R. Authoritarianism and attitudes toward the Vietnam war as reflected in behavioral and self-report measures. *Journal of Personality and Social Psychology,* 1971, *17,* 145-48.

Jackson, D. W. The dynamics of structured personality tests: 1971. *Psychological Review,* 1971, *78,* 229-48.

James, W. *The principles of psychology,* 2 Vols. New York: Holt (reprinted in one volume by Dover Publications, Inc.), 1890.

Jenkins, H. M. The effect of signal rate on performance in visual monitoring. *American Journal of Psychology,* 1958, *71,* 647-61.

Jones, J. *Prejudice and racism.* Reading, Mass.: Addison-Wesley, 1962.

Jordan, N. Behavioral forces that are a function of attitudes and cognitive organization. *Human Relations,* 1953, *6,* 273-87.

Kagan, J. Motives and development. *Journal of Personality and Social Psychology,* 1972, *22,* 51-66.

Karabenick, S. Valence of success and failure as a function of achievement motives and locus of control. *Journal of Personality and Social Psychology,* 1972, *21,* 101-10.

Karsh, E. B. Effects of number of rewarded trials and intensity of punishment on running speed. *Journal of Comparative and Physiological Psychology,* 1962, *55,* 44-51.

Katz, I. Review of evidence relating to desegregation on the intellectual performance of Negroes. *American Psychologist,* 1964, *19,* 381-99.

————. The socialization of academic motivation in minority-group children. In D. Levine (Ed.), *Nebraska Symposium on Motivation,* Vol. 15. Lincoln: University of Nebraska Press, 1967, pp. 133-91.

————. Factors influencing Negro performance in the desegregated school.

In M. Deutsch, I. Katz, and A. R. Jensen (Eds.), *Social class, race and psychological development.* New York: Holt, Rinehart & Winston, 1968.

Kaufman, H. Task performance and response to failure as functions of imbalance in the self-concept. *Psychological Monographs,* 1963, *77,* Whole No. 569.

———. *Aggression and altruism: A social psychological analysis.* New York: Holt, Rinehart & Winston, 1970.

Keller, F. S. and W. S. Schoenfeld. *Principles of psychology,* New York: Appleton-Century-Crofts, 1950.

Kelman, H. C. and C. I. Hovland. "Reinstatement" of the communication in delayed measurement of opinion change. *Journal of Abnormal and Social Psychology,* 1953, *48,* 327-35.

Kendler, M. Motivation and behavior. In D. Levine (Ed.), *Nebraska Symposium on Motivation.* Lincoln: University of Nebraska Press, 1965, pp. 1-24.

Kerlinger, F. and M. Rokeach. The factorial nature of the F and D scales. *Journal of Abnormal and Social Psychology,* 1966, *4,* 391-99.

Kerr, C. and A. Siegel. The interindustry propensity to strike — an international comparison. In A. Kornhauser, R. Dubin, and A. M. Ross (Eds.), *Industrial conflict.* New York: McGraw-Hill, 1954, pp. 189-212.

Kiesler, C. A. The nature of conformity and group pressure. In J. Mills (Ed.), *Experimental social psychology.* New York: Macmillan, 1969, pp. 235-306.

Kipnis, D. A noncognitive correlate of performance among lower aptitude men. *Journal of Applied Psychology,* 1962, *46,* 76-80.

——— and A. S. Glickman. The prediction of job performance. *Journal of Applied Psychology,* 1962, *46,* 50-56.

Kirscht, J. and R. C. Dillehay. *Dimensions of authoritarianism: A review of research and theory.* Lexington: University of Kentucky Press, 1967.

Kish, G. B. and W. Busse. Correlates of stimulus-seeking: Age, education, intelligence, and aptitudes. *Journal of Consulting and Clinical Psychology,* 1968, *32,* 633-37.

Kleinmuntz, B. *Personality measurement.* Homewood, Ill.: Dorsey, 1967.

Klinger, E. Fantasy need achievement as a motivational construct. *Psychological Bulletin,* 1966, *66,* 291-308.

———. Feedback effects and social feedback of vigilance performance: Mere coaction vs. potential evaluation. *Psychonomic Science,* 1969, *14,* 161-62.

——— and F. W. McNelly, Jr. Fantasy need achievement and performance: A role analysis. *Psychological Review,* 1969, *76,* 574-91.

Kogan, N. and M. Wallach. Risky-shift phenomenon in small decision-making groups: A test of the information exchange hypothesis. *Journal of Experimental Social Psychology,* 1967, *3,* 75-84.

Korman, A. K. Selective perception among first-line supervisors. *Personnel Administration*, 1963, *26*, 31-36.

_____. Self-esteem variable in vocational choice. *Journal of Applied Psychology*, 1966, *50*, 479-86.

_____. Self-esteem as a moderator of the relationship between self-perceived abilities and vocational choice. *Journal of Applied Psychology*, 1967, *51*, 65-67 (a).

_____. Ethical judgments, self-perceptions and vocational choice. In *Proceedings, 75th Annual Convention, American Psychological Association*, Washington, D.C., 1967 (b).

_____. Self-esteem, social influence and task performance: Some tests of a theory. Paper presented at the meeting of the American Psychological Association, San Francisco, 1968.

_____. Toward an hypothesis of work behavior. *Journal of Applied Psychology*, 1970, *54*, 32-41.

_____. Organizational achievement, aggression and creativity: Some suggestions toward an integrated theory. *Organizational Behavior and Human Performance*, 1971, *6*, 593-613 (a).

_____. *Industrial and organizational psychology*. Englewood Cliffs, N.J.: Prentice-Hall, 1971(b).

Kukla, A. Cognitive determinants of achieving behavior. *Journal of Personality and Social Psychology*, 1972, *21*, 166-74.

Kuo, Z. Y. Giving up instincts in psychology. *Journal of Philosophy*, 1921, *18*, 645-66.

Lacey, J. L. Individual differences in somatic response patterns. *Journal of Comparative and Physiological Psychology*, 1950, *43*, 338-50.

_____ and Lacey, B. C. Verification and extension of the principle of autonomic response-stereotypy. *American Journal of Psychology*, 1958, *71*, 50-73.

Landsberger, H. A. *Hawthorne revisited: Management and the worker, its critics and developments in human relations in industry*. Ithaca, N.Y.: New York State School of Industrial and Labor Relations, 1958.

Lane, I. M. and L. A. Messé. Distribution of insufficient, sufficient and oversufficient rewards: A clarification of equity theory. *Journal of Personality and Social Psychology*, 1972, *21*, 228-33.

Lawler, E. Equity theory as a predictor of productivity and work quality. *Psychological Bulletin*, 1968, *70*, 596-610.

_____. Managers perceptions of their subordinates' pay and of their superiors pay. *Personnel Psychology*, 1965, *18*, 413-22.

_____ and L. Porter. Antecedent attitudes of effective managerial performance. *Organizational Behavior and Human Performance*, 1967, *2*, 122-42.

Lawler, E. and J. C. Suttle. A causal correlational test of the need hierarchy concept. *Organizational Behavior and Human Performance,* 1972, *7,* 265-87.

Lawrence, D. H. and L. Festinger. *Deterrents and reinforcement.* Stanford, Calif.: Stanford University Press, 1962.

Lawson, R. *Frustration: The study of a concept.* New York: Macmillan, 1965

Lecky, P. *Self-consistency: A theory of personality.* New York: Island Press, 1945.

Lerner, M. J. and C. H. Simmons. Observers' reaction to the "innocent victim": Compassion or rejection? *Journal of Personality and Social Psychology,* 1966, *4,* 203-10.

Leventhal, G. S. and D. Lane. Sex, age and equity research. *Journal of Personality and Social Psychology,* 1970, *15,* 312-16.

Leventhal, H., G. Klemp, and D. Brown. Limitations of self-persuasion effects produced by subjective experience. *Proceedings of the Annual Convention of the American Psychological Association,* 1972, *7,* 267-68.

Lewin, K., T. Dembo, L. Festinger, and P. S. Sears. Level of aspiration. In J. McV. Hunt (Ed.), *Personality and the behavior disorders,* Vol. 1. New York: Ronald Press, 1944, pp. 333-78.

Lindgren, H. C. *An introduction to social psychology.* New York: John Wiley, 1969.

Locke, E. A. Relationships of goal level to performance level. *Psychological Report,* 1967, *20,* 1-68.

Mackworth, N. H. *Researches on the measurement of human performance.* London: Medical Research Council, Special Reports Series, Her Majesty's Office, No. 268, 1950.

Maddi, S. *Personality theories: A comparative appraisal.* Homewood, Ill.: Dorsey, 1968.

Maier, N. R. F. *Frustration: The study of behavior without a goal.* New York: McGraw-Hill, 1949.

_____ and L. R. Hoffman. Organization and creative problem-solving. *Journal of Applied Psychology,* 1961, *45,* 277-80.

March, J. G. and H. A. Simon. *Organizations.* New York: John Wiley, 1958.

Maslow, A. H. A theory of human motivation. *Psychological Review,* 1943, *50,* 370-96.

_____. *Motivation and personality.* New York: Harper, 1954 (2nd Ed., Harper & Row, 1970).

Masserman, J. H. *Behavior and neurosis.* Chicago: University of Chicago Press, 1943.

May, R. *Man's search for himself.* New York: Norton, 1953.

McBain, W. Noise, the arousal hypothesis and monotonous work. *Journal of Applied Psychology,* 1961, *45,* 309-17.

——. Arousal, monotony and accidents in line driving. *Journal of Applied Psychology,* 1970, *54,* 509-19.

McClelland, D. C. Notes for a revised theory of motivation. In D. C. McClelland (Ed.), *Studies in motivation.* New York: Appleton-Century-Crofts, 1955, pp. 226-34.

——. *The achieving society.* Princeton, N.J.: Van Nostrand, 1961.

——. Toward a theory of motive acquisition. *American Psychologist,* 1965, *20,* No. 5, 231-333.

——, J. W. Atkinson, R. W. Clark, and E. L. Lowell. *The achievement motive.* New York: Appleton-Century-Crofts, 1953.

McDavid, J. W. and H. Hararri. *Social psychology: Individuals, groups and societies.* New York: Harper & Row, 1969.

McDougall, W. *An introduction to social psychology* (3rd Ed., 1950). London: Methuen, 1908.

——. *Outline of psychology.* Boston, Mass: Scribner's, 1923.

McGregor, D. *The human side of enterprise.* New York: McGraw-Hill, 1960.

McGuire, W. J. The current status of cognitive consistency theories. In S. Feldman (Ed.), *Cognitive consistency.* New York: Academic Press, 1966, pp. 2-46.

Meehl, P. E. On the circularity of the law of effect. *Psychological Bulletin,* 1950, *47,* 52-75.

Mettee, D. R. Rejection of unexpected success as a function of the negative consequences of accepting success. *Journal of Personality and Social Psychology,* 1971, *17,* 332-41.

Milgram, S. Some conditions of obedience and disobedience to authority. In I. O. Steiner and M. Fishbein (Eds.), *Current studies in social psychology.* New York: Holt, Rinehart & Winston, 1965, pp. 243-61.

Miller, N. E. The frustration-aggression hypothesis. *Psychological Review,* 1941, *38,* 337-42.

——. Studies of fear as an acquired drive; 1. Fear as motivation and fear-reduction as reinforcement in the learning of new responses. *Journal of Experimental Psychology,* 1948, *38,* 89-101.

——. Some motivational effects of brain stimulation and drugs. *Federation Proceedings,* 1960, *19,* 846-54.

—— and J. Dollard. *Social learning and imitation.* New Haven: Yale University Press, 1941.

Miller, N. E., D. C. Butler, and J. P. McMartin. The ineffectiveness of punishment power in group interaction. *Sociometry,* 1969, *32,* 24-42.

Mischel, W. *Personality and assessment.* New York: John Wiley, 1968.

Montgomery, K. C. Exploratory behavior as a function of "similarity" of stimulus situations. *Journal of Comparative and Physiological Psychology,* 1953, *46,* 129-33.

Morgan, C. T. *Physiological psychology.* New York: McGraw-Hill, 1943.

Morgan, C. D. and H. Murray. Method for investigating fantasies – the Thematic Apperception Test. *Archives of Neurological Psychiatry,* 1935, *34,* 289-306.

Mowrer, O. H. *Learning theory and behavior.* New York: John Wiley, 1960.

Murray, H. A. Facts which support the concept of need or drive. *Journal of Psychology,* 1937, *3,* 27-42.

Murstein, B. *Theory and research in projective techniques: Emphasizing the TAT.* New York: John Wiley, 1963.

Newcomb, T. M. An approach to the study of communicative acts. *Psychological Review,* 1953, *60,* 393-404.

————. The prediction of interpersonal attraction. *American Psychologist,* 1956, *4,* 575-86.

————. *The acquaintance process.* New York: Holt, Rinehart & Winston, 1961.

————. Interpersonal balance. In R. E. Abelson et al., *Theories of cognitive consistency: A sourcebook.* Chicago: Rand McNally, 1968, pp. 28-51.

Nisbett, R. E. Taste, deprivation, and weight determinants of eating behavior. *Journal of Personality and Social Psychology,* 1968, *10,* 107-16.

Olds, J. and P. Milner. Positive reinforcement produced by electrical stimulation of septal area and other regions of rat brain. *Journal of Comparative and Physiological Psychology,* 1954, *47,* 419-27.

Olweus, D. *Prediction of aggression.* Stockholm: Scandinavian Test Corporation, 1969.

Osgood, C. E. and P. H. Tannenbaum. The principle of congruity in the prediction of attitude change. *Psychological Review,* 1955, *62,* 42-55.

Osgood, C. E., J. G. Suci, and P. H. Tannenbaum. *The measurement of meaning.* Urbana: University of Illinois Press, 1957.

Pallack, M. S., T. C. Brock, and C. A. Kiesler. Dissonance arousal and task performance in an incidental verbal learning paradigm. *Journal of Personality and Social Psychology,* 1967, *7,* 11-20.

Pallack, M. S. and J. S. Pittman. General motivational effects of dissonance arousal. *Journal of Personality and Social Psychology,* 1972, *21,* 349-58.

Paulus, P. B. and P. Murdock, Anticipated evaluation and audience presence in the enhancement of dominant responses. *Journal of Experimental Social Psychology,* 1971, *7,* 280-91.

Payne, R. Factor-analysis of a Maslow-type need satisfaction questionnaire. *Personnel Psychology,* 1970, *23,* 251-68.

Pepitone, A. *Attraction and hostility*. New York: Atherton, 1964.

_____. Problems of consistency models. In S. Feldman (Ed.), *Cognitive consistency*. New York: Academic Press, 1966, pp. 257-97.

Perrin, C. T. Behavior potentiality as a joint function of the amount of training and the degree of hunger at the time of extinction. *Journal of Experimental Psychology*, 1942, *30*, 93-113.

Pettigrew, T. F. Social evaluation theory: Convergence and applications. In D. Levine (Ed.), *Nebraska Symposium on Motivation*. Lincoln: University of Nebraska Press, 1967, pp. 241-311.

Porter, L. W. and E. Lawler. *Managerial attitudes and performance*. Homewood, Ill.: Irwin, 1968.

Pritchard, R. D. Equity theory: A review and critique. *Organizational Behavior and Human Performance*, 1969, *4*, 176-211.

_____, M. D. Dunnette, and D. O. Jorgenson. Effects of perception of equity and inequity on worker performance and satisfaction. *Journal of Applied Psychology*, 1972, *56*, 75-94.

Puckett, E. S. Productivity achievement: A measure of success. In F. G. Lesieui (Ed.), *The Scanlon Plan*. Cambridge, Mass.: M.I.T. Press; and New York: John Wiley, 1958, p. 113.

Radcliff, J. A. Review of Edwards Personal Preference Schedule. In O. Buros (Ed.), *Personality tests and reviews*. Highland Park, N.J.: The Gryphon Press, 1000-1005.

Rehberg, R., J. Sinclair, and W. E. Schaefer. Adolescent achievement behavior, family authority structure, and parental socialization practices. *American Journal of Sociology*, 1970, *75*, 1012-34.

Restle, F., M. Andrews, and M. Rokeach. Differences between open and closed minded subjects in learning set and oddity problems. *Journal of Abnormal and Social Psychology*, 1964, *68*, 648-54.

Rhine, R. J. Some problems in dissonance-theory research on information-selectivity. *Psychological Bulletin*, 1967, *68*, 21-28.

_____. The 1964 presidential election and curves of information seeking and avoiding. *Journal of Personality and Social Psychology*, 1967, *5*, 416-23.

Richter, C. P. Animal behavior and internal drives. *Quarterly Review of Biology*, 1927, *2*, 304-43.

Roethlisberger, F. J. and W. J. Dickson. *Management and the worker*. Cambridge, Mass.: Harvard University Press, 1939.

Rokeach, M. *The open and closed mind*. New York: Basic Books, 1960.

Rorer, L. G. The great response-style myth. *Psychological Bulletin*, 1965, *63*, 129-56.

Rosekraus, F. M. Choosing to suffer as a consequence of expecting to suffer: A replication. *Journal of Personality and Social Psychology*, 1967, *7*, 419-23.

Rosen, B. Race, ethnicity, and the achievement syndrome. *American Sociological Review,* 1959, *24,* 47-60.

―――― and R. G. D'Andrade. The psychosocial origin of achievement motivation. *Sociometry,* 1959, *22,* 185-218.

Rosenthal, R. Covert communication in the psychological experiment. *Psychological Bulletin,* 1967, *67,* 356-57.

Rotter, J. B. *Social learning and clinical psychology.* Englewood Cliffs, N.J.: Prentice-Hall, 1954.

――――. The role of the psychological situation in determining the direction of human behavior. In M. R. Jones (Ed.), *Nebraska Symposium on Motivation.* Lincoln: University of Nebraska Press, 1955, pp. 245-69.

――――. Generalized expectancies for internal vs. external control of reinforcement. *Psychological Monographs,* 1966, *80* (1, Whole No. 609), 1-28.

Rubin, I. Increased self-acceptance: A means of reducing prejudice. *Journal of Personality and Social Psychology,* 1967, *5,* 233-38.

Sales, S. M. Need for stimulation as a factor in social behavior. *Journal of Personality and Social Psychology,* 1971, *19,* 124-34.

Sanford, N. The approach of the authoritarian personality. In J. L. McCrary (Ed.), *Psychology of personality.* New York: Grove Press, 1956, pp. 253-319.

Sarason, S. Toward a psychology of change and innovation. *American Psychologist,* 1967, *22,* 227-33.

Schacter, S., N. Ellertson, D. McBride, and O. Gregory. An experimental study of cohesiveness and productivity. *Human Relations,* 1951, *4,* 229-38.

Schacter, S., R. Goldman, and A. Gordon. Effects of fear, food deprivation, and obesity on eating. *Journal of Personality and Social Psychology,* 1968, *10,* 91-97.

Schacter, S. and J. E. Singer. Cognitive, social and physiological determinants of emotional states. *Psychological Review,* 1962, *69,* 379-99.

Schacter, S. and L. Wheeler. Epinephrine, chlorpromazine and amusement. *Journal of Abnormal and Social Psychology,* 1962, *65,* 121-28.

Scott, W. E., Jr. Activation theory and task design. *Organizational Behavior and Human Performance,* 1966, *1,* 3-30.

Scott, W. Comparative validities of forced-choice and single stimulus tests. *Psychological Bulletin,* 1968, *70,* 231-44.

Seashore, S. E. *Group cohesiveness in the industrial work group.* Ann Arbor: University of Michigan, Institute for Social Research, 1954.

Seudfeld, P. and Y. A. Epstein. Where is the "D" in dissonance? *Journal of Personality,* 1971, *39,* 178-88.

Shaw, M. C. Underachievement: Useful construct or misleading illusion. *Psychology in the Schools,* 1968, *5,* 41-46.

Shaw, M. E. and P. R. Costanzo. *Theories in social psychology.* New York: McGraw-Hill, 1970.

Sheard, J. L. Intrasubject prediction of preferences for organization types. *Journal of Applied Psychology,* 1970, *54,* 248-52.

Sheffield, F. D. and T. B. Roby. Reward value of a non-nutritive sweet taste. *Journal of Comparative and Physiological Psychology,* 1950, *43,* 471-81.

Sheffield, F. D., J. J. Wulf, and R. Backer. Reward value of copulation without sex drive reduction. *Journal of Comparative and Physiological Psychology,* 1951, *44,* 3-8.

Sherif, M. A study of some social factors in perception. *Archives in Psychology,* 1935, No. 187.

Siegel, P. S. and J. B. Milty. Secondary reinforcement in relation to shock termination. *Psychological Bulletin,* 1969, *72,* 146-56.

Silber, E. and J. S. Tippett. Self-esteem: Clinical assessment and measurement validation. *Psychological Reports,* 1956, *16,* 1017-71.

Simmons, R. The relative effectiveness of certain incentives in animal learning. *Comparative Psychological Monographs,* 1924, *2,* No. 7.

Smith, C. G. and M. E. Brown. Communication structure and control structure in a voluntary association. *Sociometry,* 1964, *27,* 449-68.

Smith, P. C. and R. Curnow. Arousal hypothesis and the effects of music on purchasing behavior. *Journal of Applied Psychology,* 1966, *50,* 255-56.

Solomon, R. C. Punishment. *American Psychologist,* 1964, *19,* 239-53.

Solomon, R. L. and L. H. Turner. Discriminative classical conditioning in dogs paralyzed by curare can later control discriminative avoidance responses in the normal state. *Psychological Review,* 1962, *69,* 202-19.

Spence, K. W. *Behavior theory and conditioning.* New Haven: Yale University Press, 1956.

————. A theory of emotionally based drive (D) and its relation to performance in simple learning situations. *American Psychologist,* 1958, *13,* 131-41.

————. *Behavior theory and learning: Selected papers.* Englewood Cliffs, N.J.: Prentice-Hall, 1960.

————. Anxiety (drive) level and performance in eyelid conditioning. *Psychological Bulletin,* 1964, *61,* 129-31.

Stagner, R. Homeostasis as a unifying concept in personality theory. *Psychological Review,* 1951, *58,* 5-17.

Stedry, A. C. and E. Kay. The effects of goal difficulty on performance. *Behavioral Science,* 1966, *11,* 459-70.

Steiner, G. Introduction. In G. Steiner (Ed.), *The creative organization.* Chicago: University of Chicago Press, 1965, pp. 1-24.

Strain, G., I. P. Unikel, and H. E. Adams. Alternation behavior by children from lower socio-economic status groups. *Developmental Psychology,* 1969, *1,* 131-33.

Stricker, L. J. Review of Edwards Personal Preference Schedule. In O. Boros (Ed.), *Personality tests and reviews.* Highland Park, N.J.: Gryphon Press, 1005-12.

Sumner, W. G. *Folkways.* New York: Ginn, 1906.

Sutton, H. and L. W. Porter. A study of the grapevine in a governmental organization. *Personnel Psychology,* 1968, *21,* 223-30.

Tannenbaum, A. S. Control in organizations, individual adjustment and organizational performance. *Administrative Science Quarterly,* 1962, *7,* 236-57.

————— and R. L. Kahn. *Participation in union locals.* Evanston, Ill.: Row, Peterson & Co., 1958.

Tannenbaum, P. H. The congruity principle: Retrospective reflections and recent research. In R. Abelson et al. (Eds.), *Theories of cognitive consistency: A sourcebook.* Chicago: Rand McNally, 1968, pp. 52-72.

————— and R. W. Gengel. Generalization of attitude change through congruity principle relationships. *Journal of Personality and Social Psychology,* 1966, *3,* 299-304.

Taylor, J. A. A personality scale of manifest anxiety. *Journal of Abnormal and Social Psychology,* 1953, *48,* 285-90.

—————. Drive theory and manifest anxiety. *Psychological Bulletin,* 1956, *53,* 303-20.

Tedeschi, J. T., B. Schlenker, and T. V. Bonoma. Cognitive dissonance: Private ratiocination or public spectacle? *American Psychologist,* 1971, *26,* 685-95.

Thayer, R. E. Measurement of activation through self-report. *Psychological Reports,* 1967, *20,* 663-78. Monograph Supplement 1-V20.

Thilly, F. *History of philosophy,* 3rd Ed. Revised by L. Wood. New York: Holt, Rinehart & Winston, 1957.

Tolman, E. C. *Purposive behavior in animals and men.* New York: Appleton-Century-Crofts, 1932.

—————. Principles of performance. *Psychological Review,* 1955, *62,* 315-26.

————— and C. H. Honzik. Introduction and removal of reward and maze performance in rats. *University of California Publications in Psychology,* 1930, *4,* 257-75.

Tolman, E. C., B. F. Ritchie, and D. Kalish. Studies in spatial learning versus response learning. *Journal of Experimental Psychology,* 1946, *36,* 221-29.

Torcivia, J. M. and P. R. Laughlin. Dogmatism and concept-attainment strategies. *Journal of Personality and Social Psychology,* 1968, *8,* 397-400.

Tornow, W. W. The development and application of an input-outcome moderator test on the perception and reduction of inequity. *Organizational Behavior and Human Performance,* 1971, *6,* 614-38.

Tosi, H. A reexamination of personality as a determinant of the effects of participation. *Personnel Psychology,* 1970, *23,* 91-100.

Triandis, H. C. Cognitive similarity and interpersonal communication. *Journal of Applied Psychology,* 1959, *43,* 321-26.

———— , E. Davis, and S. Takezawa. Some determinants of social distance among American, German, and Japanese students. *Journal of Personality and Social Psychology,* 1965, *2,* 540-51.

Trexler, J. T. and A. J. Schuh. Personality dynamics in a military training command and its relationship to Maslow's motivation hierarchy. *Journal of Vocational Behavior,* 1971, *1,* 245-54.

Vacchiano, R. B., P. S. Strauss, and L. Hochman. The open and closed mind: A review of dogmatism. *Psychological Bulletin,* 1969, *71,* 271-83.

Valins, S. Emotionality and information causing internal reactions. *Journal of Personality and Social Psychology,* 1967, *6,* 458-63.

Van Zelst, R. H. Sociometrically selected work teams increase productivity. *Personnel Psychology,* 1952, *5,* 175-85.

Vernon, M. D. *Human motivation.* Cambridge, Mass.: Harvard University Press, 1969.

Vernon, P. E. Ability factors and environmental influences. *American Psychologist,* 1965, *20,* 723-33.

Vitz, P. C. Preference for different amounts of visual complexity. *Behavioral Science,* 1966, *11,* 105-14 (a).

———— . Affect as a function of stimulus variation. *Journal of Experimental Psychology,* 1966, *71,* 74-79 (b).

Vroom, V. H. *Work and motivation.* New York: John Wiley, 1964.

Walker, E. L. Psychological complexity as a basis for a theory of motivation and choice. *Nebraska Symposium on Motivation,* 1964, *12,* 47-97.

Walker, E. and R. Heyns. *An anatomy for conformity.* Englewood Cliffs, N.J.: Prentice-Hall, 1962.

Wallace, J. *Psychology: A social science.* Philadelphia: Saunders, 1971.

Walster, E., E. Aronson, and Z. Brown. Choosing to suffer as a consequence of expecting to suffer: An unexpected finding. *Journal of Experimental Social Psychology,* 1966, *2,* 400-406.

Walster, E., E. Berscheid, and G. W. Walster. New directions in equity research. *Journal of Personality and Social Psychology,* 1973, *25,* 151-76.

Warden, C. J. *Animal motivation.* New York: Columbia University Press, 1931.

Watson, G. Some personality differences in children related to strict or permissive parental discipline. In M. Harmowitz and N. Harmowitz (Eds.), *Human development: Selected readings.* New York: Crowell, 1960, 25-44.

Watson, J. B. Psychology as the behaviorist views it. *Psychological Review,* 1913, *20,* 158-77.

Webb, E. J., D. T. Campbell, R. D. Schwartz, and L. Sechrest. *Unobtrusive measures in the social sciences: Nonreactive research in the social sciences.* Chicago: Rand McNally, 1966.

Weick, K. E. and B. Nesset. Preference among forms of equity. *Organizational Behavior and Human Performance,* 1968, *3,* 400-416.

Weiner, B. New conceptions in the study of achievement motivation. In B. Maher (Ed.), *Progress in experimental personality research:* Vol. V. New York: Academic Press, 1970, pp. 67-109.

––––––. *Theories of motivation: From mechanism to cognition.* Chicago: Markham Publishing Co., 1972.

–––––– , I. Frieze, A. Kukla, L. Reed, S. Rest, and R. Rosenbaum. *Perceiving the causes of success and failure.* Morristown, N.J.: General Learning Press, 1971.

Weiner, B., H. Heckhausen, W. V. Meyer, and R. E. Cook. Causal ascriptions and achievement motivation: A conceptual analysis of effort and reanalysis of locus of control. *Journal of Personality and Social Psychology,* 1972, *21,* 239-48.

Weiner, B. and A. Kukla. An attributional analysis of achievement motivation. *Journal of Personality and Social Psychology,* 1970, *15,* 1-20.

Weinstein, M. S. Achievement motivation and risk preference. *Journal of Personality and Social Psychology,* 1969, *13,* 153-72.

Weiss, R. F. An extension of Hullian learning theory to persuasive communication. In A. G. Greenwald, T. C. Brock, and R. H. Ostrow (Eds.), *Psychological foundations of attitudes.* New York: Academic Press, 1968, pp. 109-45.

–––––– and F. G. Miller. The drive theory of social facilitation. *Psychological Review,* 1971, *78,* 44-57.

Wheeler, L. and H. Davis. Social disruption of performance on a DRL schedule. *Psychonomic Science,* 1967, *7,* 249-50.

Whitney, R. E. Agreement and positivity in pleasantness ratings of balanced and unbalanced social situations: A cross-cultural study. *Journal of Personality and Social Psychology,* 1971, *17,* 11-14.

Wiggins, N. Individual viewpoints of social desirability. *Psychological Bulletin,* 1966, *66,* 68-77.

Wike, E. L. Secondary reinforcement: Some research and theoretical issues. In W. J. Arnold (Ed.), *Nebraska Symposium on Motivation.* Lincoln: University of Nebraska Press, 1969, pp. 39-84.

Williams, S. B. Resistance to extinction as a function of the number of reinforcements. *Journal of Experimental Psychology,* 1938, *23,* 506-22.

Winterbottom, M. R. The relationship of need for achievement to learning experiences in independence and mastery. In J. W. Atkinson (Ed.), *Motives in fantasy, action, and society.* Princeton, N.J.: Van Nostrand, 1958, pp. 453-78.

Wohlwill, J. F. The emerging discipline of environmental psychology. *American Psychologist,* 1970, *25,* 303-12.

Wolfe, J. B. Effectiveness of token rewards for chimpanzees. *Comparative Psychological Monographs,* 1936, *12,* No. 5, Whole No. 60.

Wollack, Goodale, J. G., J. R. Wijting, and P. C. Smith. Development of the survey of work values. *Journal of Applied Psychology,* 1971, *51,* 331-38.

Wood, I. and E. E. Lawler. Effects of piece-rate overpayment on productivity. *Journal of Applied Psychology,* 1970, *54,* 234-38.

Woodworth, R. *Dynamic psychology.* New York: Columbia University Press, 1918.

Wrightsman, L. *Social psychology in the seventies.* Belmont, Calif.: Brooks-Cole, 1972.

Young, P. T. Food-seeking drive, affective processes, and learning. *Psychological Review,* 1949, *56,* 98-121.

———. Affective arousal: Some implications. *American Psychologist,* 1967, *22,* 32-39.

Zajonc, R. B. Social facilitation. *Science,* 1965, *149,* 269-74.

———. Cognitive theories in social psychology. In G. Lindzey and E. Aronson (Eds.), *Handbook of social psychology,* Vol. 1, 2nd Ed. Reading, Mass.: Addison-Wesley, 1968, pp. 320-411.

——— and E. Burnstein. The learning of balanced and unbalanced social structures. *Journal of Personality,* 1965, *33,* 153-63.

Zajonc, R. B., W. Heingartner, and E. Herman. Social enhancement and impairment of performance in the cockroach. *Journal of Personality and Social Psychology,* 1969, *13,* 83-92.

Zajonc, R. B. and S. M. Sales. Social facilitation of dominant and subordinant responses. *Journal of Experimental and Social Psychology,* 1966, *2,* 160-68.

Zander, A., J. Forward, and R. Albert. Adaptation of board members to repeated failure or success by their organization. *Organizational Behavior and Human Performance,* 1969, *4,* 56-76.

Zeaman, D. Response latency as a function of the amount of reinforcement. *Journal of Experimental Psychology,* 1949, *39,* 466-81.

Ziller, R. C. Communication restraints, group flexibility and group confidence. *Journal of Applied Psychology,* 1958, *42,* 346-52.

———, R. Behringer, and J. Goodchilds. Group creativity under conditions of success or failure and variations in group stability. *Journal of Applied Psychology*, 1962, *46*, 43-49.

Zimbardo, P. G. The human choice: Individuation, reason, and order versus deindividuation, impulse and chaos. *Nebraska Symposium on Motivation*, 1969, *17*, 231-307.

Zimmerman, D. W. Durable secondary reinforcement: Method and theory. *Psychological Review*, 1957, *64*, 373-83.

Zlutnick, S. and I. Altman. Crowding and human behavior. In J. F. Wohlwill and D. H. Carson (Eds.), *Environment and the social sciences: Perspectives and application.* Washington, D.C.: American Psychological Association, 1972, pp. 44-60.

Zuckerman, M., E. A. Kolin, L. Price, and I. Zoob. Development of a sensation-seeking scale. *Journal of Consulting Psychology*, 1964, *28*, 477-82.

Zuckerman, M., R. S. Neary, and B. A. Bustman. Sensation-seeking scale correlates in experience (smoking, drugs, alcohol, hallucinations, and sex) and preference for complexity (designs). *Proceedings of the 78th Annual Convention of the American Psychological Association*, 1970, *5*, 317-18.

name index

subject index